To Jo

Best

Peter Preston-Hough.

July 2015.

The war in the Far East between 1941 and 1945 is occasionally referred to as the 'Forgotten War' and this description extends to the way the campaign's air war has been analysed. However, the role of air power in Burma was vitally important to the campaign, in particular the attainment of air superiority in order to facilitate supply and close support operations. The foundation of these operations was dependent on the Allies achieving and maintaining air superiority and latterly air supremacy over the Japanese. The British lost air superiority during the initial Japanese attacks as their early warning system, aircraft, aircrew and tactics did not match their adversary's capabilities.

This book will analyse how the Allies lost air superiority during the initial exchanges, and then how technical and material difficulties were overcome before air superiority was won in 1944, and air supremacy was gained in 1945. Furthermore, the book will demonstrate how Japanese industry, their war in the Pacific, and their use of air power in Burma ultimately affected the air war's eventual outcome. The book will examine current historiography to question and corroborate existing views, as well as to reveal new information not previously published.

Dr Peter Preston-Hough is a visiting lecturer at the University of Wolverhampton and University of Chester. He lectures to undergraduates and postgraduates on aspects of air power since its inception in the twentieth century.

His areas of interest include the Royal Air Force; the Strategic Air Offensive 1940-1945; 617 Squadron in the Second World War; the Royal Air Force in the Far East 1939-1945; airborne warfare and airborne operations, particularly in Normandy and during Operation MARKET GARDEN 1944.

Dr Preston-Hough is a member of the British Commission for Military History.

COMMANDING FAR EASTERN SKIES

Wolverhampton Military Studies

www.helion.co.uk/wolverhamptonmilitarystudies

Submissions

The publishers would be pleased to receive submissions for this series. Please contact us via email (info@helion.co.uk), or in writing to Helion & Company Limited, 26 Willow Road, Solihull, West Midlands, B91 1UE.

Titles

No.1   *Stemming the Tide. Officers and Leadership in the British Expeditionary Force 1914* Edited by Spencer Jones (ISBN 978-1-909384-45-3)

No.2   *'Theirs Not To Reason Why'. Horsing the British Army 1875-1925* Graham Winton (ISBN 978-1-909384-48-4)

No.3   *A Military Transformed? Adaptation and Innovation in the British Military, 1792-1945* Edited by Michael LoCicero, Ross Mahoney and Stuart Mitchell (ISBN 978-1-909384-46-0)

No.4   *Get Tough Stay Tough. Shaping the Canadian Corps, 1914-1918* Kenneth Radley (ISBN 978-1-909982-86-4)

No.5   *A Moonlight Massacre: The Night Operation on the Passchendaele Ridge, 2 December 1917. The Forgotten Last Act of the Third Battle of Ypres* Michael LoCicero (ISBN 978-1-909982-92-5)

No.6   *Shellshocked Prophets. Former Anglican Army Chaplains in Interwar Britain* Linda Parker (ISBN 978-1-909982-25-3)

No.7   *Flight Plan Africa: Portuguese Airpower in Counterinsurgency, 1961-1974* John P. Cann (ISBN 978-1-909982-06-2)

No. 8   *Mud, Blood and Determination. The History of the 46th (North Midland) Division in the Great War* Simon Peaple (ISBN 978 1 910294 66 6)

No. 9   *Commanding Far Eastern Skies. A Critical Analysis of the Royal Air Force Superiority Campaign in India, Burma and Malaya 1941-1945* Peter Preston-Hough (ISBN 978 1 910294 44 4)

Commanding Far Eastern Skies

*A Critical Analysis of the Royal Air Force Superiority
Campaign in India, Burma and Malaya 1941-1945*

Wolverhampton Military Studies No.9

Peter Preston-Hough

Helion & Company Limited

Helion & Company Limited
26 Willow Road
Solihull
West Midlands
B91 1UE
England
Tel. 0121 705 3393
Fax 0121 711 4075
Email: info@helion.co.uk
Website: www.helion.co.uk
Twitter: @helionbooks
Visit our blog http://blog.helion.co.uk/

Published by Helion & Company 2015

Designed and typeset by Bookcraft Ltd, Stroud, Gloucestershire
Cover designed by Paul Hewitt, Battlefield Design (www.battlefield-design.co.uk)
Printed by Lightning Source Limited, Milton Keynes, Buckinghamshire

Text © Peter Preston-Hough 2015
Photographs © as individually credited
Maps drawn by George Anderson © Helion & Company 2015

Cover: Supermarine Spitfire VIII in Flight, R.A.F. Museum Hendon, photograph
reference 4288

ISBN 978 1 910294 44 4

British Library Cataloguing-in-Publication Data.
A catalogue record for this book is available from the British Library.

For details of other military history titles published by Helion & Company
Limited contact the above address, or visit our website: http://www.helion.co.uk.

We always welcome receiving book proposals from prospective authors.

Contents

List of Illustrations

List of Maps

List of Abbreviations

A.C.G.	Air Commando Group
A.C.M.	Air Chief-Marshal
A.C.O.	Advanced Chain Overseas
A.C.S.E.A.	Air Command South East Asia
A.F.T.U.	Air Fighting Training Unit
A.I.	Airborne Interception
A.L.G.	Advanced Landing Ground
A.M.E.S.	Air Ministry Experimental Station
A.O.C.	Air Officer Commanding
A.S.V.	Air to Surface Vessel
A.V.G.	American Volunteer Group
A.V.M.	Air Vice-Marshal
B.S.D.	Base Signals Depot
C.F.E.	Central Fighter Establishment
C.O.L.	Chain Overseas Low
F.A.A.	Fleet Air Arm
F.T.S.	Flying Training School
G.C.I.	Ground Controlled Interception
I.F.F.	Identification, Friend or Foe
I.O.C.	Indian Observer Corps
L.W.S.	Light Weight Set
M.A.P.	Ministry of Aircraft Production
M.R.U.	Mobile Radar Unit
M.W.O.U.	Mobile Wireless Observer Unit
O.R.S.	Operational Research Section
O.T.U.	Operational Training Unit
P.R.U.	Photographic Reconnaissance Unit
R.D.F.	Radio Direction Finding
S.E.A.C.	South East Asia Command
T.R.E.	Telecommunications Research Establishment
T.R.U.	Transportable Radar Unit
V.H.F.	Very High Frequency
W.O.U.	Wireless Observer Unit

The Wolverhampton Military Studies Series
Series Editor's Preface

As series editor, it is my great pleasure to introduce the *Wolverhampton Military Studies Series* to you. Our intention is that in this series of books you will find military history that is new and innovative, and academically rigorous with a strong basis in fact and in analytical research, but also is the kind of military history that is for all readers, whatever their particular interests, or their level of interest in the subject. To paraphrase an old aphorism: a military history book is not less important just because it is popular, and it is not more scholarly just because it is dull. With every one of our publications we want to bring you the kind of military history that you will want to read simply because it is a good and well-written book, as well as bringing new light, new perspectives, and new factual evidence to its subject.

In devising the *Wolverhampton Military Studies Series*, we gave much thought to the series title: this is a *military* series. We take the view that history is everything except the things that have not happened yet, and even then a good book about the military aspects of the future would find its way into this series. We are not bound to any particular time period or cut-off date. Writing military history often divides quite sharply into eras, from the modern through the early modern to the mediaeval and ancient; and into regions or continents, with a division between western military history and the military history of other countries and cultures being particularly marked. Inevitably, we have had to start somewhere, and the first books of the series deal with British military topics and events of the twentieth century and later nineteenth century. But this series is open to any book that challenges received and accepted ideas about any aspect of military history, and does so in a way that encourages its readers to enjoy the discovery.

In the same way, this series is not limited to being about wars, or about grand strategy, or wider defence matters, or the sociology of armed forces as institutions, or civilian society and culture at war. None of these are specifically excluded, and in some cases they play an important part in the books that comprise our series. But there are already many books in existence, some of them of the highest scholarly standards, which cater to these particular approaches. The main theme of the *Wolverhampton Military Studies Series* is the military aspects of wars, the preparation for wars or their prevention, and their aftermath. This includes some books whose main theme is the technical details of how armed forces have worked, some books on wars and battles, and some books that re-examine the evidence about the existing stories, to show in a different light what everyone thought they already knew and understood.

As series editor, together with my fellow editorial board members, and our publisher Duncan Rogers of Helion, I have found that we have known immediately and almost by instinct the kind of books that fit within this series. They are very much the kind of well-written and challenging books that my students at the University of Wolverhampton would want to read. They are books which enhance knowledge, and offer new perspectives. Also, they are books for anyone with an interest in military history and events, from expert scholars to occasional readers. One of the great benefits of the study of military history is that it includes a large and often committed section of the wider population, who want to read the best military history that they can find; our aim for this series is to provide it.

Stephen Badsey
University of Wolverhampton

Foreword

This original study into the Royal Air Force's quest for air superiority in the campaign in India, Malaya and Burma during the Second World War represents an important contribution to the historiography of the so-called 'forgotten' theatre of operations. No senior military commander, or for that matter military historian, doubts for one moment the vital nature of control of air and its importance for the successful prosecution of other operations. But beyond this, it is important to acknowledge the various levels through from local air parity through to air supremacy or dominance. These terms are often used interchangeably or too casually. Dr Peter Preston-Hough's detailed and thoughtful study explains each of these terms and applies them rigorously to the campaign in the Far East as it unfolded from 1941 through to 1945. When faced with a capable, well-equipped enemy, control of the air can never be absolute and will be constrained in some degree. This may be limited in time and space as was the case when Keith Park flew his 'big wings tactics' over the mole at Dunkirk during the Royal Navy evacuation or, in this case, where it was achieved by his predecessor over the Chindit landing grounds. The important factor for the senior commanders was to ensure that they each understood the vocabulary being employed and intuitively understood the need for joint, combined and coherent planning.

It is also clear from this book that air superiority has to be contested, gained and then maintained. The enemy clearly has a vote and may choose to cede control of the air, or may simply not have the capacity to contest it. Peter Preston-Hough does an admirable job of explaining the Japanese context at each phase of the conflict. It is evident that both (or all) sides had other strategic imperatives ranging from the priority in men and matériel being given by the British to defeating Hitler's Germany through to industrial overstretch. Building, manning and equipping a fully effective integrated air defence system was just too far beyond Britain's capacity in the early period examined in this study and this comes out very clearly from the author's analysis. Radar, early warning, intelligence, adequate communications and, last but not least, the fighters and aircrew were just not available: the Battle of Britain and its immediate aftermath had to take priority. As Britain, alone and then with increasing American support, moved into the Middle East, that theatre had higher priority. As more resources became available the pendulum in the Far East swung back in favour of the Allies. Control of the air, locally, in corridors and then more widely allowed ground commanders increasing flexibility. Peter Preston-Hough highlights the reality that even at the very end of the campaign, the Japanese retained a capability to at least hinder and disrupt Allied operations. The campaign may not have had much scholarly or popular attention, but it was no walkover for those involved.

Peter Preston-Hough's admirable study helps to rectify this substantial gap in the air power historiography as well as in the wider literature. Based as it is on his PhD thesis, it is a truly original and rigorous piece of work. At the same time, it is eminently readable and a valuable contribution to any library or collection.

Dr Peter Gray
Director: Centre for War Studies
University of Birmingham

Preface and Acknowledgements

When I started my research I have to admit to a near total ignorance of the air war in Burma and the Far East in the Second World War. Apart from knowing a little bit about Buffalos over Singapore, air transport operations and seeing some film footage of Hurricanes dropping bombs near to the Imphal Plain, I had no idea of the long and involved air campaign which was crucial to the Allies' eventual success in Burma. As my research progressed and the themes developed, I realised that the efforts of Allied service personnel stationed a very long way from home are overshadowed in academic terms by more famous events. Bookshelves are full of academic re-appraisals of the Battle of Britain or the Strategic Air Offensive, but there is nothing about the R.A.F.'s long-range bombing operations over Burma, or maritime reconnaissance sorties over the Indian Ocean. My PhD thesis is, to the best of knowledge, the first academic work about one aspect of the air war in Burma and I sincerely hope it will inspire other researchers to explore the subject not only to further historical knowledge but also to honour the Far East service personnel who were stationed a long way from home in a country with violent extremes of weather, fighting an often ruthless and relentless enemy.

It is said that writing and researching a PhD thesis is a lonely and personal activity but that is not totally true. Without the help and support of so many people a project like this would not 'take off and fly' so it is only right and proper to acknowledge the following people:

Thank you to the staff at the National Archive in Kew for finding the massive number of documents I have required for my research. Thanks are due to the staff at Churchill College Cambridge University Archive Centre for their help in producing Viscount Slim's papers and, in addition, the College's domestic staff for their assistance during my visits. Thank you to the staff at Christ Church College Oxford University Archive Centre for their forbearance producing the Portal Papers and the staff at Northwich library in Cheshire for obtaining obscure books from all over the country without once blinking their eyes.

My everlasting gratitude goes to Peter Elliot, the Keeper of Records at the Royal Air Force Museum in Hendon. Peter has been, without doubt, one of the most influential people involved in this and previous projects, always ready to field my questions or queries with good humour and expert knowledge.

Special thanks must be offered to Professor Malcolm Wanklyn for expertly proof reading the thesis.

I would like to thank the staff at Helion Publishing, in particular Duncan Rogers and Patrick Butcher, for making the transition between thesis and book a painless experience. Similarly, I would like to express my gratitude to Dr Peter Gray for agreeing to write the foreword.

Thank you to my friends, colleagues and students, far too numerous to name, who have provided support, practical advice, and listening ears for my tales of triumph and tragedy.

Thank you to Professor John Buckley who supervised the thesis with good humour, tact, understanding and sympathy. I was very lucky to have had John as my supervisor and friend, and shall always be in his debt.

I would also like to pay tribute to Pauline McClelland who was my history lecturer at Leicester Polytechnic between 1976 and 1979. Pauline was a source of great inspiration both as a lecturer and on a personal level, realizing and nurturing my interests in military history. I will never forget Pauline's interest in what I did and the encouragement she gave me throughout those three years. Thank you.

Finally to my family, past and present, thank you for your support and encouragement, but in particular my wife, Susan, who has played a huge role in putting up with absences, despair, joy and frustration to ensure the thesis and book was completed.

To you all, a sincere and heartfelt thank you.

Explanatory Notes

1. To maintain consistency 1940s place names will be used, for example, Siam instead of Thailand, Ceylon instead of Sri Lanka.

2. Japanese records. This book makes extensive reference to Christopher Shores' *Air War for Burma*. Mr Shores was assisted by two Japanese historians, Hiroshi Ichimura and Doctor Yasuo Izawa who had access to official Japanese records and their findings have been used in preparing the day to day summaries of Japanese operations and aircraft losses for this book. Therefore when 'Japanese records' are referred to, the information will have been taken from *Air War for Burma*, and suitable references will be made to the relevant page or pages in the footnotes.

3. Aircraft Nomenclature. British aircraft will be referred to by their name, e.g. Spitfire. United States aircraft initially will be referred to by the company code and name, e.g. P-51 Mustang, and after that by its name only. The exception to this will be the P-40 whose different marks were referred to by different names (Warhawk, Tomahawk, Kittyhawk) so to maintain consistency the term P-40 will be retained. The American Douglas C-47 transport aircraft was known in U.S. service as the Skytrain, but more commonly in R.A.F. service as the Dakota, and this name will be used in the book. Japanese aircraft will be referred to in the first instance by its company code and Allied code name, e.g. Ki-43 Oscar, and from then by its official Allied code name only. The following list shows a table of all the Japanese aircraft mentioned in the thesis, giving their parent company, Japanese names, Allied codenames (when given) and purposes:

Company/Code	Japanese Name	Allied name	Purpose
Kawanishi N1K1-J	*Shiden* (Violet Lightning)	George	Single-engine fighter
Kawasaki Ki-45	*Toryu* (Dragon Killer)	Nick	Twin-engine fighter
Kawasaki Ki-48		Lily	Twin-engine bomber
Kawasaki Ki-61	*Hien* (Flying Swallow)	Tony	Single- engine fighter
Kawasaki Ki-100			Single-engine fighter
Mitsubishi A5M		Claude	Single-engine fighter
Mitsubishi A6M		Zeke or Zero	Single-engine fighter
Mitsubishi G4M		Betty	Twin-engine bomber
Mitsubishi J2M	*Raiden* (Thunderbolt)	Jack	Single-engine fighter
Mitsubishi Ki-21		Sally	Twin-engine bomber
Mitsubishi Ki-46		Dinah	Twin-engine reconnaissance
Nakajima Ki-27		Nate	Single-engine fighter
Nakajima Ki-43	*Hayabusa* (Peregrine Falcon)	Oscar	Single-engine fighter
Nakajima Ki-44	*Shoki* (Demon)	Tojo	Single-engine fighter
Nakajima Ki-100	*Donryu* (Storm Dragon)	Helen	Twin-engine bomber
Nakajima Ki-84	*Hayate* (Gale)	Frank	Single-engine fighter

4. <u>Japanese Army Air Force Organisation</u>. The following table gives a guide to the J.A.A.F. operational organisation as described in the text.

Kokugun (Air Army)	Exercised the highest administrative and operational authority.
Hikoshidan (Flying Division)	Coordinated operations over a given area.
Hikodan (Air Brigade)	Each *Hikoshidan* controlled two or more *Hikodan*. Flexible in composition and size, mixed fighter and bomber formation with a small H.Q. flight of reconnaissance or photo reconnaissance aircraft. General strength of three or four *Hikosentai* plus ancillary units.
Hikosentai (Flying Operational Unit)	Basic operational unit of the J.A.A.F. with a strength of 27 aircraft. Name often shortened to *Sentai*.

Hikochutai (Flying Company-Squadron)	Three *Hikochutai* to a *Hikosentai*, each with a strength of nine aircraft. Name often shortened to *Chutai*.
Hentai (Section)	Smallest tactical formation in J.A.A.F., flight of between three to five aircraft.

The approximate comparative structure of the combatants' flying units is as follows:

R.A.F.	**J.A.A.F.**	**U.S.A.A.F.**
Group	*Hikodan*	Wing
Wing	*Sentai*	Group
Squadron	*Chutai*	Squadron

Principal Allied Commanders

This list is not exhaustive, but reflects the commanding officers referred to in the book, their rank on appointment and the date, when available, they were appointed. First names are given when available.

Date of Appointment

Air Commanders prior to December 1941
Commander in Chief, Far East
A.C.M. Robert Brooke-Popham   18th November 1940

A.O.C. R.A.F. India
A.M. Philip Joubert de la Ferte   29th September 1937

Commanders during the Japanese Invasion
R.A.F. Air Headquarters Far East
A.O.C.
A.V.M. Conway Pulford   6th March 1941

Assistant A.O.C.
A.V.M. Paul Maltby   11th February 1942

A.O.C. No 221 Group
A.V.M. Donald Stevenson   17th December 1941

India Command 1942-1943
A.O.C. in C.
A.M. Sir Richard Pierse   6th March 1942
(Promoted to A.C.M. July 1942)

A.H.Q. Bengal
A.V.M. Donald Stevenson   20th April 1942
A.V.M. Thomas Williams   1st January 1943

221 Group R.A.F.
Air Commodore H.J.F. Hunter   20th April 1942
Air Commodore H.V. Rowley   1st May 1943

222 Group R.A.F.
A.V.M. J.H. D'Albiac   13th March 1942
A.V.M. A. Lees   1st December 1942

223 Group R.A.F.
Air Commodore P.H. Mackworth   5th May 1942
Air Commodore A. Gray   2nd August 1942
Air Commodore H.J.F. Hunter   1st May 1943

224 Group R.A.F.
Air Commodore G.E. Wilson   24th August 1942
Air Commodore A. Gray   2nd January 1943

225 Group R.A.F.
Air Commodore P.H. Mackworth   2nd June 1942

Air Command South-East Asia formed on 15th December 1943
Allied Air Commander-in-Chief
A.C.M. Sir Richard Pierse   16th November 1943
Air Marshal Sir Guy Garrod (Temporary)   27th November 1944
A.C.M. Sir Keith Park   25th February 1945

Eastern Air Command (disbanded on 1st June 1945)
Air Commander (and Second in Command)
Lieutenant-General George E. Stratemeyer (U.S.A.A.F.)   15th December 1943

Assistant Air Commander
A.V.M. Thomas Williams   15th December 1943
A.M. Sir Alec Coryton   4th December 1944

Headquarters R.A.F. Burma
A.M. Sir Alec Coryton   4th December 1944
A.M. Sir Hugh Saunders   10th August 1945

Third Tactical Air Force (disbanded on 4th December 1944)
A.M. Sir John Baldwin   15th December 1943
A.M. Sir Alec Coryton   15th August 1944

Strategic Air Force
Brigadier-General Howard Davidson (U.S.A.A.F.)   15th December 1943
Air Commodore Francis Mellersh   20th June 1944

Photographic Reconnaissance Force
Group Captain S.G. Wise   1st February 1944
Colonel Minton Kaye (U.S.A.A.F.)   9th January 1945

Troop Carrier Command
Brigadier-General William Old (U.S.A.A.F.)   15th December 1943

Tenth U.S. Army Air Force
Major-General Howard Davidson   20th June 1944

221 Group R.A.F.
Air Commodore H.V. Rowley   15th December 1943
A.V.M. Stanley Vincent   17th February 1944
A.V.M. Cecil Bouchier   12th June 1944

222 Group R.A.F.
A.V.M. A. Lees   16th November 1943
A.M. A. Durston   28th March 1944

224 Group R.A.F.
Air Commodore A. Gray   15th December 1943
A.V.M. the Earl of Bandon   19th July 1944

225 Group R.A.F.
Air Commodore P.H. Mackworth   16th November 1943
A.V.M. N.L. Desoer   23rd August 1944

Chiefs of the Air Staff
A.C.M. Sir Cyril Newall   1st September 1937
A.C.M. Sir Charles Portal   25th October 1940

Land Commanders

Far East Command
Lieutenant General Sir Henry Pownall   23rd December 1941

Malaya Command
Lieutenant General Arthur Percival   May 1941

Commander in Chief India
General Sir Archibald Wavell   June 1941

Burma Corps
Major General William Slim   13th March 1942

XV Corps
Lieutenant General William Slim   June 1942

Fourteenth Army
Lieutenant General William Slim   October 1943
(Promoted to General July 1945, Knighted December 1944)

Chief of Staff China Theatre and U.S. Commander China-Burma-India Theatre
Major General Joseph Stilwell   January 1942

Long Range Penetration Force (The Chindits)
Colonel Orde Wingate   April 1942
(Promoted to Major General January 1944)

Introduction

In December 1941 Japanese forces attacked American and British bases in the Pacific and Far East with a series of well planned and executed air raids which disabled their opponents, quickly giving the Japanese air superiority. From June 1942 the Allies, notably Britain, its Commonwealth forces and America, had to reverse these early setbacks themselves to gain air superiority. By mid-1944 this had been broadly achieved. This book will critically analyse the air superiority campaign in Burma, India and Malaya between 1941 and 1945. It will demonstrate how and why the Japanese initially won air superiority through a combination of better aircraft, experienced aircrew and a successful pre-emptive counter-air campaign. The book will then analyse how, why and with what effectiveness the Allies overcame their initial weaknesses in early warning, aircraft, aircrew and air combat tactics to gain air superiority in 1944 and air supremacy in 1945. Furthermore, it will examine the crucial role Japanese industry played in failing to supply sufficient resources to the Burma front and how Japan's war in other theatres affected the eventual outcome.

Gaining and retaining air superiority in Burma was supremely important to the Allies. Air Chief Marshal Sir Keith Park, Commander-in-Chief Air Forces South Sea Asia from February 1945, was in no doubt of the importance of air superiority when he wrote the same year:

> It is however worth pausing to consider the results had enemy aircraft been allowed unrestricted use of the sky. The air supply on which the whole land campaign hinged would have been impossible, the attrition rate of our close support squadrons, which worked with accuracy and effect would have been prohibitive and the disruption caused by our strategic bombers to the enemy's communications far to the rear could not have been such as to have materially influenced the battle.[1]

As supplies and material arrived to reinforce the region in 1942, Indian ports, particularly Calcutta, had to be defended against air attack, as did Indian industry

---

1   The National Archives Kew (TNA), Air 23/4665, Despatch on Air Operations by Air Chief Marshal Sir Keith Park 1944-1945, p.22.

and the extensive airfield building programme. Air superiority in Burma assumed greater importance in 1944 when General William Slim advocated his strategy of troops standing and fighting rather than withdrawing when surrounded; troops would be resupplied by air transport and supported by ground attack aircraft, both classes of aircraft being vulnerable to Japanese fighters. Air transport was also central to General Orde Wingate's Long Range Penetration Force, more commonly known as the Chindits, and their two incursions into Burma in 1943 and 1944. Air superiority was vital to allow these aircraft to operate successfully and this book will show how and with what success this was achieved. From October 1944, the Allied air superiority campaign was assisted by the withdrawal and transfer of Japanese air units to defend their bases in the Pacific and Japan itself. Air combat between the protagonists reduced and the Allied counter-air campaign showed little return against the effort as there were fewer Japanese aircraft dispersed around many airfields. By June 1945, the Japanese Army Air Force (J.A.A.F.) had completely withdrawn from Burma leaving the Allies with unchallenged air supremacy which continued until the war ended in August 1945.

In order to provide a methodological framework, it is necessary to understand what is meant by the terms air superiority and air supremacy. Both concepts are discussed in air power literature such as Hallion and Gooch, but essentially air superiority can be considered as controlling one's airspace so as to ensure that other operations, in the air and on land and sea, can proceed without interference.[2] In 2003 Meilinger quoted the U.S. Department of Defense definitions and these give a clear description; air superiority:

> That degree of dominance in the airbattle [sic] of one force over another which permits the conduct of operations by the former and its related land, sea and air forces at a given time and place without prohibitive interference by the opposing force.

Air supremacy:

> That degree of air superiority wherein the opposing air force is incapable of effective interference.[3]

A modern definition taken from the R.A.F.'s *AP 3000 British Air and Space Power Doctrine* is "The freedom, bound by time, to use a volume of airspace for one's own purposes while, if necessary, denying its use to an opponent."[4] Air supremacy is the

---

2   Hallion, *Strike from the Sky*, p.1 and Gooch, *Air Power Theory and Practice*, p.17.
3   Meilinger, *Airwar: Theory and Practice*, p.32.
4   Anon, *AP 3000 British Air and Space Power Doctrine*, Centre for Air Power Studies R.A.F. 2009.

most desired state, where the enemy air force is incapable of effectively interfering with operations. Air superiority is the previous stage where interference is reduced to the lowest possible levels. So in essence air superiority can be likened to an aerial 'umbrella' under which air, land and sea operations may proceed. This 'umbrella' does not have to be a permanent state, as localized temporary air superiority over a battle-field may result in ground forces operating in a sterile environment secure from enemy aerial interference.

Air superiority can be achieved in a number of ways. Budiansky wrote of the 1935 *Luftwaffe* Regulation 16:

> It stated that the air forces would be called upon to perform many tasks, from supporting the army and navy to striking strategic targets. Gaining air superiority was a prerequisite for all these missions, but there were many places where the battle for air superiority would be decided: in attacks on enemy airfields and aircraft factories, in air-to-air combat, in the fire from flak units defending German troops and targets.[5]

The fundamental aim is to cause attrition to the enemy's air strength by attacking it at source in the aircraft factories or maintenance depots, and by attacking enemy airfields where there is a possibility of reducing aircraft strength as well as damaging or destroying important ancillary supplies and equipment. Attrition can also be inflicted by losses in air-to-air combat either in defensive or offensive operations, or by anti-aircraft fire defending targets.

To achieve these aims relevant factors and equipment are vital. Attacking the enemy's aircraft factories requires a suitable bombing force capable of potentially deep penetration raids. In terms of air defence an efficient early warning and command and control system is essential to prevent unnecessary combat air patrols being flown, which can prove wasteful in terms of aircraft and aircrew fatigue, and stop enemy offensive action. To complement this system, suitable, modern fighter aircraft that have the ability to climb to advantageous heights and then successfully engage the enemy with relevant combat tactics have to be deployed on well sited airfields. Offensively there is a requirement for long-range well armed fighter aircraft, capable of attacking enemy airfields whilst at the same time successfully engaging enemy aircraft in air combat. These interdiction operations are enhanced by an effective intelligence organization, which establish enemy airfield and unit activity, and direct efficient strikes. To fly and operate both categories of aircraft, well-trained and combat experienced aircrew are essential to maximize the potential of defensive and offensive aircraft to achieve air superiority.

Since 1945 the importance of air superiority in Burma and the understanding of how it was eventually achieved have received different levels of analysis. During the

---

5   Budiansky, *Air Power*, p.205.

1950s the official British histories of the Second World War began to be published, five volumes of which covered the war in the Far East, but the air war in this theatre was not given any separate volumes.[6] The five volumes cover the land war in great detail and for the most part they deal with the air war as a supporting factor to ground operations, particularly supply and ground support. Whilst the air superiority campaign is mentioned and acknowledged it is not analysed in any detail; for example there is no analysis of how the early warning organisation was established from 1942, or why Spitfire fighters took so long to reach the region. A more detailed official appreciation of the air war is given in the 'in-house' narrative series written by the R.A.F. Air Historical Branch (A.H.B.) for the government during the late 1940s and early 1950s, but not released for public viewing until the early 1970s. The narratives describe how air superiority was lost and how it was gained, and cover such factors as aircrew, aircraft and tactics and the importance of the American contribution to the counter-air offensive in 1944. However, although the narratives make good use of primary sources they fall short of critical detail in a number of areas. The establishment of the early warning organisation during 1942 is little discussed, and there is a reliance on aircraft damage claims which were probably exaggerated during the counter-air offensive in early 1944. Japanese tactics in the theatre are discussed, but there is little qualitative analysis of the effect of Japan's war in other regions on the Burma campaign. Another semi-official history of the R.A.F.'s participation in Burma was contained in the three volume set written by Richards and Saunders and published in 1953-1954.[7] Whilst using official sources, the books, intended for public consumption, lack in-depth analysis as all theatres were covered in relatively small volumes, where little in-depth coverage of many aspects of the air superiority campaign in Burma is offered. The American official history of the U.S. Army Air Force edited by Craven and Cate predictably focuses on American operations, but is nevertheless a useful source for the Allied counter-air campaign.[8] On the other hand a series of reports by the United States Strategic Bombing Survey dealing with aspects of the campaign such as Japanese air power, the China, Burma, India theatre and Japanese industry, do not present a detailed analysis of the air superiority campaign in Burma.

In books on air power written and edited by academic scholars such as Boog, Buckley, Budiansky, Cox, Gray and Meilinger, the Burma air war is either not mentioned at all, or referred to in brief terms as part of the overall war in the Pacific.[9] For example in John Buckley's *Air Power in the Age of Total War*, a full chapter deals with Japan's war against the Allies, but the war in South East Asia warrants only a few lines. However, he acknowledges that attainment of air superiority, "allowed innovatory

---

6   Kirby (ed.), *The War Against Japan*, 5 volumes.
7   Richards and Saunders, *Royal Air Force 1939-1945*, 3 volumes.
8   Craven and Cate (eds.), *The Army Air Forces in World War II*, 6 volumes.
9   Boog, *The Conduct of the Air War in the Second World War*; Buckley, *Air Power in the Age of Total War*; Budiansky, *Air Power*; Cox and Gray, *Air Power History: Turning Points from Kitty Hawk to Kosovo*; Meilinger, *Airwar: Theory and Practice*.

measures to be undertaken, notably ... the air supply of Orde Wingate's Chindits."[10] Richard Overy's *The Air War 1939-1945* takes a similar approach by subsuming the Burma war into the rest of Japan's conflict.[11] It is useful, for example, in establishing how the Pacific fighting affected Burma, but it does not deal with specific issues such as the air superiority campaign or its essential factors. However, Overy's analysis of the Japanese aircraft economy and its difficulties in providing aircraft in quantity and quality is essential in understanding why Japanese air resources were in short supply.

Specific Burma air war literature varies in analytical content. Books by Probert and Pearson offer an overall picture of the air war, but as they deal with the whole air campaign this inevitably means that any one aspect of the air offensive fails to receive a full analysis.[12] Whilst Henry Probert mentions the air superiority campaign it is generally within chapters rather than as a separate chapter. As a result, whilst he acknowledges the work entailed in establishing an early warning organisation in 1942, space prevents deeper explanation and analysis. Other books dedicated to the air war in Burma by, for example, Shores, Cull and Franks, are useful for personal accounts by combatants and the chronology of events but they often lack deeper academic analysis. Christopher Shores' *Air War for Burma*, on the other hand contains a daily record of operations which is vital as his two collaborators, Hiroshi Ichimura and Yasuo Izawa, had access to surviving Japanese military records which show the attrition rates of Japanese units.[13] Furthermore, campaign books such as those written by Allen and Latimer deal with the air war either perfunctorily or with specific reference to ground operations.[14]

There is a clear variance in how literature deals with the air superiority campaign but they generally agree that the campaign was important in allowing Allied air and ground operations to take place. The only publications that give the campaign separate sections are the A.H.B. narratives, but even those lack detailed discussion of such topics as the early warning organisation, aircraft supply, and the failures of Japanese industry to supply aircraft in quantity and quality.

Together with secondary sources, this book has made extensive use of technical, governmental and operational primary source material held at the National Archive, Kew. Furthermore, original papers appertaining to the Chief of the Air Staff, Sir Charles Portal, were consulted at Christ Church College, Oxford University, as were those of Field Marshal 1st Viscount William Slim, at Churchill College, Cambridge University, and the Air Commander of Far East Air Forces, Air Chief Marshal Sir Richard Pierse, at the R.A.F. Museum, Hendon. Its object is to bring together all the air superiority elements in one study, analyse how each element worked and how they

---

10   Buckley, *Air Power in the Age of Total War*, p.187.
11   Overy, *The Air War 1939-45*.
12   Probert, *The Forgotten Air Force* and Pearson, *The Burma Air Campaign 1941-1945*.
13   Shores, *Air War for Burma*.
14   Allen, *Burma, The Longest War* and Latimer, *Burma: The Forgotten War*.

interacted to achieve the goals of air superiority and air supremacy. It will provide the reader with new interpretations that modify or correct previously held views and it will refine the understanding of how the air supremacy campaign was conducted in Burma from 1941 until 1945.

The diversity of literature relating to the air war in Burma means there are various fundamental questions to be addressed. First the book will analyse why the early warning organisation was not established before the initial Japanese attacks, how it was built up during 1942 and 1943, and the importance of its contribution to the success of the campaign. Second, current literature does not analyse how the combined elements of aircraft, aircrew and air combat tactics contributed to the demise of Japanese air power. Third, scholarship relating to the counter-air campaign from 1942 until the end of 1943 requires examination. It was described by Craven and Cate as being unsuccessful owing to aircraft deficiencies, but the Allied air offensive during the six month period at the beginning of 1944 is said by the A.H.B. to have broken the back of Japanese air strength.[15] Thus further analysis is required to ascertain whether it achieved such a level of success as it appears Japanese aircraft strength did not deteriorate commensurately in line with Allied claims. Fourth there is the question of the extent to which individual factors such as Japanese industry, Japan's war in other theatres and the Japanese High Command contributed towards the eventual loss of air superiority. In addition to these fundamental questions two further pivotal issues will be addressed – when were air superiority and then air supremacy gained, and to what extent were the Allies and Japanese affected by priorities in other theatres? Only after all these factors have been weighed in the balance can the most fundamental question of how air superiority was won be addressed with confidence.

The structure of the book is as follows. Chapter 1 will analyse the early warning organisation in terms of the lack of equipment in Malaya and Burma prior to 8th December 1941 and the Japanese attacks. It will demonstrate how the organisation was established, despite supply and technical difficulties, during 1942 and 1943 until it achieved a level of efficiency in India in 1944 comparable with systems operating in Britain. It will also analyse the technical difficulties of providing mobile early warning facilities in adverse conditions of topography and climate when the Allies were under siege in early 1944, and then during their advance into Burma later that year.

Chapter 2 will analyse the contribution of suitable modern aircraft in their defensive and offensive roles, highlighting the tipping point in late 1943 when the Spitfire and American long-range fighters were introduced to India. Chapter 2 will also demonstrate how Allied aircrew improved in quality and quantity from mid-1942, and analyse why Japanese aircrew quality did not deteriorate in the Burma theatre. Air-to-air combat tactics will be analysed, and will demonstrate how existing tactics were improved and adapted to engage Japanese fighters.

---

15   TNA, Air 41/64, *The Campaigns in the Far East Volume IV: South East Asia November 1943 to August 1945*, p.71.

Chapter 3 will discuss the importance of an efficient counter-air campaign and how the Japanese were able to devastate British and American air strength during the first days of war. It will also analyse how the Allied counter-air campaign in 1942 and 1943 failed to achieve attritional goals against the J.A.A.F. due to a lack of suitable aircraft. Finally it will show how the introduction of long-range American fighters in late 1943 transformed the counter-air campaign into a positive operation albeit not as successfully as previously thought.

Chapter 4 will examine how the Japanese industry failed to produce sufficient aircraft in both quality and quantity for Japan's Army and Navy air arms, and how these shortages impacted on Japan's war in Burma. It will also analyse how Japan's war priorities in the Pacific, China and in the homeland affected the supply of aircraft and aircrew to Burma. Finally the chapter will show how Japanese tactics in the theatre failed to take advantage of Allied defensive weaknesses at crucial periods during the campaign, and therefore missed opportunities to disrupt Allied operations.

It is inevitable that some factors of the campaign cannot be fully analysed in a work of this nature. This study will principally deal with the Royal Air Force's air superiority campaign in Malaya, Burma and India between 1941 and 1945, although some assessment will be made of the American contribution. Whilst the American contribution to air defence was less than that of the R.A.F., its involvement in the counter-air campaign was crucial. This will be studied and analysed in Chapter 3.

The essential work of the Wireless Observer Units and the Observer Corps in relation to the early warning organisation is acknowledged in Chapter 1 without giving the units a full appreciation. Similarly although the book makes use of the intelligence agencies' appreciations of Japanese strength and losses during the campaign, and mention is made of intelligence sources in Chapter 3 in relation to the counter-air offensive, a full appreciation would have added another chapter which space did not allow. Furthermore, although R.A.F. Regiment and Army gunners manned anti-aircraft guns on the advanced landing grounds and airfields, both repelling Japanese raiders and taking a toll of enemy aircraft, space precludes a detailed analysis of their contribution. However, it is fully appreciated.

By analysing the elements of the air superiority campaign in Burma between 1941 and 1945 as a whole rather than individually, this book provides a new and crucial contribution to the understanding of the air war in Burma. In the process it sheds light on previously un-researched factors. It also corroborates some existing views, whilst examining critically and challenges some claims about the campaign which have remained largely unquestioned.

1

The Early Warning Organisation

One of the essential elements in the process of attaining and maintaining air superiority is an effective early warning system and the importance of such a system to defend against enemy air attack cannot be over emphasised. It acted as a significant enhancing or force multiplier increasing the potency of all other aspects of air superiority assets. The alternative necessitated standing patrols which would impact on the airframe life of aircraft resulting in more servicing, a costly waste of fuel and an increase in aircrews' flying hours. Moreover there was no guarantee that the patrols would effectively locate the enemy once airborne. This chapter will examine the reasons why, despite its proven value, a viable early warning system was not in place in the Far East in December 1941 and how this deficiency was resolved in India by 1944. Following the fall of Burma in the Spring of 1942, great efforts were made to equip India with an efficient defence system which included radar, supported by an Observer Corps and the formation of Wireless Observer Units, both of which would fill gaps in the radar chain. After defending India, Allied air forces moved on the offensive into Burma, and the early warning system had to be adapted to protect the temporary airfields and landing grounds characteristic of the campaign. This chapter will evaluate for the first time how this was achieved, and explain how the various technical difficulties encountered were overcome. It will also evaluate and analyse how the early warning organisation contributed to the Allies achieving air superiority in 1944 and air supremacy in 1945.

Early Warning and the British Model

The importance of an effective early warning system to defend an area against enemy air attack cannot be over emphasised. The alternative would necessitate standing air patrols which would impact on the airframe life of the aircraft resulting in more servicing, a costly waste of fuel and an increase in a pilot's flying hours. Moreover there would be no guarantee that the patrols would effectively locate the enemy once airborne on their patrols. From its beginnings in the mid-1930s, however, the British early warning system had developed to a stage that by the summer of 1940 incoming raids were being detected in sufficient time to warn the defenders of their presence and direction.

The R.A.F. system in Britain consisted of a complex organisation of radar stations that were linked to filter rooms and then to Group and Sector operation rooms which would analyse the information and warn of the raids' presence, and then control them until the enemy was sighted. This system was called Ground Controlled Interception (G.C.I.). Gaps in the radar chain, particularly at low-level, and confirmation of enemy activity were provided by the Observer Corps who manned strategically placed posts. This is, of course, a very simplified description of a complex operation which, nevertheless, proved its worth during the Battle of Britain. John Terraine quotes the reaction of the German listening service:

> The air was full of voices, calmly and systematically placing fighters here and there and guiding others back to base. It dawned on the listeners that this was part of a complex and smooth-running organisation of great size.[1]

It was, as Denis Richards observed, the product of a number of years of "careful thought and scientific refinement" which allowed R.A.F. fighters to intercept German raiders with advantages without recourse to costly standing patrols.[2] However, it must be recognized that even accounting for radar's success, the equipment, if not the concept, was in its early stages of development; incoming raids were regularly detected, but aircraft heights and numbers were often unreliably interpreted.[3]

Radar stations, Observer Corps posts and the operations rooms were linked by an efficient and reliable system of telephone landlines which were first laid in 1937, so that a radar operator on the coast would be able to report a raid securely by telephone to other links in the chain. The telephone lines were laid when the first radar stations had been built and so by 1940 were well tried and tested. A second element was the relationship between aircraft and the early warning system. Radar stations and Observer Corps positions were situated far enough forward to provide sufficient warning for R.A.F. fighters to engage the enemy in favourable conditions of height, with the sun behind them; the Hawker Hurricane Mark I and Vickers Supermarine Spitfire Mark I could attain 20,000 feet between seven and seven and a half minutes.[4] Nevertheless radar was not enough. Britain could have possessed the finest early warning system, but without reliable communications and high performance aircraft to exploit the advantage the system was incomplete.

Thus by the late Summer of 1940 Britain possessed the first integrated air defence system in the world. There were technical difficulties as the system was in its

1   Terraine, *The Right of the Line*, p.176.
2   Richards, *The Fight at Odds*, p.195.
3   Terraine, *The Right of the Line*, p.176.
4   Townsend, *Duel of Eagles*, p.479.

technological infancy, but it was good enough to be copied by the United States which adopted it for its own air defence.[5] However, although the system was used for the defence of Malta and areas of the Middle East, it had either not arrived or been fully implemented in the Far East at the outbreak of war in 1941.

Early warning in the Far East prior to war

The situation in the Far East prior to December 1941 was far removed from the model of early warning efficiency that existed in Britain. Malaya and Singapore waited for equipment behind other theatres, having "less importance and lower priority."[6] The original intention was to have 20 radar stations in Malaya, but by 1st December 1941 only six had been completed.[7] Other stations were in the process of construction, but would not play a part in trying to repel Japanese attacks. In Burma there was a problem associated with where some of the airfields had been sited. The plan to have a north-south alignment of airfields to provide "maximum operational mobility" was laudable, but:

> The Northern ones were placed too far forward in the Sittang valley where no radar warning was possible. They should have been in the Irrawaddy and Chindwin valleys, allowing radar units to be located to the East ... the airfields had been well built by the Burma Public Works Department for all weather use but they were indefensible without an efficient warning system.[8]

There were attempts to equip the region with radar cover, but moves were hindered by the difficulties in financing the equipment and staff. In September 1939 the Director of Operations, Group Captain William Coryton, asked the Air Ministry if any dates had been established to supply overseas stations with radar sets, and apparently did not receive a reply.[9] Further moves were made in 1940, but the British government showed reluctance to pay for either the equipment or the staff.[10] The provision of high grade personnel to supervise the sets met with the suggestion of a compromise; on 3rd February 1940 Squadron Leader A.V. Hammond suggested a pool of experts could be situated in Egypt and then travel to Singapore to advise when repairs were required, their expenses being paid for when necessary.[11] In March 1941 a request was made for

---

5   Craven and Cate, *The Army Air Forces in World War II, Volume One*, p.290.
6   TNA, Air 41/88, *Signals Volume V: Fighter Control and Interception*, p.55.
7   TNA, Air 41/35, *The Campaigns for the Far East, Volume I, Far East Defence Policy and Preparations for War*, p.19.
8   Probert, *The Forgotten Air Force*, p.83.
9   TNA, Air 20/2143, India and Ceylon Radar Equipment, 1939-1941.
10   Ibid, correspondence dated 24th January 1940 and 30th April 1940.
11   Ibid. Although this note refers to the radar situation in India, a similar situation existed in terms of both finance and staff in Burma and Malaya. No first name is available for Hammond.

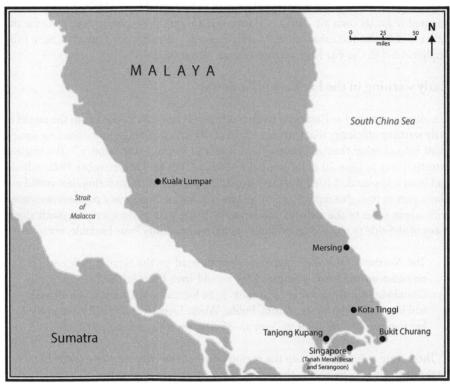

Map 1 Radar Stations in Malaya 1st December 1941

scientific officers to be posted to the Far East to work with the R.A.F., but the reply on 25th March pointed out that the Telecommunications Research Establishment (T.R.E.) was "bone dry" of suitable men unless it was of the "highest priority."[12]

The arrival of R.A.F. Buffalo squadrons in March 1941 prompted the authorities to begin to organise an early warning system.[13] The resulting structure was in place and operating successfully during exercises in August and September 1941, and would give Singapore at least 30 minutes warning of an impending raid.[14] The efforts to achieve even inconsistent coverage, however, were considerable and it is worthwhile to examine these attempts to understand the level of difficulty.

An Air Ministry report dated 17th June 1941 stated that the radar station at Tanah Merah Besar was working whilst the stations at Mersing, Bukit Chunang and

12   TNA, Avia 7/1301, Radar in the Far East, 1941-1945.
13   Probert, *The Forgotten Air Force*, p.30.
14   TNA, Air 41/35, *The Campaigns for the Far East, Volume I, Far East Defence Policy and Preparations for War*, p.42.

Tanjong Kupang were all in the process of being installed.[15] Remaining equipment was to be despatched to the area at the rate of two per month commencing in August, but there would be no Chain Overseas Low (C.O.L.) sets available before the 31st October. For Burma it was a different matter and following a radar survey of the area a subsequent report made it clear that providing cover was a difficult task. Burma's main target areas for an enemy attack would include Rangoon's dock, Syriam's oilfields and Lashio's supply depots.[16] The radar plan accepted that stations could be established in the Rangoon and Syriam areas, giving "cover against aircraft flying above 3,000 feet … [and] cover against low flying aircraft and aircraft minelayers operating over the Rangoon River."[17] However, these areas appeared to be the exception as the report stated the Moulmein area was "not ideal for R.D.F. cover, but good results can be expected over certain areas", while of the Lashio area it said:

> The terrain in this area is unfavourable for R.D.F. but the limited cover provided by a station near the aerodrome is worthwhile in view of the importance of the target. A G.C.I. type station is proposed for this area.

The oilfield was "unsuited to R.D.F. and poor results only would be obtained. At present it is not proposed to erect a station in this area." The unsuitability of the terrain in the region was clearly an obstacle to creating an adequate early warning system and would present technical challenges when radar cover was required from June 1942 onwards.

On 16th September 1941 the Air Ministry reported:

> Sufficient equipment has been allocated to the Far East pool to meet the requirement of Malaya and also of an A.C.O. station at Rangoon and the T.R.U. at Syriam … Units are being despatched at the rate of 2 per week and the priority as between Malaya and Rangoon will presumably be decided by the C. in C. Far East.[18]

However, the C.O.L. equipment allocated to Syriam could not be despatched before November as it was not yet available, and the G.C.I. for Lashio and Tavoy was unlikely to be available before the "early spring of 1942."[19] By 18th November the situation was deteriorating and the Air Ministry contacted Far East Headquarters expressing concerns that the "present R.D.F. plan gives little protection for Penang and Kota Bharu against aircraft approaching from Inland" and requesting information

---

15   TNA, Air 20/2145, Far East: R.D.F. Equipment, 1941-1942, enclosure 16A.
16   Ibid, enclosure 35A.
17   Ibid, enclosure 35A.
18   TNA, Air 20/2145, Far East: R.D.F. Equipment, 1941-1942, enclosure 36A. A.C.O. = Advanced Chain Overseas and T.R.U. = Transportable Radar Unit.
19   Ibid, enclosure 36A.

whether siting portable A.S.V. sets on hills would be feasible.[20] Far Eastern command replied on 19th November that the area between Penang and Kota Bharu was "almost impenetrable, communications not existent" and said it would report as investigations progressed.[21] Events overtook these investigations and supply of equipment to the region. On 8th December as Japanese forces attacked Malaya, the Air Ministry reported that, "It has been decided to form the following A.M.E. Stations for despatch to the Far East" and proceeded to list a number of units and personnel for deployment.[22] However, three of the units' technical staff were still training and would not be available for despatch until 20th January 1942. Similarly on 9th December, the Director of Operations reported to the Chief of the Air Staff that the remaining sets intended to fill the gaps in both high and low coverage would be despatched by the end of April 1942. A total of six G.C.I. sets were still required, three of which would be despatched from Great Britain in January, whilst the other three could be made available "at the expense of the Middle East."[23] On 24th December the Air Ministry informed Far East Headquarters that further equipment and staff were being despatched to Singapore, Malaya and Ceylon, and on Christmas Day an additional message was sent regarding equipment for Burma.[24] In every case the units would not be in position until the end of January 1942. It was a matter of too little, too late and despite requests for additional radar sets, by the time the campaign started little could be done.[25]

Previous studies of this period suggests that the Far East command had to face the Japanese with what equipment was in place but attempts to reinforce the region had been made. Throughout 1941 moves were made to supply the area with more radar equipment, but owing to demands from other theatres the sets were offered essentially too late for use. It was not merely a matter of sending radar sets for deployment either, as each site required careful surveying to gain the maximum cover against enemy aircraft. However, there were other important factors that impacted on the early warning coverage.

The size of the frontier to be defended, over 700 miles, meant that many more radar sets than were possible to supply would be needed to copy the "overlapping

20   A.S.V. = Air to Surface Vessel.
21   TNA, Air 20/2145, Far East: R.D.F. Equipment, 1941-1942, enclosure 40A.
22   A.M.E.S. = Air Ministry Experimental Station which was the name given to radar stations.
23   TNA, Air 20/2145, Far East: R.D.F. Equipment, 1941-1942, enclosure 41A.
24   TNA, Air 20/2145, Far East: R.D.F. Equipment, 1941-1942, Air Ministry to Far East H.Q. 24th December 1941.
25   TNA, Air 23/2133 and Air 23/2134, Far East Operations: Air Marshal Sir Richard Pierse personal signals, for telexes between Pierse and the Air Ministry and the Chief of the Air Staff. Pierse took command of the air forces in January 1942 and made numerous requests for additional equipment which would only arrive after this early part of the campaign was over. When Pierse arrived in India in March 1942 he was an Air Marshal, being promoted to Air Chief Marshal in July 1942.

floodlight system" that was used in Britain.[26] In addition there was the crucial factor of communications. There was a shortage of cable material in the area, and the cable laying procedure took a long time even in good conditions. In the Far East both construction and maintenance were seriously affected by the region's topography and violent weather conditions. It was practically impossible in these conditions to lay even temporary landlines, and radio sets were in short supply and were unavailable for early warning purposes.[27] The British network depended on secure telephone lines which connected radar stations with Operations Rooms and fighter airfields, but in the Far East there were too few lines, each of which passed through a telephone exchange.[28] These lines were vulnerable to enemy damage as well as sabotage by fifth-columnists.

Similar problems affected the Observer Corps. At the end of 1940 there was no Observer Corps in Malaya, and when units were formed there was little time left to train the personnel for their wartime duties. The topography also made it "impossible to establish observer posts in the mountainous country of central Malaya which caused serious gaps in the early warning system."[29] Landlines were non-existent, radio sets were in short supply and alternative methods were not always successful as Sergeant Don Purdon, a Bristol Blenheim navigator, remembered:

> For warning we had to rely on an outpost in the hills manned by Burma Frontier Force soldiers who spoke little English – communication was by heliograph. I don't think any of us could read it so we had to rely on a Burma Frontier Force counterpart first to read it and then translate from Burmese! One never knew if the flashes from the hills meant an air raid under way or whether it was a call for rations or other mundane needs![30]

However, it must not be thought that the Observer Corps were totally unprepared though as will be seen later the coverage varied from area to area as there was no common standard.

India and its pre-war quest for radar

The establishment of the early warning system in India has not received detailed attention from historians; some works make no mention of the establishment at all, whilst others refer to the efforts in varying levels of detail. Pearson and Kirby make no mention of the systems, while Richards and Saunders deals with the matter in

---

26   TNA, Air 41/88, *Signals, Volume V: Fighter Control and Interception*, p.56.
27   Ibid, p.57.
28   TNA, Air 41/35, *The Campaigns for the Far East, Volume I, Far East Defence Policy and Preparations for War*, p.42.
29   Ibid, p.41.
30   Shores, *Bloody Shambles Volume One*, p. 267.

one paragraph.[31] Probert does give the subject more attention pointing out that from having no radar sets in March 1942 India had 52 operational sets by the following December with seven filter rooms in use, together with a functioning Observer Corps.[32] There the detail finishes, Probert acknowledging the effort, "A bland statement this, concealing a vast amount of work, often highly skilled, under usually very difficult circumstances."[33] But the background to the establishment of an early warning system in India has its roots three years earlier in 1939.

The allocation of radar sets to India met with the same difficulties as Malaya and Burma owing to low priority, cost and technical problems. During 1939 the Air Officer Commanding (A.O.C.) India, Air Marshal Sir Philip Joubert de la Ferté requested allocation of a mobile set either by purchase or loan.[34] The Air Ministry opined that the requirement in India was "slight" and there were no sets available for the next twelve months.[35] Furthermore, when Joubert requested to borrow a set in March, the Chief of the Air Staff (C.A.S.) repeated no sets were available for twelve months and reminded him of the £5000 cost. The frustration of repeated delays prompted Joubert to write in April:

> Admit our requirements appear unimportant but will not be able to organise effective A/A defence North-West Frontier unless we obtain this essential unit. Operation of station at Trincomalee unlikely gives positive information of value on North-West Frontier owing to effect mountains [sic].[36]

However, the Air Ministry stuck to its position and Joubert suggested a plan to loan a radar set pending payment as it was hoped funds would be made available from the Chatfield Commission's report on the defence of India.[37] The Chatfield Commission to examine India's defences was chaired by The Lord Ernle Chatfield in 1938 and recommended India's defence should concentrate on sea communications, the modernisation of the Indian Army and re-equipment of R.A.F. squadrons, whilst spending less on defending the North-West frontier. The plan to borrow a radar set floundered through cost questions as the Committee was exploring how reorganisation and re-equipment costs could be spread over five years as it believed more than one radar set was required for India's defence. After being asked to explain

31 Pearson, *The Burma Air Campaign 1941-1945*; Kirby (ed.), *The War Against Japan, Volume I*; Richards and Saunders, *The Fight is Won*, p.308.
32 Probert, *The Forgotten Air Force*, p.113.
33 Ibid, p.114.
34 TNA, Air 2/3172, Overseas and Colonies; Burma; R.D.F. Station, 1939-1945, letter 9th March 1939.
35 Ibid, enclosure 1B.
36 Ibid, 17th April 1939. It is to be noted that even at that time doubts were being expressed about the efficiency of radar in mountainous regions.
37 TNA, Air 23/691, Information for Chatfield Commission, 1937-1938.

his position Joubert wrote to Air Vice-Marshal Richard Peirse who was Deputy Chief of the Air Staff (D.C.A.S.):

> ... a mobile R.D.F. station is essential as the backbone of the air defence of the North-West of India .... I could not tolerate for much longer the present situation where certain vital targets in North-Western India are exposed to attack with but the most rudimentary organisation for their protection ... I consider myself the best judge of what is required out here, and I merely ask the Air Ministry to order this material and send it out in advance of the implementation of the Chatfield Report. I am rather cross about this, and I hope you will be able to help me. Time-wasting of this nature is more than irritating.[38]

At the beginning of October 1939 it was agreed to loan one set to India, but the war in Europe meant supplies to India and elsewhere lacked priority, the India Office being informed on 22nd October that the delivery estimate was "a good deal too optimistic."[39] However, there were signs that the necessity of an observer system equipped with wireless to complement the radar was being considered as the proposed location of the set at Peshawar was thought to be of little value and this approach would eventually become an integral part of the overall early warning plan in areas where radar, through technical reasons, would not work.[40]

Although the provision of three radar sets for India was acknowledged on 18th December 1939 the provision had to take its turn "in the order of priority for supply of equipment to ports abroad."[41] To assist the Governments of India and Burma to decide what types of radar they required a survey would examine various factors; details of current available radar sets; their costs; the rate of production; and the situation regarding reconnaissance and "execution of works of installation for ports abroad."[42] However, there were difficulties as a mobile radar set would not be available before the second half of 1940 and:

> The production of the expensive C.O. sets is high and the limitation of supply will be the various work surfaces needed for their installation. The cost of this set including work surfaces would be 10 Lakhs, but while it is the set recommended

---

38   TNA, Air 2/3172, Overseas and Colonies; Burma; R.D.F. Station, 1939-1945, letter dated 7th June 1939.
39   TNA, Air 2/4125, Communications; Request from Air Officer Commanding for additional HF D/F set and mobile RDF set on deferred payment terms, 1939-1940, enclosure 11A.
40   Ibid.
41   TNA, Air 20/2143, India and Ceylon Radar Equipment; 1939-1941. The three sets were for Bombay, Calcutta and Karachi.
42   Ibid, letter dated 17th January 1940.

for ports it seems little doubt that weaker and less expensive sets would in some cases be sufficient.[43]

A further difficulty was finding suitable R.A.F. staff to operate the sets, and those operatives supplied by India would have to be trained in Britain at additional cost.

1940 heralded a new round of discussions about Indian radar requirements. The Signals Branch enquired on 1st January what types of sets (and cost) were recommended for the defence of the Indian ports and what set was of likely use for the detection of surface vessels.[44] Edmund Dixon of the Radio Detection Committee replied that the problem had been "tentatively considered" with different types of radar (mobile, ordinary and low) probably being suited for the various locations, whilst the cost of the equipment was "not known as a fact", but the estimates made "were sufficiently good for [your] purposes."[45] The optimism was tempered when Joubert (now back in Britain as an R.D.F. advisor) realistically dealt with priorities:

> Much depends, however, upon whether – as is the case at the moment – we are to be faced continually with a state of emergency in this country. Continuance of these emergencies will naturally add to the already considerable delays in production.[46]

Moreover on 18th January comprehensive results of the R.D.F. committee's enquiries were published and the report covered the types and cost of equipment:

> No definite <u>rate of production</u> can be given at present. The rate is altered as emergencies arise and as the production of one type is advanced and of others retarded when the present home emergency programme has been completed.[47]

If these emergencies did not occur, the MB2 mobile set would be available in May 1940. The mobile MB1 set would be sent to Egypt in February and the C.H.L. set would be available for overseas deployment in June. Radar equipment's siting was vital to its efficiency and whilst the report made reference to site surveys in Malta, Aden and Egypt, India is notable for its absence. However, there were still questions relating to the types of radar set, their costs and the numbers of operating staff. For example, in January 1940 the Director for Training was asked if he could supply an estimate of training costs and he replied that it was unlikely he'd "be able to supply an

---

43   Ibid, 10 Lakhs would have equated to approximately £66,800 in 1940.
44   TNA, Air 2/4125, Communications: Request from Air Officer Commanding for additional HF D/F set and mobile RDF set on deferred payment terms, 1939-1940.
45   Ibid, handwritten note on enclosure 19A.
46   Ibid, Joubert to the War Cabinet Office, 10th January 1940.
47   Ibid, the underlining appears in the report.

estimate for some time as we've not had a regular course at a training establishment", indicating that overseas stations had not been considered for radar deployment.[48]

On 3rd February 1940 the Air Ministry reported that the Chiefs of Staff had completed a review of military rearmament policy in the Middle East and India.[49] It was clear that force increases depended on the strategic situation and ultimately it would be "a long-term policy and we cannot at present foresee when it will be possible to send the additional squadrons to India"[50] In terms of radar:

> R.D.F. would be a valuable asset if it would work satisfactorily in vicinity of Frontier mountains. Technical possibilities are being considered and arrangements are being made for an R.D.F. expert now proceeding to Egypt and Aden to go on to India to carry out investigations.[51]

Before the expert arrived, the Air Ministry contacted the A.O.C. India, Air Marshal Sir John Higgins, to state that the mobile set as previously ordered was "not recommended for use on the Frontier owing to echoes off hills" and two inexpensive alternative sets were to be ordered for experimental purposes.[52]

India's ports were visited by Flight Lieutenant J.F. Atherton between 29th March and 13th April 1940, and he filed his report to the A.O.C. India on 18th April 1940.[53] Atherton visited Karachi, Bombay, Cochin, Madras, and Calcutta and he reported that the radar system was to provide cover from air and sea attacks:

> The first four ports require protection against enemy shipping and ship-borne aircraft. In the case of Calcutta, only detection of aircraft required, as the port is some considerable distance up the HOOGLY RIVER [sic].[54]

Atherton made general recommendations that Karachi, Bombay, Cochin and Madras would be best served by the C.O.L. equipment that would give cover to a distance of 50 to 60 miles, but was not adapted to give an aircraft's height, whilst assisting coastal guns to detect shipping in conditions of bad visibility; the report stressed that in the latter case it would only be an additional aid and not take the place

---

48 Ibid, loose minute 26.
49 Ibid, Air Ministry to A.H.Q. India.
50 Ibid.
51 Ibid.
52 Ibid, Air Ministry to Higgins, 7th March 1941. The experimental sets were for use from aircraft which would assist in coastal defence.
53 TNA, Avia 15/370, Radar: Overseas Stations; Sites and Layouts of RDF stations in India, 1940-1942, Report on Possible Provision of R.D.F. at Defended Ports in India. No first name is available for Atherton.
54 Ibid, p.6. The Hooghly River is a distributary of the River Ganges. The capital letters are contained in the report.

of a seaward patrol. For Calcutta a full C.O. station was suggested which would detect aircraft flying at 10,000 feet at a range up to 80 to 100 miles, the height being determined to plus/minus 2,000 feet. Cost had to be balanced against efficiency:

> The cost would be in the neighbourhood of £60,000 to £70,000. Should this cost be prohibitive, an M.B. (Mobile) set could be employed at about a tenth of the cost. This would give the same facilities as a C.O. but with a range of approximately only 35 miles.[55]

Atherton reported on numerous technical difficulties. Karachi was deemed unsuitable for a C.O. station, "since there might be considerable difficulty due to fixed echoes from the mountains in the north", but a C.O.L. set mounted in nearby Manora "might be expected to detect a cruiser at 20,000 yards and aircraft at 50 – 60 miles." Topographical difficulties were noted at Bombay as the most suitable sites on Malabar Hill or Cumbatta Hill were rendered unsuitable by the "numerous buildings," whereas Sambhu Packhadee had results similar to Karachi."[56] Cochin provided difficulties as the terrain was very flat and not much above sea level, which posed a technical problem as the contemporary C.O.L. set required a height of "at least 60 feet above sea level" for it to work. Atherton did note that a new type of tower mounted equipment would eventually become available, but the cost of providing solid foundations for towers of 340 or 360 feet on waterlogged land a considerable distance inland was high:

> There would be no such difficulty for a C.O. station in the Cochin area but I have presumed that the cost of such a station would be considered too high for the port.[57]

Madras had three possible sites: the roof of the Navy Office; the Pallawava Hills which had good range against aircraft but not ships; and the north end of Madras which was low lying. Here the radar equipment would work better if it was mounted on towers. The terrain around Calcutta was also flat but, for Atherton, there were no "technical difficulties" selecting a suitable site for either C.O. or mobile stations, but the "problem of siting a station in this district is, however, tactical rather than technical, being a question of communications, power supplies, internal security, etc."[58] Problems were not confined to the Eastern coast as the threat to India in 1940 was perceived as coming from the Soviet Union in the north-west and two other reports show that the frontier had similar technical difficulties siting equipment in

55   Ibid, p.2.
56   Ibid, p.3.
57   Ibid, p.4.
58   Ibid, p.5.

mountainous regions.[59] The T.R.E. were researching the problems, but a solution was not likely to happen quickly as various trials had failed to produce a satisfactory set for overland use and further research was unlikely to bear results for another six months.[60]

The delay would carry on into 1941 when radar sets were in short supply owing to the increasing demands of the Middle East and Soviet Union:

> It is understood the India Stores Dept. have now ordered the necessary equipment for these four stations. They appear so low on the list of priority of R.D.F. requirements in general, that it is unlikely that the materials will be forthcoming for many months to come.[61]

By 20th June 1941 the likelihood of India receiving radar receded when the Air Ministry told A.H.Q. India that although R.D.F. cover was to be provided at Hong Kong and Ceylon, "The provision of equipment for India has been postponed until 1942."[62] Atherton wrote that his surveys had been limited by:

1. The comparatively undeveloped state of plans for the air defence of India.
2. The reluctance of the Government of India to spend any money on R.D.F.
3. The then limited knowledge of the performance of different types of R.D.F. equipment.[63]

Atherton's findings require comment. The plans for the defence of India had assumed attacks were going to come from the north-west rather than from the north-east or east and the early warning system was based on the assumption that possible attacks were likely to come from this direction. Radar technology worked well over Britain, or in Malta, but India's mountainous regions presented a different situation, thus giving scientists new challenges. If Atherton was fundamentally correct, he was partially mistaken in his statement that India was reluctant to spend any money on radar. India had to construct its conventional forces and a brief examination of the situation following the Chatfield Commission will show India's dilemma.

---

59   TNA, Avia 15/370, Radar: Overseas Stations; Sites and Layouts of RDF stations in India, 1940-1942, note from Air Ministry to A.H.Q. India, 29th April 1940. Bayly and Harper, *Forgotten Armies*, p.77, refer to a book written by Victor Bayley, *Is India Impregnable?*, which was "symptomatic" in speculating "the Russians and Afghan rebels would try to invade the 'treasure house of the world' as the Great Mughals had called India."
60   Ibid, T.R.E. to A.H.Q. India, 10th September 1940.
61   TNA, Air 20/211, India: General Papers, Air Ministry, letter 1st January 1941.
62   TNA, Air 20/2145, Far East: R.D.F. Equipment, 1941-1942, Air Ministry to H.Q. Far East, 24th December 1941. At the time of the Japanese attacks in December, neither Hong Kong nor Ceylon were covered.
63   TNA, Avia 15/370, Radar: Overseas Stations; Sites and Layouts of RDF stations in India, 1940-1942, report 19th December 1941.

The Chatfield Commission of 1937-1938 had proposed a contract, along with recommendations to increase the size of India's armed forces, which would have increased India's air defence units.[64] However, no judgement had been made on the size of the air forces. This decision was to wait until the C. in C. India visited Britain in 1939 but the visit never took place. From 1939 to 1941 India started a rapid programme to modernize its armed forces and in particular its army for overseas service in the Middle East and Iraq. The bulk of India's resources therefore went to increase conventional technology such as artillery and tanks, whereas radar was not seen as a priority. It was in its infancy and did not work in certain geographic locations. Moreover it was expensive, not only to purchase, but also to staff with personnel from Britain. This was undoubtedly a pragmatic approach, but one which eventually resulted in India being left bereft of any radar equipment until the Spring of 1942.

As the Japanese attack was starting on 8th December the Air Ministry decided to form eleven A.M.E. Stations; five C.O.L.s; three T.R.U.s; and three mobile units all of which were going to be allocated to a Far East pool.[65] The A.O.C. would deploy the sets to meet requirements in Malaya, Burma, Ceylon and possibly the Dutch East Indies and Manila. The Air Chiefs in Britain were obviously confident of India's security as it was not mentioned in the memo. Two days later a memo referred to India's radar provision, recalling Atherton's 1940 report to install equipment at the Eastern ports, but India would have to wait:

> In view of the present situation in the Far East, it is considered that a review of the R.D.F. requirements has become necessary ... The Director of Plans stated in a memo dated 29/11/1941 that the Chief of Staff had decided that the Far East was to take priority over India as regards the supply of equipment.[66]

This reinforced the decision of June 1940 that India's radar would be delayed until 1942, but as the situation deteriorated in Malaya, A.H.Q. India were told on 23rd December that the Air Ministry were sending R.A.F. technical officers "for preparation of the R.D.F. plan for India and Burma" and these officers' presence was to be hastened.[67]

On Christmas Eve 1941 A.H.Q. India were informed that two Mobile Radar Units (M.R.U.s) were being sent to Calcutta and two more M.R.U.s to Madras, together with personnel from Britain at the end of January 1942. Four days later the deployment

---

64 TNA, Air 23/691, Information for Chatfield Commission, 1937-1938.
65 TNA, Air 2/7200, Radar and Radio Countermeasures (Code B, 61): Provisions of R.D.F. equipment use in A.C.S.E.A. including India, 1940-1943.
66 Ibid, memo, 10th December 1941.
67 TNA, Air 20/2144, India and Ceylon Radar Equipment, W.T. and R.D.F. stations, 1941-1942, Air Ministry, Whitehall to A.H.Q. India.

was reinforced when six stations were to be forwarded with their staff by 15th January 1942 to India Command; Colombo and Trincomalee each were to receive one station, and two stations each were being sent to Calcutta and Madras.[68] The latter two moves were significant as there is nothing to suggest that these stations were being sent to either location as staging posts, and therefore it can be assumed they were going to be established in an early warning role. However, despite these intentions the sets were still in Britain in February.[69]

Japan attacks

The Japanese invasion of the Far East has been described many times and it is not intended to repeat it again here. It is, however, pertinent to examine how the early warning system in the region had a direct effect on the subsequent outcome. The first Japanese daylight attacks on 8th December on Malaya were not detected. After a sustained day of attacks the Japanese destroyed 60 out of 110 operational Allied aircraft and "the British air effort had almost ceased within twenty-four hours of the opening of hostilities."[70] When warnings were given they were inconsistent either because of technical problems or the ground controllers misreading information. 21 Squadron R.A.A.F. were placed on immediate readiness at 06:45 hours on 8th December; ten minutes later five Japanese bombers appeared over their airfield. No order to scramble having been received it was left to the squadron to take-off on its own initiative as Squadron Leader Bill Allshorn later recalled:

> As the pilots were putting on their parachutes and the aircraft were being warmed, I looked up to see a stick of bombs leave the enemy formation and realized it was too late for take-off.[71]

There were also communication problems:

> There were practically no signals specialists available to us, and very little equipment. We had to rely on asking assistance from the local AA unit for our telephone equipment … which literally must have been some of the first that were ever made, were totally unreliable. The observer system which I had to use had been organised by fighter ops Kallang, and under it we were unable to get reports on enemy aircraft direct from the observer posts, but got them through the railway station master at Kuala Lumpur. Owing to the delays attendant on

---

68 Ibid, report dated 28th December 1941.
69 Ibid, there are various reports in the file showing the stations had not been despatched.
70 Kirby, *The War Against Japan, Volume I*, p.191.
71 Cull, *Buffaloes over Singapore*, p.44.

this system, we usually got our warnings that the Japanese were 40 miles away, just as the raid was on.[72]

By 16th December early warning cover became so poor that air patrols had to be flown to provide warning against surprise attacks.

In Singapore the situation was better at first as the radar stations were giving at least 30 minutes warning of attack. However, the R.A.F. Brewster Buffalo fighters, with their slow rate of climb, were "taking all that time to climb to 25,000 ft, the bombers' normal height, and without V.H.F. they could not be informed of the raiders' movements."[73] After 15th January the situation deteriorated when the radar station at Mersing withdrew in the face of the Japanese advance and the reduction of warning time led to aircraft either being caught on the ground, or being late taking off. When Hurricanes arrived in January the available warning time left them, even with a superior rate of climb, struggling to reach height to engage raiders. Eventually the weight of Japanese numbers matched against the attrition and maintenance difficulties of the R.A.F. told and Singapore fell on 15th February.

Before Singapore had fallen, British forces had withdrawn to Sumatra to re-organize on two airfields known as P1 and P2. The island had no radar units and had to rely on a group of Dutch Observer Corps volunteers whose efficiency was questionable. They were:

> Stationed at points on concentric circles around the town with a radius of 50-100 kilometres. The volunteer observer corps was full of enthusiasm but lacked experience, and warnings were consequently erratic.[74]

The Japanese attacked Allied airfields on Sumatra in the same manner as Malaya and Singapore. Even though some successes were achieved by Allied aircraft flying from P2, the overwhelming weight of Japanese attack proved too much for the defenders and the island was evacuated on 18th February. The campaign moved to Java where two radar sets were quickly erected in Batavia and a warning system was soon established:

> Efficient operation and filter rooms were quickly connected to the Dutch Observer Corps, the fighter airfields, the anti-aircraft defences of Batavia and the air operations room in Bandoeng. The Dutch did everything they could to help and even staffed the filter and operation rooms with volunteer youths and women whose alertness and enthusiasm ... could hardly have been better.[75]

---

72   Squadron Leader William Harper, 453 Squadron, quoted in Ibid, p.71.
73   Probert, *The Forgotten Air Force*, p.53. The Buffalo fighter will be discussed in Chapter 2.
74   Kirby (ed), *The War Against Japan, Volume I*, p.355.
75   Ibid, p.432.

This was an improvement on previous events as a Hurricane pilot, Sergeant Terence Kelly, recalled:

> Apart from the operations room now running well, there were to the North, on the myriad islands in the Sunda Straits, watchers who reported the approach of enemy aircraft. Thus, for the first time, there was fair warning and the chance of climbing high enough to engage the enemy if not in equal numbers, at least otherwise on reasonable terms.[76]

Despite this improvement the defenders were short of aircraft and spares and were in no position to sustain consistent and repeated losses which the air fighting caused, and eventually the Hurricanes were reduced to untenable numbers against a numerically superior enemy.

In Burma there was a familiar story of early warning deficiencies when Japanese attacks commenced at the end of December 1941. The terrain in Burma had made establishing radar and observer posts difficult as there was only one radar set in Burma situated to the East of Rangoon which supported a chain of observer posts linked by unreliable telephone lines.[77] It was not ideal as:

> Its efficiency may be judged by the fact that only on one occasion did the warning which it gave of the approach of enemy aircraft arrive earlier – and then only by a few minutes – than that given by the men of the Observer Corps.[78]

Unlike Malaya and Singapore's Observer Corps, in Burma the Observer Corps were a well-trained and established organisation which represented an early defence provision by the Burmese Government. For example, at Rangoon various listening posts were linked by Post Office telephone lines via a central exchange to a combined operations room, which was reminiscent of the British model. The warning situation improved from mid-January 1942 when the radar set was moved from Moulmein to Rangoon and notable successes were achieved in the period from 23rd to 29th January when R.A.F. and American Volunteer Group (A.V.G.) pilots claimed 50 Japanese fighters and bombers destroyed. Air Vice-Marshal Donald Stevenson, A.O.C. 221 Group, wrote that the warning had been good from both the radar and the Burma Observer Corps, with the R.A.F. and A.V.G. being well controlled.[79] However, "there were limits to what one set could do", and the Japanese ground and air advance forced the Allies' meagre numbers of aircraft to withdraw to Magwe.[80] This airfield would

---

76   Kelly, *Hurricane over the Jungle*, p.136.
77   Richards and Saunders, *The Fight Avails*, p.59.
78   Ibid, p.59.
79   TNA, Air 2/7787, Far East Air Operations in Burma January to May 1942, A.V.M. Stevenson's despatch.
80   Probert, *The Forgotten Air Force*, p.85.

receive a radar set and cover from the Observer Corps but the system could not cope under sustained attack:

> The observer posts did all they could but amid growing confusion and damage to communications the system could not cope, and the radar not only suffered from a very low rate of serviceability but was incorrectly sited ... under such a weight of carefully planned attack Magwe was always going to be overwhelmed.[81]

Magwe was the precursor to actions over the island of Akyab. Some aircraft were at Akyab and were joined by a few survivors from Magwe, but owing to a lack of early warning and repeated Japanese raids over a 72 hour period from 27th March, their destruction meant the air forces in Burma virtually ceased to exist.

The final major action took place in Ceylon at the end of March 1942 and only 50 serviceable Hurricanes and two Fleet Air Arm squadrons of Fairey Fulmars were available for fighter defence.[82] Three designated Ceylon A.M.E.S. stations remained unpacked on the dockside and technical staff faced a huge effort to get a system working.[83] When the Japanese attacked on 4th April the radar station at Ratmalana was not working and as a result the defenders received no warning. Despite being at a tactical disadvantage the Hurricanes and Fulmars claimed 27 Japanese aircraft destroyed (an exaggerated claim) for the loss of fifteen Hurricanes and four Fulmars. The action left sixteen Hurricanes serviceable and "It had not been a good day for the rapidly improvised defences, though the enemy had failed in their main object, namely to inflict a 'Pearl Harbor' on the Eastern Fleet."[84] On 9th April the Japanese launched an attack on Trincomalee, but the enemy were spotted by a patrolling Catalina flying boat, and the radar station at China Bay was able to direct British aircraft to engage the Japanese with an advantage. Although outnumbered and sustaining eleven losses, the British claimed 24 enemy aircraft destroyed, again an exaggeration, but enough to cause some consternation to the Japanese, who admitted their losses had been higher than the British claims. The radar had made an obvious and important difference despite the control system being improvised:

> At the time of the raids no filter room had yet been established in Ceylon and the two radar stations reported direct to the temporary Fighter Operations Room at Colombo and the Gun Operations Room at Trincomalee respectively.[85]

---

81   Ibid, p.92.
82   Ibid, p.98. The Fulmar was a single engine, two seat carrier-borne aircraft.
83   TNA, Air 20/2144, India and Ceylon Radar Equipment, W.T. and R.D.F. stations, 1941-1942. The A.M.E.S. stations were 542, 545 and 546.
84   Probert, *The Forgotten Air Force*, p.100.
85   TNA, Air 41/88, *Signals Volume V: Fighter Control and Interception*, p.63.

Both actions on Ceylon demonstrated how crucial an early warning system was to the defenders in terms of allowing them to gain sufficient height to engage their enemy.

Reinforcements 1941-1942

Priority plans were made to rectify the deficiencies in early warning coverage in the Far East. The Air Ministry stated their intention to form five C.O.L.s, three A.C.O.s, and three mobile G.C.I. stations for use in Malaya, Burma, Ceylon, and possibly the Dutch East Indies and Manila.[86] There were soon problems with the proposed time scales. Personnel required for the mobile G.C.I. stations were being trained in Britain and would not be despatched to the Far East until 20th January 1942. Similarly the technical equipment was being made in Britain and the target date for its assembly was 20th January, arrangements being made "for shipment in the first available convoy after that date."[87] Transport times meant the equipment would not reach the region until the middle of February. Furthermore, the C.O.L. and A.C.O. stations' sites remained to be selected, which was a complex task even when not undertaken under enemy fire. This was indicative of British problems for the next few months. Firstly, the equipment were not standard items and had to be specially built or transferred from other theatres; secondly, personnel had to be trained; and thirdly there was the logistical difficulties of transporting the units from Britain to the Far East. Moreover, the Japanese advance was so rapid as to negate any attempt to reinforce the early warning organisation.

Attempts to reinforce radar units during this period were problematical. Messages show the numerous units that were to be despatched, and these convey the difficulties unfolding. On 24th December four radar units were listed for despatch to Calcutta and Madras at the end of January 1942, but the Air Ministry made it clear that "No, repeat no, diversion R.D.F. equipment from Middle East can be made."[88] By 13th January 1942 permission was sought to divert number 258 A.M.E.S. which was en route to Iraq, from Bombay to Rangoon to assist its defence. Furthermore, on 8th February the Director of Operations acknowledged that radar cover in Burma was lacking as "the hills [are] said to make it impractical; NORGROUP asked for diversion of the Wireless Observer Units now en route to Iraq."[89] The urgency was obvious, but the difficulty was that despatch and production was linked to high demand and it is clear that there was little if any chance that the equipment would arrive in time.

---

86   TNA, Air 20/2145, Far East: R.D.F. equipment, Report: A.M.E.S. for Far East
       Command, 8th December 1941.
87   Ibid.
88   TNA, Air 20/2144, India and Ceylon radar equipment: W.T. and R.D.F. stations, Air
       Ministry to A.H.Q. India, 24th December 1941.
89   Ibid, D. of S. to D. of O., 8th February 1942. NORGROUP was the name given to the
       R.A.F. in Burma at that time.

This can be demonstrated by examining what happened to some of the units intended for service in the region.

The 8th December 1941 report listed four C.O.L. stations, two A.M.E.S. and three G.C.I. stations which would be despatched for Far East service on 20th January 1942.[90] However, on 15th March 1942 none of these units had reached their destination; all but two were still in transit to the Far East, whereas the remaining two had been diverted to Australia. On 24th December four stations were designated to be despatched to Calcutta and Madras respectively by the end of January 1942. However, on 15th March only two were en route, whereas the other two had not yet been despatched from Great Britain. These two examples are typical of the efforts to equip the region with radar for the next few months as despatch and delivery dates were routinely delayed. Equipment would take three or four weeks to arrive and, except in the case of mobile units, another few weeks to establish; but the Air Ministry gave an estimation that the mobile units could go into operation within four to seven days of arrival. By 28th March there was only one working radar unit in India, number 258 A.M.E.S. based at Mathurapura, south of Calcutta, while seven further A.M.E. stations were in situ in Ceylon.

While the reinforcement of radar units to the region had been too late, there was a bonus as all the units intended for the Far East were diverted to India where they would eventually be used to establish an air defence system. Reports from 15th and 30th March 1942 show a total of 37 units of all varieties being either despatched, diverted, or en route by sea to the Indian ports of Madras, Calcutta, Karachi and Bombay.[91] It is apparent that the authorities had started to recognize the importance of India's air defence as on 26th February Edmund Dixon wrote to the Radio Defence Committee:

> It becomes clear that the defence of the Far East is to be centred on India …
> The Air Staff has already recognized the new importance of India by appointing a Radio Officer and a Scientific Officer from the Middle East, DCD party to make surveys for R.D.F. ground stations at the main defended areas and ports in India, Ceylon and Burma. Meanwhile a Radio Installation and Maintenance Unit has been started at the R.A.F. depot at Karachi.[92]

A memorandum dated 4th March 1942 acknowledged that some form of early warning was essential in all defended areas, whilst the installation, maintenance and administration of such systems required "considerable skill" as well as an intimate

---

90   TNA, Air 20/2144, India and Ceylon radar equipment: W.T. and R.D.F. stations, report dated 24th December 1941.
91   TNA, Avia 15/370, Radar: Overseas Stations; Sites and Layouts of RDF stations in India, 1940-1942.
92   Ibid, Report: Proposed C.T.B. representative in India, report dated 26th February 1942.

knowledge of the "workings of … fighter defence and air raid warning controlled in the United Kingdom by Fighter Command."[93] The siting of radar equipment was acknowledged as being of supreme importance to obtain the best results and Squadron Leader J.W. Findlay, an expert in siting radar equipment, was despatched from the Middle East to India.[94] It is unclear from the report or its background whether Burma was expected to fall, but the document makes clear provision for equipment to be pooled in India prior to deployment, or to be transferred there in the event of territories being overrun.

In April 1942 early warning units were beginning to arrive in India and Ceylon, and further target dates for the arrival of additional equipment were in August and September. The monsoon period between June and October gave the Allies time to rebuild and for equipment to arrive resulting in 52 radar sets being operational in India and Ceylon in December 1942.[95] In the meantime an early warning policy was formulated.

On 22nd June 1942 A.H.Q. India informed its command of its policy of providing early warning cover to target areas.[96] The long-term policy was:

  i)   R.D.F coverage along the length of the coast of India and of Ceylon,
  ii)   Extension of inland coverage making the maximum use of R.D.F.,
  iii) Ground Observer systems for the reporting of low flying aircraft and where high cover only exists,
  iv)   Ground Observer system for reporting aircraft in areas uncovered by R.D.F.[97]

Based on figures from the experience of the Air Defence organisation in Great Britain the report quoted the minimum distance between a hostile aircraft being detected and its target was 80 miles for a successful interception to occur. In India:

[I]t will not be possible for some considerable time to provide anything approaching complete coverage, either overseas or overland.[98]

The reasons for this were given as: a lack of R.D.F. equipment; lack of communications for the ground observer system; lack of Wireless Observer Units; and a shortage of trained Indian Observer Corps personnel. The report concluded that all elements of the early warning system would have to be integrated to make the best possible use

---

93   Ibid, Ground R.D.F. in Areas under A.H.Q. India, report dated 4th March 1942.
94   No first name is available for Findlay.
95   TNA, Air 41/63, *The Campaigns in the Far East: Volume II, Malaya, Netherlands East Indies and Burma, 1941-1942*, p.49.
96   TNA, Air 23/2037, Raid Warning System, 1942-1944, report 22nd June 1942.
97   Ibid, p.1.
98   Ibid, p.8.

of resources and that the establishment of effective ground control and filter rooms were vital.

A.V.M. Stevenson added to the policy on 8th July issuing the Fighter Directif Number 2.[99] The defence of Calcutta was paramount and Stevenson pointed out that if invasion happened, "it would be a military disaster of the first magnitude."[100] Intelligence sources led the British to believe that the scale of Japanese air attack from the land and sea on Calcutta was approximately 300 to 400 aircraft and would have to be countered by a determined defence. It was considered that the Japanese range of attack was at least 300, if not 600 miles from the port which would give the Allies some degree of early warning.[101] Stevenson reported that overland the R.A.F. would receive 200 miles warning from the Observer Corps, whilst high raids routed over the sea would give 70 miles warning from the radar equipment supported by Observer Corps and local plotting procedures. This figure was obviously at odds with the minimum distance quoted in the A.H.Q.'s report in June. The provision for high level radar cover did not pose as big a technical difficulty as that of providing low-level cover, as Stevenson admitted such cover would only give a likelihood of:

[A]t least some minutes' warning ... to get our fighters off the ground to meet the scale of attack ... we may expect to get sufficient warning to enable us, in emergency, to get our fighters off the ground.[102]

The installation of three chain stations to cover Calcutta from attack from the south and south-east was in progress, and as the report was being written one became operational. The effort to establish an early warning chain was immense and in order to gauge the difficulties it is pertinent to analyse aspects of the establishment process before assessing how effective the system was by the end of 1942.

As the radar organisation was being established in India in 1942, the Indian Observer Corps (I.O.C.) was expanded to support the early warning system. Formed in 1940 to face a possible threat from the Soviet Union in the north-west, the I.O.C. consisted of railway staff reporting through their station masters who passed the information on by telephone to an air defence centre.[103] This was unsatisfactory as the railway staff had their own duties to perform, and this led to time lags of "great length."[104] There then began a period where the I.O.C. was bedding in as a separate organisation which met problems of recruitment, class and pay, but by the beginning of 1942 it was starting to become formalised. In April 1942 plans were formulated to

99   TNA, Air 23/4408, Air Defence Fighter Directives, 1942. The spelling of Directif is used in the original document.
100 Ibid, point 1.
101 Ibid, point 16.
102 Ibid.
103 TNA, Air 23/5420, History of the I.O.C., 1943-1945, enclosure 3A.
104 Ibid.

construct five observer belts around the east and south of Calcutta and its industrial areas, linked by wireless and telephone to the control rooms. In addition some observer posts were to be placed on boats in the mouth of the Ganges. The posts provided an essential addition to the early warning system at low-level. In trials carried out by an aircraft flying between 1,000 to 1,500 feet, plots were accurately made at 75 miles to the north-east and 50 miles to the south-east by the I.O.C.[105] For the rest of 1942 the observer cover was refined although obstacles such as low telephone line priority and poor communications had to be overcome.[106] For example in October it was reported that the reports received over the Kharagpur to Barang railway telephone line were "generally worthless."[107]

The survey process that preceded that of the radar units covered 40 technical, geographical and administrative aspects ranging from soil composition and drainage to expected direction of attack, to medical facilities and defence to transport, emphasising the point that planning was essential if radar equipment was to operate effectively. A typical report for a T.R.U. site on Grubb's Island on 11th April 1942 showed the exact location, radar coverage and even the scale of rainfall, for weather conditions were to play a significant part in determining how radar would work in such a hostile climate. If weather was one problem, electrical supply could be another. Pilot Officer Sarawate surveyed Calicut for an M.R.U. on 29th August and reported that as the power line was a mile away from the proposed site the possibility of obtaining a mains supply had to be considered. He recommended:

> The 11 Kv supply could be brought up to domestic site stepped down there and ½ of l.t. line run to supply the station. Mr Raja Iyengar of the W.C.E.S. Co Ltd has been asked to supply the estimate.[108]

This question of paying for facilities should not be overlooked. In the same report Sarawate wrote, "Land value in Calicut is extremely high. Hence the area for the domestic site is restricted to 2½ acres only."[109] Another consideration was the local population and their living conditions. Sarawate surveyed a site in Nagercoil on 20th August and considered the impact on rice paddy fields and holy areas around Nagercoil and Kanyakumani.[110]

105 TNA, Air 23/2038, Indian Observer Corps, 1942-1944, report to Sir Richard Pierse.
106 In September 1942 there existed a gap of 22 miles north of Calcutta owing to no telephone wire being available.
107 TNA, Air 23/2038, Indian Observer Corps, 1942-1944, report, 26th October 1942.
108 TNA, Avia 15/371, Radar: Overseas Stations (Code 41/4): Sites and Layouts of RDF stations in India, 1940-1942, report by Pilot Officer Sarawate, point 36. There is no first name available for Sarawate.
109 Ibid, point 40.
110 Ibid, report 20th August 1942, point 40.

The same process for each site had to be conducted and as an example of the difficulties which often had to be faced it is pertinent to examine a report from November 1942.[111] A team of six were tasked to survey a site around Hingol firstly for an R.D.F. site, and then to determine whether transport could reach the area. The expedition started from Karachi and passed along winding roads with sheer drops, followed by small tracks which only allowed speeds of eight to ten mph. As the track became smaller and less accessible so attempts were made to find access to the site across what was thought to be a dry river bed but one of the trucks sank six inches into the soft bed, and it took six hours to extricate the vehicle. Following a night in camp the party continued its journey and three more attempts were made to find an accessible track going west this time with the help of native guides but, "this also failed and information obtained from villagers indicated that the track had been lost in sand and shrub."[112] The party was forced to turn back as their rations and petrol were running out. Another attempt to find the track was made on the return journey, but it was found to be impassable owing to soft sand dunes. The report's conclusion stated that there was "no approach to Hingol by road to convey the M.R.U. type equipment."[113]

Apart from surveying radar sites during 1942 there were a number of technical and administrative problems which made the establishment of a viable early warning system harder to achieve. The British Chiefs of Staff had recognized the technical difficulties of using radar in mountainous regions in 1940 stating a mobile set was "not recommended for use on the Frontier owing to echoes off hills."[114] The mountains surrounding radar sites created 'permanent echoes' which caused distortion and interference on radar screens and when these problems arose solutions were sought from the scientists at the T.R.E. in Malvern. In June 1942 a request for help to deal with 'permanent echoes' was forwarded to the T.R.E. who replied that a number of solutions were available to counter the difficulties, notably using specific types of G.C.I. radar and portable sets sited on flat ground in the centres of "saucer shaped regions."[115] This solution represented theoretical research work but there were only two pieces of suitable equipment manufactured with five under construction. The sets were experimental and would not be ready for operational use for six to eight weeks, raising concerns:

111 TNA, Avia 15/370 Radar; Overseas Stations; Sites and Layouts of RDF stations in India, 1940-1942, report 22nd/23rd November 1942.
112 Ibid.
113 Ibid, p.2.
114 TNA, Air 2/4125, India Command: Request from A.O.C. for additional High Frequency Direction Finding Set and mobile R.D.F. set, 1939-1940, report dated 7th March 1940.
115 TNA, Avia 15/370, Radar: Overseas Stations; Sites and Layouts of RDF stations in India, 1940-1942, report dated 11th June 1942, point 2.

The experiments we have done on reducing the effects of permanent echoes by the use of coherent pulses are not considered sufficiently advanced to promise any applications for this in India within a year.[116]

Furthermore, staff at the Ministry of Aircraft Production (M.A.P.) thought the best solution of dealing with permanent echoes was the careful siting of the correct choice of equipment and warned that an operational light-weight set suitable for transportation by mule would be unlikely to reach India until early 1943. Atherton's visit to Indian towns in 1940 had also raised doubts as to whether the radar units would work in some areas without costly high aerial towers.[117] Construction of towers and gantries to assist the low-level coverage faced both supply and technical problems. Wood and local specialized labour were in short supply and a proposal was made to use steel to erect the structures. However, it was quickly identified that the I.F.F. interrogator signals could be adversely affected by the towers' steel construction. It was admitted that "the whole question of fitting I.F.F. aerials for tower-type C.O.L. stations had been overlooked and they had no scheme for even the timber tower C.O.L."[118] Ultimately, and largely due to there being no guarantee when a solution was forthcoming, the towers were built of a mixture of steel and wood.

In addition there were the harsh weather conditions. In Bengal at 8am in June the temperature was recorded at 83 degrees Fahrenheit (F), with a relative humidity of 91% whilst the maximum day temperature in the shade reached 103 degrees F. A priority was to redesign the equipment as two major components, the condenser and transformer, failed under such conditions. The radar equipment had to be able to withstand 90% humidity and 100 degrees F. Air conditioning units would have provided a solution to the problem but they were in short supply in India:

A large number of faults due to dampness and tropical conditions are recorded. This points to the need for air-conditioning plants, but owing to the priority given to hospitals there seems little chance of obtaining plants for AMES.[119]

The situation did not improve as the year continued; of the 47 radar stations in service in India in November 1942 only nine had locally sourced air-conditioning units.[120]

---

116 Ibid, point 5.
117 TNA, Avia 15/370, Radar: Overseas Stations; Sites and Layouts of RDF stations in India, 1940-1942, Atherton's report, 18th April 1940.
118 TNA, Air 2/7200, Radar and Radio Countermeasures (Code B, 61): Provisions of R.D.F. equipment use in A.C.S.E.A. including India, 1940-1943, report by Flight Lieutenant Paul Taylor, 9th September 1942.
119 TNA, Air 20/1518, A.C.S.E.A. Ground Radar Reports, October 1942.
120 TNA, Avia 15/370, Radar: Overseas Stations; Sites and Layouts of RDF stations in India, 1940-1942, A.H.Q. India to Ministry of Aircraft Production, 15th December 1942.

An important element in ensuring radar equipment worked to its best advantage was the use of aircraft to calibrate the devices. It was recognized by the Far East command on 4th March 1942 that it was "vitally important" for height-finding radar to have aircraft calibration:

[A] number of aircraft will be required to be made available specifically for the purpose. No action has yet been taken to establish the necessary calibration flights and recommendations are awaited after investigations, but operational aircraft can be used.[121]

On 29th April India Command recommended that nine Blenheims should form three flights to serve India's purposes, while a Catalina should be used for calibration duties over the Indian Ocean.[122] However, there was a conflict between using aircraft for calibration when there were shortages in the Far East:

The supply of aircraft to India will not be sufficient for a considerable time to equip Operational Squadrons and there is therefore no point in establishing calibration flights. If A.H.Q. India considers it essential to have calibration flights they will have to form these from their own resources.[123]

Operational necessity took priority with the inevitable result:

Very few stations are calibrated. The number of calibration flights is negligible. This is due to difficulties in obtaining aircraft.[124]

Progress was thus extremely slow in establishing calibration flights and radar efficiency suffered until the middle of 1943 when specific flights were formed.

As 1942 ended, and in spite of the various problems, there were 52 radar stations covering Ceylon and India, particularly Calcutta. The system was not perfect. The lack of designated calibration flights resulted in height discrepancies, whilst it was admitted that the low-level cover, despite the I.O.C., was "extremely weak."[125] The

121 TNA, Air 2/7200, Radar and Radio Countermeasures (Code B, 61): Provisions of R.D.F. equipment use in A.C.S.E.A. including India, 1940-1943, enclosure 44B, p.1.
122 The Blenheim was a twin-engine bomber and the Catalina was a twin-engine flying boat.
123 TNA, Air 2/7704, Air Ministry and Ministry of Defence: Registered Files. Royal Air Force: Air Command Southeast Asia (Code B, 67/37): R.D.F. organisation: India, enclosure 10A.
124 TNA, Air 20/1518, A.C.S.E.A. Ground Radar Reports; Squadron Leader H. M. Barkla's report to India Command on 29th September 1942. No first name is available for Barkla.
125 TNA, Air 2/7200, Radar and Radio Countermeasures (Code B, 61): Provisions of R.D.F. equipment use in A.C.S.E.A. including India, 1940-1943, Quoted in report from Director of R.D.F. who stated that the low cover, under 3,000 feet was extremely weak and "no substantial improvement was likely for some time to come."

monsoon period had given the Allies time to establish an early warning system and as it ended in September R.A.F. squadrons were scrambled daily to investigate unidentified aircraft detected by the early warning organisation. From September to the end of the year the majority of interceptions resulted in friendly aircraft being found either because they had strayed away from planned routes or had failed to activate their I.F.F. equipment. The frustrations of intercepting friendly aircraft rather than hostile ones, together with occasional controlling inexperience showed in squadrons' operations books. For example, 135 Squadron's diarist wrote on 19th November 1942:

> The Squadron was scrambled at 11.05 hrs together with the remainder of the wing for '15 plus bogeys' 10 miles South of base, angels 20. Hope runs high – Hurricanes tore around the sky – R/T 'mutterings' filled the air – finally at 11:10hrs plots faded – so what??[126]

All fighter squadrons had similar entries in their record books and while there were obvious frustrations the fact that aircraft were being intercepted showed that the system was starting to work.

In August 211 A.M.E.S. encountered problems from operator difficulties, storms, flooding and insects shorting out electrical components. During the last week in August the station had been missing aircraft and plots because their tracking had been completed on the reciprocal heading which had not been realized:

> This came as a considerable shock when we were beginning to pride ourselves on our plotting, having passed 1004 plots at an average of 3 per minute over the last week. Faulty plotting found mainly due to W/T errors and plotting on the reciprocal probably due to faulrt [sic] relay switching.[127]

258 A.M.E.S. also reported that "native cross talk was heard on the line during the day" when plots were telephoned to their filter room.[128] Despite these early difficulties things improved for the radar stations as exemplified by 544 A.M.E.S. based at Dum Dum who on 8th, 18th and 23rd November 1942 were congratulated by filter room staff on their "excellent tracking" of test flights or friendly aircraft.[129]

The system's efficiency was tested when the Japanese began a series of attacks on Chittagong in December 1942 and it is pertinent to examine five occasions on which Japanese aircraft were intercepted. On 5th December a mixed Japanese force of 50

---

126 TNA, Air 27/949, 135 Squadron Operations Record Book, 19th November 1942. 'Bogey' was the codename for an unidentified contact or sighting; 'angels' was code for 1,000 feet, hence 'angels 20' would translate as 20,000 feet.
127 TNA, Air 29/172, 211 A.M.E.S. Operations Record Book, 30th August 1942.
128 TNA, Air 29/175, 258 A.M.E.S. Operations Record Book, 26th July 1942.
129 TNA, Air 29/181, 544 A.M.E.S. Operations Record Book, 8th November 1942 to 23rd December 1942.

Ki-43 Oscar fighters and 25 Ki-48 Lily bombers attacked Chittagong where six R.A.F. Curtiss P-36 Mohawk fighters from 155 Squadron were at readiness. Six Mohawks were scrambled but their squadron diarist recorded that the flight was "warned late, our pilots not able to inflict much damage."[130] The late warning resulted in the fighters being met at a disadvantage by the Japanese escort, albeit during the ensuing fight an Oscar was shot down. Five days later Hurricanes from 135 Squadron were scrambled to counter another mixed force of fighters and bombers raiding Chittagong, and although another Japanese fighter was destroyed there is no mention in the Squadron's record book that radar was involved in the interception. The raid was actually detected by staff from the I.O.C. as recalled by Sergeant Bill Davis, a 136 Squadron pilot, "There was no radar of course; warning came from local observer corps people, and the warning on this occasion was just too short."[131] The late warning put the defenders at a disadvantage and the Hurricanes were caught climbing losing four aircraft and two pilots.[132] On 15th December a Japanese fighter escorting a raid on Chittagong was shot down by Hurricanes from 79 Squadron, but there is no mention in either the Squadron's Operations Record Book or Daily Air Summary if radar detected the raid. It was not until the night of 22nd/23rd December that radar and the control organisation played a significant role in detecting and controlling a successful interception. At 00:15 hours six Hurricanes were scrambled when enemy aircraft were detected approaching from the south and according to 17 Squadron's record book, "Wing Commander O'Neill was flying with the Squadron on a G.C.I. control."[133] During the course of the attack the Hurricanes were guided to their targets by the ground organisation and attacked two bombers; Japanese records show both crash landed.[134] The 248 A.M.E.S. diarist recorded:

> Three enemy aircraft plotted from South East; taken over Calcutta and out due East. Informed by filter room that there were two tally ho's [sic].[135]

The 544 A.M.E.S. diarist recorded:

> [I]nstructed by Filter officer to log following message, 'Particular praise given to Diamond Harbour for the very satisfactory plotting, as a result of which two "Tally Hos" were made.'[136]

130 TNA, Air 27/1037, 155 Squadron Operations Record Book, 5th December 1942.
131 Franks, *Hurricanes over the Arakan*, p. 94.
132 Shores, *Air War for Burma*, p.39.
133 TNA, Air 27/235, 17 Squadron Operations Record Book, 23rd December 1942.
134 Shores, *Air War for Burma*, p.44.
135 TNA, Air 29/174, 248 A.M.E.S. Operations Record Book, 23rd December 1942.
136 TNA, Air 29/181, 544 A.M.E.S. Operations Record Book, 23rd December 1942.

The feat was repeated the following night when Hurricanes from 293 Wing were successfully guided to counter night bombers raiding Calcutta, and a Japanese aircraft was successfully destroyed. The interceptions over the two nights were of particular note as the Hurricanes were guided to the raiders purely by the ground control organisation as they did not carry their own Airborne Interception (A.I.) equipment.

Finally as 1942 closed Calcutta's air defences consolidated with an early warning system that was starting to show signs of efficiency, which would increase with experience and technical improvements. Some of the problems, such as those posed by the weather and the topography, would not be completely solved by the end of hostilities in 1945, and this made the provision of early warning difficult as the campaign moved from defence to offensive operations in 1944.

1943

1943 was a further year of rebuilding as the Allies were not strong enough to invade Burma until 1944. Two early Allied campaigns of 1943 had mixed success. Firstly the limited campaign to strike along the west coast of Burma from November 1942 to retake Akyab failed in its objective as superior Japanese land forces were able to push the Allied advance back into India. The second campaign was Colonel Orde Wingate's first penetration raid into Burma between February and May 1943 with the Long Range Penetration force, which later became known as the 'Chindits'.[137] While there is debate as to whether the raid had any strategic value, it did prove to be a morale boost as it showed what ordinary troops of the line could achieve, and it demonstrated the value of air supply. The development of air supply would be an essential part of Army commander Lieutenant General William (Bill) Slim's future strategy, and this would depend on Allied air superiority and a reliable early warning system over the supply zones.

R.A.F. Defensive Operations

The air defence of north-east India at the beginning of 1943 started to improve from the previous year. There were more Allied fighters, Hurricanes were starting to be equipped with V.H.F. radios and the early warning system was slowly improving. The effectiveness of the early warning system was demonstrated during two Japanese night raids on Calcutta in January 1943. Japanese air raids at the turn of the year lacked the magnitude of raids on European cities, but were enough to terrify the civilian population into evacuating the city, "which led to considerable

---

137 The name Chindit was derived from Chinthé – the name of the mythical creatures that guarded Burmese Pagodas. The name Chindit was not recognized until 1944. Orde Wingate was promoted to Colonel when he arrived in India in 1942, and was subsequently promoted to Major General in 1944.

disruption of public services."[138] A flight of A.I. equipped Bristol Beaufighters had arrived from the Middle East and on 9th January one aircraft was vectored to intercept a Japanese raid on Calcutta.[139] Expertly directed to the raiders' vicinity by ground controllers, the R.A.F. crew used the aircraft's A.I. set to detect and shoot down three Japanese bombers, the destruction of all three being confirmed. The feat was almost repeated on 15th January when a Beaufighter intercepted another night raid on Calcutta and shot down one Japanese bomber. As the civilian population returned to their city the effect of these radar-equipped fighters on Calcutta life was profound:

> The four Beaufighters had more than earned their keep; their presence had effectively denied the enemy the right to bomb the most important strategic target in India. It would be another year before they reappeared.[140]

The combination of radar, ground controlled interception, experienced crews and high performance radar equipped aircraft had been highly successful, but the same was not yet true of the day fighter effort.

During the first six months of 1943 the J.A.A.F. raided Indian ports, notably Calcutta, and Allied airfields engaged in supporting the First Arakan offensive. Whilst some Japanese aircraft were successfully intercepted the radar problems encountered during at end of 1942 were still present. On 27th January 136 Squadron were scrambled six times during the day finding nothing, and on 20th March the squadron diarist recorded, "Ten aircraft were scrambled at 09.00 and seven aircraft at 11.30. No enemy aircraft were encountered in the 2½ hour flying involved."[141] 135 Squadron experienced similar difficulties; on 6th January their diarist recorded that the Squadron, "were scrambled for supposed bogeys. The usual myth."[142] However, on other occasions Japanese aircraft were intercepted and destroyed following radar detection. A notable success was achieved on 27th March when a force of Hurricanes from 79 and 135 Squadrons destroyed nine unescorted Lily bombers during an attack

138 Probert, *The Forgotten Air Force*, p.128.
139 Ibid, p.128; Cab 79/16, Records of the Cabinet Office, November to December 1941; Air 23/5141, Fighter Defences: North-east India. Probert wrote that the raids caused Pierse to call for night fighter assistance in December but it had been called for earlier than that. A request had been refused on 8th December 1941 when the Chiefs of the Air Staff had pointed out to the Far East Commander that Malta was doing well without such equipment. On 13th September 1942 a stronger case for the deployment of suitably equipped night-fighters was made by Air Headquarters Bengal, and in December orders were sent to the Middle East for the Beaufighters to make the journey.
140 Probert, *The Forgotten Air Force*, p.129.
141 TNA, Air 27/952, 136 Squadron Operations Record Book, 27th January 1943.
142 TNA, Air 27/949, 135 Squadron Operations Record Book, 6th January 1943.

on Cox's Bazaar.[143] The defenders had sufficient warning of the raid and were able to climb to an advantageous height at which the bombers could be successfully attacked. However, this advantage was not always provided and squadrons complained that they were warned too late. On 1st April 67 Squadron were scrambled to intercept a raid against Feni airfield but took off "too late to be in a good position to attack" whilst on 9th April with only five minutes' warning they were caught by 16 Japanese fighters whilst climbing.[144] Pilots' views were mixed:

> By about March 1943, we had some radar and it wasn't so bad. The usual thing was to climb away to the North and get to 20,000 feet then turn round and start to take an interest in what was going on. Height was always a problem with radar and quite often Control would suddenly change the enemy's height by 10,000 feet – above or below! There was a lot of guess work – it was more of an art than a science.[145]

There was obviously some work to be undertaken before the early warning system was satisfactory and the next section will analyse what steps were taken to overcome the various problems, and how successful they were by the year's end.

Problems and Solutions

Apart from the perennial supply difficulties, the effects of extreme weather, high humidity and topography had already been experienced throughout 1942 as the radar system was established. None of these physical factors could be eliminated and it was therefore the scientists' task to find workable remedies to the various problems.

New questions emerged as radar equipment became operational. For example, in 1942 it was found that both temperature and humidity affected radar readings, but in 1943 it transpired that while there was an effect on normally sited stations, placing a set on higher ground resulted in an even greater error.[146] The problems raised questions for the 1944 campaign. Reports showed that in country similar to the Imphal Plain long-range permanent echoes made the detection of high flying aircraft "less secure."[147] It was subsequently suggested that one remedy would be to increase the

---

143 Franks, *Hurricanes over the Arakan*, p.176 and Shores, *Air War for Burma*, p.74. This was due to the Japanese fighter escort failing to make their rendezvous thus leaving the bombers to their fate.
144 Shores, *Air War for Burma*, pp.78-81.
145 Sergeant Bill Davis quoted in Franks, *Hurricanes over the Arakan*, p.211.
146 TNA, Air 20/5701, O.R.S. Report N1, 20th March 1943.
147 TNA, Air 23/2835, Visits to India Command Air Defence System, Report 261, 20th April 1943.

number of radar sets guarding a target, but this would have an obvious supply implication as radar equipment was in such high demand.[148]

The introduction of the Operational Research Section (O.R.S.) early in 1943 helped to identify difficulties and suggest practical remedies. Whilst some solutions could be addressed locally, India Command relied on scientists and radar experts in Britain to provide the necessary research and advice. In India the situation warranted sending a radar expert, Squadron Leader J.W. Findlay, to Britain between April and July 1943 to visit radio and radar establishments. There were three purposes for his visit; to study new R.D.F. equipment and techniques; to collect information for the manufacture of R.D.F. components and spares; and liaison with establishments to provide better inter-change of information.[149] It can be also assumed that Findlay researched available light-weight radar sets in view of Allied plans for the 1944 campaigns.[150] The trip was relatively successful in finding solutions to technical difficulties. One reoccurring problem had been caused by 'permanent echoes' on ground sited radar equipment, and the T.R.E. scientists developed a device which resulted in a 'coherent pulse method' which eliminated the phenomena. However, Findlay reported, "The project is unlikely to be in the production stage (if production is decided upon) in less than eighteen months."[151] The supply of other equipment presented further obstacles as the categories of radar Findlay examined had long delivery dates. For example, a contract for 132 Type 11 radar sets, which offered a possible solution to reception in mountainous country would not start production until November 1943 and then would be supplied at a rate of only eight per month. Furthermore, Findlay's mission to find a light-weight set ran into difficulties. He saw a set which could be housed in a tent or mounted on a variety of vehicles which good crews could make ready for action in two hours, and normal crews in up to eight hours.[152] However, he concluded that further research was required on this light-weight set as it was:

[C]urrently unsuitable owing to its weight and should be modified so that its weight was less than 1000lbs, 60 lbs weight per unit and the total number of units were less than 20.[153]

---

148   TNA, Air 2/7201, Provision of R.D.F. Equipment for use in A.C.S.E.A. including India. Report dated 22nd July 1943 shows some equipment would not be in the region until December 1943.

149   TNA, Avia 7/889, R.D.F. Stations – India; Report on visit to U.K. by Squadron Leader J.W. Findlay 21st April to 18th July 1943. No first name is available for Findlay.

150   Findlay's visit did not cover radar purely as an air-defence tool as some of his report covered various navigation and blind-bombing aids which were in operation with Bomber Command in Europe. Gee, H2S and Oboe are all mentioned.

151   TNA, Avia 7/889, R.D.F. Stations – India, Findlay's report, p.8.

152   Ibid, p.3.

153   Ibid, p.3.

Plans to carry these sets into action to cover the advanced landing grounds during the advance into Burma were important to the planning staffs' considerations and in a later section it will be examined how it was proposed to transport the sets by mule.

Finlay had been successful in his objective to establish closer communications with the establishments in Britain and he wrote the visit was, "very satisfactory … good interchange of information … agreed further exchanges would take place."[154] Secondly the fact that Findlay had been present at planning discussions made a difference when dealing with the scientists and technicians engaged in solving the region's problems, as records show subsequent regular, friendly correspondence between the establishments regarding technical difficulties. Lastly he was able to describe the various solutions and have an input into new radar sets in developmental stages that would not have been sent to the region as prototypes. The drawback was the speed at which research and production of new devices could be carried out.

Although radar could not be said by 1943 to be still in its early infancy, it was held back by a number of demands being made on radar scientists by different theatres and units. The bombing campaign in Europe demanded developments in blind bombing and navigation devices such as H2S, Oboe, and Gee. The campaign against German submarines also involved intensive research to develop and improve Air to Surface Vessel (A.S.V.) equipment for Coastal Command. The Far East added to the research programme as it had identified new phenomena connected to extremes of temperature, humidity and topography that radar scientists in the late 1930s had not envisaged. Furthermore, given the complexity of radar equipment and the limited manufacturing base in Britain it would take time for the sets to be developed, tested and manufactured.[155] Thus although India's problems could not be solved immediately there were solutions available for the future. However, there is an important point to be made. Findlay's visit and the subsequent correspondence between the establishments showed the Far Eastern Theatre of operations had not been forgotten by the scientists, as is often thought. Research and development was clearly in hand to solve the technical difficulties, but circumstances dictated that the remedies would take time and India Command had to remain patient.

The Human Factor

Technical problems were not the only obstacle to developing an early warning system as operator errors in operation and filter rooms were highlighted during O.R.S. investigations throughout 1943.

One difficulty lay with the accuracy of estimating and reporting aircraft heights and in May the O.R.S. wrote:

---

154 Ibid, p.3.
155 Moves were made to purchase radar equipment from the Australians and Americans, and enquiries were made in India to recruit technical staff to manufacture sets in the region.

It is readily apparent ... that the accuracy of estimating is low. While operators cannot be expected to estimate numbers of aircraft with mechanical accuracy, a higher degree of accuracy should be obtainable if proper instruction were given; this could possibly be arranged with Supervisors where they are available.[156]

and in June:

It appears ... that Stations are not following existing instructions re frequency of height readings and it is suggested that the position be reviewed and fresh instructions issued, taking into account the type of station and, in the case of M.R.U.s, the type of height switch fitted.[157]

Furthermore, there were inaccuracies counting aircraft numbers and investigations showed differences between stations, for example:

Counting of single aircraft in the Chittagong Filter Room area is not so accurate as in the Ballygunge Filter Room area. The percentage inaccuracy is 8.5% as compared to 5.7%.[158]

Solutions were not technical but required better training and adherence to accepted operational methods. Wing Commander J.F. Wright commented on these points on 8th June 1943 writing, "There is room for considerable improvement in operations at some of the R.D.F. stations."[159] He also made reference to two recent conferences where the delegates "decided that Operator Supervisors are essential to raise the operational efficiency of the system."[160] Wright pointed out that plotting by Wireless Telephony (W/T) in the Bengal area lost about 50% of plots whereas in Ceylon only 10 to 20% was lost and concluded, "The difference in the efficiency of the two areas is due to DRILL. (The procedure is the same in both areas.)"[161] The importance of increased training and practice in procedures was to be demonstrated later in December when the Japanese raided Calcutta in force and the interception failed owing to procedures breaking down.

---

156 TNA, Air 20/5708, O.R.S. Memo NB2, May 1943.
157 TNA, Air 20/5709, O.R.S. Memo NB3, June 1943.
158 TNA, Air 20/1514, O.R.S. Memo NB8, November 1943.
159 TNA, Air 23/2835, Visits to India Command Fighter Defence System; Report by Wing Commander J.F. Wright on the Air Reporting Organisation with special reference to Filter Rooms in the India Command, p.1. No first name is available for Wright.
160 Ibid.
161 Ibid p.4, his capital letters.

Defence to Offence

In January 1943 the threat to north-west India from Germany in the Caucasus began to decrease as the German Army Group B was in the process of defeat in Stalingrad and was in danger of being "bottled up in the Caucasus" by Soviet forces.[162] This diminished threat led to the acknowledgement by Far Eastern commanders that:

> [I]ncreased Russian resistance and the development of definite counter-offensives together with our successes in North Africa have greatly reduced the threat of German land or air operations against Karachi. It has indeed become so remote that even assuming German successes during 1943 against Russia towards the Caucasus, it could not materialize earlier than April 1944.[163]

Simultaneously the Japanese fleet was occupied in the Pacific and the threat to Ceylon and the eastern coast of India was considered to be similarly reduced.[164] Combining this reduced level of threat with a shortage of trained personnel and a need to install more radar stations in the north-east of India, radar deployment was revised. Some stations would be reduced to a care and maintenance basis, other stations under construction were left to be completed but no equipment would be installed, whilst other stations were cancelled. As equipment and staff became available plans were formulated to utilise radar and the early warning facility further afield.

Observer Developments and 1944 Plans

Throughout 1943 the I.O.C. continued to evolve efficiently with early plans to form 20 mobile wireless companies for advance warning which eventually would be experienced enough to work without R.A.F. assistance.[165] In May the first four Indian Mobile Wireless Observer Units (M.W.O.U.) took over from the R.A.F. W.O.U.s in the Manipur area freeing the airmen for duties further afield.[166] The M.W.O.U.s would play a significant role when the Allies fought in eastern India and some observer units were withdrawn to furnish posts east and south-east of Imphal:

---

162 Calvocoressi, Wint and Pritchard, *Total War*, p.500.
163 TNA, Air 23/5139, Fighter Defences North West India, letter from Air Ministry to AHQ India 2nd January 1943, and Air 2/7200, Radar and Radio Countermeasures (Code B, 61): Provisions of R.D.F. equipment use in A.C.S.E.A. including India, 1940-1943, for a similar appraisal, 8th April 1943.
164 TNA, Air 2/7200, Radar and Radio Countermeasures (Code B, 61): Provisions of R.D.F. equipment use in A.C.S.E.A. including India, 1940-1943, A.H.Q. India memo, 8th April 1943.
165 TNA, Air 23/2038, Indian Observer Corps, I.O.C. Policy, 27th February 1943, p.4.
166 Ibid, Letter John MacDonald to Air Vice-Marshal Thomas Williams, 6th May 1943.

Although the Army had been well East of Imphal since December, we were only just getting wireless unit posts deployed East of Imphal in late April, early May. Wireless unit personnel for the screen East of Imphal had been sitting at Imphal since January.[167]

The work of the W.O.U.s was extremely dangerous as small groups were sent many miles ahead of the front, occasionally with Ghurkha guards, to report by Morse code the passage of aircraft. Leading Aircraftman Ron Collis wrote of his time with 2/3 W.O.U. in 1943:

> The posts were set at intervals of about 15-20 miles and as high as possible. My post, Thenzawi, sat at about 6,000' [feet] spectacular views but murder to get to. There was a march of at least 60 miles to be undertaken and not a single yard was flat.[168]

Each post consisted of three ground observers and three wireless operators, one of the former nominally a corporal and in charge of the post. Collis' post was eventually taken over by the Indian Army observers in June 1943 to relieve R.A.F. personnel for duties elsewhere, Collis eventually being posted to the mobile radar unit in Tamu. Observer posts such as these will feature in the siege at Imphal which will be described later.

Plans for the 1944 campaign to re-take Burma depended on air transport to deliver supplies, men and matériel to the battlefront, and therefore Advanced Landing Grounds (A.L.G.s) would be essential to provide forward airstrips for transport aircraft. Air supply would be vulnerable to enemy fighter attack and it was imperative that the A.L.G.s were defended by ground based anti-aircraft guns and fighter aircraft assisted by an early warning system, but its implementation was to prove difficult.

One question was how an early warning system could be provided to protect A.L.G.s:

> Apart from a few ports and railheads without adjacent airfields, the problem can in effect be reduced to that of the aerial defence of advanced landing grounds ... particularly in the second phase of assault during Combined Operations.[169]

Securing an A.L.G. would take place in two phases: the initial landing would be protected by continuous fighter cover, and the second, a consolidation phase, would

167 TNA, Air 20/5240, Operational Filter Rooms in India, Wright's Report 8th June 1943, p.1.
168 Burma Star Website, www.burmastar.org.uk/wou2.htm, 2/3 W.O.U. Wireless Observer Units, website accessed 29th May 2007.
169 TNA, Avia 7/889, O.R.S. Report S1, 20th April 1943, p.1.

involve fighters operating from local, possibly captured, airfields.[170] An effective early warning system would therefore be necessary to avoid standing patrols once the second phase had been achieved, but there were drawbacks. High level raiders up to 23,000 feet could be detected with reasonable accuracy, but:

> There is no simple solution for the problem of detection of low-fliers in mountainous country unless it is possible to deploy R.D.F. sets or W.O. Units in advance of the vulnerable point.[171]

Thus the danger to the A.L.G. was from low-flying raiders which would evade detection until above the geometrical skyline.[172] The report had no illusions as to the threat as, "the problem of the provision of adequate warning of a low-flying attack on an A.L.G. surrounded by hills will generally be insuperable."[173] To counter the threat radar sets required to be positioned at least 20 miles ahead and for W.O.U.s 40 to 50 miles which, in the latter case, was thought to be impossible and would result in the "greater part of the responsibility … fall[ing] to R.D.F. raid reporting."[174] But if it was deemed impossible to station men with radios 50 miles ahead of the A.L.G.s there was little chance to position a radar set, albeit light-weight, 20 miles ahead. It will be remembered that while the subject was being debated in April 1943, Squadron Leader Findlay was in Britain and he concluded that the current light-weight set was too heavy and needed to be broken down into smaller units. It was considered that in order to detect low-flying raiders a powerful set employing a very narrow radio wavelength and capable of detecting aircraft up to 50 miles would be suitable. Such equipment had transport implications:

> The necessary aerial would be of such a size and its turntable in consequence so massive that its transportation by anything except a heavy vehicle would be out of the question.[175]

Equipment of this size obviously could not be carried by air, and would rely on being brought by ship to a convenient port, and then transported, if possible, by road.

---

170 Ibid, O.R.S. Report S1, 20th April 1943, p.1.
171 Ibid, p.1. The O.R.S reported that "the ultimate limit of aircraft detection is set by the geometrical skyline. In practise moreover this means the horizon as seen almost without exception from a valley."
172 The O.R.S. calculated that if the skyline was less than 32 miles from the A.L.G. raiders travelling at 240 mph would reach it in less than the eight minutes required to scramble the first section of fighters, and subsequent sections of fighters would be unable to scramble until the dust had settled from the first section's take off.
173 TNA, Avia 7/889, O.R.S. Report S1, 20th April 1943, p.2.
174 Ibid p.3.
175 Ibid p.1.

Furthermore, there were the factors of weather and accessibility. Heavy rains would reduce most roads to muddy tracks unsuitable for heavy vehicles and therefore the heavier the radar equipment the less chance there was of moving forward.

Here were the planners' difficulties. Firstly, a multi-functional radar set which possessed the ability to detect high and low-level raiders, and was light enough to be transported relatively easily did not exist. The Type 11 which was hoped would fulfil these factors was being developed in Britain, but its production would not start until November 1943 at the earliest.[176] This date would have been good news to the planners who actually expected the equipment not to be ready until the autumn of 1944.[177] Secondly, because there was no suitable radar set available, a system had to be devised using four fundamental types of set mobilised to varying degrees in seven different forms. There was also the problem of how to transport the various types and sizes of set given the topographical and climatic factors.

Transportation of the radar equipment would have to take place in various stages, firstly from the supply camps in India to the A.L.G.s, then to the operational site, and then, if necessary, from one operational site to another. The latter stage was important to consider firstly if the Allies' advance progressed and secondly if the Japanese overran a forward radar base. The initial stage of moving large and small radar equipment did not present a problem as it could be flown into the A.L.G. by transport aircraft and once there the light-weight set (L.W.S.) could be used temporarily while the heavier G.C.I. equipment was assembled and installed. After that the L.W.S. could be moved as far forward by mule or by jeep to provide the necessary defensive early warning. Both modes of transport would depend on the equipment being small enough to be carried by mule team on suitable roads for a vehicle, even as small as a jeep, to traverse, but more than one jeep would be necessary:

> We have found that at least five jeeps are required to carry one crated L.W.S. with its W/T R/T set and spares and test gear excluding crew and barrack equipment.[178]

There was also the question of whether the equipment would provide the warning required. India Command reported that as a result of their research with correctly sited G.C.I. sets in Imphal the equipment could give fair cover against high-flying aircraft but negligible cover against those at a lower level. The L.W.S. was not considered to be suitable in its present state, "Light Weight Set has the neither range, necessary interception facilities nor the proven operational performance of G.C.I."[179] It was

176 TNA, Avia 7/889, R.D.F. Stations: India; Findlay's report, p.8.
177 Ibid, O.R.S. Report S1, 20th April 1943.
178 TNA, Air 2/7984, R.A.F. A.C.S.E.A.; Radar Requirements; Air Ministry to HQ SEAC 10th December 1943.
179 TNA, Avia 7/889, R.D.F. Stations: India, Report S1, 20th April 1943, p.3.

therefore necessary to find a method to transport the more efficient G.C.I. equipment to forward areas and some work had begun. In February 1943 A.H.Q. India reported to Whitehall that G.C.I. equipment had been installed on an 80-foot barge with a further intention to install three C.O.L. sets:

> [F]or use Arakan coast or similar region. Intention is to overcome transportation difficulties thus enabling station to be sited on inland water in localities when road access impossible.[180]

By April the plan had advanced sufficiently to include the barge mounted radar sets in the first planning stages to secure A.L.G.s as the light-weight sets, G.C.I. and mobile C.O.L. equipment would either be established on land, or mounted on barges offshore.[181] Furthermore, throughout the year work was carried out to install light-weight sets on a jeep for greater mobility and G.C.I. sets onto a D.U.K.W. for use either offshore or on the inland waterway system as an alternative to the barge concept.[182] These developments showed ingenuity which would eventually assist in the provision of a radar screen over forward areas.

The Spitfire Arrives

The Spitfire's contribution to attaining air superiority in the Far East will be discussed in Chapter 2 but the introduction of the fighter version in October 1943 provided an essential element in providing an efficient air defence capability in conjunction with the early warning system.[183] The lack of an appropriate fighter during 1942 and 1943 had been identified by the O.R.S. who reported in June 1943:

> The comparatively poor performance of our fighter aircraft has a decisive influence on the difficulties of interception, and the provision of improved fighters would be the most important single contribution towards a successful fighter defence.[184]

The difference between the Spitfire and Hurricane to air defence was significant; the Spitfire Mark V had a service ceiling of 38,500 feet and a rate of climb to 20,000

---

180 TNA, Air 2/7201, Provision of R.D.F. Equipment for use in A.C.S.E.A. including India. A.H.Q. India to Air Ministry Whitehall, 23rd February 1943.
181 TNA, Avia 7/889, R.D.F. Stations: India, Report S1, 20th April 1943, p.3.
182 The D.U.K.W. was an American built six-wheeled amphibious vehicle. D indicated a vehicle designed in 1942, U meant utility, K indicated driven front wheels, W indicated two powered rear axles.
183 The first Spitfires in India were photographic reconnaissance variants (P.R. Mark IVs) which arrived in October 1942 and served with 681 Squadron.
184 TNA, Air 20/5628, O.R.S India, Report S2, 14th June 1943.

feet of 7 minutes 48 seconds, whilst the tropicalised Hurricane, on paper, would only attain 34,000 feet and reach 20,000 feet in 8 minutes 20 seconds.[185] This difference was observed in an eight day period from 8th November 1943 when a series of reconnaissance missions flown by Ki-46 Dinahs were intercepted by Spitfires following ground detection and control by radar; three Dinahs were destroyed.[186] The height ranging problems were still a problem and Sergeant Guy Watson later recalled a 10th November interception:

> The radar was very bad on height finding, extraordinarily bad. We always seemed to be 1000 feet or even 2000 feet below them, whereas we should have been above them.[187]

However, another pilot engaged in the same interception reported that he had reached 30,000 feet and the Dinah was 1,500 feet below him.[188] Despite the height problems, in a matter of a few days the Japanese reconnaissance capability had been nullified by the combination of the early warning system guiding the Spitfires to advantageous interception heights in a way not previously seen during the Hurricane's service as front line defender.

Despite these early successes engagements at the end of 1943 suggested that there was still work to be done in terms of radar accuracy, operator proficiency and fighter control. On 23rd November a formation of Japanese fighters flew an early morning reconnaissance against Chittagong in the hope of engaging some of the newly arrived Spitfires. Sixty-six Hurricanes and Spitfires were scrambled to engage the raiders, but virtually no contacts were made as the lead squadrons had failed to receive correct radio channels and the radar plot had been confused by the Japanese formation splitting into two.[189] On 28th November 12 Japanese bombers with their escort of six fighters attacked Feni from 30,000 feet but the defending Hurricanes and Spitfires were below the raiders' height and did not catch them until they had turned for their bases. One day later radar detected an enemy formation of 12 plus aircraft flying at 20,000 feet towards the Arakan and five squadrons of Hurricanes and one Spitfire squadron were scrambled to intercept, but fighter controllers' mistakes, combined with radar deficiency, misinterpreted the raiders' height. Only a few of the defenders made contact with the enemy; 67 Squadron's Hurricanes were attacked out of the sun as they were too low, whilst the Spitfires from 615 Squadron were too high, "The height was all wrong. Our controller had got us in position and we found the Japs

185 Price, *Spitfire Mark V Aces 1941–45*, p.87 and Anon, *Jane's Fighting Aircraft of World War II*, p.129.
186 The Ki-46 Dinah was a twin engine reconnaissance aircraft capable of flying at 34,450 feet. Its maximum speed was 391 mph at 19,685 feet.
187 Franks, *Spitfires over the Arakan*, p.44.
188 Flight Sergeant Willie Hyde referred to in Ibid, p.44.
189 Ibid, p.50.

were well below us; they were just specks in the distance."[190] Owing to the Spitfires' superior speed they were able to catch some of the Japanese fighters and during the engagement claimed one fighter probably destroyed and four damaged.[191] Apart from the problems of establishing accurate height readings, the controllers had to adapt to the Spitfire as a much faster climbing aircraft than the Hurricane, but experience and practice would eventually make control more efficient. However, a defining moment for the fighter control organisation occurred during the Japanese raid on Calcutta on 5th December.

The Japanese planned a major raid on Calcutta which was given the codeword of 'Ry Ichi-go' (Dragon First) and included fighters and bombers drawn from the J.A.A.F. and the J.N.A.F.[192] Approximately 128 Japanese aircraft flew towards Calcutta docks and 65 Hurricanes and Spitfires were scrambled to intercept, but the Japanese route took them to the south of Chittagong and the defending aircraft lacked the range to make contact; only one Spitfire engaged the enemy and its pilot had to force-land when he ran out of fuel. When Japanese bombers reached their target only two squadrons of Hurricanes were left to engage, but the defenders could not get through the Japanese fighter screen and the bombers went unmolested. An hour later another Japanese raid arrived over the city and the defenders were on the ground refuelling after the first raid; a flight of specially adapted night-fighter Hurricanes was scrambled and as a result eight of them were shot down when Japanese fighters attacked from above. This is a simplified account of the raid's engagement as the interception was both confusing and difficult to relate, however, the outcome was "an unhappy episode for the R.A.F. and a tactical coup for the Japanese."[193]

The Japanese had raided Calcutta at extreme range and caused damage and disruption to the city which was out of proportion to the weight of bombs they dropped; within a day of the raid a squadron of Spitfires returned to Calcutta for its defence. The O.R.S. investigated the raid and reported its initial findings on 31st December 1943, criticizing the way the raids had been picked up by controllers in the first instance, and how the second raid had been treated as a mass attack spread over heights between 10,000 and 20,000 feet when it was known from radar reports to consist of a few aircraft all flying over 25,000 feet.[194] The fighter controllers were criticised for the use of night-fighter Hurricanes to intercept the second raid, as they had been patrolling at too low a height while the other aircraft had been refuelling and did not have time to gain sufficient altitude. A further criticism was levelled at the controllers who

190 Pilot Officer Arthur Carroll, 615 Squadron, quoted in Ibid, p.56.
191 Shores, *Air War for Burma*, p.120.
192 This was the only occasion in the Burma Campaign where the J.A.A.F. and J.N.A.F. jointly undertook a raid.
193 Probert, *The Forgotten Air Force*, p.160. Franks, *Spitfires over the Arakan*, pp.60-77, and Shores, *Air War for Burma*, pp.125-129, for other detailed accounts.
194 TNA, Air 20/5694, O.R.S. Report N.8, Analysis of Raid on Calcutta, December 1943.

made no use of 79 Squadron's aircraft as they were on 'command guard' and were only scrambled to get them out of the danger area.

Human error in detecting and controlling the raid was the only reason given for the interception's failure, no blame apportioned to the operational radar equipment. In a later report submitted by the O.R.S. on 12th March 1944, plotting stations were said to have shown "preferential treatment" of hostile tracks to the detriment of friendly tracks which may not have given the controllers a true picture of where formations of aircraft, particularly friendly, were placed.[195] It was concluded that the stations had not adhered to their standing instructions by failing to report all tracks, friendly and hostile, and the duty filter controller should have warned them to "adhere to normal procedure."[196] It will be recalled that similar observations had been made in May 1943 and clearly the lessons had not been learned at the end of the year. Furthermore, on 26th December during a raid on Chittagong confused controlling had resulted in some Spitfires failing to make contact with the enemy formation whilst others had been sent too far to the east.[197] Additional training and practice would be necessary if operational efficiency was to be improved. It was fortunate that Spitfires were arriving in the region during this period to assume the interception role from the Hurricane as the Calcutta raid had shown it had reached the end of its life as an interceptor.

The value of the Spitfire with better control was demonstrated on New Year's Eve 1943 when one squadron intercepted a mixed Japanese force of six bombers and nine fighters who were attacking the Arakan. 136 Squadron had climbed to 30,000 feet and their controllers successfully vectored them to a position 9,000 feet above the Japanese formation, which suited R.A.F. tactics and the Spitfires' capability. Consequently three bombers were shot down, two force landed, one was heavily damaged, and one fighter was lost; R.A.F. losses amounted to one Spitfire whose pilot was rescued.[198] The action showed the power of such aircraft if the radar and control system could operate efficiently.

1944

The first six months of 1944 proved crucial for Allied air superiority in Burma. Three major engagements at the Battle of the Admin Box, the two sieges at Kohima and Imphal, and the second Chindit operation required air superiority to protect vulnerable transport and close air support sorties in Burma. In February 1944 Japanese air strength was approximately 270 aircraft, by the end of June this figure had been

195 TNA, Air 20/5717, O.R.S. Report NB14, Comparison of Radar Effort on Hostile and Friendly Tracks during Calcutta Raid December 5th 1943.
196 Ibid.
197 Franks, *Spitfires over the Arakan*, pp.88-89.
198 Shores, *Air War for Burma*, p.142.

reduced to 125 aircraft of all types.[199] The reduction is explained by a combination of factors; air-to-air combat attrition, a programme of interdiction raids against Japanese airfields, and transfer of Japanese aircraft to other theatres of operation. These elements will be examined in depth in other chapters of this book. This section will focus on analysing radar developments during the first half of 1944, and discussing the contribution the early warning system made to air defence.

Spares, Transport and Personnel

Even though great efforts had been made to improve the early warning capability in 1943, difficulties persisted. Weather and topography, permanent echoes, delayed equipment supply, spare parts arriving late and damaged, remaining transport problems, and trained personnel were scarce.

During 1943 T.R.E. radar developments designed to improve equipment for Far East operations had proved encouraging, but delivery dates had mainly been scheduled for early to mid-1944. As equipment arrived, the R.A.F. experienced an acute shortage of spares to maintain sets already in the theatre. In February 1944 Air Command South East Asia (A.C.S.E.A) radar experts reported:

> Air Ministry Harrogate … stated that a critical stage in the production capacity had been reached, and that a delay of about three months was anticipated before any further issue of the required spares could be expected.[200]

The situation in India was so serious that fully functioning radar sets were "robbed" of vital components in order that both operational and training units could be kept working.[201] The relevant spares had been ordered in December 1943. A.C.S.E.A. brought the situation to Whitehall's attention in May 1944 who replied in August, "There seems to be no valid reason why they were overlooked but the matter is now being pursued with vigour by the Equipment Branch concerned."[202] In June A.C.S.E.A. reported that a number of Type 57 sets had been delivered without the full pack of six months' spares originally planned. Furthermore, spares shortages were not restricted to radar equipment as A.C.S.E.A. reports show deficiencies in spares for portable generators vital for use with light-weight portable radar sets.[203]

One overriding reason for the spares' shortage was the decision at the ARCADIA Conference in January 1942 to make Germany the first priority. This decision can be

---

199 TNA, Air 41/64, *The Campaigns in the Far East Volume IV: South East Asia November 1943 to August 1945*, p.70.
200 TNA, Air 20/1515, Ground Radar Report, February 1944. A.C.S.E.A was formed as part of South East Asia Command in September 1943.
201 Ibid, Ground Radar Report March 1944. The term "robbed" is taken from the report.
202 Ibid, Whitehall to A.C.S.E.A., 4th August 1944.
203 Ibid, Ground Radar Report, June 1944.

demonstrated by reference to the provision of test equipment for the friendly aircraft I.F.F. system. Early in 1944 A.C.S.E.A. had indicated that no test gear had been received for its I.F.F. equipment and there was "considerable difficulty ... maintaining the full efficiency of the equipment as a result."[204] Their only solution was to 'borrow' some equipment from a newly arrived mobile unit for use at existing stations. A month later the command stated:

> The position regarding deficiencies remains substantially unchanged. It has recently been drawn to this Headquarters' attention that test gear already in the command is rapidly deteriorating and will become unserviceable through fair wear and tear.[205]

A similar warning followed in May, but it was not until August that Whitehall replied:

> At present their [sic] are large demands by A.E.A.F. and Ninth Air Force which first must be met. The rate of production of test gear is not sufficient to meet the existing large demands. In general after the requirements of A.E.A.F. have been met, India receives a share of all arising off contract.[206]

Whitehall continued by listing a number of pieces of equipment that were en route and those which were remaining to be sent, but it is clear that none of it was likely to arrive quickly.

An additional problem existed with spare parts arriving either broken or damaged. In March out of 204 items shipped to India 38% were found to be defective, in May 84 valves out of 110 were found to be broken and in June 56 valves out of a possible 195 were delivered damaged.[207] These breakages were due to two main factors; poor handling over the long passage from Britain and inadequate packing for delicate spare parts. Even though moves were made to improve matters breakages continued to be a problem throughout the year; in December the lack of spare valves for the Type 57 station was so acute that A.C.S.E.A. warned that a number of stations were in danger of being closed.

Additionally there were problems with material imported from the United States. Despite the equipment being efficient and relatively plentiful it did not always arrive on time, spares were broken and ancillary equipment did not work properly. In April A.C.S.E.A received notification that 22 American sets were allocated for delivery

204 Ibid, Ground Radar Report, March 1944.
205 Ibid, Ground Radar Report, April 1944.
206 Ibid, Whitehall to A.C.S.E.A., 2nd August 1944. Allied Expeditionary Air Force (A.E.A.F.) and the U.S. Ninth Air Force operated in Europe.
207 TNA, Air 20/1519, Senior Radar Officer Reports, March, May and June Reports.

to the Far East between May and June, with two years' worth of spares accompanying each set.[208] However, when the first of seven much anticipated air transportable sets arrived in June, they were all delivered incomplete and not one constituted a working station.[209] The sets had to be checked and overhauled at a Base Signals Depot (B.S.D.) instead of being transported directly to the forward operating areas; during the checking process waterproof seals had to be removed which caused damage and ultimately, further delays.[210] The portable power supply was bedevilled by difficulties caused by the extreme climate and an inherent design fault. The generator's engine ran at high temperatures resulting in greater wear and tear on its moving parts. Furthermore, when the generator was operated in forward areas it had to be situated in a pit firstly to shield it from enemy shrapnel, and secondly to reduce noise from its loud engine. However, placing the generator into a pit resulted in the engine running at an even greater temperature and ultimately a larger requirement for spare parts.[211]

Transport

Providing radar cover in Burma and its surrounding regions proved a challenge given its inhospitable terrain and adverse weather conditions. Even when suitable equipment existed there was the additional problem of transporting it to suitable sites to provide efficient early warning.

Fitting radar sets to water-borne vessels gave favourable reception from the good reflecting surface open expanses of water would provide. It was ideal to fit efficient G.C.I. equipment onto the bows of a Landing Ship Tank [L.S.T.]. This had been successful in North Africa, but it needed to be tested in Burma. Such a test would, of course, depend on the provision of a L.S.T.[212] Progress slowed dramatically owing to every type of landing craft being requisitioned from around the world for the proposed invasion of France in June 1944. However, more success was achieved by fitting lightweight warning sets to 85 foot steel barges, the first of which (5048 A.M.E.S.) became operational in February 1944. Moored off St Martin's Island, the C.O.L. was near to the area of land operations and detected enemy aircraft that did not come within range of other stations.[213] But there were some difficulties; the engine system interfered with the radar equipment, and operating in an offshore swell adversely affected the reception. These faults aside the barges proved extremely useful and 5048 A.M.E.S. played

---

208 TNA, Air 2/7201, Provision of R.D.F. Equipment for use in A.C.S.E.A. including India, Whitehall to A.C.S.E.A., 21st April 1944.
209 TNA, Air 20/1519, Senior Radar Officer Reports June. An identical situation occurred in January 1945 with seven additional AN/TPS-2 sets.
210 TNA, Air 41/12, *Signals: Volume IV Radar in Raid Reporting*, p.403.
211 TNA, Air 20/1519, Ground Radar Reports, June.
212 TNA, Air 20/5693, O.R.S. report N7, 8th January 1944.
213 TNA, Air 20/1518, Ground Radar Report, February 1944.

a vital role during the land battles at Buithidaung and Maungdaw during the battle of the Admin Box.

Radar was also fitted to a variety of different motor vehicles and trailers to move the equipment ahead of advancing troops. The vehicles were given a series of code names and each combination showed both invention and ingenuity. 'Turkey' was a G.C.I. set which was carried by transport aircraft to an A.L.G., and then transported up to five miles further by jeep. This could be operational in 48 hours and was used at Myitkyina airfield after the Americans' occupation on 24th July 1944.[214] 'Mountain Goat' was a light-weight set carried by jeeps and was designed for use in inaccessible forward areas; in April 1944 nine sets were available for operation.

'Hawk' consisted of a G.C.I. station using light-weight components and V.H.F. and I.F.F. facilities, all of which were housed in one covered vehicle; but after operational trials in September 1944 only four were ever completed. 'Falcon' was a transported aerial with equipment taken from surplus anti-aircraft gear which was found particularly valuable during the campaign in central Burma in April 1945. During the spring of 1944 trials were carried out by fitting a light-weight set with wireless equipment onto an amphibious DUKW vehicle to enable radar cover to be transported on inland waterways; the DUKW was thus transformed into the 'Goose.' The 'Buffalo' consisted of a light-weight set mounted on a Ford vehicle which was large enough to carry all the radar technical equipment and wireless communications, with an additional jeep attached for general purposes.

These schemes were developed through the necessity of providing radar cover, but there were delays in production. In April it was reported that delays were being encountered with radar vehicle construction because of lack of production facilities, material supply difficulties or delays in design approval.[215] Despite hopes that the building programme would proceed, out of these systems only the 'Buffalo' and the barge mounted set were in operational use in time to make an impact during the first six months of 1944.[216] They all became useful during the latter stages of the campaign in Burma, but by that time the J.A.A.F.'s operations had reduced in intensity, and the rate of Allied advance had become so rapid that the mobile radar units could not keep pace with the army's progress.[217] Furthermore, radar units would solely rely on motor transport to carry the radar sets into action despite earlier experiments with alternative methods. It will be recalled that during 1943 a proposal was made to break a light-weight set into small enough parts to carry by mule. In May 1944 it was discovered

---

214 TNA, Air 41/12, *Signals: Volume IV Radar in Raid Reporting*, pp.383-384, for a full
     description of all these transported radar devices.
215 TNA, Air 20/1518, Ground Radar Report, April 1944.
216 A 'Buffalo' was stationed at Tamu on 21st December 1943 and was able to provide
     important cover during the initial stages of the Kohima siege, but was overrun on 18th
     March 1944 and had to re-locate.
217 TNA, Air 20/1518, Ground Radar Reports, December 1944.

5048 A.M.E.S. Barge. (Source: TNA, Air 20/1518, A.C.S.E.A.,
Ground Radar Reports, 1st October 1942 to 31st October 1944)

Mountain Goat. (Source: TNA, Air 20/1518, A.C.S.E.A., Ground Radar Reports, 1st October 1942 to 31st October 1944)

Rear of a 'Buffalo'. (Source: TNA, Air 20/1518, A.C.S.E.A., Ground Radar Reports, 1st October 1942 to 31st October 1944)

The 'Goose'. (Source: TNA, Air 20/1518, A.C.S.E.A., Ground Radar Reports,
1st October 1942 to 31st October 1944)

that the packages could not be reduced into small enough parts without "considerable modification" and the project was abandoned.[218]

Personnel

Problems affecting supply, spares and transport were exacerbated by the shortage of trained radar personnel from operators to mechanics. As the radar system in the Far East expanded, greater numbers of personnel were required but policy dictated that Germany was to be defeated first and personnel were kept in the European Theatre. The Air Historical Branch narrators give additional reasons for the shortages.[219] These were: inevitable war casualties; distances from Britain for reinforcements to travel; internal distance and transport problems within the Command's boundaries;

---

218 Ibid, May 1944.
219 TNA, Air 41/12, *Signals: Volume IV Radar in Raid Reporting*, p.378.

and sickness peculiar to the region.[220] Deficiencies in British personnel were made up by recruiting and training officers and men of the Royal Indian Air Force to act as operators and mechanics which proved successful. However, the lack of trained personnel, particularly at the beginning of 1944, coupled with equipment shortages, forced a decision to close down unnecessary stations to free both staff and equipment for re-deployment. Radar stations in Western Bengal were considered to be worth placing on a care and maintenance basis, whilst stations on India's west coast could be closed completely owing to the lack of threat.[221] This logical policy of closing radar stations as the advance moved east continued until August 1945.

Air Defence January to June 1944

From January 1944 the campaign moved away from ports and airfields to the battle-front where air superiority would prove decisive in allowing air transport and ground support aircraft to carry out their tasks. The early warning system would play a role in obtaining and maintaining air superiority with varying degrees of success. The next section will analyse the contribution of the early warning system during the battle of the 'Admin Box', the initial stages of Major General Orde Wingate's second Chindit operation (Operation THURSDAY), and the sieges of Kohima and Imphal. All four actions overlapped and ran concurrently, so to maintain clarity each will be dealt with separately.

The 'Admin Box'
The Allies planned to capture the airfield on Akyab Island which would be an important acquisition for air operations when the Allies moved towards Rangoon. A sea-borne landing was unfeasible owing to the lack of suitable shipping, the alternative was an advance along the western Burmese coast through Maungdaw and Buthidaung which was undertaken by soldiers of the 5th and 7th Indian Divisions; on 9th January 1944 both Divisions were in Maungdaw. The Japanese decided to invade India with a two-pronged thrust towards the major supply areas around Imphal, and the campaign's approval was signed two days after the Indian Divisions had occupied Maungdaw. On 4th February the Japanese 55th Division moved north and split the 7th Indian Division east of Buthidaung, and from there a defensive position was formed around the village of Sinzweya. This position was known as the 'Admin Box', owing to the numbers of clerks, typists and other support troops who fought during the siege.[222]

---

220 The sickness factor is often overlooked as the climate and conditions bred disease, particularly for newly arrived personnel, and an examination of the radar stations' Operations Record Books regularly shows staff being sent to hospital.
221 TNA, Air 20/1518, Ground Radar Report, February 1944.
222 Allen, *Burma: The Longest War*, pp.150-190, and Latimer, *Burma: The Forgotten War*, pp.221-238 for full accounts of the battle.

The eventual victory at the 'Box' was notable in that it was the first time the Japanese Army had been defeated by Allied forces in Burma. Previously the Japanese encircled Allied troops, cutting them off from lines of communication and supply before inflicting a defeat. Lieutenant-General Slim planned to turn these encircled positions into strongholds capable of withholding enemy pressure while other forces moved in to attack the Japanese. Vast amounts of supplies had been stockpiled in rear areas as a precursor to this tactic and once the Japanese had circled the 7th Indian Division orders were issued to supply the troops by air.[223] The achievement and maintenance of air superiority was a vital factor in protecting largely undefended transport aircraft and vulnerable ground attack aircraft from the Japanese fighter force which had sufficient numbers to cause problems. Furthermore, R.A.F. fighters would need the early warning organisation to provide warning of approaching enemy aircraft and avoid costly standing patrols.

The area around Maungdaw, Buthidaung and Sinzweya was fortunate in having established radar coverage which spanned from Agartala in the north to Ramu and Cox's Bazar in the south. The radar units consisted of a mixture of Mobile Radar Units, (M.R.U.s), Ground Controlled Interception units (G.C.I.) and Chain Overseas Low units (C.O.L.).[224] The system had been tested on 15th January 1944 when a series of Japanese fighter sweeps flew over the Maungdaw-Buthidaung area in retaliation for Allied ground attack operations against Japanese troops.[225]

The early warning system detected the enemy formations in sufficient time to allow Spitfires to scramble and reach a height to attack the Japanese aircraft. After what was described as "excellent controlling", the Spitfires destroyed five Japanese fighters and damaged a number of others; this was the largest single loss of Japanese fighters over Burma to that date and three of the Japanese pilots were experienced veterans.[226] On 16th January a Dinah reconnaissance aircraft was detected, intercepted and destroyed by Spitfires from 615 Squadron and on 20th January a formation of 100 Japanese fighters stacked at heights from 10,000 to 24,000 feet were successfully attacked from 30,000 feet by Spitfires. Whilst only one Japanese aircraft was lost following a forced landing from this engagement it demonstrates the early warning and control systems were adequately prepared to deal with medium to high flying enemy aircraft flying over the area.

The air battle in support of the 'Admin Box' took place between 4th February to 22nd February and during that time Japanese sorties consisted of large scale fighter

223 Latimer, *Burma: The Forgotten War*, p.226.
224 TNA, Air 41/12, *Signals: Volume IV Radar in Raid Reporting*, Appendix 38, p.612. The system was enhanced on 1st February when 6168 A.M.E.S. and its barge was declared operational and was moored off St Martin's Island.
225 Shores, *Air War for Burma*, p.148.
226 Ibid, p.148; Franks, *Spitfires over the Arakan*, p.121; TNA, Air 27/953, 136 Squadron Operations Record Book, 15th January 1944; Air 27/2096, 607 Squadron Operations Record Book, 15th January 1944.

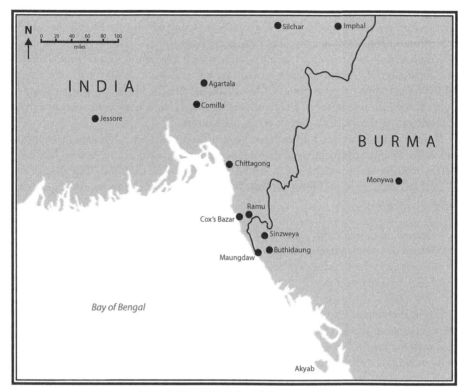

Map 2 The Admin Box February 1944

sweeps, escorted bomber raids and ground attack sorties in support of Japanese troops by fighter aircraft equipped with bombs. On nine out of eighteen days of the battle R.A.F. fighters intercepted Japanese aircraft, and on the remaining days both air supply and ground support operations were allowed to continue free from aerial interference, even though they ran considerable risk from ground fire.

The early warning and control organisation in the Arakan acquitted itself well during operations in this period. On 4th February 70 Japanese fighters were engaged on a sweep in support of ground troops but radar units detected the incoming aircraft in time to give two Spitfire squadrons time to make height before the formation was intercepted. Similarly on 5th February a high flying Dinah was detected, intercepted and destroyed, while later in the morning Spitfires were scrambled to 28,000 feet to meet a formation of 70 Oscars. The Japanese aircraft were spotted flying 15,000 feet below the Spitfires and this gave the R.A.F. an advantage in their attack. Similarly on 15th February an 81 Squadron pilot recalled that "Our interception at 2000 feet above and up sun was ideal."[227] The value of the system was demonstrated on 8th February when a formation of Douglas C-47 Dakotas was escorted by twelve Hurricanes of 134 Squadron during a supply drop. The Hurricane pilots heard by radio of the approach of "15 plus bandits" heading in their direction which gave some aircraft time to escort one formation of transports back to Chittagong and some to stay with the others whilst they dropped their supplies.[228] However, despite the Hurricanes' attempting to fight off the Japanese fighters, a Dakota was lost when the screen was penetrated, thus demonstrating the vulnerability of transport aircraft.[229]

Despite these successes for the radar system there were some indications of future problems. It will be remembered that a reoccurring problem for the system had been height reading and prediction. On 10th February while 81 and 607 Squadrons had been placed in a good position to attack, Flying Officer Bill Andrews, 615 Squadron, wrote in his diary:

> Scrambled down South again near Buthidaung at 22 grand [22,000 feet] ran into about 40+ Jap fighters at about 25 grand. Shattering! ... We must have the height or we have had it. We could have had it but control gave them at 18,000 feet – someone boobed![230]

Flight Lieutenant Jimmy James, 607 Squadron, later remembered, "the Ops. people were picking up the Jap aircraft a lot earlier although they were not always too accurate with the height."[231] Apart from equipment deficiencies or operator error, the difficulty in height reading was hindered by the Japanese adopting new tactics of stacking their formations from ground level to 20,000 feet. This would counter the R.A.F. tactic of gaining height before their dive and zoom manoeuvre, and would make the fighter controller's task harder to accurately position fighters to attack. Previously, with the exception of occasional low-level activity, the Japanese fighters and bombers had not chosen to fly at low-level against Allied territory giving the radar a detection advantage. Later during the sieges of Imphal and Kohima the Japanese altered their tactics and flew low under the radar cover giving the defenders little time to respond effectively. This resulted in the defenders not totally relying on the early warning organisation. Standing patrols were carried out during the period and the Dakotas

---

227   Flight Sergeant Albert Swan quoted in Franks, *Spitfires over the Arakan*, p.180.
228   TNA, Air 27/947, 134 Squadron Operations Record Book, 8th February 1944; Shores, *Air War for Burma*, p.157.
229   Shores, *Air War for Burma*, p.158. The transport crews were disconcerted by the appearance of the Japanese fighters in strength and it took the Commanding Officer of Troop Carrier Command, Brigadier- General William Old to personally lead a flight of transports in a supply drop to raise morale.
230   Franks, *Spitfires over the Arakan*, p.169.
231   Ibid p.207.

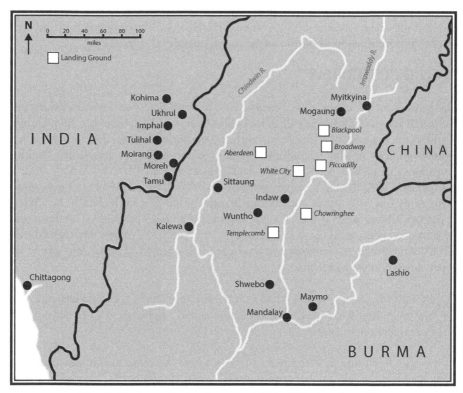

Map 3 North-east India, Burma and China March to June 1944

were escorted by Hurricane squadrons during their supply operations as a matter of course.[232]

The air defence of the 'Admin Box' lasted for eighteen days and even though, according to Japanese records, only five of their aircraft were destroyed and a few more damaged, it had been ultimately successful.[233] In that time the ground troops had been supplied by air and R.A.F. fighters had largely kept Japanese aircraft away from interfering with the supply dropping operations. The established early warning and control system had played an important role in detecting incoming raids giving sufficient time to allow fighters to gain a height and attacking advantage. However,

---

232 TNA, Air 27/158, 11 Squadron (Hurricane) Operations Record Book , 1st January 1944 to 30th June 1944, and Air 27/352, 31 Squadron (Dakota) Operations Record Book, 1st January 1944 to 30th December 1944, "Our comparatively small losses were due to excellent co-operation and ability of Fighter Aircraft."

233 Shores, *Air War for Burma*, pp.156-165.

the Japanese had flown at heights which radar was very capable of detecting in good time but subsequent events over Operation THURSDAY's landing grounds, and over Imphal and Kohima, would prove a bigger challenge for the system.

Operation THURSDAY

The problem of providing early warning in a forward area was encountered during the initial stages of Operation THURSDAY, the second Chindit expedition. Unlike the first, the majority of Wingate's troops, 10,000 out of 12,000, flew into advanced landing grounds in gliders, and once on the ground engineers established landing strips for subsequent supply operations by transport aircraft.[234]

Operation THURSDAY began overnight on 5th/6th March 1944 but the original plans to fly into two strips, codenamed Broadway and Piccadilly, had to be altered at the last minute when it was thought Piccadilly had been blocked by the Japanese. Broadway was chosen as the only site to accept the incoming gliders until 6th March when a second strip at Chowringhee was opened. The scale and importance of the air supply operation were immense:

> By 11th March the two strips had seen the landings of 579 C47s and Dakotas, and 74 gliders. 9,052 personnel, 187 mules and 175 ponies, and 254.5 tons of stores had been delivered.[235]

The landings came as a complete surprise to the Japanese and it was not until 10th March that their bombers and fighters strafed and bombed Chowringhee after flying over Broadway; ominously this formation had not been detected. There had been no provision in the plan to take radar sets to Broadway, but the Japanese attack combined with a reconnaissance flight over Broadway prompted A.V.M. Sir John Baldwin, Air Commander Third Tactical Air Force, to write to A.C.M. Pierse on 10th March suggesting some fighters were deployed.[236] Following a survey on 10th March a detachment of six 81 Squadron Spitfires was sent to Broadway together with a servicing party, some signal personnel and a light-weight radar set. However, Broadway was not in the best position to site radar equipment, being surrounded by 1,000 feet high hills, and trees over 100 feet high which affected the radar's reception, whilst the set could only give warning of aircraft flying due north or south at a range of 25 miles. Flying Officer Alan Peart later recalled:

---

234 Ibid, p.168.
235 Ibid p.173. After 13th March most supplies were air dropped to the troops who had moved on from the landing area.
236 TNA, Air 23/7655, Operation THURSDAY: Allied landings in N.E. Burma. Letter Baldwin to Pierse 10th March 1944.

From an air defence viewpoint it was most vulnerable being close to the enemy fighter bases and having no early warning except for a small mobile experimental radar with a short range.[237]

The Spitfires arrived on Broadway on 12th March and on the following day 40 Oscars attacked it. The radar had given some warning, but during the scramble one Spitfire only just left the ground when it was shot down and its pilot killed. The remaining Spitfires managed to climb and engaged the Japanese fighters, destroying one and causing another to force land.[238] Air Commodore Stanley Vincent, A.O.C. 221 Group, had personally witnessed the Japanese attack which destroyed three American light aircraft and wounded some soldiers. Vincent concluded that the order to scramble had taken too long to reach the fighters once the raid had been declared hostile by U.S.A.A.F. personnel manning the operations room.[239] Whatever the reason for the delay the result was the Spitfires had taken off late:

> Today 30 plus enemy fighters tried to strafe our new base. R.D.F. was very bad, only got five minutes warning. Sergeant Campbell and I were last to scramble. Bounced over 'drome – Campbell killed immediately.[240]

Despite Vincent praising the quality of the British aircraft and their pilots, if the system could not provide adequate warning, neither the advantage of man nor machine could be capitalized upon.[241]

The detachment of Spitfires to Broadway ended on 17th March following a raid by 15 Oscars on the landing ground.[242] The first warning was of 4 plus aircraft approaching the area travelling fast and low at a distance of 25 miles which was on the edge of the set's detection limit. Squadron Leader William Whitamore, the commanding officer of 81 Squadron, had experienced false alarms in the past and decided to wait for further information. A second warning gave the Japanese position as 15 miles away and at this the pilots strapped themselves into their aircraft. The final warning gave the Japanese as 10 miles away and at this two aircraft (piloted by Whitamore and Peart) took off, the rest of the detachment being held on the ground. There was

---

237 Shores, *Air War for Burma*, p.179.
238 Ibid p.180.
239 TNA, Air 25/913, 221 Group Operations Record Book, 13th March 1944. Visit to Broadway by A.O.C. 221 Group, 13th March 1944.
240 Flying Officer Larry Cronin quoted from his diary in Franks, *The Air Battle of Imphal*, p.32.
241 TNA, Air 25/913, 221 Group Operations Record Book, 13th March 1944. Visit to Broadway by A.O.C. 221 Group 13th March 1944. Vincent wrote; "Spitfires proved themselves superior to the Oscars and their pilots the masters of the enemy pilots."
242 Franks, *The Air Battle of Imphal*, p.34. According to Cronin, the previous day the Spitfires had "only just got off [the ground]."

insufficient time for the Spitfires to take off and make height before they engaged the Oscars, and subsequently Whitamore was shot down and killed, Peart's aircraft was badly damaged, and the rest of the aircraft on the ground were either destroyed or badly damaged; one pilot was killed as he sat in his aircraft waiting to take off. Peart recalled:

> Whitamore and myself had only just left the ground when the Oscars arrived. We had no height, little airspeed and were definitely with our pants down in a rather helpless position to stop the first attack.[243]

and according to Flying Officer Larry Cronin:

> At last the Japs have woken up to the fact that if they come in low enough over the hills our Radio Location won't be able to pick up them up until it's too late.[244]

It was decided that the detachment was to end and in future the squadron would remain at readiness at their airfield waiting for a telephone call when an enemy attack was expected.[245] It was anticipated that the Spitfires could be over Broadway in 40 minutes, and if fitted with overload tanks they would be able to intercept the Japanese fighters as they made their escape. This plan's obvious drawbacks were demonstrated on 18th March when Japanese fighters raided Broadway completely destroying what was left of the light-weight set without being intercepted by 81 Squadron whose diarist recorded, "our efforts to intercept from this range were fruitless."[246]

Plans were proposed to use the three landing sites at Piccadilly, Broadway and Aberdeen as radar bases to give a triangulation effect for better coverage; a mobile operations room would be established at Aberdeen and all three bases would be linked by V.H.F. radio sets.[247] Following siting surveys at the end of March, 221 Group reported with "regret" their findings.[248] Broadway was considered unsuitable for resident fighters owing to their vulnerability to low-level attack, whilst as there were no plans to turn Piccadilly into a stronghold it was not possible to place a radar set there.

---

243   Shores, *Air War for Burma*, p.183.
244   Ibid, quoted from Cronin's diary.
245   TNA, Air 23/1945, Report by Air Commander 3rd Tactical Air Force on Operation THURSDAY. Signal from 221 Group H.Q. to 3rd Tactical Air Force, 18th March 1944, p.2.
246   TNA, Air 27/678, 81 Squadron Operations Record Book, 18th March 1944.
247   TNA, Air 25/913, 221 Group Operations Record Book, 1st March to 31st March 1944. Précis of a conference held at 221 Group to discuss the control of fighter aircraft at an Advanced Landing Ground in Burma, 27th March 1944.
248   Ibid, Appendices, Fighters at Broadway, 4th April 1944 and TNA, Air 25/913, 221 Group Operations Record Book, 1st March to 31st March 1944, Siting Recce at Aberdeen and Piccadilly by Wing Commander W.D.A. Smith (181 Wing) and Squadron Leader D.W. Rowson (221 Group). No first names are available for Smith or Rowson.

Aberdeen had been carefully surveyed and had been declared unsuitable for radar as it would only give limited cover to the south and south-west, with even less cover to the north. The defence of Broadway and Aberdeen would therefore have to rely on local anti-aircraft guns and Spitfires flying from Imphal or Kangla.

Probert described the radar and fighter detachment to Broadway as a "gallant effort" but in essence it was a failure.[249] The three Japanese raids received short warning from radar leaving the fighters insufficient time to take off and climb to height. This came as no surprise as Flight Lieutenant Atherton had pointed out how hills affected radar signals in 1940, and similar problems had been encountered during the siting surveys during 1942.[250] It will also be recalled that during the A.L.G. investigations in 1943 the O.R.S. had stated a light-weight set would need to be placed 20 miles ahead of the point to give defenders sufficient warning.[251] Given that the set had a range of 25 miles the O.R.S. recommendation would give the defenders 45 miles of warning, whilst at Broadway they had only 25 miles. The interceptions on 13th and 17th March had both been delayed, firstly by indecisive controllers and then by an experienced squadron commander who was waiting for firm evidence of the raid, but while it is possible to place some blame on these factors, the root cause of the raids' successes was the lack of efficient early warning.

Imphal and Kohima

The Japanese advanced westwards towards Imphal and the garrison at Kohima where troops were instructed to remain and fight whilst their supplies were brought to them by air. The sieges at these locations have been well documented in various publications such as those written or edited by Louis Allen, Jon Latimer, John Colvin and Woodburn Kirby, but the role played by the early warning system in combination with the fighter defence has received little analysis in these books.[252] The next section will analyse how the early warning system performed in the defence of the transport and close support effort.

The Area and its Early Warning System

The topography and situation within both areas were quite different. The battle area at Kohima measured 700 x 900 x 1,100 yards and the battle at times resulted in fierce hand to hand fighting, famously across the width of the Governor's tennis court. There was no room to operate conventional aircraft to take off and land, so supplies

---

249   Probert, *The Forgotten Air Force*, p.176.
250   See p.41 of this book.
251   TNA, Avia 7/889, O.R.S. Report S1, 20th April 1943, p.1.
252   Allen, *Burma, The Longest War*; Latimer, *Burma: The Forgotten War*; Colvin, *Not Ordinary Men*; and Kirby (ed.), *The War Against Japan, Volume IV*.

had to be dropped by parachute and, therefore, there was no opportunity for reinforcements to be landed or casualties evacuated. Imphal Plain covered 700 square
miles, its valley was 25 miles long and 10 miles at its widest point. There were six
airfields within the boundaries, two being all-weather strips, which allowed supplies
to be brought directly to the valley and wounded and non-essential personnel to be
evacuated. Furthermore, offensive aircraft were able to fly close support sorties from
these airfields whilst Spitfires operating from the same bases provided air defence.
The Imphal Plain was covered by a well-established early warning system consisting
of radar, observer posts, filter and control rooms, the majority of which had been
in place since late 1943. For instance 857 A.M.E.S., operating a G.C.I. set which
played a significant part detecting Japanese aircraft during the siege, had been in Buri
Bazar on 1st September 1943 before moving to Mungai on 7th December and Moirag
on 21st January, finally returning to Buri Bazar on 1st April.[253] In addition to these
stations advanced radar sets were situated to the east, for example, 6168 A.M.E.S. at
Tamu, 383 at Ukhrul and 857 at Moirang.[254] This established system was strength-
ened by mobile wireless units stationed in the hills to the east of the advanced radar
units. From the middle of 1943 W.O.U.s had been deployed to the east of Imphal to
give additional early warning cover, in particular against low-flying aircraft:

> In view of recent Jap tactics – low altitudes and under radar cover – you are asked
> to consider advisability of deploying a certain number of W.O.U. posts as far
> forward as possible. This would assist the controller in passing information to his
> fighters and the possibility of effecting an interception on these low attacks.[255]

In March the W.O.U. companies had 50 posts established but as will be discussed
shortly, their effectiveness was diminished when the Japanese advanced westwards.

Despite the area having relatively good coverage there were familiar problems
which reduced the early warning. The mountains surrounding Imphal created permanent echo difficulties and to counter this, radar stations were sited in locations which
attempted to provide compromises between overlapping cover and solving technical
problems. However, the scale of the country resulted in stations being spread thinly
providing weak spots where there was little or no coverage. Furthermore, there was no
radar equipment to detect low flying raiders. As a result, even though the G.C.I. sets
could cope adequately with high-flying aircraft as Japanese reconnaissance aircraft

---

253   TNA, Air 29/184, 857 A.M.E.S. Operations Record Book, 1st October 1942 to 31st
October 1945.
254   TNA, Air 26/267, 181 (Signals) Wing, Operations Record Book, 1st June 1943 to 31st
December 1944; Air 29/178, 383 A.M.E.S. Operations Record Book, 1st February 1943
to 31st March 1945; Air 29/184, 857 A.M.E.S. Operations Record Book, 1st October
1942 to 31st October 1945.
255   TNA, Air 23/2037, Raid Warning System, memo 3rd T.A.F. to 224 Group, 9th February
1944.

discovered to their cost, it was "practically impossible to track enemy aircraft if they flew in at a sufficiently low altitude."[256] The Japanese raiders capitalized on this deficiency by splitting their formations into high and low sections, composed of multiple or single aircraft, thus making the fighter controllers' task harder to keep track of friendly or enemy aircraft given the difficulties with I.F.F. equipment. To compound these problems some of the R.A.F. mobile wireless units had been replaced by inexperienced sections from the Indian W.O.U. Corps which resulted in a lower standard of detection.[257]

Potentially the greatest threat to the air security of Imphal and Kohima resulted from the loss of the advanced radar stations to the east. During the Japanese Army's advance westwards units had to be withdrawn and re-sited, or moved back into the security of the Plain. For example 569 A.M.E.S. at Wabagai had to move its location owing to the proximity of the Japanese advance on 18th March. Once in Senjam Khuhou the staff erected their technical equipment in 36 hours before being forced to move again on 7th April.[258] When 569 first moved on 18th March it had been replaced by a light-weight set operated by 6168 A.M.E.S. which in turn had to withdraw inside the Plain at Moreh before succumbing to artillery fire on 27th March.[259] This was typical of events which were replicated at various sites over the March to April period.[260] Furthermore, nearly all of the 50 observer posts had to be evacuated and redeployed sometimes with the loss of their equipment, leaving serious gaps which enemy aircraft could penetrate.[261]

The eventual success of the air defence of Imphal and Kohima can be attributed to various interlinking factors. Interdiction raids on Japanese airfields, conservation of Japanese aircraft strengths, and Japanese aircraft not flying in poor weather gave Allied transport aircraft time to fly supplies in and casualties out. All these factors played a role in clearing the skies over Imphal and Kohima, and often overshadowed the part played by the air defence fighters operating over Allied territory, with the result that the part played by the early warning system has been overlooked or misrepresented. The Air Historical Branch authors suggest that the loss of the advanced radar sites was offset by the long-range American interdiction raids on Japanese airfields.[262] Similarly the Official History states:

256 TNA, Air 41/12, *Signals: Volume IV Radar in Raid Reporting*, p.392.
257 TNA, Air 41/64, *The Campaigns in the Far East Volume IV: South East Asia November 1943 to August 1945*, p.87.
258 TNA, Air 29/182, 569 A.M.E.S. Operations Record Book, 1st November 1943 to 31st October 1945.
259 TNA, Air 41/12, *Signals: Volume IV Radar in Raid Reporting*, p.393.
260 Ibid, p.393 and TNA, Air 26/267, 181 Signals Wing Operations Record Book, 1st June 1943 to 31st December 1944.
261 TNA, Air 23/5420, Indian Observer Corps: History.
262 TNA, Air 41/12, *Signals: Volume IV Radar in Raid Reporting*, p.393.

The interception of enemy aircraft proved difficult owing to the withdrawal of the wireless observer screen covering the plain, and to the blanketing of radar by the surrounding hills. There was therefore little warning of incoming raids and interceptions were infrequent.[263]

Both these statements are not totally accurate as the early warning system, despite its deficiencies, performed reasonably well and assisted defending fighters to intercept Japanese formations.

The Early Warning System in Action

The lack of advanced radar posts, observer posts and low-level radar resulted in weak spots which Japanese aircraft exploited. On 17th April Kangla airstrip was attacked without prior warning and four days later on 21st Kangla was attacked again without warning, the 81 Squadron diarist writing:

In the late afternoon there was some excitement when 8 Oscars suddenly appeared over Kangla Strip. Without due warning 3 bombs were dropped but none landed near the airstrip or aircraft.[264]

On 22nd April 20 Oscars attacked Tulihal airfield at 0700 hours damaging a section of Beaufighters; one was destroyed and two were damaged, but anti-aircraft gunners claimed one Japanese aircraft destroyed and others damaged.[265] The low-level attacks were complemented by Japanese aircraft roaming over Allied airspace practically immune from detection. On 11th April three Spitfires were escorting six Dakotas on a sortie to Aberdeen strip and were attacked by a number of Japanese fighters without warning from the ground. The Spitfires were able to fight off their opponents and despite no losses to the Japanese no transport aircraft were lost or damaged. On 23rd April a 62 Squadron Dakota was returning from a supply drop over Sapam and was attacked without warning by two Oscars; fortunately the R.A.F. pilot was able to evade his attackers and the aircraft was only slightly damaged.

The danger of allowing Japanese fighters to break through to the vulnerable transport aircraft was demonstrated on 25th April during a supply drop to troops at Sapam. The early warning organisation correctly identified a number of Japanese aircraft heading towards Imphal and Spitfires were scrambled together with some American P-38 Lightnings which were returning from an interdiction sortie. The Japanese aircraft were intercepted and the Allied pilots claimed two destroyed, two probably

---

263 Kirby, (ed.) *The War Against Japan, Volume IV*, p.245.
264 TNA, Air 27/679, 81 Squadron Operations Record Book, 21st April 1944.
265 Shores, *Air War for Burma*, p.209. Despite the claim no Japanese aircraft were recorded as lost.

destroyed and five damaged, but the action had not prevented some Japanese fighters breaking through to attack the Dakotas.[266] Three R.A.F. Dakotas were lost, and two U.S.A.A.F. transport aircraft were reported lost making the overall loss five valuable aircraft and crews.[267]

Protecting transport aircraft from enemy interference presented A.C.S.E.A. with a dilemma; clearly the early warning organisation could not be totally relied on to detect roaming Japanese fighters, whilst those flying at low-level were practically undetectable. At the same time aviation fuel was in short supply on the Plain so that constant air patrols were potentially wasteful particularly when it is remembered that the Japanese did not fly on every day of the siege. The solution was the establishment of a designated air corridor along which transport aircraft would fly and fighters patrol during the hours of daylight when transports were flying. While this can be regarded as a compromise between constant air patrols and interception, it proved successful. After the corridor's introduction only one Allied aircraft was lost to enemy fighter action within its confines. This was on 17th June when a 99 Squadron Vickers Wellington 'cut the corner' rather than flying along the air corridor with its patrolling fighters and flew into the path of a number of Oscars.[268]

Despite the problems with gaps and low-level cover, the early warning system performed quite well during this period when raiders were flying at medium to high altitudes. On 12th April Spitfires were scrambled to meet a formation of Oscars over Imphal which Number 4 Filter Room reported as 12 plus aircraft at 20,000 feet; a successful interception resulted although no Japanese aircraft were lost.[269] On 17th April 30 Spitfires were scrambled to meet a combined formation of 62 Japanese bombers and fighters en route to Imphal at approximately 25,000 feet. In addition to the Spitfires, 12 P-51 Mustangs of the American Air Commando Group were diverted from a bombing raid to intercept the Japanese formation. The subsequent interception was successful starting with detection by radar. Number 4 Filter Room reported "tracking and station performance excellent" whilst Flying Officer Peart recalled:

We climbed hard under instruction from the controller and intercepted a large force of the enemy. There were six bombers at a medium altitude, say 15,000

---

266 Ibid, p.210 and TNA, Air 24/1286, Daily Operational Summaries, Nos. 596-656, 1st April 1944 to 31st May 1944.
267 Shores, *Air War for Burma*, p.211; TNA Air 27/584, 62 Squadron Operations Record Book, 25th April 1944; Air 27/1159, 194 Squadron Operations Record Book, 25th April 1944 and TNA, Air 24/1286, Daily Operational Summaries, Nos. 596-656, 1st April 1944 to 31st May 1944.
268 Between 30th April and 5th July 1944, 14 transports were lost in the region to a combination of flying accidents, mechanical failure and weather.
269 TNA, Air 29/165, Number 4 Filter Room Operations Record Book, 12th April 1944.

feet, with covering fighters up to 30,000 feet. We positioned ourselves and then attacked the top cover.[270]

Four Japanese fighters were destroyed and a fifth was seriously damaged when the pilot had to force land at his airfield.[271] On 6th May Number 4 Filter Room tracked a formation of 9 plus aircraft which grew to 20 plus aircraft flying at 10,000 feet towards Imphal; 12 Spitfires were scrambled and following the interception a Japanese Oscar was lost. The radar system was of particular value when high flying reconnaissance aircraft flew towards Imphal; on 26th April, 28th April and 1st May, 857 A.M.E.S. with its efficient mobile G.C.I. equipment detected and controlled the interceptions and on each occasion the interception was successful with Spitfires destroying three Dinahs.

The value of the advanced observer posts despite so many being withdrawn and overrun during the Japanese advance was demonstrated towards the end of the Imphal siege. On 29th May Number 4 Filter Room reported that Post 146 M.W.O.U. at had made visual contact with six enemy aircraft at 9000 feet and there had been "no radar warning."[272] Spitfires were scrambled but failed to find the raiders, but when 857 and 383 A.M.E.S. detected the Japanese aircraft Spitfires were successfully directed on to the enemy fighter sweep.[273] On 8th June Post 146 M.W.O.U reported a visual sighting of "15 hostiles … [which] circled Bishenphur area and went out low. Not seen outside the valley by radar."[274] These aircraft were not tracked or detected by any radar units in the area with the result that they attacked Hurricanes engaged on tactical reconnaissance duties; no warnings were given and one Hurricane was lost, three more damaged.[275] Nine days later Post 146 again reported a visual sighting of 20 hostile aircraft at 8,000 feet flying north and fortunately a Spitfire was airborne on an air test as were patrolling Spitfires in the air corridor. The air test Spitfire found the Japanese fighters first and called other R.A.F. fighters to the area where a successful interception resulted in five Japanese aircraft being destroyed, one of the pilots, Sergeant Major Tomesaku Igarashi, being an experienced 'ace'.[276]

Failure and Successes

It must be acknowledged that Japanese tactics had been largely unsuccessful as their aircraft had not flown every day or overwhelmed the air defence system despite the fact that continuous low-level or free roaming attacks could have caused chaos among

270 Franks, *The Air Battle of Imphal*, p.78.
271 Shores, *Air War for Burma*, p.207.
272 TNA, Air 29/165, Number 4 Filter Room Operations Record Book, 29th May 1944.
273 Ibid and TNA, Air 27/2124, 615 Squadron Operations Record Book, 29th May 1944.
274 TNA, Air 29/165, Number 4 Filter Room Operations Record Book, 8th June 1944.
275 Shores, *Air War for Burma*, p.242.
276 Ibid, p.244.

transport aircraft and forced them to fly at night with the inevitable result of decreased supply tonnage. One reason was that Japanese commanders were aware of potential shortages that such operations could result in and followed a conservation policy. However, whilst these factors may be used to explain Japanese tactics they overshadow the part played by the air defence fighters and in particular the early warning system over Imphal and Kohima. With the wisdom of hindsight it is clear that the Japanese could have made more efficient use of its resources to disrupt the Allied air operation, but nevertheless it is important to analyse the part played by the early warning system in relation to the attacks it faced during the period rather than in the context of what the Japanese failed to do.

The Imphal Plain was similar to the Admin Box in that it had an established early warning system and was similar to the landing ground at Broadway in that it could not detect low-level raiders with any kind of success. One reason for this was that the radar equipment was still lacking in technology appropriate for the topography of the country. The Chief Radar Officer reported a 24th May raid as follows:

> Six enemy aircraft were reported at 3000 feet by an O.P. and were not seen by 5071 A.M.E.S. This failure is attributed to P.E.s and the low altitude at which the aircraft were flying.[277]

Low-level cover was improved by wireless observer units and the obvious benefits of this organisation were demonstrated in the raids in late May and early June. However, the early warning cover was not helped by the advanced radar units and observer posts withdrawing into Imphal to avoid capture or being overrun by Japanese land forces, with the remaining observer posts being thinly spread out along a wide and inhospitable terrain.

If the low-level cover was difficult to provide, radar warning of Japanese raids at higher altitudes proved more successful. The need to provide protection for transport aircraft has been discussed at length earlier and the loss of five aircraft on 25th April showed their vulnerability against fighter attack. This action saw the introduction of an air corridor which fighters patrolled which was in addition to regular escort duties carried out by R.A.F. squadrons. The presence of these patrols and escorts provided an important deterrence as between 29th March and 22nd June there were just two occasions on 11th and 26th April when Dakotas were attacked by Japanese fighters whilst being escorted by Hurricanes and Spitfires respectively. Furthermore, there is no record of any aircraft being attacked whilst flying within the protection of the air corridor. To complement these defensive patrols, the early warning system gave fighters warning to scramble or divert from other tasks in each successful interception during the siege period. For example, on 26th April Hurricanes were escorting

---

277 TNA, Air 20/1518, Chief Radar Officer's Reports, February to July 1944. O.P. = Observer Post and P.E. = Permanent Echoes.

Dakotas on a supply drop when the radar organisation warned of the approach of enemy fighters whilst also scrambling Spitfires from ground bases to intercept, and on 17th June ground observers from a M.W.O.U. provided warning of an incoming raid which assisted firstly an aircraft performing an air test and then patrolling fighters to intercept the Japanese aircraft.[278] During the interceptions of this period there were some familiar problems of height prediction and ground controlling, but the interceptions resulted in Japanese aircraft being engaged and prevented from reaching the transports. Research in Japanese records for Shores' *Air War for Burma* shows that between 29th March and 22nd June approximately 20 Japanese aircraft were destroyed as a result of the air fighting over Imphal and Kohima. This might not be a large figure, but the primary aim was to keep the Japanese fighters away from the transport aircraft and maintain local air superiority over the battlefield. This was achieved by the defending fighters assisted by the early warning system, for without it costly air combat patrols would have had to be flown with deterorious effects on fuel consumption, airframes and pilot fatigue.

June 1944 to August 1945

After Imphal was relieved the Japanese retreated eastwards short of supplies and manpower, and although there remained much bitter ground fighting before the war ended, the J.A.A.F. in Burma had been numerically reduced by attrition and aircraft withdrawn for use elsewhere. From September 1944 until May 1945 the Japanese air effort was limited to reconnaissance sorties and a series of nuisance raids which caused minor damage, but ultimately had little effect on Allied operations. The next section will analyse the contribution of the early warning system in the Far East from June 1944 to August 1945.

Technical Problems, Old and New

The technical problems posed by topography, weather, humidity and mountain ranges described in this chapter continued to pose difficulties for the rest of the war and in many cases would not be solved until years later. Shortages of trained staff were resolved by training courses or by the closure of radar stations in rear areas and the re-deployment of staff. Closure of radar stations began in September 1944; 180 Signals Group reported in December 1944 that three A.M.E.S. stations were to close, three more to be placed in care and maintenance, whilst two more were to be

---

278 Shores, *Air War for Burma*, pp.212-212 and pp.242-244; TNA, Air 24/1286, Daily Operational Summaries, Nos. 596-656, 1st April 1944 to 31st May 1944 and TNA, Air 24/1287, Daily Operational Summaries, Nos. 657-717, 1st June 1944 to 31st July 1944.

reduced to a two-watch system.[279] This was typical as demands for staff and equipment increased, and the threat of Japanese air attack diminished. Supplies of equipment caused familiar difficulties with sets arriving incomplete, broken or not arriving at all.[280] At some stations equipment and training were still found to be deficient. During an inspection visit to the Sambre filter room on 1st May 1945 it was found that some equipment was obsolete whilst some staff were ill-equipped to deal with signal interference.[281]

New research units were established in an effort to solve the technical difficulties. In June 1944 a Radio Experimental Unit was set up to carry out research duties previously carried out by the Base Signals Unit. It would:

> [U]ndertake and coordinate research and experimental work on Wireless and Radar problems which arise within the command, and on the adaptation of radio equipment existent in the command to meet the specialised requirements of this theatre of operations.[282]

On 7th March 1945 there was a proposal to form a Radio Development Unit in Ceylon. It was recognised that future operations in tropical and sub-tropical climate conditions would require "quick improvisation" as the campaign continued.[283] Attempts to solve the permanent echoes problem had been carried out in Scotland's mountainous regions and the Far East from mid-1943, but by March 1945 trials were still inconclusive and no answers would be available by August 1945.[284] It was recognized that the humidity and rainfall likely to be encountered as the forces moved through Burma would penetrate radar equipment, and great efforts were carried out to tropicalise the kit.[285] Remedial work to waterproof radio and radar equipment in the field was undertaken and this led to the formation of the Mobile Waterproofing Unit in 1945.[286]

By the end of 1944 it was recognised that more experimental work needed to be carried out in respect of the Far East's particular demands. Between 2nd December

279 TNA, Air 26/264, 180 Signals Wing Operations Record Book, 1st July 1943 to 31st August 1945, "Nos. 281, 224 228 A.M.E.S. are to be closed down and dismantled. Nos. 590, 248, 568 to be placed on a care and maintenance basis. Nos. 851 and 15059 A.M.E.S.s to be placed on a two watch system."
280 TNA, Air 20/1519, Senior Radar Officer Reports India Command. In November 1944 the Senior Radar Officer reported that no complete Type 63 A.M.E.S. had been received in the Command and out of 150 cases that were shipped, 51 were untraced.
281 TNA, Air 20/5697, O.R.S. Report N15, May 1945.
282 TNA, Air 29/1209, Radio Experimental Unit (India) Operations Record Book and Appendices, 1st May 1944 to 28th February 1945.
283 TNA, Avia 7/1306, R.D. F. in the Far East, 1944-1945.
284 TNA, Avia 7/2209, Radar in Mountainous Regions, 1943-1945.
285 TNA, Avia 7/2618, Tropicalisation of Mobile Ground Radar Equipment, 1945.
286 TNA, Air 20/1519, A.C.S.E.A. Ground Radar Reports, 1944-1945.

1944 and 13th January 1945, Group Captain W.C. Cooper of the Ministry of Aircraft Production, (M.A.P.) and Mr Watson of T.R.E. visited the area to establish whether there was an opportunity to reinforce the influence of the Controllerate of Communications Equipment (C.C.E.) and they concluded that it "became increasingly evident that radio development effort in the theatre was essential."[287] Pointing out that the distances from the United Kingdom and United States and vast distances within the theatre were not assisting development, they reported that the operation to liberate Burma required "technical preparations to serve a number of D-Days."[288] They found the theatre:

> [H]as necessarily had to accept radio equipment chosen for it in the United Kingdom and the United States taking second place to the needs of the European Theatre ... no evidence was forthcoming of a detailed study of operational requirements in relation to radio equipment which should be made available as distinct from that which is being supplied.[289]

Cooper and Watson recommended that a developmental effort be made in the Far East and United Kingdom, taking into account the "continuing demands of the European Theatre" and this needed to be started within five months from February 1945 prior to the monsoon period beginning. The findings were enough to convince the Air Ministry that the organisation would be worthwhile and its approval was granted in February 1945. From the end of March 1945 radio and radar scientists, technicians and R.A.F. experts were recruited either voluntarily or by requisition.[290] Many of the staff volunteered to travel to India on short service commissions from research establishments and the T.R.E. with appropriate adjustments to their service conditions. The requirement to send suitable personnel to the Far East is demonstrated by the case of Flying Officer W.J. James of the 2nd Tactical Air Force in Europe who received a posting to India on 9th April, less than a month before the end of the European war:

> We have decided to select you for duty as a ground radar specialist for the Calcutta section of the C.C.E. organisation in India ... you should try to complete your tour of duty with the 2nd T.A.F. before the end of this month since we are planning for you to leave this country for India between the middle and end of May,

---

287 TNA, Avia 7/2737, Far East Radar Organisation, 1944-1945. There are no first names available for Watson or Cooper.
288 Ibid.
289 Ibid.
290 TNA, Avia 7/1303, R.D. F. in the Far East, 1945, contains correspondence and posting details.

and you will, of course, need to undergo a medical examination, be vaccinated and receive various inoculations before leaving for India.[291]

However, many of the staff recruited for the venture never arrived in India and those that did continued their research at a slower peacetime pace.

There was no indication in March 1945 that the war would end in August, and no assurances that the J.A.A.F. would cease to be a threat by May that year, let alone that the re-capture of the Burmese west coast ports would be virtually unopposed.[292] This organisation was at least twelve months late in its conception and might have produced answers to problems which the O.R.S. on their own could only report on, or the smaller units investigate without access to better scientific equipment. The organisation was recognized as being needed in the theatre, but by the time the personnel and equipment arrived the radar organisation was beginning to get smaller and disband owing to the lack of Japanese air threat.

The speed of the Allied advance through Burma posed new challenges to the early warning organisation. Defence of static targets such as cities or strongholds had previously been the main priority, but from July 1944 the Japanese retreated with Allied forces in pursuit and its front line assets had to be defended. Both air transport and close support operations required warning against enemy air attack, as did their defending fighters, and to provide effective early warning radar equipment had to be placed in advance of the fighter base. This cover ideally required a light-weight radar set and a method to transport it. A true light-weight and portable set having the capability to detect high and low flying aircraft in the difficult terrain had long been a desire of the Command, and some sets started to become available during 1945.

Transport and the Light-Weight Set

There were two methods by which radar sets could be transported to their positions, by air in the case of equipment such as the 'Turkey' or by road as in the case of the 'Mountain Goat'.[293] Although a helicopter had been used for the first time in the theatre it was neither big nor powerful enough to lift a series of radar components over long distances.[294] Lifting equipment by air proved successful for captured airfields and advanced landing grounds. 6178 A.M.E.S.' light-weight radar set and crew had been flown into Mawlaik by glider on 29th November 1944 and the station gave "excellent

---

291 Ibid, enclosure 46. There is no first name available for James.
292 Plans to retake the Western Burmese ports had called for elaborate early warning systems carried on barge and ship, with provision for rapid radar deployment once ashore. However, the Japanese abandoned the ports before the Allied landings.
293 'Turkey' was a hand-turned, air-transportable G.C.I. set. Please see pp.75-77 of this book for transport methods.
294 Y'Blood, *Air Commandos Against Japan*, p. 116. An American helicopter had been used to rescue downed airmen on 24th April 1944.

service" until being withdrawn the following February.[295] Similarly a 'Turkey' was flown into the captured airfield at Myitkyina by the Americans on 24th July 1944 and gave a reasonable range of warning. Transporting these devices by air was ideal if there were airfields for aircraft or gliders, but other methods were necessary and principally this involved fixing the set to a motor vehicle and transporting the unit by road. The bad road conditions which prevailed in some Burmese regions were suited for the 'Mountain Goat'; 6171 A.M.E.S. was able to move its vehicles at Sittang on 19th November and this deployment was found to be "very useful."[296] The 'Hawk' light-weight G.C.I. equipment mounted on a covered vehicle was reported to be "very promising" but only four were ever built following its operational trials in September 1944.[297]

Despite the relative promise of vehicle mounted equipment there were still problems. The majority of the equipment was not light enough to traverse the poor road network and many vehicles bogged down following the monsoon period. Even during the dry season, radar vehicles struggled to maintain the pace of the advancing armies. During the advance on Rangoon the mobile equipment advanced with the Army on the outer flanks' main roads and railways but the plan was unsuccessful, "This scheme of deployment was not a success, and some units were left idle while waiting information as to where they should be deployed."[298] This confusion was brought on by the requirement to provide early warning cover in a situation where the equipment was unsuitable for the circumstances. As will be discussed later, the provision of effective and alert anti-aircraft artillery able to keep pace with the front line troops would have provided a good defensive substitute.

Transport was one difficulty and early warning equipment was another. Light-weight sets had been required for over two years, and even though technology was improving, a set which fully met the needs of the Far East Command was slow to arrive. A series of radar sets were trialled or introduced from August 1944 and whilst some were adequate others did not represent a significant advance over existing equipment. For example, the Type 63 set was considered to be of "considerable value" but was not thought to be the "final answer to problems of light-weight coverage in mountainous country."[299] In November it was reported that trials on a light-weight Type 61 set had not shown it to be significantly different than the earlier Type 57, but even so it was considered to be of great value for light warning cover against low flying aircraft.[300] Lastly the 'Falcon' air transportable light-weight set which started trials in

295 TNA, Air 41/12, *Signals: Volume IV Radar in Raid Reporting*, p.395.
296 Ibid.
297 TNA, Air 20/1519, A.C.S.E.A. Ground Radar Reports, 1944-1945.
298 TNA, Air 41/12, *Signals: Volume IV Radar in Raid Reporting*, p.400.
299 TNA, Air 20/1519, A.C.S.E.A. Ground Radar Reports, 1944-1945, October 1944 report.
300 Ibid, November 1944 report.

October 1944 and by April 1945 was described as being "most useful" for its range of deployments.[301]

From the end of 1944 the rate of Fourteenth Army's advance presented the command with the problem of how to supply early warning. The December 1944 Senior Radar Officer's report stated:

> Radar cover near the front lines is not as satisfactory as it should be for the following reasons:
>
> 1. Speed of Forward Movement
>
> 2. Difficulties in Transportation
>
> 3. Reluctance to cut down number of 'elaborate static establishments' in rear areas and no release of personnel to man units in the forward areas.[302]

The front line was 150 miles from the Allied air bases and this made it difficult for fighters to mount 'loiter' patrols over the front line. The alternative was an early warning system that could be transported with the front line troops. From January 1945 the Radar Officer's monthly report regularly contained requests for light-weight radar and in January stated " requirement for the newer types of LW set are increasing" whilst describing the success of the light-weight set flown into Akyab after the landing, "results were excellent. This incident illustrates the value of light-weight, robust sets under the conditions of this theatre."[303] The conditions at Akyab looking over water were different to those in the Burmese jungles and mountainous regions and the light-weight sets had a limited usefulness in the latter.

Operations and Difficulties Providing Low Flying Defence

The difficulties provided by the lack of specific radar equipment, and its means of transportation were to play a part in how effectively the Allies' front line was defended against air attack. As the relationship was close the next section will analyse the elements of air defence and early warning as one rather than in isolation.

The period from the end of the monsoon in 1944 until the last aerial combat on 29th April 1945 saw the Japanese engage in high and low attacks. As in late 1943 and early 1944 the Allied early warning system was enhanced by the introduction of the Spitfire and any incursion by medium to high-flying raiders was likely to result in a successful interception. On four occasions between 24th September and 7th October 1944, Spitfires intercepted and destroyed four Dinahs at high altitude directly as a

---

301 Ibid, April 1945 report.
302 Ibid, December 1944 report.
303 TNA, Air 20/1519, A.C.S.E.A. Ground Radar Reports, 1944-1945, January 1945 report.

result of successful detection by radar.[304] Furthermore, on 5th November Spitfires intercepted a formation of Oscars over Palel at 12,000 feet and destroyed one of these aircraft.[305] However, at lower levels the results were not as good. During the morning of 8th November Oscars were en route to strafe front line positions and encountered Dakotas on supply operations; despite some Spitfires being scrambled no interception was made. Later the same day, Oscars entered the same area finding more transports and once again attacked at low altitude. As a result of both these attacks six R.A.F. and U.S.A.A.F. Dakotas were lost, and on neither occasion were the attackers detected by radar.[306] In December a series of low-level attacks began against Allied airfields and front line positions which the early warning system could not cope with. On 13th December six Oscars attacked Kalewa airfield without detection, but worse was to follow in January 1945. The distance from the Allied fighter bases to the front line gave the J.A.A.F. an opportunity to attack in greater numbers since the Imphal siege in June 1944.[307] Although the attacks were described as nuisance raids they still were unpleasant for the troops and caused occasional losses among transport supply aircraft.[308] On 11th January Lilys attacked Ye-U airfield, whilst later in the day Oscars attacked a road convoy on the Shwebo-Ye-U road without detection. The following day Oscars en route to Shwebo found an airstrip at Onbauk where Dakotas were dropping supplies or unloading on the ground; two Dakotas were lost in the air and two on the ground; the attack was not detected by any early warning units.

Such attacks caused damage on a small scale but did not seriously affect the Allied advance as the "land battles continued unimpeded by the Japanese 5th Air Division."[309] During the first months of 1945 there was a feeling of resignation that little could be done to counter the low-flying threat as, "The ground radar system was in general unable to give assistance in dealing with these raids."[310] The alternative to providing early warning cover was to provide patrols over the battle area which increased in intensity as the Allied advance continued and this table shows the increased patrolling sorties in comparison with the scrambles recorded in March 1944:

304 Shores, *Air War for Burma*, pp.263-270.
305 Ibid, p.281.
306 Ibid, p.282.
307 Ibid, p.302.
308 TNA, Air 20/1519, A.C.S.E.A. Ground Radar Reports, 1944-1945, November 1944 report. The report states, "Japanese air activity increased again over the previous month and reached a nuisance level."
309 TNA, Air 41/64, *The Campaigns in the Far East Volume IV: South East Asia November 1943 to August 1945*, p.217.
310 TNA, Air 20/1519, A.C.S.E.A. Ground Radar Reports, 1944-1945, January/February 1945 report.

	Scramble	**Patrol**	**Escort**
1944			
March	334	469	210
1945			
January	8	1755	312
February	51	2063	144
March	47	2330	156
April	7	1667	80
May	7	1192	35
June	4	616	15
July	11	10	19[311]

The increased patrol figures from February 1945 clearly show how the R.A.F. tried to counter the remaining Japanese air threat in lieu of a viable early warning system. However, the work of the W.O.U.s continued to provide a measure of early warning from the ground. By 1st November 1944 there were no static civilian observer posts left, the organisation becoming an entirely military entity relying on wireless communications and total mobility. As the Allied advanced progressed, the W.O.U.s were regularly re-positioned over a 400-mile land front, as well as in marine craft which doubled in an air sea rescue role.[312] The warning these units gave was important in local defence, "In practically every case, the warning was delivered in time for the Ack-Ack crews to be quite ready to receive the enemy." This is an important point because as fighter defence became harder to provide, local anti-aircraft defence assumed greater responsibilities, and this will be discussed shortly.

The Allies were now on the offensive. The J.A.A.F. was depleted by a combination of air-to-air combat, unit transfers, and the continuing interdiction raids on their airfields by long-range American fighters which had been complemented by raids by carrier launched Fleet Air Arm aircraft. By March 1945:

> So considerably had the 4th *Hikodan* been affected by this attrition, that offensive fighter sorties, which had numbered 100 in January and 54 in February, had fallen to only 22 in March, and those all by night.[313]

The inability to provide low-level early warning coverage over the front lines was not so serious owing to a lack and weight of Japanese opposition, for if they had possessed more aircraft and had chosen to pursue a low-level attack strategy the Allied advance

---

311 TNA, Air 25/910, 221 Group Operations Record Book, 1st January 1944 to 30th
     September 1944.
312 TNA, Air 23/5420, History of the I.O.C., 1943-1945.
313 Shores, *Air War for Burma*, p.347. A *Hikodan* was an Air Brigade.

may have been delayed. That is, of course, conjecture as there were many factors at play during the last eight months of the war, but the question of whether it was possible to provide low-level early warning was recognized by the Air Ministry.

During May 1945 representatives from the Central Fighter Establishment (C.F.E.) visited the Far East to examine the fighter defence organisation and their report's second conclusion reads, "There is a need in Burma for the development of low radar cover."[314] This could not have caused any surprise as this subject had already been repeatedly brought to the attention of the Air Ministry and the T.R.E. since 1942. The difficulty of providing cover over the battlefront in Burma caused Wing Commander E. Drew, Senior Radar Officer, to write a paper issued on 10th August 1945 entitled 'Low Radar Cover and Fighter Control'.[315] Drew argued that there was no requirement for low-level radar cover in places where airforces operated in direct support of the Army:

> Low Cover radar equipment is unsuitable for the control of offensive operations and the provision of defence against low flying aircraft imposes conditions on the fighter organisation of the force which is incompatible with an offensive conduct of Air Operations.[316]

Drew made his comparison with the conditions in southern England during 1943 when German low-level attacks were countered by a system which involved radar stations having the advantage of operating over sea and based on high ground and directly communicating with fighter squadrons on readiness. The success of the system was due to two factors; operating over sea gave better radar results than over land, and communications between elements of the organisation was "first class." Drew pointed out that aircraft in this situation had to be kept on a high state of readiness, which in a battlefield scenario was not possible as it was more profitable to act offensively. A parallel was drawn with the North African campaign where Air Marshal Arthur Coningham, Officer Commanding 1st Tactical Air Force, withdrew the defensive element of his fighter force from the battlefront reasoning that low-level nuisance attacks were difficult to defend against, and the damage and casualties they caused were small. Coningham therefore left the defence against low-level raiders to mobile anti-aircraft batteries.[317] There was clearly a judgement as to whether the effort expended to provide cover over a battlefront was worthwhile, particularly in such a harsh environment as Group Captain T.F. Maloney, Drew's senior officer, made clear:

---

314 TNA, Air 64/29, Visit to South East Asia by the Tactics Branch of the Central Fighter Establishment, 1st February to 7th April 1945, Report No. 27.

315 TNA, Air 23/2112, Provision of Low Radar Cover in Burma 1945. No first name is available for Drew.

316 Ibid.

317 Coningham continued this strategy when he commanded the 2nd T.A.F. during the Normandy campaign in 1944.

The warning to be obtained from low cover over land will vary with the terrain but is not likely to be early in hilly country. The decision therefore rests on the balancing of the effort expended against the results obtained.[318]

Maloney considered the C. F. E.'s representatives had undertaken their task incorrectly as their enquiries had been made with the "operational staffs of the Groups" rather than with the specialist signal staff. This was disingenuous as various signals staff had been highlighting the deficiencies with low-level capabilities since 1943 and their views were identical to those expressed by their operational colleagues.[319] Providing low-level radar in the Far Eastern conditions was too difficult for 1945 technology as offensive operations in the Middle East and Europe had demonstrated and the better option was to provide an anti-aircraft artillery facility. Until radar could be placed ahead of the front line, or even in aircraft flying above the battlefield, commanders had to accept the risk of nuisance air raids.

Conclusions

The contribution of the early warning organisation in the Far East has been discussed, usually in the context of the failure in Malaya and in the Chindit insertion in 1944. However, this chapter represents a fuller evaluation and analysis of how the system failed in 1942 and how it became an effective organisation by the beginning of 1944. It has also demonstrated the importance and contribution of the early warning organisation to the air superiority campaign despite technical and supply challenges.

When the Japanese attacked in 1941 much of the Far East was not covered by an early warning organisation based on the British model. Due to the low priority of the region, financial constraints and equipment shortages, very few radar sets were sent there and were in place prior to the initial attacks. Similarly the Observer Corps were not properly organised to one standard throughout the region, which exacerbated early warning deficiencies. However, early warning failures were not the only reason for the loss of air superiority. The British model had shown that the system had to be fully integrated, with the early warning organisation working with suitable modern fighters to achieve successful interceptions in the defenders' favour. The Buffalo did not possess sufficient performance to make use of the available warning, even when the radar and observer systems were working correctly. Thus a modern early warning system in the Far East would not have yielded overwhelmingly successful results. Furthermore, pre-war technical surveys had shown some areas, particularly mountainous regions, would present particular siting difficulties given the state of the equipment available in 1941 and this factor featured repeatedly during the next few years.

---

318 TNA, Air 23/2112, Provision of Low Radar Cover in Burma 1945, loose minute sheet. No first name is available for Maloney.
319 TNA, Air 20/1519 series for Radar Officer's Reports for this period.

The defence of the east India ports was of paramount importance from June 1942 as supplies were transported into the ports, and the extensive airfield building programme was underway. By December 1942 52 radar sets were in operation and this marked an enormous achievement by technicians in the field in the face of adverse topographical weather conditions. This marked a big improvement over the beginning of the year, and it assisted the defenders during the December raids to intercept and neutralise the Japanese night bomber threat. However, the system was not perfect. Technical problems made height estimation difficult and this was made worse by the lack of a suitable fighter to complete an integrated air defence. Like the Buffalo before, the Hurricane did not have sufficient performance to quickly achieve an advantageous interception height and radar problems magnified its shortcomings. However, when the Spitfire fighter was introduced at the end of 1943 and controllers adapted to its performance, the early warning organisation was able to play a full role in a properly integrated system which, by the beginning of 1944, was comparable to the defence of the south-east of England. Raids were routinely intercepted and dispersed, and the threat of reconnaissance Dinahs was neutralised.

However, despite these successes the Allies found it harder to provide early warning when operating in mobile situations. The importance of protecting transport aircraft and close support aircraft during the first months of 1944, as well as conserving precious fuel by not flying standing patrols, cannot be overstated. However, the action at Broadway showed that even the Spitfire required sufficient warning and the cover proved harder to provide at Imphal when the Japanese overran radar and observer positions to the east of the Plain. Whilst some of the early warning gaps could be filled by observer units there were never enough personnel to fill the recommended ten-mile gap between posts. Furthermore, when the Allies began to advance into Burma, early warning proved extremely hard to provide owing to the speed of the advance and Burma's topography.

While some of the difficulties can be attributed to personnel shortages, it is clear that scientific circumstances played a part. Radar equipment of the period worked well in the environment it was designed for, the coast of England looking over the reflective surfaces of the sea, and these criteria applied to the defence of Calcutta. From the pre-war surveys in the Far East it was clear that technical conditions caused by the weather and topography would affect existing radar equipment. Research needed to be carried out to overcome these difficulties and provide specialist radar, such as the light-weight set that could be dismantled and carried by mule. Unfortunately for the Far East commanders, their research requests came at the same time as a limited number of scientists were faced with many requests for radar developments in other theatres of war. This is not to say that the Far East was ignored. This chapter has effectively demonstrated that scientists were aware of the problems and were making active steps to remedy them as the copious correspondence, personal visits and ingenious solutions (e.g. the Goose) show. The problems of providing a light-weight transportable radar set that could provide high and low cover in mountainous, high humidity terrain however was just beyond the capabilities of an over stretched scientific organisation in the middle of a world war.

Despite these difficulties the early warning organisation played an important role in achieving Allied air superiority. In combination with night-fighters in 1943 the threat of Japanese night bombers was neutralised for nearly a year leaving Calcutta free to get on with its work in the ports and manufacturing industries. Even though there were interception problems with the Hurricane, the early warning system provided a measure of warning which negated the requirement for costly standing air patrols, and the Hurricanes were able to disrupt the incoming raids, even at cost to themselves, thereby preventing Japanese aircraft from reaching their targets. The system eventually reached fruition in India with the introduction of better aircraft like the Spitfire and this chapter has shown the importance of the relationship between early warning and the aircraft employed to achieve an integrated defence. Furthermore, even though the system experienced some difficulties during the first months of 1944, the warning it provided was responsible for the majority of aircraft being shot down or repelled during fighter interceptions. Therefore despite the difficulties, the early warning organisation played a crucial role in achieving air supremacy in 1945.

2

Aircrew, Tactics and Aircraft

The Japanese gained air superiority over the Allies in 1941 and early 1942 by exploiting British and American weaknesses in aircrew quality, air fighting tactics and obsolete aircraft. Chapter 1 showed how the early warning organisation was initially poor, and how the Allies improved the system in defence and attack. This chapter will analyse the initial weaknesses in aircrew, tactics and aircraft, and then show how their individual improvements contributed to the attainment of air superiority.

In addition to an efficient early warning system the maintenance of air superiority depends on three factors: aircrew that are well-trained and experienced for combat; relevant air tactics to engage the enemy; and aircraft of sufficient quantity that are suitable for the task they are engaged on. These factors are interdependent as, for example, it would be useless to have excellent aircraft without the pilots or tactics to exploit them, whilst trained and experienced pilots would be at a disadvantage without modern aircraft. From December 1941 until June 1942, the Japanese possessed the advantage in all these factors and were able to gain air superiority over their opponents, whose aircraft, aircrew and tactics were relatively poor in comparison.

From June 1942 the Allies endeavoured to strengthen their resources as well as build on the tactics and combat experience gained through air fighting during the first months of the war with Japan. Allied pilots improved in quality due to better initial training, the transfer of experienced aircrew to India, and in-theatre training which was relevant to combat conditions over the Burma area. This improvement began during the 1942 monsoon with the influx of experienced squadrons into the theatre and continued in 1943 and beyond with the formation of the Air Fighting Training Unit (A.F.T.U.) in Calcutta. As Allied pilots improved, the quality of their Japanese opponents did not significantly deteriorate even though their aircraft were largely unchanged, which was in contrast to their colleagues in the Pacific. Both Japanese Navy and Army pilots in the Pacific were sent into combat from 1944 with insufficient training owing to a growing lack of training resources. This chapter will analyse why Japanese pilots held superiority over the Allies in the first engagements in 1941 and early 1942, and show why the quality of Allied pilots improved whilst that of the Japanese fighter pilot remained constant.

The fundamental Allied air fighting tactic of dive and zoom had been established in early exchanges and was recognized as the best way to counter Japanese fighters' manoeuvrability until the end of air combat in 1945. Whilst thought by some to have been an innovation, the tactic had its origins in the First World War and was developed during the inter-war years in different guises. This chapter will analyse its development from its origin through its use by the *Luftwaffe* in 1940, to its importance in the Far East campaign and the ways in which the Allies adapted it to counter Japanese innovations in early 1944.

Whilst aircrew and tactics improved from June 1942, the provision of aircraft for the air superiority campaign lagged behind owing to the priority given to the war against Germany. Initially Malaya and Burma were equipped with the Buffalo which was thought unsuitable for air combat against the Germans, but owing to R.A.F. over-confidence was considered a match for Japanese fighters. The Buffalo was replaced by the Hurricane which initially fared little better, but from October 1942 it remained the principal R.A.F. air superiority fighter albeit in later variants until early 1944. The 'Germany first' policy resulted in the delay of a suitable defensive fighter, the Spitfire, until September 1943 followed by significant long-range offensive fighters, the Lightning and Mustang, from November 1943. These aircraft were ultimately crucial in both defence and attack, particularly the American long-range fighters which made a significant contribution to the counter-air campaign from January 1944. This chapter will show why the Far East was equipped with unsuitable aircraft at the beginning of the war and analyse the impact better aircraft had on the campaign once they were deployed to the theatre and to what extent this was important in gaining air superiority.

Part One – Aircrew

When the Far East war began, Japanese aircrew were highly trained and had considerable combat experience from their encounters with the Chinese and Soviets during the late 1930s. Japanese ability compared with Commonwealth pilots who had a mixture of flying experience varying from combat gained during the Battle of Britain to those who had recently graduated from flying schools. As the war progressed Allied aircrew became more proficient through a mixture of accrued experience and better primary and later operational training in which pilots were taught a variety of skills from air combat to methods of ground attack. Whilst Allied aircrew improved, Japanese aircrew quality in the Pacific deteriorated as a result of attrition and the difficulties in training suitable quantities of pilots in times of shortages. However, as the quality appeared to deteriorate in the Pacific this section will determine whether it actually did so in the Far East and analyse whether Japanese efficiency in late 1944 was affected by pilot quality.

The Japanese Army Air Force (J.A.A.F.) had its roots in 1909 with the establishment of a military balloon association, some Army aircraft participating in reconnaissance and bombing operations in 1914 in China and again in 1918-1922 during their Siberian expedition into the Amur basin. There were various reasons for the intervention into Siberia: firstly to assist local groups who were resisting the Bolshevik regime that had seized power from the Kerensky government; secondly, to assist the European Allies who feared war equipment would fall into Bolshevik hands; and thirdly, to secure potential economic investment rights.[1] The intervention brought Japan "little profit and no glory" although the J.A.A.F. gained some experience in reconnaissance and bombing operations.[2] Its first fighter units were established in 1919 after a French delegation visited Japan to advise the Army on aerial matters. They also introduced specific fighter types such as the French Nieuport.[3] In April 1921 a branch of the *Tokorozawa* Flying School was established in Akeno to train fighter pilots which became an independent body in 1924, whilst the Aviation Branch itself became independent in May 1925.[4] The Japanese Naval Air Force (J.N.A.F.) had similar roots as the Army with the military balloon association in 1909, but split away in 1912 to conduct its own investigations using foreign built floatplanes.[5] Naval aviators participated in the First World War using floatplanes in reconnaissance and bombing missions although this was the only contribution Japanese Naval aircraft made during the war. However, during 1916 a flying unit (the *Yokosuka Kokoutai*) was formed at Yokosuka training aircrew and testing new aeroplanes. This formed the basis for an expansion of training units which had increased by four in 1930 with plans to organize another 17 *Tais* (units).[6] The Navy received assistance from Great Britain and in 1921 a British mission visited Japan to teach new techniques and train pilots on new aircraft including fighters. As the 1920s and 30s progressed both Air Arms grew in size and the Japanese aircraft industry developed their own aircraft such as the *Nakajima* Type 91, or the *Nakajima* Type 3, rather than building European types under licence.

While the J.A.A.F. and J.N.A.F. were expanding and taking delivery of aircraft, aircrew training developed accordingly. The expansion of flying training units resulted in many more trained pilots, with Army schools producing 750 pilots a year at the outbreak of war in 1941, whilst Navy schools were producing about 2,000 a year.[7] Although the Army concentrated on pilot training at the expense of other aircrew categories, by 1941 Navy training units were designed to train 2,500 navigators, bomb aimers, gunners and flight engineers.[8] Aircrew were specially selected for their physical fitness and academic excellence, Bergerud describing the former as follows:

1   Storry, *A History of Modern Japan*, pp.157-159.
2   Ibid.
3   Hata, Yasuho and Shores, *Japanese Army Air Force Fighter Units and their Aces 1931-1945*, p.1.
4   Ibid, p.1.
5   Hata, Yasuho and Shores, *Japanese Naval Air Force Fighter Units and their Aces 1932-1945*, p.1.
6   Ibid, Footnote, p.1.
7   TNA, Air 48/69, U.S.S.B.S., *Japanese Air Power*, p.34.
8   Ibid.

Cadets were put through a gruelling physical program that included hanging from an iron pole with one hand, swimming, holding one's breath, walking on hands, standing on heads, diving off a platform onto the ground, and wrestling. Poor performance in this program could result in the shame of expulsion.[9]

The flying training graduation rate could be low; J.N.A.F. pilot, Saburo Sakai recalled that out of his class of 1,500 in 1937, only 75 were accepted.[10] Such selection and acceptance criteria ensured the Japanese air arms were elite bodies confident of their abilities and with considerable flying experience. Captain Minoru Genda of the J.N.A.F. stated the average flying experience of naval pilots at the beginning of the war was between 800 to 1,000 hours with a minimum of 200 to 300, whilst the 600 pilots engaged on the attack at Pearl Harbor had an average of 600 flying hours to their credit.[11] The average flying experience of both Army and Navy pilots operating in the Philippines and Malaya in 1941 was between 500 to 600 hours and the squadron and flight commanders much more, Genda stating about 2,000.[12] This was in contrast to R.A.F. fighter pilots trained in Britain:

[P]ilots still, during the winter of 1940 – 1941, went forward to squadrons after only 10 – 20 hours flying at the O.T.U., and Fighter Command found that at the end of January that some 300 out of 1461 pilots in the first line were unfit for operational duties.[13]

Moreover, 50 per cent of the J.A.A.F. pilots had combat experience against the Chinese and Soviets, whilst 10 per cent of the J.N.A.F. pilots had similar experience fighting the Chinese.[14] The Army's experience against the Soviets was particularly important:

Japanese Army Air Force officers now attribute a considerable part of the skill of Army pilots during the first days of the war to the lessons learned while fighting the Soviets.[15]

This combined experience was to prove beneficial in the early fighting against the British and Americans in 1941-1942.

---

9   Bergerud, *Fire in the Sky: The Air War in the South Pacific*, p.324.
10   Saburo Sakai quoted in Bergerud, *Fire in the Sky; The Air War in the South Pacific*, p.324.
11   Bergerud, *Fire in the Sky; The Air War in the South Pacific*, p.525. Genda planned the Pearl Harbor attack.
12   TNA, Air 48/69, U.S.S.B.S., *Japanese Air Power*, p.35 and Bergerud, *Fire in the Sky; The Air War in the South Pacific*, p.325.
13   TNA, Air 41/4, *Flying Training, Aircrew Training 1934-1942*, p.505.
14   Ibid, p.35.
15   Ibid.

On 7th December 1941 the Japanese possessed two elite, highly trained and well armed air forces and their performance over the next few months surprised the British and Americans. Pre-war propaganda gave Allied pilots an erroneous view of the Japanese:

> On the quality of Japanese pilots, we had been told and we had read – in rather silly articles – that they couldn't fly and they couldn't see! But we quickly found out that we were up against some of the most experienced pilots in the world.[16]

and:

> [V]ery misleading rumours were current about Japanese pilots and their capabilities ... we were told that a Japanese pilot could not fly over 20,000 feet![17]

Intelligence relating to Japanese pilots' abilities had not been passed to R.A.F. pilots as Flight Lieutenant Tim Vigors later recalled:

> I am of the opinion that many aircraft and lives were lost during the first weeks of the war owing to the complete absence of any sound intelligence reports on the performance of Japanese fighters and the ability of their pilots.[18]

Senior British officers expressed disbelief at the Japanese abilities as A.V.M. Donald Stevenson, A.O.C. 221 Group, wrote, "The performance of the Japanese aircraft of all types and the accuracy of their high level bombing had come as an unpleasant surprise."[19] A.V.M. Paul Maltby, Deputy A.O.C., R.A.F. Far East, doubted the Japanese were responsible:

> My general impression at the time was that either the Japanese pilots had reached a suspiciously high standard of training, or that German pilots were leading these flights.[20]

The perception that Germans were leading the attacks was assisted by some Japanese aircraft being misidentified for German types as there were various sightings

16   Pilot Officer Jack Storey quoted in Franks, *Hurricanes over the Arakan*, p.19.
17   Squadron Leader Frank Howell quoted in Cull, *Buffaloes over Singapore*, p.94.
18   TNA, Air 41/63, *The Campaigns in the Far East, Volume II, Malaya, Netherlands East Indies and Burma 1941-1942*, p.62. Vigors had previously fought in the Battle of Britain.
19   TNA, Air 2/7787, *Operations: Far East; Air Operations in Burma, January to May 1942*; Despatch by A.V.M. Stevenson, 1942-1948, p.47.
20   TNA, Air 23/2123, Operations of the R.A.F. during the campaigns in Malaya and Netherlands East Indies: report by Air Vice-Marshal P.C. Maltby, 1st January 1941 to 31st December 1942, p.6.

of Ju87s, Bf109s, Bf110s and *Heinkel* bombers, whilst there were reports that some captured airmen were wearing German uniforms. Brian Cull quotes correspondent Cecil Brown writing later that Lieutenant Peter Court of a Dogra regiment said:

> [O]ne of the planes shot down had a German pilot, wearing a Luftwaffe uniform ... everyone I talk to say there are German pilots, but I can't find anyone who's actually seen and talked with one.[21]

Toland wrote that Stalin believed some Japanese pilots had been trained in Germany whilst others engaged in the attacks were German:

> Curiously, he was convinced that Japanese air successes would not have been possible without the Germans, who – according to one secret report – had contributed fifteen hundred aircraft and hundreds of pilots.[22]

There is no evidence to suggest either German aircraft or aircrews were involved in these early and successful attacks, and it is now clear that Japanese aircrew were experts in their own right. Their Commonwealth opponents in 1941 did not match this expertise.

In contrast to the Japanese at the start of December 1941 the British and Commonwealth pilots had a patchy record of experience. Whilst squadron and flight commanders were ex-Spitfire and Hurricane pilots with experience fighting the Germans in Europe and the Middle East, many of their pilots had no combat experience and limited flying time. When the Buffalo arrived in the Far East in February 1941 its squadrons were formed from scratch with some experienced pilots, some inexperienced, and others who had transferred from other squadrons.[23] The first two Buffalo squadrons, 67 and 243, drew selected pilots from Blenheim units, whilst some pilots transferred from flying the Vickers Vildebeest biplane.[24] 488 Squadron R.N.Z.A.F. was composed of New Zealand pilots of "fundamentally excellent material, but with a low standard of flying experience" some of whom had arrived from flying training school having trained on biplanes and with no operational training.[25] Furthermore, not all the pilots were suited for fighter operations. A.V.M. Maltby wrote of 21 Squadron R.A.A.F. which had originally flown C.A.C. Wirraways:

---

21   Cull, *Buffaloes over Singapore*, p.59. Cull does not state which Dogra regiment Court was serving with.
22   Toland, *Rising Sun,* p.248.
23   TNA, Air 2/7787, Operations: Far East; Air Operations in Burma, January to May 1942; Despatch by A.V.M. Stevenson, 1942-1948, p.40.
24   TNA, Air 41/35, *The Campaigns in the Far East Volume I*, p.13 and Cull, *Buffaloes over Singapore* , p.16.
25   Cull, *Buffaloes over Singapore*, p.44.

It will be observed, therefore, that the pilots of this squadron had not been selected originally for fighter aircraft and some were not in fact entirely suitable for this role.[26]

Sergeant Rex Weber wrote in his diary, "So eventually I finished by volunteering for fighters, but I might say that I have little faith in myself as a fighter pilot."[27] Squadron Leader William Harper commanding 453 Squadron R.A.A.F. later recalled:

> The aircrew personnel of no. 453 Squadron, with the exception of the Flight Commanders, were pilots straight from F.T.S., and some of them told me when I questioned them, that they had no desire to be fighter pilots and had been given no choice in this matter.[28]

The newly posted squadron pilots entered an intensive and difficult period of training. There was a lack of experienced flying instructors to train the new pilots to an Operational Training Unit (O.T.U.) standard and as a result they were often trained by their squadron and flight commanders. The Buffalo squadrons suffered, in Maltby's view, from a poor standard of gunnery, and he concluded this was due to too few and slow target drogue towing aircraft, lack of cine-gun equipment and the shortcomings of the aircraft's guns. There was:

> Continual trouble with the .5 gun and synchronising gear. This was largely overcome by local modification by October 1941. Nevertheless many pilots were still not altogether confident about their armament.[29]

The combination of inexperienced pilots and new aircraft resulted in inevitable flying accidents and whilst some of the accidents were the result of pilot error, others were caused by engine failure or other mechanical defects.[30]

On 8th December 1941 these combat inexperienced pilots met the Japanese air forces with its combat ready aircrews. Despite the disparity, the Commonwealth

---

26 TNA, Air 23/2123, Operations of the R.A.F. during the campaigns in Malaya and Netherlands East Indies: report by Air Vice-Marshal P.C. Maltby, 1st January 1941 to 31st December 1942, paragraph 78. The Wirraway was an armed version of the North American Harvard trainer built under licence by the Commonwealth Aircraft Corporation (C.A.C.).

27 Cull, *Buffaloes over Singapore*, p.19.

28 Ibid, P.23.

29 TNA, Air 23/2123, Operations of the R.A.F. during the campaigns in Malaya and Netherlands East Indies: report by Air Vice-Marshal P.C. Maltby, 1st January 1941 to 31st December 1942, paragraph 81.

30 Cull, *Buffaloes over Singapore*, pp.23-26. Cull quotes the total Far East Command accident figures between January and September 1941 as 67 accidents, 22 aircraft write-offs, 31 serious damage and 48 fatalities.

pilots' inexperience cannot be used as the only reason why the Japanese were ultimately successful in Malaya and Singapore. Chapter 1 demonstrated the lack of an effective early warning system, and the quality and quantity of Japanese fighter aircraft must also be taken into consideration. It is clear that many of the pilots had flying ability, but there was no substitute for combat experience against a determined foe especially when the other factors are considered. Furthermore, during the period between the opening of hostilities and the Hurricane's arrival in January 1942 there was insufficient time to train replacement pilots:

> Our reinforcements consist of nine Australian Sergeant Pilots; unfortunately they were not operational and we were apparently expected to train them all in one Buff on a bomb-torn aerodrome. So now do you wonder why 453 is getting properly brassed off?[31]

Things did not improve when Hurricanes arrived. On 15th January 1942 51 Hurricanes were delivered in crates to the Far East and after assembly and test flights were put into action against the Japanese. Within fourteen days these aircraft had suffered severe losses:

> 17 had been written off
> 7 damaged but repairable
> 2 damaged and repairable by the squadrons
> 21 available for operations immediately
> 4 serviceable within 24 hours[32]

Given that these aircraft, according to Air Chief Marshal Sir Charles Portal (Chief of the Air Staff), should have "swept the Japanese from the sky" there was clearly a problem and he contacted Maltby on 8th February:

> At a time when so much depends on you and those under you, who are fighting a historic battle against great odds and under tremendous difficulties, I am most reluctant to add to your labours. I should nevertheless be glad to receive privately from you some indication of the causes of the very moderate success of the Hurricane against the Japanese on occasion when interceptions are made.[33]

Portal displayed some ignorance of Japanese capabilities:

31   453 Squadron diarist quoted in Cull, *Buffaloes over Singapore*, p.176.
32   Christ Church College, Oxford University, Portal Papers, File One, Prime Minister's Minutes, January to March 1942.
33   TNA, Air 8/612, Operation of Hurricanes in the Far East, Portal to Maltby, 8th February 1942.

Intelligence here do not credit Japs with high performance and we hoped on arrival of more experienced fighter pilots that you would make tea with them if only you could make interceptions. We all feel that at least occasional infliction of really heavy casualties on Jap Air Force such as Hurricanes achieve in Burma is to be expected and would have enormous effect.[34]

Maltby attributed some of the problems to poor morale, the lack of adequate early warning, the weight of Japanese bombing and mounting battle casualties.[35] However, he made clear that pilot quality played a significant part:

First squadrons not homogenous units but collection of individuals, great majority from O.T.U.'s who could not shoot and not well-trained in fighting tactics ... Later squadrons had majority experienced pilots withdrawn before sailing and replaced by O.T.U. trainees.[36]

Maltby's message prompted Portal to instigate an enquiry into the allegation that better pilots had been removed, telling Prime Minister Winston Churchill:

It does not surprise me to learn that those of them who were but newly trained when they left England should have been found weak in air gunnery when first sent against the enemy on their arrival.[37]

This was corroborated by Pilot Officer Jerry Parker who later recalled that after initial training he had arrived at the O.T.U. in Usworth in February 1941 and after flying solo on the Hurricane had only one lesson in wartime flying on the aircraft owing to bad weather.[38] After posting to 232 Squadron he flew convoy protection roles but found there were restrictions on non-operational flying:

Such restrictions were probably the cause of our not practising aerial gunnery; we were allowed one short burst apiece using one of our eight guns at a ground target and another at a towed drogue target.[39]

Portal's enquiry into the allegation that better pilots had been removed revealed a number of unfortunate events.[40] Whilst examination of the squadrons' rosters revealed

---

34   Ibid.
35   Ibid, Maltby to Portal, 17th February 1942.
36   Ibid.
37   Ibid, Portal to Churchill, 17th February 1942.
38   Cull Brian, *Hurricanes over Singapore*, p.8.
39   Ibid, p.8.
40   TNA, Air 8/612, Operation of Hurricanes in the Far East, P.S. (unidentified) to Portal, 24th February 1942.

that no pilots had been exchanged before sailing, some less experienced pilots had gone by sea instead of making a long overland flight. Of the original 24 pilots sent to Singapore, consisting of four flight commanders and 20 pilots from 17, 135, 136 and 232 Squadrons the enquiry stated, "The pilots sent by ship would be immobilised for a long period at sea and were probably not the pick of the bunch." Similarly 14 more pilots from 242, 258 and 605 received the comment, "Here again, the least well-trained pilots were probably sent on the long sea route."[41] The report makes an important point as the emergency in Singapore occurred after the squadrons had set sail for its Middle East destinations where it was likely the pilots would have had more time to acclimatise to combat condition:

> All these 38 pilots were at sea before the need to reinforce Singapore arose and there was nothing very much we could do about improving their quality.[42]

Furthermore, Maltby later observed that the situation in Malaya was so desperate that there was no time to form the Hurricanes into defined units, or to acclimatise to the conditions and Portal confirmed to Churchill:

> In the Far East emergency there was nothing to be done except to try to get what pilots and aircraft we could to Singapore in time. This alone was the reason for the unfortunate mixture fragments from various sources.[43]

Portal's report to Churchill was an accurate summary of the inquiry's findings but failed to mention the fact that 232 and 258 Squadrons:

> [H]ad done a journey half way across the world and would have arrived in Singapore at a time when conditions were going bad. Even if they had contained crack pilots they would not therefore have had much chance to show what they could do.[44]

This reinforces the point that the inexperience of Commonwealth pilots was only one factor in explaining Japanese superiority, others being the lack of early warning and inadequate aircraft.

---

41   Ibid, p.1.
42   Ibid, p.1.
43   TNA, Air 23/2123, Operations of the R.A.F. during the campaigns in Malaya and Netherlands East Indies: report by Air Vice-Marshal P.C. Maltby, 1st January 1941 to 31st December 1942 and TNA, Air 8/612, Operation of Hurricanes in the Far East, Portal to Churchill, 24th February 1942.
44   TNA, Air 8/612, Operation of Hurricanes in the Far East, P.S. to Portal, 24th February 1942.

While pilots gained experience in combat against the Japanese, many of them, including more experienced pilots, were lost in action, therefore leaving a partial vacuum. The situation did not alter significantly until the defence of Rangoon. By that time some experienced pilots had reached Burma with 17 and 135 Squadrons and the Allied effort included the American pilots of the A.V.G. with their P-40s. The Americans were basically mercenaries employed by the Chinese government and some of the pilots had been recruited from non-fighter units. Colonel Claire Chennault, air advisor to the Chinese government, had recognized the importance of intensive training and put the recruits through training consisting of five to eight hours per day on aerial combat theories, section attacks and knowledge of their aircraft.[45] In air fighting between 23rd and 29th January the R.A.F. and A.V.G. claimed 50 Japanese bombers and fighters destroyed, and between 24th and 25th February 37 Japanese aircraft destroyed.[46] Conditions over Burma had changed for the fighter pilots. Whereas neither the Hurricane nor P-40 were ideal, they were better than the Buffalo and took advantage of the improved early warning system to gain height. However, although pilot and aircraft quality improved during this period, the gradual reduction in aircraft numbers and removal of sufficient early warning coverage eventually resulted in the Allied air cover diminishing before the fall of Burma.

R.A.F. pilot and aircrew training improved as the war progressed. At the beginning the expansion programme concentrated on increasing numbers; in 1934 the R.A.F. trained 300 new pilots, whereas in 1941 the number had increased to 22,000 thanks to an expansion of training schemes at home and also in the Commonwealth and America.[47] The scramble to train aircrew experienced various problems such as lack of facilities, insufficient instructors and a lack of suitable aircraft, and in the race to train more pilots quality was initially sacrificed for quantity:

A pilot's pre-squadron flying experience rose from 150 hours in 1934 to 350-450 in 1942. The quantitative expansion came first, and lack of reserves made it necessary to sacrifice quality to quantity in 1940 and 1941, but quantitative expansion and a solution to the problems of operational training made possible a great qualitative expansion at the beginning of 1942.[48]

Whilst the quantitative expansion began at the start of 1942 the Far East experienced some difficulties establishing a fighter O.T.U. with a number of aircraft including Hurricanes and Curtiss Mohawks, which were short of spare parts.[49] Designated 151

---

45   Heiferman, *Flying Tigers: Chennault in China*, p.27. Further details of the A.V.G. training can be found in Chennault, *Way of a Fighter*, and Ford, *Flying Tigers: Chennault and the American Volunteer Group*.
46   Probert, *The Forgotten Air Force*, p.87.
47   TNA, Air 41/4, *Flying Training, Aircrew Training 1934-1942*, p.28.
48   Ibid, p.46.
49   TNA, Air 41/71, *Flying Training, Volume Two, Part Three: Operational Training*, p.946.

O.T.U. on 28th July 1942, its 18 allotted aircraft resulted in its only being able to train 20 pilots at a time, but with nearly 300 more requiring tuition. Between July and March 1943 the unit concentrated on training pilots from the Indian Air Force, but in June 1943 following a review of fighter pilot requirements it was planned to expand the O.T.U. to train 100 pilots per month, with shorter course times, but the planning depended on deliveries of aircraft from Britain. The plan was not expected to reach fruition until early 1944, but in the event all O.T.U.s were transferred to the Middle East. Despite these problems all pilots and crews were arriving fully trained and after jungle training were ready to join their squadrons.[50]

The American experience was similar to that of the British. At the outbreak of war, training organizations were placed on a war basis and initially shortages of aircraft and instructors had to be overcome which eventually succeeded owing to its resources and great pool of aircrew recruits. For example, at the end of December 1942 93,000 men were awaiting aircrew classification prior to training and in April 1943 over 60,000 were in aircrew colleges at over 150 institutions.[51] In December 1943 the Americans had 74,000 pilots in various stages of training on 55 week courses, 45 of which were spent flying. This eventually resulted in a vast pool of well-trained pilots reaching operational units.[52]

In addition to better pilots and training, many of the Allied reinforcements brought combat experience to the theatre. In late 1942, the newly arrived 79 and 607 Hurricane Squadrons brought extensive combat experience from Europe, and Beaufighter crews which arrived in January 1943 to counter the Japanese night bomber operations had considerable experience from combat operations in the Middle East. Furthermore, in early 1944, 81 and 152 Squadrons, equipped with Spitfires were posted to India from the Middle East and Italy, bringing combat experience gained against German units. Similarly the Americans were able to bring in experienced pilots. For example the fighter pilots of the 1st Air Commando Group (A.C.G.), commanded by Lieutenant Colonel Philip Cochran and Colonel John Allison, were hand-picked:

> The lure of combat duty and the secret nature of Project 9 made recruiting simple. Lieutenant Colonel Cochran said, "We were allowed to bring in from anywhere – if we knew a man's name, we'd send for him. We knew them through our time in the Air Force."[53]

---

50   Ibid, p.950.
51   Craven and Cate, *The Army Air Forces in World War II, Volume VI*, pp.562-563.
52   Ibid, pp.568-578. Between 1st July 1939 and 31st August 1945 America trained 193,440 pilots.
53   Wagner. *Any Place, Any Time, Any Where*, p.25. Project 9 was the original name given to the A.C.G. at its inception.

Therefore, there was an influx of experienced pilots and aircrew reaching the Far East, but together with their comrades already in the theatre the majority undertook important additional operational training.[54]

Operational training for aircrews in the Far East was carried out at the Air Fighting Training Unit (A.F.T.U.) at Armada Road, Calcutta. The unit was formed in April 1943 under the command of Wing Commander Frank Carey, an ex-Battle of Britain pilot who had recent experience fighting the Japanese over Burma in 1942. The unit was quickly in operation and on 10th July:

> Air Fighting Training Unit Amarda Road now training 60 pupils comprising of 16 pilots on pilot gunnery instructors course plus 2 possible attachments from USAAC – 3 weeks, 30 bomber aircrew on refresher course – 3 weeks, 6 navigators on bombing leaders course – 6 weeks and 6 air gunners on gunnery leaders course – 6 weeks.[55]

The unit's importance was recognized:

> Our main operational success coming winter will depend upon tactics and firing of our very rapidly increasing SE fighter force. 4 squadrons will come from Middle East and need training on tactics against Japanese. 3 squadrons are converting to Spitfires. Air fighting, and tactical instruction our success depends very largely on the AFTU which must therefore operate and train and be administered by the best men we can put into it.[56]

Fighter pilots were instructed in facets of air fighting such as gunnery and deflection shooting, and also in the essential dive and zoom tactic. Shortly after receiving its Spitfires in September 1943, 615 Squadron attended the A.F.T.U. between 16th and 31st October and its Operations Record Book shows the course contained deflection shooting, range estimations and drogue and cine-gun attacks.[57] Furthermore, American pilots attended the unit to learn the essentials of air fighting in the Far East; 459th Fighter Squadron (F.S.) Lightning pilots attended Amarda Road in February 1944 and impressed the instructors with the rapid development of their new skills.[58] The importance of this specialized and on-going training cannot be over-emphasised. A.C.M. Pierse wrote, "the A.F.T.U. is doing very good work and has led to considerable improvement in the standard of shooting and fighting efficiency of

---

54   The Air Commando Group did not attend the A.F.T.U.
55   TNA, Air 2/8229, Establishment of A.F.T.U. and A.F.D.U. AHQ India to Air Ministry Whitehall, 10th July 1943.
56   Ibid, 19th August 1943.
57   TNA, Air 27/2123, 615 Squadron Operations Record Book, 1st November 1943.
58   Stanaway, *P-38 Lightning Aces of the Pacific and CBI*, p.79.

fighter squadrons."[59] Similarly American General Howard Davidson wrote to Carey on 12th March 1944 following the 459th's first attack, "We are indebted to you for the fine training you have given them. Accept our sincere thanks."[60] A.V.M. Thomas Williams, A.O.C. Air Headquarters Bengal, expanded on the American's message, "Positive rules in combat are what we are striving for and I am satisfied your course is accomplishing this."[61] This was clearly an important training attribute which provided theatre pilots with expert, and relevant, knowledge of their enemy.

As the Allies developed their training organization the Japanese similarly increased their programme firstly by forming 18 new training units with the intention of providing a year's flying training for officers and enlisted men. As the pace of war increased the Japanese formed another two new training groups, one late in 1942 and another in early 1943, this expansion providing the J.A.A.F. with 2,700 pilots in both 1942 and 1943, whereas the J.N.A.F. produced 2,300 in 1942 and 2,700 in 1943.[62] Although there was a steady stream of new pilots, the United States Strategic Bombing Survey (U.S.S.B.S.) pointed out that during those two years both Japanese Army and Navy pilots suffered a decline in their flying hours prior to entering combat due to the necessity of quickly replacing pilots lost in the early encounters. Replacing mounting losses after the early Pacific battles became a priority and in 1943 the Japanese decided to re-organize and expand pilot training by increasing the number of intermediate units from 18 to 48, and by forming new units specifically to provide primary training.[63] Similar re-organization occurred in 1943 when operational training units were formed to give new pilots specific training for their role, as the equivalent R.A.F. units did. Until that time Japanese operational squadrons provided their pilots with this necessary training, but this had the potential of interfering with combat operations.

The Japanese expanded training programme was designed to produce 30,000 pilots per year, but this rate was not attained owing to shortages of fuel, aircraft and attacks on Japanese training bases by Allied aircraft. Between 1st January 1944 and 1st January 1945 the J.N.A.F. and J.A.A.F. each trained 16,000 aircrew. As this figure was not broken down into classifications it is therefore safe to assume that the figure of 30,000 pilots was not achieved.[64] Pilots suffered from a reduction in accrued flying hours before entering combat which, depending on sources, ranged from between 100 to 400 hours. In an intelligence report written in April 1945 a figure of 200 hours was quoted; in another 1945 intelligence report 300 to 400 hours was quoted; and in the U.S.S.B.S. report of 1946 the pilots are supposed to have reached their combat status

59 TNA, Air 23/4308, Despatch of Air Operations Period 1st January to 30th June 1943, p.5.
60 Franks, *Frank 'Chota' Carey*, p.139. Davidson was the Air Commander of the Tenth Air Force.
61 Ibid, p.138.
62 TNA, Air 48/69, U.S.S.B.S., *Japanese Air Power*, p.35.
63 Ibid.
64 Ibid, p.36.

with only 100 hours.[65] The lack of relevant flying experience could make the difference between life and death in combat. For example at the Battle of the Philippine Sea in June 1944 the main body of the 1st Air Flotilla were new graduates from flying schools with 100-150 hours in their logbooks to replace 45% losses suffered over Bougainville and Rabaul the previous November.[66] In the subsequent air battles American pilots claimed over 500 Japanese aircraft destroyed, many of these as a result of Japanese pilots' inexperience and the action became known as the 'Great Marianas Turkey Shoot.' Consistent pilot losses were experienced throughout the Pacific Theatre as Japanese aircrews and pilots fell behind that of their American opponents, but did this deterioration play a part in damaging Japanese operations in Burma?

Firstly the J.N.A.F. can be discounted from the Far Eastern analysis as they were withdrawn to other areas after the 1942 monsoon and, apart from occasional operations, such as the joint raid on Calcutta on 5th December 1943, were not encountered again. The departure left the J.A.A.F. as the Allies' opponent but a reduction in its pilots' quality is questionable. The authors of the Air Historical Branch (A.H.B.) narrative wrote:

> There is no doubt, however, that his air forces in Burma felt the impact of poor long-term planning in his training organization for his replacement pilots and aircrews were generally inferior in quality than those who took part in their initial offensives.[67]

However, the narrative does not identify when the deterioration occurred, and it does not give any specific evidence of Japanese aircrew inferiority. Analysis of commanding officers' despatches from such as A.C.M. Sir Richard Pierse, A.C.M. Sir Keith Park, A.V.M. Thomas Williams and Major-General George Stratemeyer, particularly those from late 1943 until May 1945, reveals nothing to indicate a deterioration of Japanese aircrew quality which would have been apparent from their pilots' combat reports.[68] Similarly an analysis of all Spitfire squadrons' Operations Record Books from October 1944 to May 1945 reveals no comments about their adversaries' abilities at a time when other theatres, for example the Pacific, were reporting a decline. In the U.S.S.B.S. report on air operations in Burma the authors wrote of Japanese aircrew between 1st June 1944 and 1st June 1945, "Japanese pilots and

---

65 Anon, *The Organisation of the Japanese Army and Navy Air Forces in 1945*; Air 40/2689 Monthly Reports on Japanese Air Force, MN7 Developments in the J.A.A.F. Training Organisation 1st April 1945; TNA, Air 48/69 U.S.S.B.S., *Japanese Air Power*, p.35.

66 Hata, Yasuho and Shores, *Japanese Naval Air Force Fighter Units and their Aces 1932-1945*, p.90. A Japanese Air Flotilla (*Koku-sentai*) was a land based Air Attack Force, a subsidiary of a Base Air Force.

67 TNA, Air 41/64 *The Campaigns in the Far East; Volume IV South East Asia November 1943 to August 1945*, p.44.

68 Stratemeyer was the Air Commander, Eastern Air Command.

air crews, with the possible exception of those based in the extreme rear areas, were tough, experienced, and resourceful fighters."[69] In December 1943 S.E.A.C. asked the Air Ministry and the Americans in the South-West Pacific if there was a deterioration in Japanese aircrew standard as a result of training deficiencies or the lack of first class pilots. The Americans answered that there was a general deterioration in standards owing to the heavy combat losses endured by Japanese forces, but the Air Ministry replied, "Reports reaching us suggest that pilots are below standard prevailing at breakout of war but that there is not yet any serious deterioration of quality."[70] Furthermore, during the first crucial six months of air fighting in Burma in 1944 the Allies apparently encountered a skilful and respected enemy and if there was a deterioration in quality it was not mentioned by pilots quoted in books such as Norman Franks' *The Air Battle of Imphal*.[71] The Allied Weekly Intelligence Summary makes no mention of aircrew quality until 9th April 1944 when the report mentions the withdrawal of Japanese bomber units following recent losses for replacement and training.[72] Similarly on 4th June 1944 medium bombers were withdrawn after experiencing serious losses, but the analysts believed that the forthcoming monsoon would give the units necessary time for training as it was "believed many crews are very inexperienced."[73] Crucially, however, the intelligence summaries give important clues about the fighter pilot quality in Burma. On 8th October it was reported that the 50th and 64th *Sentais* were "old and experienced units which have operated in this theatre for well over two years, while 204th made its first appearance in December 1943 in the combined raid on Calcutta."[74] On 29th October the summary reported on the 19th October Fleet Air Arm (F.A.A.) attack on Sumatra when 12 Oscars were encountered. The intelligence officers thought a small fighter unit had been based in the area for some weeks. The F.A.A. pilots made reference to:

> The seemingly ill-trained pilots and poor showing of the intercepting aircraft, it does seem more likely that they were drawn from this unit *rather than from the well-trained and experienced units in Burma*.[75]

There were various factors to explain why Japanese pilot quality did not deteriorate in the Far East. Firstly the tempo of their operations was much slower, for example, than those in the South-West Pacific; Japanese air activity tended to be at a high intensity for a few days followed by up to a fortnight when no operations were carried

69   R.A.F. Museum, Hendon, U.S.S.B.S. Report, *Air Operations in China, Burma, India*, p.13.
70   TNA, Air 23/7674, Air Command South Sea Asia. Japanese Air Forces; organisation, report 14th December 1943.
71   Franks, *The Air Battle of Imphal*.
72   TNA, Air 24/1297, S.E.A.C. Appendices, Intelligence Branch April 1944 No.21.
73   TNA, Air 24/1299, S.E.A.C. Appendices, Intelligence Branch June 1944 No.29.
74   TNA, Air 24/1305, S.E.A.C. Appendices, Intelligence Branch October 1944 No.47.
75   Ibid, No.50, my italics.

out. This inactivity was due to a policy of aircraft conservation and to the weather conditions over Burma which precluded aerial operations by both sides, and gave the aircrews time for rest, recuperation and local training when practicable. Furthermore, there was no air activity during the two monsoon periods of 1942 and 1943 which gave the aircrews additional time away from operations. Whilst some Japanese fighter pilots were sent away to other theatres on detachment during the monsoons, there is no evidence to suggest entire squadrons were redeployed.

Crucially there was the additional factor of aircrew attrition which appears to have been lower than in the Pacific Theatre. Dr Yasuo Izawa and Hiroshi Ichimura researched Japanese records for this period and Christopher Shores used their findings in *Air War for Burma*. Using the figures as a minimum statistic for Japanese fatalities in air-to-air defensive operations gives this table:

Against the RAF

	1943	1944	1945
Fighter Pilots	8	17	4
Bomber Crews	24	4	2
Reconnaissance Crews	4	9	3

Against the USAAF

Fighter Pilots	22	4	3
Bomber Crews	8	8	0
Reconnaissance Crews	0	1	0[76]

These figures are for the entire year and it can be assumed that such losses could be easily replaced. The statistics above are from air-to-air interceptions, but aircrew attrition during counter-air operations did not yield any more significant results. For example during the intensive counter-air campaign between 1st January and 31st July 1944 Japanese aircrew fatalities during Allied action over their lines were 23 pilots and one bomber crew killed which demonstrates the difficulties in attacking the enemy on his own territory.[77] Whilst aircraft could be destroyed when parked on the airfields, unless the aircrews were in the machine or in close proximity they would escape injury or death; many of the fatalities reported were as occupied aircraft were taking off, landing or taxiing. Allowing for these numbers only representing fatalities and not those aircrews who were injured, the losses do not appear to have impacted adversely upon Japanese aircrew quality which was still high during the first half of 1944.

In October 1944 the J.A.A.F. started to transfer units away from Burma to other theatres, including the defence of Japan itself. As these units withdrew there is no evidence that aircrew quality diminished as aircraft quantity gradually reduced to

---

76   Shores, *Air War for Burma*, pp.48-378.
77   Ibid, pp.146-252.

negligible numbers by April 1945. Therefore it would appear from the available evidence that the Allies fought a resourceful enemy whose skill was undiminished during the Far East campaign.

Part Two – Air-to-Air Tactics

From October 1942 the quantity and, eventually, the quality of Allied aircraft improved and this will be described in the next section. Throughout the war Japanese fighter aircraft remained dangerous adversaries owing to their light design and high manoeuvrability at low speeds. The Oscar remained the principal Japanese fighter in the Burma Theatre until 1945 but even then it was regarded with respect by Allied pilots. To counter their manoeuvrability Allied pilots adopted the dive and zoom tactic where the attacker gained the advantage of height before diving at high speed through the enemy formation, and then 'zooming' up before repeating the action. This was a fundamental air fighting tactic and was still taught to British and American pilots in 1945. However, the tactic as employed specifically in the Far East is over-looked. Mike Spick's *Fighter Pilot Tactics*, for example, which mentions dive and zoom in other conflicts fails to mention the Far East separately.[78] This section will analyse the background to the dive and zoom tactic from the First World War and discuss its significance for Allied combat operations in the Far East.

During the First World War Anthony Fokker had devised interrupter gears which allowed a machine gun to fire through the propeller arc without damaging it and this equipment was fitted to the Fokker E-1, a monoplane of "clean design and good performance" which had an "ability to make long, almost vertical dives."[79] This ability was exploited into a tactic which Jones described as drawing "inspiration from the hawk", but can be recognized as the dive and zoom attack.[80] Jones described how the German pilot cruised at height above the German lines awaiting his victim, before swooping down from behind, firing a long burst of fire before continuing to dive past out of range, "If the British aeroplane was not shot down ... the German pilot would climb again and continue his swift diving attack."[81] With the German introduction of the machine gun equipped fighter it was a logical for tactics to be devised for its use and it was natural for its pilots to develop methods to make the best use of the fighter's capabilities. After testing the Fokker E-1 Oswald Boelcke became aware of its advantages devising four basic principles of air fighting, "height advantage; attacking out of the sun; the use of cloud for concealment; and close range."[82] These formed the basis for all future air fighting.

78   Spick, *Fighter Pilot Tactics: The Techniques of Daylight Air Combat*.
79   Jones, *Official History of the War in the Air, Volume Two*, p.149.
80   Ibid, p.150.
81   Ibid, p.150.
82   Barker, *The Royal Flying Corps in World War 1*, p.106.

During the inter-war period the lessons of the First World War were developed. In 1925 a former Royal Flying Corps (R.F.C.) pilot, Major Oliver Stewart, wrote *The Strategy and Tactics of Air Fighting*, which was based on the experiences of First World War pilots. It contained the essentials:

> [T]he value of surprise, gained by height and a position up-sun; how to quarter the sky; the use of the bounce (called the dive and zoom attack); the need to turn into the enemy if attacked.[83]

As Boelcke and his contemporaries had discovered, the main essentials of air fighting, height and surprise, would require the aircraft to be at height above the enemy which must necessarily impact on aircraft design and operation. For example in 1934 the *Design and Tactics of Air Defence of Great Britain Fighters* prophetically stated:

> The rate of climb demanded for fighters also has to be increased with every improvement in the speed of enemy bombers … it may be that the time is approaching when we must modify the method of handling our fighters and get them off the ground earlier than at present. It may even be necessary in very special circumstances to establish standing patrols; this will involve the use of aeroplanes with much greater endurance.[84]

This was written before the introduction of an integrated early warning system but gives a strong indication of the importance of height advantage, and in the absence of an early warning system, a fast climbing aircraft. It was reinforced in the R.A.F.'s 1937 *Manual of Air Tactics* as was the importance of surprise:

> Surprise is the most potent of the incalculable factors in air fighting. The chance of achieving surprise always exists. Superiority in armament or in performance will not save a pilot from almost certain destruction if he allows himself to be surprised.[85]

The 1937 Manual was concerned with attacking bombers in tight sections of three fighters in the 'number one' and 'number two' attacks, but whilst the dive and zoom attack is not specifically mentioned, reference is made to 'pecking attacks'. In this the attacking fighters, taking advantage of the enemy's blind spots with diving and converging attacks, would "withdraw to a position from which he can repeat the

---

83   Bungay, *The Most Dangerous Enemy*, p.261.
84   TNA, Air 16/305, *Design and Tactics of Air Defence of Great Britain Fighters*, 11th May 1934, p.3.
85   TNA, Air 10/1430, *R.A.F. The Manual of Air Tactics* Chapter VIII, 1937, paragraph 24.

manoeuvre."[86] Once again this manoeuvre could be quickly adapted into a dive and zoom to take advantage of the fighter's height and performance.

With the advent of the Second World War the two main European protagonists started with different tactical formations. The RAF flew in rigid sections of three aircraft which necessitated the two wingmen concentrating on flying in formation with the leader rather than keeping a watch for enemy aircraft. However, as a result of their experiences in the Spanish Civil War, the *Luftwaffe* adopted a more flexible formation of four aircraft (*Schwarm*) which were split into two pairs of aircraft called a '*Rotte*'. The *Rotte* was the basic fighting unit and enabled the leader to concentrate on fighting whilst his wingman kept a vigil 200 yards above, behind and slightly to one side in an extension of Boelcke's tactics.[87] When the R.A.F. and *Luftwaffe* met over France and Britain in 1940, the superiority of German tactics soon became apparent and their aircraft formations were adopted by the British at first on an ad-hoc and then official basis. While the British and German formations may have differed, the fundamental principles of height advantage and surprise were equally important to both.

Following extensive combat during the Battle of Britain the South African ace, Squadron Leader Adolphus 'Sailor' Malan, devised ten rules for air fighting, which were published by the R.A.F. to assist other pilots and rule number four was "Height gives you the initiative."[88] Paramount to gaining the height initiative was the early warning and control system employed by the RAF in 1940 which prevented costly standing patrols, whilst ensuring the defending fighters had sufficient time to be manoeuvred into advantageous attacking positions. While these were both fundamental factors, tactics had to be adapted to take advantage of the fighter's capabilities. For example, during the Battle of Britain the *Luftwaffe* found the Bf109 could be out-turned by the Spitfire and Hurricane in combat and "countered [this] by using dive and zoom tactics."[89] Sixteen months later, the R.A.F. used these same tactics against the Japanese.

Whilst these lessons had been learned and developed into, for example, wing formations by the end of 1940 in Europe and the Middle East, at the end of 1941 British and American pilots in the Far East had to adapt their tactics to suit a different and dangerous enemy. However, the potential of Japanese fighter aircraft and their pilots had been recognized during the late 1930s during the Chinese–Japanese war. Colonel Claire Chennault had firsthand experience of Japanese fighter aircraft and their pilots and he later wrote of the high quality of the Japanese pilots' training and cocky

---

86   Ibid, Chapter VIII, paragraph 44.
87   Spick, *Fighter Pilot Tactics: The Techniques of Daylight Air Combat*, pp.43-44.
88   Kaplan and Collier, *The Few*, p.116.
89   Spick, *Fighter Pilot Tactics: The Techniques of Daylight Air Combat*, p.61. It should be recognized that another reason for *Luftwaffe* pilots diving away from their R.A.F. adversaries was the realization that the non-fuel injected British Merlin engine would cut out if put straight into a dive. The solution at first was for the R.A.F. pilot to perform a half-roll and later a float was inserted into the engine's carburettor.

aggressiveness.[90] Furthermore, he observed that Japanese fighters sacrificed armour to achieve greater manoeuvrability in comparison to U.S. fighters, which made them dangerous to dogfight, "In a turning tail-chasing dogfight they were poisonous."[91] As Chinese pilots were engaging their Japanese enemies, four Soviet fighter squadrons arrived at the end of 1937 equipped with a mixture of the manoeuvrable *Polikarpov* I-15 biplane and fast *Polikarpov* I-16 monoplane. In response to the Japanese aircraft the Soviets used their powerful fighters to dive away from their opponents and, offensively, to attack using the dive and zoom.[92]

Observing and participating in the aerial combat gave Chennault a respect for the Japanese pilots' capabilities which complemented their aircraft, and he was able to pass his experience to the American Volunteer Group pilots in 1941. The A.V.G. were equipped at the time with an early version of the Curtiss P-40 which was heavily armed, fast and robust but was not capable of matching the high manoeuvrability of Japanese aircraft. Lecturing to his pilots Chennault said:

> You can count on a higher top speed, faster dive, and superior firepower. The Jap fighters have a faster rate of climb, higher ceiling, and better maneuverability. They can turn on a dime and climb almost straight up. If they can get you into a turning combat they are deadly. Use your speed and diving power to make a pass, shoot and break away ... Close your range, fire and dive away.[93]

One of Chennault's pilots confirmed his leader's instructions:

> Chennault told us that we had a sorry airplane, as fighters go. That it had two things; diving speed and gunfire. If we used those, we could get by with it. If not, we were going to get shot up, cold turkey. He told us: never stay in and fight; never try and turn; never try to mix it with them. All we could do was to get altitude and dive on them and keep going – hit and run tactics.[94]

One unidentified A.V.G. pilot was interviewed on his return to America after combat in October 1942:

> If he was above me my first movement would be away from him and down. There's nothing you can do to combat those fellows, when they have the advantage ...

---

90   Chennault, *Way of a Fighter*, p.57.
91   Ibid.
92   Spick, *Fighter Pilot Tactics: The Techniques of Daylight Air Combat*, p.44.
93   Chennault, *Way of a Fighter*, p.113.
94   Flight Leader George Paxton quoted in Ford, *Flying Tigers*, p.78.

After you've got out of the proximity of the battle, climb up to altitude, and come back into the fracas again.[95]

The Americans took advantage of the tactic and took it into the Pacific Theatre as will be shown later and together with their adoption of R.A.F. formations, were in a reasonable position to engage the Japanese.[96]

When R.A.F. squadrons engaged the Japanese from 8th December 1941 many pilots had not experienced aerial combat whilst some had fought the Germans and Italians. In Europe and the Middle East it was customary to climb into the formation and then engage in a turning dogfight exploiting the Spitfire's or Hurricane's manoeuvrability. However, as described earlier, this tactic could not be used by the Buffalo against the Nate, Oscar or Zero. The R.A.F. pilots were quick to realize their opponents' capabilities:

> The Army 97 [Nate] could turn right inside the Buffalo and I was a little too long in realizing the extent of their manoeuvrability.[97]

and:

> If you were mixed in a dogfight with a Zero, the outcome was very clear. Very quickly you were a dead man.[98]

It is not clear whether the R.A.F. pilots were aware of the dive and zoom tactic at this time, but the prerequisite for its implementation was height and owing to the lack of adequate early warning and the Buffalo's slow climb rate it would have been difficult to use. Other methods of countering the Japanese fighters were tried. Sergeant Ross Leys remembered a First World War tactic whereby if a pilot found himself within a circle of attacking fighters he would fly inside the circle in the opposite direction and break up the enemy formation.[99] Flight Lieutenant Mowbray Garden recalled trying an unusual method:

> There were three of them in formation on my tail and I could not out-turn them. I was dying for an excuse to bail out, until I remembered the advice of Flt Lt Tim Vigors, which was to the effect that when you think all is lost and death and destruction are imminent, just shut your eyes, work the rudder left and right,

---

95 TNA, Air 23/5280, Japanese Air Tactics – Fighter Aircraft, Some Japanese Air Tactics, 23rd October 1942, enclosure 8A, pp.1-3.
96 Chennault told his pilots to forget their pre-war formations and adopt the R.A.F. two-aircraft sections from European experience at the end of 1940.
97 Flight Lieutenant Tim Vigors quoted in Cull, *Buffaloes over Singapore*, p.64.
98 Sergeant Greg Board quoted in Ibid, p.69.
99 Ibid, p.76.

open the throttle to maximum and 'pudding basin' the control column. I did just that and when I opened my eyes there was not an aircraft in the sky.[100]

Both these measures showed the pilots using a previous generation's experiences or a tactic born out of necessity, but neither involved the dive and zoom technique. However, when height was attained the dive and zoom was used. Sergeant Geoff Fiskin shot down five Japanese aircraft in a week over Singapore in a Buffalo and later attributed his success to the dive and zoom tactic:

> The only thing to do was to get as much height as possible above any Japs before making an attack – preferably two or three thousand feet – when you could make the initial attack and have enough speed created in the dive to get round for a second go, even if it meant putting your feet on the dash board and blacking out slightly. This did not always work as the Jap planes outnumbered us by 10-20 to one, but when it did we got victories. When it did not we got out and lived to fight another day.[101]

The timing of Fiskin's experiences is important in tracing the evolution of the dive and zoom tactic in the Far East. The fifth of his victories was scored on 21st January over Singapore which was a couple of months before the R.A.F. and the A.V.G. shared an airfield whilst defending Rangoon. It is not recorded if the Americans had been in contact with the R.A.F. to share their tactic, or whether the latter had not been able to implement it owing to the Buffalo and lack of early warning. It is possible that individual pilots remembered past accounts of the stories of First World War pilots' tactics as Sergeant Leys had, or been forced to adapt tactics as learned in the pre-war years, e.g. the pecking attack and there were enough serving pilots trained in the 1938 Air Fighting Manual. Furthermore, experience was a vital element in addition to taking advice. For example, after the first Hurricanes saw action over Singapore in January 1942 casualties were sustained even though their pilots had been advised of the "inadvisability of getting involved with 'dog-fighting' owing to the navy 'O's [Zero] small turning circle."[102] An unidentified Buffalo pilot reported:

> The R.A.F. boys flying them [the Hurricanes] began to mix it with the Zeros which we knew was practically impossible. The Zero was just about the nippiest,

---

100 Ibid, p.119. By 'pudding basin' Garden means pushing the control column around as if stirring with a spoon.
101 Ibid, p.157.
102 TNA, Air 23/2123, Operations of the R.A.F. during the campaigns in Malaya and Netherlands East Indies: report by Air Vice-Marshal P.C. Maltby, 1st January 1941 to 31st December 1942, paragraph 379.

most highly manoeuvrable fighter in the world. They buzzed around the Hurricanes like vicious bees.[103]

However, later in January, even though the Hurricanes were outnumbered, the pilots achieved better results using the dive and zoom tactic as, "with the realization that 'dog-fighting' did not pay, the revised 'in and out' tactics adopted gradually gave increasing success."[104]

As the air fighting subsided over Singapore, Malaya, Java and Sumatra the Japanese focus switched to Burma and for the Allies the defence of Rangoon. For the first time R.A.F. and A.V.G. squadrons shared the same airfields at Mingaladon (Rangoon) and benefitted from an exchange of their combat experiences:

> Many of the A.V.G. pilots were fine and exceptionally good and experienced, but they all had the mark of the mercenary about them – which of course they were. They did, however, impart what experience they had to the R.A.F. pilots which was very welcome.[105]

The R.A.F. and A.V.G. pilots achieved better success against Japanese raiders over Burma due to an improved early warning system which gave the squadrons more time to climb to height to make the full use of the dive and zoom tactic which, together with more powerful aircraft, demonstrated the viability of the tactic.[106]

The first months of fighting the Japanese had taught the British and Americans several basic lessons that remained relevant for the rest of the war. Japanese fighters were extremely manoeuvrable and were not to be engaged in traditional dog-fights by the heavier Allied fighters such as the Hurricane and P-40. The basic First World War doctrine of height and speed was still relevant when intercepting the Japanese and the former could be best achieved by an efficient early warning system giving defenders ample time to climb higher than the raiders. Lastly the best tactic to engage the Japanese was the dive and zoom method which exploited the rugged Hurricane's and P-40's high diving speed and superior armament. This was also applicable to the Spitfire on its introduction to India in late 1943 and American types in 1944 as, despite their superior rate of climb and performance, they could not match the Oscar's manoeuvrability. It must also be remembered that during 1942 the lessons taught by Chennault had been reinforced by action in the Pacific where the manoeuvrability of the Zero and Oscar at low speeds had caused American flyers concerns, and as a result

---

103 Cull, *Hurricanes over Singapore*, p.36.
104 TNA, Air 23/2123, Operations of the R.A.F. during the campaigns in Malaya and Netherlands East Indies: report by Air Vice-Marshal P.C. Maltby, 1st January 1941 to 31st December 1942, paragraph 382.
105 Group Captain Frank Carey quoted in Franks, *Frank 'Chota' Carey*, p.102.
106 Probert, *The Forgotten Air Force*, p.88.

the dive and zoom was soon advocated, but as late as January 1945 the following was deemed necessary to be included in an American instructional book:

> Since it has been obvious that our planes could be outmaneuvered by Japanese planes such encounters have been avoided. "DON'T DOGFIGHT WITH THE JAP" has been a repeated warning to our fighter pilots, and this admonition is still appropriate … When attacking Jap fighters at slower speeds, Allied pilots have been using "hit-and-run" tactics, making single attacks then breaking away in a high speed climb or dive.[107]

The tactic was reinforced by a cartoon (opposite).

The instruction not to dogfight but use 'hit and run', bounce or dive and zoom tactics is repeated in most tactical documents published between 1942 and 1945, but putting it into practice was not always straightforward.

Typically on 19th March 1943, 43 Squadron, flying Hurricanes, were scrambled to intercept a raid on Feni but the ground control gave the raiders height as 25,000 feet and the interceptors were at 20,000 feet thus failing to engage.[108] More height led to better results. For instance on 1st April 1943 Hurricanes from 615 Squadron were scrambled to intercept a mixed force of bombers and fighters attacking Feni airfield and quickly reached 27,000 feet before diving on the enemy formation. The attack was successful and the Hurricane pilots claimed two bombers destroyed, two probably destroyed, five damaged and one fighter damaged, for the loss of one Hurricane.[109] The importance of height was recognized in Tactical Memorandum No 33 of 22nd April 1943:

> [I]n order to inflict casualties on the enemy fighters, our fighters must have the height advantage. This should be exploited because on all occasions when our fighters have gone into the attack from above the enemy, they have scored outstanding victories and the enemy casualties have been high.[110]

The memorandum continued:

> Controllers must get the fighters off the ground at the first warning. They should not wait to have a raid identified as hostile. It is much better to have several false alarms than miss a big raid.[111]

---

107 TNA, Air 40/2217, Japanese Fighter Tactics For Air Combat Intelligence Officers, p.34.
108 Franks, *Hurricanes over the Arakan*, p.171.
109 Ibid, pp.181-182, and Shores, *Air War for Burma*, p.78.
110 TNA, Air 23/5297, Air H.Q. India: Tactical Memoranda, 1942-1943, p.1.
111 Ibid, p.3.

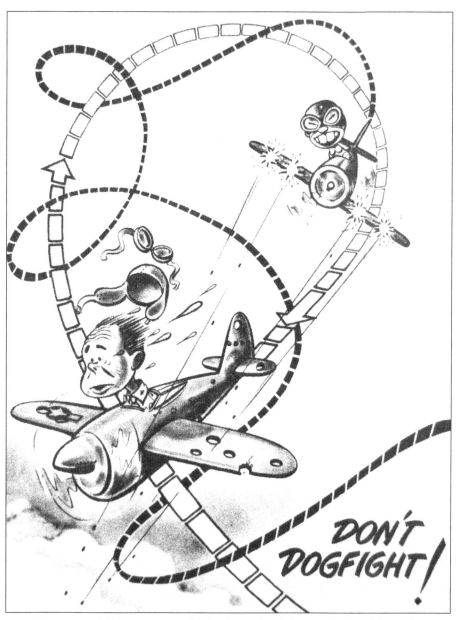

U.S. Instructional Cartoon. (Source: TNA, Air 40/2217, Japanese Fighter Tactics for Air Combat Intelligence Officers)

However, even though the radar cover improved during 1943 the Hurricane was unable to climb quickly enough and it would require a better fighter to counter the Japanese.

The Spitfire arrived in India in September 1943 with a powerful and superior rate of climb which gave the Allies a defensive edge. Capitalising on the improved early warning system the Spitfires were able to intercept the reconnaissance Dinahs, and once the controllers were used to manoeuvring the Spitfires into position, the pilots were able to use the dive and zoom tactic to good effect. On 31st December 1943, 136 Squadron was scrambled to intercept a raid on Chittagong and the ground controller was able to manoeuvre the Spitfires into a favourable position at a height of 30,000 feet:

> For me it was one of those days when everything went right. Using maximum combat revs and full throttle I made a series of dive and climb attacks on the fleeing formations, making use of my superior speed from my dives to elude the fighters.[112]

The pilots claimed a total of eight bombers and three fighters destroyed for the loss of one Spitfire and, although these Japanese losses are probably an over-estimate, this clearly showed the value of the tactic.[113] For the next few weeks through January 1944 similar successful interceptions took place with Spitfire squadrons inflicting losses on Japanese raiders, but the tally began to slow as circumstances worked against the Spitfire. There were only four operational Spitfire squadrons defending a large front against superior Japanese numbers, for example on 5th February 12 Spitfires intercepted over 100 aircraft over Bawli Bazaar. Despite these odds the defenders were still able to break up the formations and use their dive and zoom advantage on occasions where possible. However, the Japanese had started to develop tactics intended to negate the Spitfire's advantages.

Basic Japanese fighter formations were of a v-shape (vic) of three aircraft similar to the British formation but they did not fly in such a rigid pattern. Later in the war the Japanese adopted the Allied four aircraft formation in the Pacific when their aircraft improved in performance, but for the slower Oscar the three aircraft formation was more common. When engaged Japanese aircraft flooded the sky as recounted by an unidentified A.V.G. pilot:

> Because once you made contact with them the sky looks as if you have hit a beehive. They're all over the place, and you will never find one of them close, I mean, very seldom.[114]

---

112 Flight Lieutenant Gordon Conway quoted in Franks, *Spitfires over the Arakan*, p.100.
113 Shores, *Air War for Burma*, p.142.
114 TNA, Air 23/5280, Japanese Air Tactics – Fighter Aircraft, Some Japanese Air Tactics, 23rd October 1942, enclosure 8A, page 2.

Similar experiences from the Pacific Theatre defined the formation:

> [F]ighters made large circles at different altitudes, one above another. If one of the lower fighters were attacked, it dived to avoid contact. The next high fighter immediately dived same action. Usually the Japanese fighter attempted to attack from behind and slightly below.[115]

Furthermore, the American Pacific ace, Major Richard Bong, wrote in February 1944, "The Japs darned near always outnumbered us, and it seemed we were always finding ourselves in a mess of enemy fighters."[116] The Japanese brought these tactics to the Far East at the beginning of 1944 and this was reported in a Tactical Extract:

> New gambits such as the defensive circle and the use of separate formations which appear to have been disposed with the idea of enticing Spitfires to 'mix-it' at medium and low levels … at layers between 18 to 24,000 feet … They later began flying in different directions and executing defensive circles. Many more aircraft appeared to be flying between ground level and 10,000 feet and it is considered that in all roughly 100 enemy aircraft were airborne.[117]

Spitfire pilots were now faced with a counter to the dive and zoom; if the Japanese fighters were stacked at varying heights it meant the Spitfires would fly through one layer of Japanese fighters and then continue to encounter others in their dive and subsequent climb. For example on 9th February 1944 three sections from 615 Squadron reported intercepting over 50 Japanese aircraft "at all heights from 15,000 feet to deck level."[118] Whilst Japanese formations could be disrupted and disorganised their tactics made it difficult for the R.A.F. pilots to shoot down their adversaries and new tactics were required.

In September 1944 Japanese tactics were categorised by Allied tacticians and counter measures devised by the A.F.T.U. were published for instructional use.[119] The first Japanese formation was described as the 'Beehive' where a "formless conglomeration of Jap fighter aircraft" flew at heights between 17,000 feet and ground level, their random directions giving the impression the formation was disorganized.[120] Second was the 'Squirrel Cage' where Japanese fighters performed a variety of aerobatics which took them in different directions, which also filled the sky with aircraft giving

115 Ibid, Notes on Japanese Air Tactics, 3rd August 1942, enclosure 10A, page 3.
116 TNA, Air 23/2862, Air Tactics ACSEA, 1st January 1944 to 31st December 1944, Four Tips for a Fighter Pilot by An "Ace", p.1.
117 Ibid, Tactical Extract No 4.
118 TNA, Air 27/2124, 615 Squadron Operations Record Book, 9th February 1944.
119 TNA, Air 23/4672, Japanese Fighter Tactics in Burma, 1st January to 31st December 1944, Part II Fighter Position on Burma Front.
120 Ibid, p.9.

the impression that a dogfight was in progress. Lastly was the 'Decoy Ducks' where a Japanese fighter was painted in a bright colour (usually silver) which stood out against the jungle background, its purpose was to lure unsuspecting Allied fighters into a trap, as other Japanese fighters would be ready to pounce.[121] To meet these formations the Allied pilots were left with two options, either to engage or leave the vicinity. If the Japanese had the height advantage then the advice was to dive away at 400 mph before climbing in a right hand turn as the pursuing Japanese fighters could not cope with such a manoeuvre. However, if the Allied pilots had the height advantage then their formation should consist of three boxes of four aircraft, line abreast with 700 feet height differences between each box.[122] On engaging the enemy the middle box containing the formation leader would attack one Japanese aircraft, and when the rest of the Japanese formation dived or climbed the other two boxes would attack them from above. In addition Spitfire pilots were taught the 'rolling attack' which made use of their height advantage when a Japanese aircraft was directly below. As the Japanese aircraft disappeared under the Spitfire's wing the pilot would turn his aircraft in the opposite direction whilst performing a barrel roll to bring his guns onto the target when the manoeuvre was completed. Despite the intricacies of these manoeuvres the document made it clear that even in September 1944 pilots "entering this theatre of war from the Middle East or Europe ... [had] to make radical changes to their outlook" by disregarding any preconceived ideas about the Japanese being poor pilots or shots, and imagining they could use the same tactics they used against the Germans against the Japanese, "The exact opposite is the case."[123] The dive and zoom attack was the fundamental tactic from which all else was founded, but:

> Whereas the Hun used to dive and climb or "bounce" our aircraft as a set method of attack, this is the only correct method of attacking the Jap. This point is illustrated in the 2 cartoons which are attached. The effect of them is DON'T DOG FIGHT THE JAPS BUT BOUNCE HIM.[124]

Although these tactics had been presented and developed by the A.F.T.U., Allied squadrons in the field were also finding solutions to the Japanese tactics as the Tactical Memorandum refers to both Lightnings and Spitfire pilots working

121 Franks, *Hurricanes over the Arakan*, p. 31. Pilot Officer Underwood stated he saw aircraft "painted in quite brilliant colours." Although reported as a tactic by Allied aircrew there is no evidence to say this was a deliberate Japanese tactic, and it is possible that the shiny silver Japanese fighters may simply have not been painted in camouflage.
122 TNA, Air 23/4672, Japanese Fighter Tactics in Burma, 1st January to 31st December 1944, Part II Fighter Position on Burma Front, p.10.
123 Ibid, p.12.
124 Ibid.

R.A.F. Instructional Cartoon (1). (Source: TNA, Air 23/4672, Japanese Fighter Tactics in Burma, 1st January to 31st December 1944, Part II Fighter Position on Burma Front, p.12)

R.A.F. Instructional Cartoon (2). (Source: TNA, Air 23/4672, Japanese Fighter Tactics in Burma, 1st January to 31st December 1944, Part II Fighter Position on Burma Front, p.12)

out "counter-measures which have been effective" to the Beehive and Squirrel Cage formations.[125] As with the pilots in 1941 and 1942 practical experience at squadron level was vital to solving immediate problems during combat conditions.

* * *

By April 1945 the J.A.A.F. had withdrawn from Burma to other areas and theatres closer to Japan leaving air supremacy to the Allies. As this withdrawal continued a party from the Tactics Branch of the Central Fighter Establishment in Britain visited India and Burma. The subsequent report admitted that recent air-to-air combats had been infrequent and that their findings were based on past experiences but continued, "As the principles have remained constant it is reasonable to assume they will prove of use in the future."[126] The report is an accurate summary of not just what happened in the few months around their visit but also what had occurred for the preceding three years and serves well as a conclusion to this section. Although most Allied fighters had the advantages of straight and level speed, dive and zoom they were unable to match Japanese fighters at low speeds for manoeuvrability and so the "basis of Allied Tactics is avoidance of infighting with the Japanese whose manoeuvrability gives them a clear advantage."[127] To counter this:

> Allied fighters employ a high speed attack, if possible from above and astern, breaking away after the attack at speed to a sufficient distance away from the enemy to allow unmolested positioning for another attack.[128]

This is another way of describing the dive and zoom, which amounts to a vindication of the tactic and the pilots that adopted it during the first few months of the Japanese war.

Thus the formulation of relevant air fighting tactics played an integral role in attaining air superiority over the Japanese. Air fighting tactics used against German adversaries were clearly irrelevant against highly manoeuvrable Japanese fighters and the adoption of the dive and zoom manoeuvre proved effective for the rest of the war. Furthermore, it was vital that pilots were instructed in its application, particularly those who transferred from other theatres, and the A.F.T.U. was central to this. However, the air fighting tactics cannot be viewed in isolation. The success of dive and zoom depended on an effective early warning system to allow fighters to attain

---

125 TNA, Air 23/4672, Notes on the Japanese and Recent Fighter Tactics in Burma, Part II Fighter Position on Burma Front, p.10.
126 TNA, Air 23/2835, Visits to India Command Fighter Defence System, Tactics Branch Visit No 5, Report on visit to South Sea Asia by the Tactics Branch of the Central Fighter Establishment, Tactics Branch, p.16.
127 Ibid, p.17.
128 Ibid.

superior height but, in turn, the tactic required high performance fighter aircraft that could capitalize on the height and the tactic. Whereas the Buffalo and Hurricane had struggled to achieve height even when the early warning system was working, the Spitfire capitalized on improved warning facilities and its superior performance to make effective use of the dive and zoom.

Part Three – Aircraft

In December 1941 Japan's aircraft, particularly their fighters, were better in many respects than their Allied counterparts. The Japanese had been fighting over China since the mid 1930s and their aircraft had been adapted and improved during operational use. The *Nakajima* Ki27 Nate was a monoplane fighter that first flew in 1936 and following testing entered service against the Chinese in 1937. The Nate typified Japanese fighter design which placed manoeuvrability above armament or armour protection; equipped with two .303 machine guns it was both light and compact.[129] *Nakajima* used its experience of the Nate to improve the design which led to the Oscar which became Japan's main fighter over Burma between 1941 and 1945. The Oscar was a low wing monoplane powered by a radial engine and had fully retracting main wheels. It was fitted with two .303 machine guns and had no armour protection, but this reduced the weight and, combined with its compact size, ensured the aircraft was extremely manoeuvrable.[130] The final main fighter type encountered by the Allies was the J.N.A.F. aircraft carrier based *Mitsubishi* Type 0 known to the Allies as the Zeke or Zero.[131] Similar in appearance to the Oscar, this aircraft was another example of the Japanese philosophy of manoeuvrability at the expense of weight and size although as opposed to the Oscar's meagre armament, the Zero carried two .52 machine guns and two 20mm cannons.[132] The first prototype was flown in April 1939 and after further development saw service against the Chinese in 1940 where its outstanding performance was first witnessed.

Despite these aircraft seeing service in China during the years before December 1941, their operational capabilities came as an "unpleasant surprise" to the Allies.[133] The Nate and its Naval counterpart, the A5M Claude, had a fixed undercarriage which looked like outdated technology in Western eyes and may have "blinded the

---

129 A comparative table of fighter aircraft types for 1941-1942 is attached in Appendix I.

130 See Appendix I.

131 The Zeke was more commonly known as the Zero and this name will be used in this book.

132 The Zero's similarity to the Oscar proved a problem to Allied pilots. Long after the Japanese Navy Air Force had left the Far East in 1942, Allied pilots were reporting encounters with Zeros when in fact they had been fighting the Oscar.

133 TNA, WO 106/2540, Malaya Command Operations: despatch by Major General A.E. Percival, January to February 1942.

powers-that-be to the truth."[134] Despite its showing against the Chinese Air Force over Chongqing in August 1940 where six Japanese Navy pilots claimed 57 Chinese aircraft destroyed, the Allies did not see the Zero as a threat.[135] Colonel Claire Chennault, air advisor to Chiang Kai-shek and later commander of the American Volunteer Group in 1941, had, however, warned the Americans of the Zero's capabilities and General George Marshall (U.S. Army Chief of Staff) conveyed the message to the "army commanders in Hawaii and the Philippines, but they paid no attention."[136] Chennault wrote that he had warned the American War Department of the Japanese aircraft types, but later found that the information on the Nate was missing from official files and that the U.S. technical dossier in use at the time of Pearl Harbor contained no information about the Zero.[137] The British Air Ministry received reports of the Zero from various sources. These had allegedly been passed to A.H.Q. Far East but the reports either did not arrive or were lost among other intelligence reports.[138] Probert wrote:

> Minds long conditioned to a belief in Japanese inferiority were not to be so readily changed. Indeed the performance data about the Zero … was not circulated to stations; apparently a senior officer strongly denied the possibility of the Japanese possessing such an aircraft and took no action.[139]

In May 1941 a Zero was shot down in China and intelligence reports of its performance, tankage, range and armament were forwarded to Singapore and London in September, but a lack of staff, "resulted in the technical information not being passed to the R.A.F. squadrons."[140] This was to prove a disadvantage to operational pilots in combat as Flight Lieutenant Tim Vigors later recalled:

> I am of the opinion that many aircraft and lives were lost during the first weeks of the war owing to the complete absence of any sound intelligence reports on the performance of Japanese fighters and the ability of their pilots.[141]

---

134 Shores, *Bloody Shambles Volume One*, p.40. The 'Claude' was a low wing monoplane Naval fighter of compact appearance with an open cockpit and fixed undercarriage.
135 Ford, *Flying Tigers: Chennault and the American Volunteer Group*, p.40.
136 Ibid, p.44.
137 Chennault, *Way of a Fighter*, p.16.
138 Elphick, *Far Eastern File, The Intelligence War in the Far East 1930-1945*, p.167.
139 Probert, *The Forgotten Air Force*, p.27.
140 Ibid, p.167 and Shores, *Bloody Shambles Volume One*, p.40.
141 TNA, Air 41/63, *The Campaigns in the Far East, Volume II, Malaya, Netherlands East Indies and Burma 1941-1942*, p.62.

Another operational squadron commander reported that some of his pilots "were astonished to meet monoplane fighters."[142] However, by the time the R.A.F. squadrons met Japanese fighters in December 1941 the British had sent its fighter defence to the Far East but the aircraft chosen did not match Japanese fighters.

The American Brewster Buffalo had been designed in 1935 to a U.S. Navy carrier-borne fighter requirement. The aircraft had a short fuselage, mid-set wings and retractable undercarriage, with an armament of four .5 inch Colt machine guns, two in the wings and two in the aircraft's nose. The British placed an order for 170 Buffalos in 1940 but after three were trialled in Britain in September 1940 it was found that they were unsuitable for European service owing to their poor performance and weak armament. The aircraft was not thought suitable for carrier use by the Royal Navy as Air Chief Marshal Sir Charles Portal (Chief of the Air Staff) wrote to Churchill on 21st January 1941, "It appears that the Brewster does not fold and does not possess arrester hook. It is therefore unsuitable for embarking in carriers."[143] The remainder of 167 aircraft were sent to Malaya where 76 and 243 Squadrons were formed in February 1941, joined by 453 Squadron R.A.A.F. and 488 Squadron R.N.Z.A.F. in October 1941.[144]

Although the Buffalo's dimensions were comparable to Japanese fighters its operational performance did not match that of its adversaries. In July 1941 a test report compared the Buffalo's performance with what was known about the Zero:

	Zero	Buffalo
Rate of climb to 13,000 ft	4.3 minutes	6.1 minutes
Speed at 10,000 ft	315 mph	270 mph
Speed at 20,000 ft	295 mph	292 mph[145]

It was found, however, that 292 mph could not be obtained in Malaya and a maximum speed of 280 mph was considered a truer figure. It was thus at a disadvantage against Japanese bombers as Flight Lieutenant Jack Mackenzie later recalled, "It was difficult to even catch up with the enemy bombers – it was just too slow and completely unsuitable for the job it was given to do."[146] An unidentified Australian pilot added, "Bombers outpacing fighters – you've got to f***ing well laugh!"[147]

---

142 Unidentified squadron commander quoted in Ibid, p.63.
143 Christ Church College, Oxford University, Portal Papers, File One, Prime Minister's Minutes, January to March 1941. The reference to 'fold' means the wings did not fold for below deck storage.
144 Probert, *The Forgotten Air Force*, p.28. These four squadrons were later joined by 21 Squadron in Malaya, and 67 Squadron which was stationed in Burma.
145 TNA, Air 41/63, *The Campaigns in the Far East, Volume II, Malaya, Netherlands East Indies and Burma 1941-1942*, p.44.
146 Cull, *Buffalos over Singapore*, p.93.
147 Ibid, p.118.

The Buffalo's weight combined with its underpowered engine gave it a poor rate of climb which, has been demonstrated earlier, was crucial in fighter operations against the Japanese. Tactics evolved to counter the Japanese fighters' high manoeuvrability in December 1941 called for Allied aircraft to climb above the attackers and use their speed to dive through formations before zooming up to height for another dive. However, owing to the unreliability of the early warning organisation in giving adequate warning, the Buffalo was forced to fight at unsuitable heights whilst climbing to meet enemy formations. Over Singapore the Buffalos needed at least 30 minutes warning to reach 24,000 feet at which the Japanese flew, but this time was identical to that given by the early warning system, "The air defence was thus handicapped by the short warning received as well as by the poor performance of the Buffalos compared with the Zero fighters."[148]

Did the British have any alternatives to the Buffalo? Intelligence sources had warned of Japanese fighter capabilities and whether these warnings were mislaid or misinterpreted there was an over confidence in the Buffalo's abilities. At a meeting of the Chiefs of Staff in London in 1941:

[The] Vice Chief of the Naval Staff advocated the despatch of Hurricanes to Malaya, but his opposite number on the Air Staff insisted that "Buffalo fighters would be more than a match for the Japanese aircraft that were not of the latest type."[149]

Air Chief Marshal Sir Robert Brooke-Popham, C. in C. Far East, wrote to Air Marshal Sir Arthur Tedder on 4th August 1941, "I like the Buffalo as a fighter especially its armament which is four guns."[150] However, there were aircraft shortages in 1940 and 1941 to consider. On 8th November 1940 Portal wrote to Churchill:

Last week there were more than 425 Hurricanes and Spitfires in the Storage Units ... This surplus is falling fast ... Will you please stop shipments abroad now? Production is falling too.[151]

Spitfires and Hurricanes were in short supply and were required for the defence of Great Britain, European operations, Middle East and Greek operations, and could not be spared for the Far East. Furthermore, after the German invasion of the Soviet Union in 1941, 240 Hurricanes were promised by Churchill to Stalin in addition to

148 Kirby (ed), *The War Against Japan, Volume I*, p.286.
149 Cull, *Buffalos Over Singapore*, p.13. The opposite number was A.C.M. Sir Wilfred Freeman.
150 TNA, Air 23/1350, Correspondence with Air H.Q. India, Far East and Armed Forces India. Tedder was the Commander of R.A.F. Middle East Command.
151 Christ Church College, Oxford University, Portal Papers, File One, Prime Minister's Minutes, October to December 1940.

200 P-40s taken from American deliveries, both suitable for Far Eastern service. The deployment of Buffalos to Malaya was therefore the product of a number of factors: an acute fighter shortage; an aircraft unsuitable for operations against German types; and a misguided optimism that the Buffalo was a match for Japanese aircraft. Even so it was the most modern R.A.F. aircraft stationed in the Far East which included the torpedo carrying Vildebeest, a fabric and strut biplane, considered obsolete in the mid-1930s. Major General Arthur Percival, G.O.C. Malaya, later wrote:

> I was far from feeling happy when I was told that our fighters were a type which I had not heard of as being in action elsewhere, i.e. the ... Buffalo. However, a fighter was a fighter and we were in no position to pick and choose at that time.[152]

Squadron Leader Gerald Bell, commanding 243 Squadron, recalled:

> However, we were proud to be flying the Buffalo which was, despite its obsolescence, modern compared to the other aircraft which the command was equipped.[153]

The Buffalo's service operators had mixed views. Pilot Officer Terry Marra recalled, "As a combat aircraft it was hopeless. As an aircraft to fly it was beautiful – it really was."[154] Marra listed difficulties including the engines using excessive oil, the machine guns failing to fire, and a ceiling of 22,000 feet on a hot day. Squadron Leader Wilfred Clouston, 488 Squadron, remembered:

> All of us who had been on decent aeroplanes – Spitfires and Hurricanes – thought Buffalos were terrible things. They didn't have the climbing ability ... They were too slow to get up to altitude and were cumbersome things ... It was a good aeroplane, but not for fighting. The gun platform was particularly poor.[155]

For those pilots used to the reliability and firepower of the Spitfire and Hurricane the armament of the Buffalo was poor. Kapitan Pieter Tideman of the Royal Netherlands East Indies Army Military Air Service stationed in Java and Sumatra, for example, wrote that "our armament was too little and too light."[156] Additionally the .5 inch Colt machine guns fitted to the Buffalos of 21 Squadron R.A.A.F. were prone to corrosion in their electrical systems and the solution was to replace the .5 inch guns

---

152 TNA, WO 106/2540, Malaya Command Operations: despatch by Major General A.E. Percival, January to February 1942. Written in 1945 after his release from Japanese captivity.
153 Cull, *Buffalos over Singapore*, p.14.
154 Ibid, p.6.
155 Ibid, p.28.
156 Ibid, p.7. The Royal Netherlands Air Force was formed in March 1953.

with .303 inch machine guns.[157] Groundcrews' opinion was unfavourable as Leading Aircraftman (L.A.C.) James Home recalled:

> I always said this aircraft was a disaster and now I was seeing further confirmation. It was short, fat and stunted like a beer barrel fitted with an engine, and when the engine started up it couldn't make up its mind whether to continue running or cough up its innards and report sick … I hated to think how any of our Buffalo pilots felt when they faced the Zero – one thing for sure, he needed to be brave.[158]

Mechanic, L.A.C. Helsdon Thomas remembered:

> Spot welds would break on the box section undercarriage. Rivets were discovered in the fuel lines, fuel pumps and carburettors. Big-end bearings had a habit of cracking up and depositing white metal into the scavenger filters.[159]

Many of these faults were discovered during training in 1941 and before the Japanese attacks of December and also later, when as a result of air fighting, the disparity between Japanese aircraft and the Buffalo became apparent modifications in the field were made. At the end of December 1941 the aircraft stationed at Sembawang (Malaya) had been reduced in weight by 1,000lbs by removing two of the four guns and halving the ammunition, whilst further weight reduction was made by lightening the radio equipment, removing the external radio mast and removing any non-essential equipment such as the Verey pistol and cockpit heater. Furthermore, the aircraft was filled with 80 gallons of fuel rather than the usual 130 gallons, but the pilot still had to pressure the fuel system by means of a hand pump from the cockpit at above 18,000 feet.[160] Nevertheless the total weight reductions improved the fighter's performance by 30 mph, giving it more manoeuvrability with the result:

> That with these improvements our Buffalo fighters were able to almost match the Zeros in performance. Now our fighter pilots were gaining confidence after initially having been given a hard time in battle.[161]

These modifications did not however solve the problems of attrition. By the end of December 1941 the numbers of serviceable Buffalos had decreased substantially

---

157 Ibid, p.36.
158 Ibid, p.7
159 Ibid, p.14.
160 TNA, Air 41/63, *The Campaigns in the Far East, Volume II, Malaya, Netherlands East Indies and Burma 1941-1942*, p.79.
161 Group Captain J.P.J. McCauley, Sembawang's Station Commander, quoted in Cull, *Buffalos over Singapore*, p.99. No first name is available for McCauley.

and those remaining aircraft faced greater numbers of Japanese fighters. Buffalos had been lost during the squadrons' training period in 1941 as a result of flying accidents, whilst approximately 21 were lost in the initial attacks on British aerodromes on 8th December. As air fighting progressed through December and January 1942, aircraft continued to be lost during air and ground operations; for example, on 14th December 453 Squadron did not have a single serviceable aircraft available and later on the evening of 22nd December out of 15 aircraft which had started the day only four were left serviceable.[162] By 18th January 1942 only 24 Buffalos in Malaya were still serviceable.[163]

Despite the Buffalo's faults not every pilot was dissatisfied with the aircraft. Kapitan Tideman flew the aircraft in Java and recalled:

> The Brewster was a good, sturdy fast fighter, with two half-inch armour plates behind the seat. She would take a hell of a beating. My view is that our drawback during the fighter actions was not an inferior aeroplane, but that we had too few of them and also our armament was too little and too light.[164]

Tideman's views may have been influenced by the fact that the Dutch Buffalo was a newer variant with a 1,200 hp engine rather than the R.A.F.'s 1,100 hp motor and this improved its performance. Similarly R.A.F. pilot Sergeant Geoff Fisken test flew every Buffalo that left the assembly area in Seletar in 1941 before flying operationally with 243 Squadron and later recalled:

> We did hours and hours of it [testing]. That was the main thing, we built up more hours. We had about 150 hours in Buffalos before the war started, so we knew what they would do and what they were like. I got a couple of trips in Hurricane Mk IIBs that 488 Squadron had in Singapore and I didn't think the Hurricane was as good as a Buffalo.[165]

Sergeant James Macintosh of 488 Squadron was in a dogfight with Zeros on 18th January and remembered, "I proved twice in the course of this combat that the Buffalo was equal to the manoeuvrability of the Zero."[166] On 1st February 1942 a mock dogfight was staged between a Hurricane flown by Wing Commander Frank Carey and a Buffalo from 67 Squadron flown by Sergeant Gordon Williams. At heights above 20,000 feet the Buffalo was found to be superior, at heights around 16,000 feet the aircraft were evenly matched, and below that height the Hurricane

---

162 Probert, *The Forgotten Air Force*, p.53 and TNA, Air 41/63, *The Campaigns in the Far East, Volume II, Malaya, Netherlands East Indies and Burma 1941-1942*, p.61.
163 Probert, *The Forgotten Air Force*, p.53.
164 Shores, *Bloody Shambles Volume One*, p.65.
165 Cull, *Buffalos over Singapore*, p.223.
166 Ibid, p.147. Macintosh was awarded two Zeros probably destroyed.

had the edge.[167] Furthermore, in July 1941 during handling trials at the Royal Aircraft Establishment in Farnborough the Buffalo's aileron handling was found to be "exceptionally effective" whilst test pilots "considered them to be a definite improvement on the Hurricane and Spitfire fabric covered ailerons."[168] The report does not mention what heights these trials were carried out at but it would seem likely that it was at over 20,000 feet which gave a misleading impression as the Japanese fighters chose to fight below those heights. However, despite these favourable comments the Buffalo did not perform well in the theatre for a variety of reasons discussed earlier and as fighting continued plans were made to send better aircraft to the region.

After the initial Japanese successes on 8th and 9th December 1941 the decision was taken on 10th December to reinforce the R.A.F. in the Far East. Pre-war reinforcement plans called for aircraft to be sent from the Middle East at the end of 1941, but fighting there initially precluded any diminution of its fighter strength. Early plans to send P-40s were cancelled as it was felt the aircraft was too new in British service as there was little operational experience with the aircraft as well as a shortage of spare parts.[169] It would also take too long for fighters to be sent from Britain, but a solution was found in diverting two fighter wings, each equipped with Hurricanes, which were destined for service in the Caucasus and northern Persia. 51 crated Hurricanes with 24 pilots drawn from 17, 135,136 and 232 Squadrons together with enough maintenance equipment and staff for two squadrons were diverted to the Far East. But the reinforcement plan was problematical. The decision to send the Hurricanes had been made on 10th December, but they would not arrive until 15th January.[170] Following a superb effort by ground crews to assemble the aircraft, the first Hurricanes were ready to fly within 48 hours of their arrival but air superiority in Malaya had already been lost to the Japanese during the preceding six weeks. Moreover, these Hurricanes could not be regarded as reinforcements but rather as replacements for the Buffalos lost during December 1941 and within days many of the Hurricanes were lost. On 29th January Portal told Churchill of the fate of the 51 Hurricanes: 17 had been written off and nine were damaged; four could be serviceable within 24 hours; and only 21 available for immediate operations.[171] An additional 48 Hurricanes taken from the Middle East arrived during the next week but again they were replacements for losses rather than reinforcements. Sergeant Terence Kelly, a Hurricane pilot with 258 Squadron, thought the 98 Hurricanes which arrived at the beginning of 1942 should have been

167 Shores and Cull, *Bloody Shambles Volume Two*, p.256 and Franks, *Frank 'Chota' Carey*, p.96. Carey was an experienced Battle of Britain pilot who arrived in the theatre with the Hurricane replacements in January 1942, and Williams was an experienced Buffalo pilot.
168 TNA, Avia 6/2442, Handling Tests on Buffalo, July 1941.
169 TNA, Air 41/63, *The Campaigns in the Far East, Volume II, Malaya, Netherlands East Indies and Burma 1941-1942*, p.84.
170 The squadrons were told of the diversion on 17th December.
171 Christ Church College, Oxford University, Portal Papers, File One, Prime Minister's Minutes, January to March 1942.

held back until all were available to fly in mass formations against the Japanese rather than in "penny-numbers."[172] A.V.M. Paul Maltby, Deputy A.O.C. Malaya, was aware of the implications of using the pilots and their aircraft as soon as they had been assembled but:

> [E]vents had moved too fast and the stake was too high for delay to be accepted; and the Hurricanes had to be used immediately they had been erected and tested.[173]

Aircraft were put into action as soon as possible with the effect that numbers began to diminish with every operation. For example in eleven days 232 Squadron lost 18 Hurricanes, at least seven more damaged in combat, with two more destroyed on the ground; nine pilots were killed and four seriously wounded.[174]

There were also various technical problems with the Hurricanes which affected its performance. The original 51 Hurricanes diverted to the Far East were Mark IIBs, but the performance figures in the aircraft manual were not matched by its performance in Malaya and Burma. The IIB was equipped with twelve .303 machine guns which, with their ammunition, added nearly 1,000lbs to its overall weight compared to the Mark I which had eight guns.[175] Furthermore, as the Hurricanes had been destined for Middle East service they were fitted with a large sand filter in a cowling underneath the aircraft's nose which could not be removed. These two factors reduced the aircraft's speed by 30 mph and pilots considered the handling and manoeuvrability were affected detrimentally. Pilot Officer Jerry Parker, a pilot with 232 Squadron, recalled:

> We never got a good performance from our Hurricanes in Singapore. Although for marksmen of our calibre a congregation of machine guns was desirable, the extra four guns must have weighed at least half a ton. The Hurricanes became not only slow, particularly in the climb, but also very heavy and unwieldy in manoeuvre.[176]

Following their early combat with the Japanese A.V.M. Conway Pulford, A.O.C. Singapore, wrote to Portal on 23rd January 1942 to state the Hurricane was struggling to match Japanese aircraft and informed him that four guns were to be removed to

---

172 Kelly, *Hurricanes Versus Zeros*, p.25.
173 TNA, Air 23/2123, Operations of the R.A.F. during the campaigns in Malaya and Netherlands East Indies: report by Air Vice-Marshal P.C. Maltby, 1st January 1941 to 31st December 1942, paragraph 376.
174 Cull, *Hurricanes over Singapore*, p.69.
175 See Appendix I.
176 Cull, *Hurricanes over Singapore*, p.25.

improve performance.[177] Portal's reply on 24th January shows a misunderstanding of the realities:

> Strongly recommend you should not remove your four guns from the Hurricanes. Actual experiments here have shown that effect on the total ceiling is only 300 feet and rate of climb negligible. Manoeuvrability is unaffected.[178]

Furthermore, on 2nd February Portal wrote to Pierse advising him that Hurricanes were en route to him from the Middle East despite them being "hard pressed" and added, "Hurricanes should do well against JAPANESE aircraft whose performance is not very high."[179] Despite Portal's recommendations, individual squadrons did remove four guns from some of their Hurricanes which improved the aircraft's abilities. In addition there was also a concern that the Far East had not been sent the best aircraft available, particularly in later consignments from the Middle East. Percival wrote of the original Hurricanes, "These machines were not the most modern type of Hurricane" whilst part of the later Middle East shipment of Hurricanes included some Mark I aircraft which were obsolete.[180] Of the original 'Burma' Hurricanes Franks wrote:

> Most had been ferried in from the Middle East and not all were new aircraft! It was suspected that new aircraft for the Far East were 'pinched' by various senior people along the way, and substituted for 'war weary' types. Several arrived with their Form 700s noted 'For training use only'.[181]

Ten Mark I Hurricanes had been sent with some Mark IIBs on H.M.S. *Indomitable* in February 1942 with an additional 26 flying by air to India, and later in the month the Far East command was informed that 50 more Hurricane Mark Is were being sent.[182] These 50 aircraft were largely untropicalised but were sent specifically to India to train fighter squadrons. It was perhaps understandable that older aircraft were sent from the Middle East as they were engaged in their own fighting, but once in India there was every possibility that some of these aircraft would be used for operational duties when shortages prevailed.

Hurricane squadrons found fighting the Japanese as difficult as the Buffalo squadrons. The continuing lack of adequate early warning against Japanese air attack resulted

177   TNA, Air 8/612, Operation of Hurricanes in the Far East, January to February 1942.
178   Ibid.
179   TNA, Air 23/2133, Far East Operations: A.O.C.-in-C. Air Marshal Sir Richard Pierse, personal signals to and from Air Ministry. Portal's capitals.
180   TNA, WO 106/2540, Malaya Command Operations: despatch by Major General A.E. Percival, January to February 1942, p.102.
181   Franks, *Hurricanes over the Arakan*, p.26. A Form 700 is an aircraft's logbook.
182   TNA, Air 2/7655, Movements: Despatch of Hurricanes to the Far East by Carrier, 1942.

in their being caught on the ground or whilst climbing to meet the enemy formations. On 27th January an unheralded raid on Kallang (Singapore) cost the newly arrived 488 Squadron four of its Hurricanes destroyed and another nine written off as unserviceable, all whilst being refuelled.[183] On Sumatra on 7th February a late warning for an air attack on Palembang 1 airfield resulted in three burnt out Hurricanes and a further 11 damaged, while the Hurricanes taking off faced difficulties as Air Commodore Stanley Vincent, A.O.C. 226 Group, reported:

> Once again the warning came late, and once again the inexperienced pilots found the Japanese more than a match. The Hurricanes were unable to gain height in time and were attacked in ones and twos immediately after taking off.[184]

These were common incidents during the retreat from Singapore through Java and Sumatra and although the early warning system did improve slightly when Burma was invaded and gave the defending Hurricanes and P-40s from the American Volunteer Group some degree of time to respond.

The pilots also showed varying degrees of experience which gave rise to suspicions that the best pilots had not been sent with the original 51 Hurricanes. After investigation Portal wrote to Churchill on 24th February:

> Of the four squadrons, you will remember that the first to arrive consisted of the least experienced pilots of the four squadrons destined for Iraq and south Russia. Not very much was expected of them.[185]

When the situation deteriorated experienced pilots who should have gone to the Soviet Union and Iraq were diverted to Burma where Portal reported, "they seem to have done quite well."[186] Portal's comments reflected the necessity of using the pilots without time being allowed for training or to instil an esprit de corps. It was important to get aircraft and pilots to Singapore as quickly as possible in the circumstances:

> This alone was the reason for the unfortunate mixture of fragments from various sources. If we could have delayed the Japanese advance for the time necessary for these squadrons to shake down and train together, they would have undoubtedly have given a much better account of themselves.[187]

---

183   488 Squadron had been re-equipped with Hurricanes following the loss of their Buffalos.
184   Cull, *Hurricanes over Singapore*, p.108. There were two airfields on Sumatra, Palembang 1 (P1) and Palembang 2 (P2).
185   TNA, Air 8/612, Operation of Hurricanes in the Far East, January to February 1942.
186   Ibid.
187   Ibid, p.2.

This echoed Maltby's observation that there was no time for the pilots to acclimatise to the local conditions, although in his despatch he pointed out that some of the pilots had gained experience in the Battle of Britain.[188]

The need to reinforce the Far East during those months reached desperate lengths. The experiences with the Buffalo and latterly with the Hurricane showed that it was not merely a matter of throwing any aircraft into the fighting as the J.A.A.F. and J.N.A.F. were resourceful, well equipped and well-trained. Moves were nevertheless made to send numbers of Gloster Gladiator biplane fighters to Malaya from the Middle East. As late as 23rd July 1941 General Archibald Wavell, C. in C. Middle East, wrote to Tedder about a visit he made to Risalphur in India:

> Found R.A.F. Squadron training as fighter squadron with Audax machines. Most modern aircraft possessed in India. Does this not make your heart bleed? Could you not now spare some Gladiators, as many as possible, to enable pilots this squadron to be trained in comparatively modern machines.[189]

Wavell appeared to be asking for Gladiators as training machines rather than operational aircraft, but Tedder's reply on 25th July made it clear that the aircraft were unsuitable for transfer, "It does but my heart's blood does not produce fighters. Do not think flight of our very part worn Gladiators practicable from here to India."[190] In February 1942 Portal exhorted Tedder to send as many Hurricanes as he could spare to Pierse, adding he had noticed that 46 Gladiators were stationed in the Middle East. Portal added:

> Propose offering these to ABDAIR as they are desperately short of fighters and Gladiator manoeuvrability may prove useful against Japanese aircraft.[191]

Tedder replied that of the 46, only 26 were serviceable, with five additional aircraft serviceable in a fortnight but the remaining were unserviceable. Of those that were in flying condition some had been given to the French, others were unarmed and used for metrological flights, whilst others were used for communication purposes in the desert and their removal would create additional problems for his command as they would have to be replaced by precious Hurricanes. Pierse entered the debate, writing:

---

188 TNA, Air 23/2123, Operations of the R.A.F. during the campaigns in Malaya and Netherlands East Indies: report by Air Vice-Marshal P.C. Maltby, 1st January 1941 to 31st December 1942, paragraph 376.
189 TNA, Air 23/1350, Correspondence with Air H.Q. India, Far East and Armed Forces India.
190 Ibid, Tedder to Wavell, 25th July 1941.
191 Ibid, Portal to Tedder, 10th February 1942. ABDAIR was the air element of the American-British-Dutch-Australian (ABDA) Command.

Grateful for your proposal but even if Gladiators available consider them to be completely outclassed by enemy fighters who even now meet Hurricanes and P-40s on equal terms.[192]

This seemed to have ended the matter, but on 19th March A.V.M. John D'Albiac, A.O.C. 222 Group, wrote to Pierse and the Middle East A.H.Q. that if Hurricanes and Spitfires were not available for transfer to his command he would accept the 46 Gladiators Tedder had previously offered.[193] Pierse intervened by advising against the Gladiators firstly on the grounds they were part worn and secondly because "another type … will complicate already overstretched maintenance organisation."[194] No Gladiators were ever sent to the Far East, but the episode shows firstly how desperate the theatre was for fighters and secondly how this desperation manifested itself in senior commanders who should have understood the situation better.

Buffalos and Hurricanes were not the only Allied fighter engaging Japanese aircraft during this period. The Americans had a number of P-40Bs, a monoplane which had similar dimensions to the Hurricane and was armed with two .5 inch guns in the fuselage and four .3 inch guns in the wings. Used against the Japanese in Java and the Netherlands East Indies by 17th Pursuit Squadron (Provisional), the aircraft acquitted itself well despite a shortage of numbers but it found the Japanese aircraft's manoeuvrability challenging:

It [P-40] could outdive the Japanese fighters, was faster in level flight, and was better armored. But the enemy plane seemed to have more range, could outclimb the P-40, and was more maneuverable. For the American pilot to risk a dogfight was to flirt with suicide.[195]

During the early part of the Burma campaign the P-40 was used by the American Volunteer Group (A.V.G.), which consisted of U. S. Army and Navy pilots employed by contract by the Chinese Government and commanded by Claire Chennault. At first only 43 of the original 100 aircraft delivered were serviceable whilst Chennault found half of his 100 pilots had never flown fighter aircraft and a dozen had not even seen a P-40.[196] An intensive training programme was initiated based on Chennault's experiences of advising Chinese pilots against the Japanese during their air battles in the late 1930s. When the battle for Burma began Chennault rotated his squadrons between China and Burma, but he ensured that one squadron alone was based in

---

192 Ibid, Pierse to Tedder 12th February 1942.
193 TNA, Air 23/1350, Correspondence with Air H.Q. India, Far East and Armed Forces India.
194 Ibid, Pierse to A.O.C. 222 Group, 22nd March 1942.
195 Craven and Cate, *The Army Air Forces in World War II, Volume One*, p.401.
196 Chennault, *Way of a Fighter*, p.111. Chennault wrote that by March 1942 18 of these pilots were still not classified for combat operations.

Burma and resisted demands that all his aircraft should be deployed there. On 23rd and 25th December the A.V.G. and 67 Squadron (Buffalos) claimed 36 Japanese aircraft destroyed; between 23rd and 29th January American P-40s and R.A.F. Hurricanes claimed 50 Japanese fighters and bombers destroyed; and on 24th and 25th February 37 more Japanese aircraft were claimed destroyed.[197] Although probably over-estimates these were potentially better results than previously achieved, but were the aircraft the prime factor? The P-40 was a similar aircraft to the Hurricane and its pilots were slightly more experienced using the dive and zoom tactic as taught by Chennault to counter Japanese fighter capabilities. However, the deciding factor was the efficiency of the Burma Observer Corps and the radar unit based at Rangoon which gave the defenders a better chance of achieving sufficient height. Both the P-40 and Hurricane had a high diving speed which suited the dive and zoom tactic which the advantage of height made possible but only if sufficient warning could be achieved:

> If a man got off the ground thirty seconds before his mates, he could grab an extra 500 to 800 feet of altitude before the Japanese arrived – an edge that could mean the difference between living and dying.[198]

During the early months of attacks against Burma the early warning system coped well providing the defenders with sufficient warning, but once the radar equipment was forced to move from Rangoon and the Japanese air forces moved into the evacuated airfields in large numbers the conditions in Malaya were replicated.[199]

Once the 1942 monsoon was over there was, at first, little Japanese aerial activity over the Burmese front but in December regular attacks began on the airfields at Chittagong and Feni. These continued into 1943 when the Japanese raided targets that had a direct bearing on the Allies' first Arakan campaign, in particular seeking to disrupt the support given to the ground forces by Allied aircraft. From then the Hurricane held the line against Japanese attacks until better aircraft were available, and the Beaufighter was introduced to make a significant impact in the air superiority campaign as a night-fighter.

Despite the Hurricane's shortcomings against Japanese fighters in the absence of a reliable early warning system, it became the principal R.A.F. day fighter in the Far East Theatre from May 1942 until the beginning of 1944. As R.A.F. reinforcements arrived from May 1942 onwards they were equipped with either the IIB or IIC variant, many of which had already seen service in the Middle East. Three of the squadrons,

197 Probert, *The Forgotten Air Force*, pp.86-88.
198 Ford, *Flying Tigers: Chennault and the American Volunteer Group*, p.202.
199 Kirby (ed), *The War Against Japan, Volume II*, p.151.

79, 607 and 615, had flown Mark IIBs in Britain whilst their Operations Record Books show them re-equipping with IICs in India between June and August 1942.[200]

The Hurricane IIC was not a significant advance on other versions of Hurricane in the theatre other than in terms of its armament; both the IIB and IIC had the Merlin XX engine as its powerplant and the IIC was longer than the IIB by one inch.[201] Whereas the IIB was initially equipped with twelve or eight .303 machine guns, the IIC was fitted with four 20mm cannons which gave greater hitting power, but added to the Hurricane's performance problems. The IIB, with twelve guns, had a maximum weight of 7340 lbs whereas the IIC, with cannons, had a maximum weight of 7640 lbs, some 300 lbs heavier.[202] The cannons' weight, in Sergeant Bill Davis' opinion, made the Hurricane IIC challenging to fly in combat. After fighting a Japanese fighter he recalled:

> As I was spinning down I wondered whether the aircraft had any damage but it came out of the spin all right. The Hurricane IIB was pretty good at recovery from a spin, but the IIC with cannons wasn't so clever.[203]

The additional weight increased the time it took the IIC to climb to 20,000 feet to 9.1 minutes as compared to the IIB's time of 8.4 minutes.[204] These figures are taken from official sources but in addition the Hurricanes had transferred from the Middle East equipped with heavy sand filters and they had already completed a number of combat flying hours. Combined together, these factors reduced the aircraft's manoeuvrability and its rate of climb still further. The Hurricane's overall speed caused additional problems not only when intercepting enemy fighters and bombers, but also whilst escorting friendly aircraft such as the Vengeance dive-bomber:

> I think this was the first time Vengeances operated, or at least it was our first escort to them. It was rather embarrassing for us, because once they'd dive-bombed and pulled up their dive brakes, and cleared the area, they left us behind. We couldn't keep up with them in our old Hurricanes.[205]

200 TNA, Air 27/664, 79 Squadron Operations Record Book, 1st March 1937 to 31st December 1941; TNA, Air 27/665, 79 Squadron Operations Record Book, 1st January 1942 to 31st December 1943; Air 27/2093, 607 Squadron Operations Record Book, 1st March 1930 to 31st December 1943; Air 27/2123, 615 Squadron Operations Record Book, 1st June 1937 to 31st December 1943.
201 TNA, Supp 9/1, British Types, 1941-1945.
202 See Appendix II.
203 Franks, *Hurricanes over the Arakan*, p.93.
204 TNA, Supp 9/1, British Types, 1941-1945.
205 Sergeant Bill Davis quoted in Franks, *Hurricanes over the Arakan*, p.171.

The combination of a low rate of climb with a relatively slow speed made it difficult for the aircraft to intercept the high flying and quick Japanese reconnaissance aircraft, the Ki-46 Dinah. Flying Officer Gordon Conway (136 Squadron) later recalled:

> One of our difficulties was our inability to get to height in time to intercept Japanese high-flying recces; they would fly with impunity over our bases providing the target material for the next raids.[206]

Sergeant Barney Barnett remembered, "Scrambled to 27,000 feet at noon. Jap recce ... passed 800 yards off, couldn't catch the bugger!"[207] The Hurricane therefore needed much assistance from the early warning organisation but this was not always forthcoming.

Whilst the Hurricane had not improved as a fighter, the early warning organisation had advanced from the early days of December 1941. In December 1942 there were 52 operational radar sets stationed from Ceylon to north-east India, but despite the increase in radar coverage it was not enough to assist the Hurricanes in achieving sufficient height during interceptions. Conway recalled:

> Our success was limited by poor early warning, the lack of precise radars, and the comparatively poor performance of the Hurricane at the height the Zeros chose to fight.[208]

Flight Lieutenant Paddy Stephenson, 123 Squadron, remembered:

> The 42/43 ops were not the most brilliant pages of the history of the Hurricane. We were controlled at maximum range and seldom had height advantage, so essential when the Jap fighters had manoeuvrability.[209]

However, the early warning system occasionally gave the Hurricanes sufficient time to attain height. On 1st April 1943 17 Hurricanes from 67 and 615 Squadrons were scrambled to meet a raid on Feni by 27 Ki-21 Sally bombers which were escorted by Oscars from the 50th and 64th *Sentais*.[210] Good early warning gave the Hurricane pilots the chance to climb to 27,000 feet thereby gaining a significant advantage to use their dive and zoom tactics on the Japanese formations.[211] The six Hurricanes from 67 Squadron had taken off too late to get into a good position to attack, claiming only one Japanese fighter as damaged, but 615 Squadron had been in a perfect position

206 Probert, *The Forgotten Air Force*, p.129.
207 Franks, *Hurricanes over the Arakan*, p.183.
208 Probert, *The Forgotten Air Force*, p.129.
209 Franks, *Hurricanes over the Arakan*, p.212.
210 Shores, *Air War for Burma*, p.78.
211 Franks, *Hurricanes over the Arakan*, p.181.

and claimed three destroyed, two probable and six damaged bombers and fighters.[212] A few days earlier, on 27th March, the early warning system gave four Hurricanes of 79 Squadron and seven of 135 Squadron sufficient time to climb to 20,000 feet and intercept a raid of between 15 to 18 Lilys on Cox's Bazaar. The Japanese fighter escort failed to rendezvous and the Hurricanes were left to attack the bombers without enemy fighter interference. Flying Officer Robert Windle later recalled:

> On the 27th we caught about 25 bombers and really did them over. I remember being surprised how fast their bombers could go. They took quite a bit of catching and didn't have anything in the way of escort. They kept their formation in spite of what they were copping from us.[213]

Despite the bombers' speed they were no match for the Hurricanes; the squadrons claimed eight destroyed, five probably destroyed and four damaged.[214] These two engagements demonstrate what the Hurricanes were capable of in favourable circumstances provided they had adequate early warning, their superior armament allowing them to be effective against Japanese bombers. It must also be recognized that the Hurricane's four cannons could also prove devastating against the lightly built and mainly unarmoured Japanese fighters as Conway recalled:

> I gave this Oscar a burst of cannon and he literally fell apart. He seemed to stop in mid-air. His port wheel came down, his flaps, and with pieces flying off all round, he flicked and spun vertically into the sea just by the airfield.[215]

The Hurricane could pose a serious threat to the Japanese given the right circumstances and it was clear that its heavy armament could take advantage of light Japanese fighter construction. Nevertheless it was clear that a better day fighter was required to take air superiority from the Japanese. However, before the Spitfire arrived the R.A.F. took delivery of an aircraft which made a significant effect on the air superiority campaign by night. However, this is much less well known and seldom discussed.

While the Hurricane was holding its own against Japanese fighters during this period it did not substantially alter the balance of air superiority. The first aircraft type which significantly altered the course of events was the Bristol Beaufighter night-fighter variant which arrived in January 1943. The Beaufighter was a twin-engine monoplane that carried a crew of two and a powerful armament of four 20mm cannon and six .303 inch machine guns.[216] The aircraft had proved itself as an excellent

---

212 Shores, *Air War for Burma*, p.78.
213 Franks, *Hurricanes over the Arakan*, p.176.
214 TNA, Air 24/1282, Daily Operational Summaries Nos. 141 – 250, 1st January 1943 to 30th April 1943.
215 Franks, *Hurricanes over the Arakan*, p.205.
216 See Appendix II.

long-range interdiction aircraft in the Middle East and significantly as a very efficient night-fighter when equipped with Airborne Interception (A.I.) radar over Britain from early 1941. The first squadron (Number 27) had arrived with its Beaufighters in India during December 1942 in an interdiction role but owing to technical difficulties was not able to attain full operational status until February 1943.[217] 27 Squadron was the only Beaufighter unit in this role until 177 Squadron arrived in October 1943 but owing to the numbers of tasks allotted to it was unable to make a significant effect on Japanese strength during the counter-air offensive as will be discussed later. However, in its night-fighter role the Beaufighter made an impact within a few days of its arrival in India.

Between 20th and 27th December 1942, the Japanese conducted night bombing raids on Calcutta which, while not on the scale of European bombing raids, had a significant effect on the city's life. Calcutta's port was receiving supplies important for building up Allied strength in the Far East, whilst its factories were producing material for the war effort. The raids caused 25 killed and 139 injured but no buildings of any substance collapsed and the only military target, the oil refinery, was only slightly damaged.[218] Despite this over 350,000 people left the city and although many skilled workers stayed in the mills and factories the public services suffered most:

> The absence of cleaners left the city with piles of rotting rubbish in the streets; despite mid-winter the stench grew and there was a danger of Calcutta becoming the centre of an epidemic.[219]

It was imperative to stop the Japanese raiders before the next suitable night bombing period and the situation deteriorated further. A.C.M. Pierse requested a flight of night-fighters from the Air Staff and he was quickly sent a flight of A.I. equipped Beaufighters from 89 Squadron in the Middle East. These aircraft became the nucleus for 176 Squadron which served in the Far East for the rest of the war.

Eight Beaufighters arrived at Dum-Dum airfield (Calcutta) on 14th January 1943 with a mixture of Mark I and VI aircraft. All these aircraft were equipped with A.I. radar and their crews had considerable experience of intercepting Axis aircraft in the Middle East. Within a day of arriving the Squadron was in action at 21.45hrs. On 15th January Flight Sergeant Arthur Pring and his radar operator, Warrant Officer Cyril Phillips, were vectored to intercept a raid on Calcutta:

217 Innes, *Beaufighters over Burma, No.27 Squadron, R.A.F. 1942-1945*, p.51.
218 TNA, Air 41/36, *The Campaigns in the Far East Volume III, India Command*, p.66.
219 Ibid.

Various vectors given G.C.I. A.I. contact made 2256 by F/Sgt Pring. Three E/A destroyed (modified Army 97 H/B) 20 miles S.S.W. of Khuha Confirmed by F/O Gray.[220]

The three Sallys were from the 98th *Sentai* and all were confirmed by the Japanese as lost in the action.[221] Four nights later on 19th January three Lilys from the 8th *Sentai* approached Calcutta whilst two Beaufighters from 176 Squadron were on patrol. Flying Officer Charles Crombie and his radar operator Warrant Officer Ray Moss were controlled onto the incoming raiders:

F/O Crombie and Sgt Fisher scrambled. F/O Crombie vectored by G.C.I. on to 4 Army 97 H/B approaching Calcutta up Hoogly [sic] River. Two E/A destroyed (confirmed) and a further probable.[222]

According to Japanese records only one of the bombers was destroyed whilst the others returned to their base, whilst Crombie and Moss had to safely abandon their aircraft after it had been hit by Japanese defensive fire.[223] In two nights the Japanese had lost four bombers and the obvious power of the Beaufighter operating at night caused the commander of the 5th *Hikodan* to order the immediate cessation of night raids on Calcutta.[224] The interceptions had a dramatic effect on the night offensive on Calcutta as Japanese raids virtually ceased for a year and the life of the city quickly returned to normal as fears of the raids diminished. 176 Squadron's Operations Record Book shows a series of practice scrambles, training and patrols for the next few months but no actual interceptions of Japanese raiders.

As opposed to early actions in the theatre all the necessary factors were present for the Beaufighter's success as a night fighter. The aircraft was modern, fit for purpose, well armed and capable of intercepting night raiders, particularly bombers. The crews were also well-trained in their tasks and all had brought experience with them from the Middle East; Pring and Phillips had already shot down three Axis bombers over Egypt and Malta. Lastly the crews had at their disposal excellent A.I. radar which they efficiently exploited. Furthermore, it should be recognized that by the end of 1942 radar coverage of Calcutta had improved significantly and this was paramount in assisting 176 Squadron's crews:

[I]t must be remembered that the success of the Beaufighters belonged in part to the greatly improved warning system without which the Beaufighters could not

---

220 TNA, Air 27/1112, 176 Squadron Operations Record Book, 16th January 1943.
221 Shores, *Air War for Burma*, p.50.
222 TNA, Air 27/1112, 176 Squadron Operations Record Book, 20th January 1943.
223 Shores, *Air War for Burma*, p.53.
224 Ibid.

have positioned themselves near enough to enemy aircraft to make use of their A.I. radar equipment.[225]

The Beaufighters and their crews had shown the Japanese could be beaten at night. However, whilst it possessed long range, it did not have sufficient performance to engage Japanese single-seat day fighters, and now it was a matter of waiting until Spitfires arrived to complete the process by day. However, it would take until September 1943 for them to arrive. The next section will discuss why it took so long for this fighter to arrive in the Far East.

The Spitfire is one of the most iconic fighters of the Second World War and like the Hurricane had the distinction of serving from the first day of the war until the last although its later marks were bigger and faster. Earlier in the war the Spitfire's capabilities were such that German aircrew in the Battles of France and Britain claimed they were shot down by this aircraft rather than the Hurricane which Peter Townsend has described as 'Spitfire Snobbery'.[226] The first fighter Spitfire to reach India in late 1943, the Mark V, was armed with two 20mm cannon and four .303 inch machine guns, and crucially had a rate of climb, on paper, to 20,000 feet, nearly two minutes faster than the Hurricane IIC.[227] Given this rate of climb and a service ceiling of 37,000 feet it was ideal to take advantage of the dive and zoom tactics as well as intercepting the high flying Japanese Dinah reconnaissance aircraft.

The Spitfire's arrival in India however was delayed by over eight months as proposals to send the aircraft can be traced to December 1942. A.V.M. Ronald Ivelaw-Chapman, Director of Planning, wrote on 20th December:

> I think the time has come when we must raise the question of creating a Spitfire pattern in India from its present, somewhat nebulous level to one of a rigid programme.[228]

Despite 100 Spitfires being produced per month for the TORCH landings, Ivelaw-Chapman proposed to eventually re-equip all the single-engine fighter squadrons in India with Spitfires, except those equipped with Hurricanes for fighter-reconnaissance duties. He also wanted to form a small "spearhead" of Spitfire squadrons for air defence before the 1943 monsoon began in May 1943.[229] The shipments would begin in January with enough aircraft to equip one squadron and later shipments would

225 TNA, Air 41/36, *The Campaigns in the Far East Volume III, India Command*, p.39.
226 Townsend, *Duel of Eagles*, p.237. During the Battle of Britain three German aircraft were shot down by Hurricanes for every two by Spitfires.
227 See Appendix II.
228 TNA, Air 2/5498, India Command: Spitfires for India, 1942-1943, report 20th December 1942.
229 Ibid.

increase to a level where two squadrons per month would be equipped.[230] However, by the start of the monsoon not one Spitfire was despatched to India let alone a squadron's worth. The delay was mainly due to production difficulties as well as the commitment to provide other overseas commands and Fighter Command in Britain. Furthermore, at the beginning of 1943 Britain was honouring its commitment to the Soviet Union by sending refurbished Spitfire Vs and new Hurricanes.[231] In March 1943 a revised delivery date of May 1943 was given:

> You have recently ruled that the allotment of Spitfires to overseas commands, including Australia, is to be 290 a month and that 25 of these are to be sent to India from May onwards.[232]

Despite some discussions on whether the Spitfire Vs destined for India should have different performance parameters as regards engine and wing configurations, May was still quoted as the start of the shipments to India:

> India's quote is 25 per month beginning in May and Spitfire V production dies in November, so after that month the despatches to India will consist of Vs (re-conditioned), VIIIs or IXs. The quota of 25 is calculated to re-equip about five of India's fighter squadrons with Spitfires by the end of 1943.[233]

On 16th April 1943 A.H.Q. India was informed by the Air Ministry that 25 tropicalised Spitfires per month were to be sent by sea starting in May and "The flow should start to arrive in India about mid-August."[234] However, the timetable of aircraft to be sent in May was not adhered to despite the Mediterranean being opened for supply ships in May 1943; four were despatched on 15th June with a further 22 on June 28th but these aircraft did not reach India until the end of August and there were some additional problems. Pierse asked for sufficient spares to be sent in advance of the Spitfires' arrival but according to one squadron pilot there was a breakdown in communications:

---

230 Ivelaw-Chapman was keen to emphasise that the Spitfires were to replace the Hurricanes and were not in addition.
231 TNA, Air 20/3904, Russia – Supply of Hurricanes and Spitfires; Price Alfred, *The Spitfire Story*, pp.139-140. The Soviets were unhappy with the supply of refurbished Spitfire Vs and would have preferred to receive Mark IXs and it took a visit of a three man Soviet Military Delegation to the Vickers factory to convince them of the quality of the refurbishment work.
232 TNA, Air 2/5498, Spitfires for India, D.W.O. to C.A.S. 11th March 1943. It will be noted that only 25 of the 290 Spitfires mentioned, 8.6%, were allocated for India.
233 Ibid, D.O. Ops to V.C.A.S. 29th March 1943. Mark IX Spitfires were never sent to India. Against the last two lines of this passage an unidentified hand has written in pencil, "doubtful."
234 Ibid.

I can recall the uproar when it was discovered that we had no spares so flying was restricted … Apparently some base type in Delhi, when all these bits and pieces were consigned to our theatre of war, knew we didn't have any Spits, so sent them back to the Middle East. What a shambles![235]

Bengal Command reported:

We are at present faced with a situation where we have Spitfire aircraft in the Command which we cannot operate as the unit equipment has not arrived, although warning of the arrival of these aircraft was given over three months previously.[236]

Despite these early setbacks the Spitfire eventually arrived in India with 607 Squadron taking delivery of their new aircraft in early September 1943 followed over the next month by 615 and 136 Squadrons.

The introduction of the Spitfire to India was clearly a planned but protracted move and one which brings into question another description of the deployment. In April 1943 Wing Commander Paul Richey, a fighter pilot with vast experience of European operations, arrived in Delhi and was given the job of assessing fighter tactics in India by the A.O.C. Bengal Command A.V.M. Thomas Williams. After visiting squadrons and assessing how the defenders dealt with raids on India, Richey submitted his reports in May 1943. These were critical of procedures and pressed for the introduction of Spitfires into the theatre. Richey later related the story to Norman Franks that Williams said:

Of course there is no doubt the Hurricane is not up to the job and we must have Spitfires. Bill Williams called me into his office, smilingly congratulated me on the report, then took out a pair of scissors and said, "There's just one thing I can't let through." He then proceeded to cut out the sentence about Hurricanes and Spitfires, and destroyed it saying "That's true, and both you and I know it, but we must never let the boys [the pilots] suspect it – it would destroy morale." As if they didn't know it![237]

Richey submitted his report to the Fighter Operations H.Q. in Delhi and soon after, Williams told Richey, "Paul we're getting Spits! How would you like to take command of the first Wing?"[238] Franks wrote:

---

235 Flying Officer Wilfred Goold, quoted in Franks, *Spitfires Over The Arakan*, p.22.
236 TNA, Air 23/1926, Despatch on Air Operations Bengal Command, 21st June 1943 to 15th November 1943, paragraph 29.
237 Richey, with Franks, *Fighter Pilot's Summer*, p.200.
238 Ibid.

As far as Paul was concerned, he had helped, by whatever means, to get Spitfires to the fighter pilots in India/Burma and they started to arrive in October 1943.[239]

There is obviously a disparity in this account as by the time Richey had submitted his report in May Spitfires were en route to the theatre although there is no evidence to disprove Richey's reports helped promote future acquisition of this valuable aircraft.

By the middle of September 1943 the first Spitfire Vs had been accepted into service and instantly impressed their pilots, "Golly – the thrust after the Hurricane! It literally forced me into the seat and by the time I'd settled myself I was at a couple of thousand feet."[240] Flying Officer G. Falconer recalled:

> We did the same work with the Spits as we did with the Hurries, a bit faster though! They were a real break for us, as the extra speed, manoeuvrability and better vision gave us a better chance to do something about the air raids we were getting.[241]

Despite the pilots' enthusiasm the Spitfire's short range proved a problem in the Far East as it had in Europe, especially given the multiplicity of tasks allotted to it. A.V.M. Williams wrote:

> While the Spitfire remains an outstandingly fine fighter for defence and for combat within a narrow range, it cannot really pull its weight in this theatre unless satisfactorily pressurised jettison tanks of 60-90 gallons are provided. These I have asked for repeatedly, so far without result.[242]

and Pierse, on 6th November 1943:

> Spitfire or Mustangs of the latest type are what we want. I am impressed with reports of the latter and, if they come up to expectations, I shall press for the Mustangs because of their longer range.[243]

But the R.A.F. never received the Mustang in India. It continued to use the Spitfire, which was eventually equipped with long-range fuel tanks in 1944.[244]

---

239 Ibid, p.202.
240 Flight Sergeant Frank Wilding quoted in Franks, *Spitfires over the Arakan*, p.25.
241 Ibid, p.27. There is no first name available for Falconer.
242 TNA, Air 23/1926, Despatch on Air Operations Bengal Command, 21st June 1943 to 15th November 1943, Appendix J.
243 TNA, Air 23/2153, Minutes to S.A.C.S.E.A. 1943-1944.
244 There were some initial technical difficulties with the Spitfire's 90-gallon tank at first as it would not jettison without slowing the aircraft down.

Although the Spitfires arrived in September they were not in proper action until early November as the squadrons were required to train on their new aircraft and to attend the A.F.T.U.. 615 Squadron participated in its first scramble with the Spitfire on 4th October 1943 when one aircraft took off to intercept a Japanese reconnaissance aircraft, and although the Japanese aircraft was not found the Squadron diarist recorded the "performance of the Spitfire was most gratifying in climbing power, manoeuvrability and speed."[245] On 16th October the Squadron went to the A.F.T.U. for a fortnight's course on air fighting and tactics, which included deflection shooting, range estimation and camera gun attacks on towed drogues.[246] It should be noted that the squadron had considerable combat experience with their Hurricanes but the course ensured these pilots would make the best use of their Spitfires, and this, of course, applied to the other two equipped units. The first three 615 Squadron successes are indicative of the climbing ability and speed which had been long awaited in the theatre. On 8th November, two Spitfires were scrambled to intercept a Dinah flying over Chittagong. Catching it at 25,000 feet and sending it down, "they overhauled it easily and shot it down in flames."[247] There was further success on 10th and 16th November when Dinahs were once again intercepted at 29,000 and 26,000 feet respectively. Both were shot down.

A.H.Q. India had stressed to 222 and 225 Groups how vital the destruction of reconnaissance aircraft had been in the Mediterranean Theatre stating it was of "cardinal importance" in India to achieve the same result.[248] As the Spitfires had been able to intercept the Dinahs which the Hurricanes could not, they had blinded Japanese planners to Allied movements whose reconnaissance sorties were thereafter limited to short-range flights over the Burma front rather than long range missions over ports and installations.[249] The interception of Dinahs by Spitfires was thus a major contribution to the Allies' war effort as between December 1943 and February 1945, 17 Dinahs were destroyed by Spitfires.

The Spitfire Mark V began to be phased out of production in late 1943 and India started receiving the definitive two-stage Merlin powered Mark VIII variant in January 1944. The Mark IX, mentioned earlier, which did not see service in the Far East, was a stop-gap measure introduced to counter the German *Focke-Wulf* Fw190 in Europe until the Mark VIII was introduced into operational service.[250] The Mark VIII was powered by a more powerful Merlin engine and although it was slightly

---

245 TNA, Air 27/2123, 615 Squadron Operations Record Book, 4th October 1943.
246 Ibid, 1st November 1943.
247 Ibid, 8th November 1943.
248 TNA, Air 23/2194, Demi-Official Letters between A.O.C-in-C India and A.O.C. Bengal (later 3rd T.A.F.), 2nd November 1943.
249 TNA, Air 41/64, *The Campaigns in the Far East; Volume IV South East Asia November 1943 to August 1945*, p.39.
250 The stop-gap Mark IX was produced in greater numbers than the Mark VIII, 5,665 against 1,658.

bigger and heavier than the Mark V its performance was improved giving it a rate of climb to 20,000 feet of 6.7 minutes and a ceiling of 40,500 feet.[251] The Mark VIII was considered as one of the best Spitfires produced as it had a number of refinements such as the four bladed propeller, a retractable tailwheel which gave the aircraft an extra 5 mph and multi-ejector exhausts which increased speed by another 4 mph.[252] The first two squadrons equipped with the Mark VIII, 81 and 152, had seen extensive service in the Mediterranean flying Spitfires and brought with them valuable combat experience. However, flying the Spitfire VIII against nimble Japanese fighter aircraft was not easy as Flying Officer Dudley Barnett, a Mark VIII pilot from 136 Squadron, noted in his diary:

> A bad day. 81 got a completely new opinion of Japs. Reckon M.E. and U.K. squadrons would be very surprised. Most of their (81's) [sic] aircraft u/s for rippled skins and warped engine bearings! We've a bit of it too.[253]

This was written after air combat in February 1944, and clearly the Spitfire's technical advantage over the Oscar was not enough to completely counter the latter's advantage in manoeuvrability.

While there was a steady increase of Spitfire squadrons in the theatre there were never enough to satisfy demand. By Christmas 1943 there were three Spitfire squadrons in India, at the end of January 1944 this had increased to six, although two of these had only just arrived from the Middle East and one (155) was converting its Mohawks to the Spitfire VIII. On 5th December 1943 the Japanese mounted a series of raids against Calcutta, comprising bombers and fighters, which did not cause much damage, but did amount to a moral victory as few of their aircraft were shot down. The R.A.F. report of the raid was highly critical of the way defending fighters had been controlled from the ground. It also submitted that Hurricanes were now obsolete as interceptors.[254] There were no Spitfire squadrons available in the immediate area. All three were scrambled from distant bases throughout the raid; only one aircraft from 136 Squadron made contact at the aircraft's maximum range before crash landing out of fuel.[255] After a few more raids when ground controllers were criticized for their directions, the controlling began to improve significantly with the result that Spitfire pilots were able to intercept successfully. For example, on 31st December 136 Squadron intercepted a raid on minesweepers off Akyab, climbing to 30,000 feet

---

251 See Appendix III.
252 TNA, Air 16/1162, Lecture on the Development of the Spitfire by Group Captain Worstall, 1946, p.8. No first name is available for Worstall.
253 Shores, *Air War for Burma*, p.162.
254 TNA, Air 20/5696, O.R.S. Report Number N.8. The R.A.F. pilots claimed one Japanese fighter destroyed, one probably destroyed and four damaged; their losses amounted to eight Hurricanes lost.
255 After the raid 136 Squadron was recalled to Calcutta for defensive duties.

before diving on the Japanese formation 9,000 feet below; the R.A.F. pilots claimed eight bombers and three fighters destroyed.[256] Clearly the Spitfire was a match for the Japanese but the lack of numbers was a drawback. Flight Lieutenant Gordon Conway remembered:

> The controllers had only three Spitfire squadrons to play with and obviously couldn't afford to launch the whole force in case we were all caught on the ground refuelling at the same time. So their tendency was to scramble a single squadron in response initially, and we would normally be out-numbered until a second squadron was sent to help, when it became clear that the raid wasn't a feint and needed more response.[257]

The controllers and defenders were not assisted by the early warning system's inaccurate estimates of the numbers of Japanese aircraft; on 4th February 136 Squadron was scrambled to meet a raid initially thought to consist of 20 aircraft, but it grew to 100. Conway remembered, "Our hitherto high scoring rate slowed to a trickle, for under such pressure the problem was how to survive."[258] This was to be a regular occurrence. On 5th February 607 Squadron were scrambled to intercept a raid near Bawli Bazaar which grew from 12 aircraft to over 100; on 12th April ten Spitfires engaged over 30 Oscars and on 17th April two Spitfire squadrons engaged 50 Oscars escorting six bombers. Furthermore, it was not merely a matter of aircraft numbers because, as explained earlier, the Japanese adopted new tactics to counter the Allied dive and zoom. They stacked their aircraft formations from low to high level so that as the R.A.F. fighters dived through the 'Beehive' formation they would find themselves surrounded by Japanese fighters.[259] During the 5th February raid the Japanese fighters were flying between low-level and 18,000 feet, and on 17th April from low-level to 30,000 feet with bombers flying in the middle at 15,000 feet. Given these circumstances the Spitfires and supporting Hurricanes could only hope to break up and disrupt the Japanese raids, rather than destroy Japanese aircraft en masse.

The next obstacle was the varying efficiency of the early warning and controlling organisation because the Spitfire, even accounting for its excellent rate of climb, required early warning and accurate height information. Accurate information was not always possible. Between November 1943 and February 1944 various raids were reported giving heights that were either too low or too high. Speaking of intercepting a Dinah, Sergeant Guy Watson remembered:

---

256 Shores, *Air War for Burma*, p.142. Both 615 and 136 Squadrons had been scrambled to meet this raid, but only the latter made contact.
257 Franks, *Spitfires Over The Arakan*, p.114.
258 Ibid, p.147.
259 TNA, Air 23/2640, Allied Fighter Aircraft – Tactics, 1943-1945.

> The radar was very bad on height finding, extraordinarily bad. We always seemed to be 1,000 or even 2,000 feet below them, whereas we should have been above them.[260]

and Flight Sergeant Bill Davies recalled:

> Quite an important factor in radar controlled interceptions was the lack of accurate height finding. It was always disconcerting to have the target's height suddenly change by the odd ten thousand feet. This was not the controller's fault as interpreting their gear in those days was more of an art than a science.[261]

However, when the controllers and radar got it right, the Spitfires were able to achieve good results; as noted earlier on 31st December 136 Squadron was successfully directed to intercept the raid over Akyab, Flight Lieutenant Conway writing, "it was one of those days when everything went right."[262] Similar comments were recorded in connection with successfully intercepted raids on 15th January, "By excellent controlling"; 5th February, "excellent control" and 15th February; "up sun and ideal."[263]

As the campaign moved east into Burma it became more difficult for the Spitfire to operate successfully because of shortcomings in the early warning system. A detachment of 81 Squadron Spitfires VIIIs stationed at the Chindit landing ground at Broadway was covered by a mobile light-weight radar set, but it only gave short warning of Japanese attack. On 13th March 1944 40 Oscars attacked the landing site and the radar gave the detachment little time to take off and meet the raid and one Spitfire was destroyed as it became airborne:

> Today 30 plus enemy fighters tried to strafe our new base. RDF very bad; only got five minutes warning. Sergeant Campbell and I were last to scramble. Bounced over 'drome – Campbell killed immediately.[264]

Four days later the Japanese attacked Broadway again and caught 81 Squadron; two pilots were killed, one on the ground, five aircraft were destroyed and one badly damaged.[265] Subsequently 81 Squadron withdrew from Broadway to Kangla and from then onwards the protection of Broadway depended on air patrols, or once the landing

---

260 Franks, *Spitfires Over The Arakan*, p.44.
261 Ibid, p.158.
262 Ibid, p.100.
263 TNA, Air 27/953, 136 Squadron Operations Record Book, 15th January 1944; TNA, Air 27/2094, 607 Squadron Operations Record Book, 5th February 1944; Flight Sergeant Albert Swan, 81 Squadron, quoted in Franks, *Spitfires Over The Arakan*, p.180.
264 Flying Officer Larry Cronin from his diary quoted in Shores, *Air War for Burma*, p.180.
265 See Chapter 1, p.87 of this book for the description of this action.

ground was under attack the squadron would be alerted by telephone.[266] Once the siege of Imphal began, Spitfire squadrons were sent to defend the Plain but suffered from a lack of early warning which became progressively worse as the Japanese advanced towards Imphal and overran radar and observer positions. The Japanese took advantage of the weak spots in the warning chain by flying low and breaking their formations into small sections of two or three which made both detection and interception difficult. Patrols by Allied aircraft were not considered to be feasible as fuel needed to be transported into Imphal and could not be wasted. The Allies countered this threat in a number of ways. As soon as unidentified aircraft were reported approaching the area fighters were immediately scrambled to save time and if the weather favoured a Japanese attack aircraft were sent to known exit points to catch the raiders as they returned to their home bases. Furthermore, squadron pilots were positioned on hilltops around Imphal equipped with aircraft pattern radios to report on raiders' progress directly to the defending pilots.[267] The eventual solution was the adoption of an air corridor for transport aircraft to fly along which was patrolled by Allied fighters during daylight hours. All these elaborate methods assisted in protecting the transport and ground attack aircraft, and it should not be forgotten that important attrition was being afflicted on Japanese units by the Americans' counter-air offensive.

Between October 1944 and May 1945 Japanese raids became infrequent and spasmodic; Japanese assets reduced as a result of attrition and transfer, and the remaining raids were usually carried out at low-level and in small numbers which presented the defenders with problems. A.C.M. Sir Keith Park wrote in his despatch:

> Even when the temporary halt around Mandalay and Spitfires were able to occupy the Shwebo and Monywa airfield groups, air supply was proceeding over a hundred and thirty mile front which the four available squadrons of Spitfires were hard pressed to cover in conjunction with their other defensive duties.[268]

As the Fourteenth Army pushed eastwards and captured airfields the possibilities of providing effective early warning diminished owing to the inconsistent mobile radar sets and speed of the Allied advance. Fortunately as Japanese air assets reduced, their raids became more of a nuisance value than a serious threat. They caused some damage but never enough to seriously interfere with the Allied progress through Burma. Moreover the Spitfire continued to successfully intercept Japanese reconnaissance

266 TNA, Air 41/64, *The Campaigns in the Far East; Volume IV South East Asia November 1943 to August 1945*, p.79 and Franks, *The Air Battle for Imphal*, p.35.
267 TNA, Air 41/64, *The Campaigns in the Far East; Volume IV South East Asia November 1943 to August 1945*, pp.86-88.
268 TNA, Air 23/4665, Despatch on Air Operations by Air Chief Marshal Sir Keith Park, 1st January 1944 to 31st December 1945, p.19. Park had assumed command of A.C.S.E.A. on 25th February 1945.

aircraft and provide important air patrols but the number of scrambles and air activity reduced significantly in the first few months of 1945:

	February 1945	May 1945
Scramble	51	7
Patrols	2,063	1,192
Escorts	144	35[269]

While its role as an interceptor decreased the Spitfire soon found employment as a ground attack fighter in support of the Fourteenth Army advance.

Allied Aircraft engaged in the Counter-Air Offensive

The preceding section demonstrated how the right types of aircraft in conjunction with other criteria made a positive contribution towards air superiority in the defensive role. This section will analyse the relative effectiveness of Allied aircraft types when engaged in the counter-air offensive role.

The counter-air offensive in the Far East had an important role particularly when effective early warning systems and defensive fighters were lacking as was sometimes inevitable with a front stretching over 700 miles. Following the initial Japanese attacks in December 1941 the R.A.F. attempted to reduce Japanese air strength by attacking enemy airbases with Buffalo fighters or Bristol Blenheim bombers. The twin-engine Blenheim was classified as a high-speed bomber before the war but by 1942 it had been rendered obsolete by single-engine fighters which were faster and more manoeuvrable. Most of the Blenheims in the Far East in December 1941 were the Mark I, which could carry a 1,000 lb bomb load. It was armed with two machine guns, one being located in a power operated dorsal turret, but its top speed of 285 mph at 15,000 feet was insufficient to protect it against enemy fighters.[270] On 9th December six Blenheims from Butterworth airfield in Malaya attacked Japanese airfields at Singora and Sungei Patani without fighter escort; three of the Blenheims were lost. During the same afternoon the remaining Blenheims were detailed to return to Singora, but as they were taking off a low-level raid by Japanese aircraft destroyed and damaged all but one aircraft which was already airborne. The Blenheim's pilot, Squadron Leader Arthur Scarf, decided to continue to the target alone where he attacked enemy aircraft and buildings before being overwhelmed by enemy fighters on his way home.[271] Despite such acts of bravery this and similar attacks did little to reduce Japanese air strength.

269 TNA, Air 41/64, *The Campaigns in the Far East; Volume IV South East Asia November 1943 to August 1945*, pp.370-391.
270 TNA, Supp 9/1, British Types 1941-1945.
271 Bowyer, *For Valour: The Air V.C.s*, p.263 and Lake, *Blenheim Squadrons of World War 2*, p.89. Scarf died after successfully landing his aircraft and subsequently received the Victoria Cross. The other two members of his crew survived the attack.

A counter-air offensive in 1941 was unlikely to succeed as the Allies had too few suitable aircraft and these were committed to too many tasks against a superior enemy.

The events at the beginning of December 1941 had demonstrated the attributes of a successful offensive fighter. For example, the Japanese Zero which had the operational range of a bomber, with the armament and manoeuvrability of a fighter albeit at the expense of armour and pilot protection. At the start of 1942 Wavell asked the Air Ministry to provide long-range fighters for the Eastern Command but his request met with some difficulties as, in the main, such aircraft did not exist. The R.A.F. had long asked for a true long-range fighter that could escort bombers whilst retaining the ability to defend itself but nothing had been forthcoming. Portal told Churchill in May 1941:

> The long-range fighter whether built specifically as such, or whether given increased range by fitting extra tanks, will be at a disadvantage compared with the short range high performance fighter.[272]

Both the Spitfire and Hurricane had been designed as short-range interceptors, and neither had the range to participate in deep interdiction operations without auxiliary fuel tanks. Portal was correct about the difficulty of successfully adapting the Hurricane as its performance with long range tanks in the Far East did not match that of Japanese fighters, but the lack of any development in adapting any other fighter, such as the Spitfire, would eventually prove a serious oversight.[273] The only operational British long-range aircraft available at the beginning of 1942 were the De Havilland Mosquito, which was only just entering service in Britain, and the Beaufighter which was in demand in Europe and the Middle East as an interdictor and night-fighter. The Air Ministry informed A.H.Q. India on 21st April 1942 that the Mosquito was experiencing "teething problems" and:

> The need for long-range fighters your command already fully realized here and ways and means of providing Beaufighters are being urgently considered in consultation Admiralty.[274]

The Beaufighter was introduced into Far East service at the end of 1942 but its impact on the counter-air offensive was minimal owing to its lack of numbers. The Americans possessed the P-40 which had a longer range than the Hurricane with a similar performance, but these aircraft were largely based in the north of India

---

272 Terraine, *The Right of the Line*, p.703.
273 Ibid, Appendix G, p.703. Terraine considered the problem to be a blind spot in Portal's war direction, as Portal believed a long-range fighter could never hold its own against a short-range fighter.
274 TNA, Air 23/2135, Far East Operations: A.O.C.-in-C., Air Marshal Sir Richard Peirse; personal signals to and from the Air Ministry, 1942.

defending the transport route into China and were in short supply. There were therefore limited resources for a counter-air offensive at the end of the monsoon in October 1942.

The only suitable aircraft the R.A.F. possessed was the American built Curtiss P-36 Mohawk, a single-engine fighter aircraft armed, in British service, with six .303 inch machine guns and provision for bombs and auxiliary fuel tanks.[275] Common to most American aircraft the Mohawk had a large internal fuel capacity which gave the aircraft a range of 620 miles in comparison to the Hurricane IIC's 460.[276] This long-range ability made the aircraft ideal for bomber escort and interdiction operations, and combined with its manoeuvrability made it popular with its pilots:

> Make no mistake, the Mohawk was a good aircraft. Beautiful to fly, very manoeuvrable and very reliable. A number of pilots returned safely to base with cylinder pots shot up; a bullet anywhere in the cooling system of a Merlin and you'd had it. The Cyclone air-cooled engine of the Mohawk could take a lot of punishment and still put-put along. The weaknesses of the Mohawk were, of course, poor height performance and lack of fire power – six machine guns was not very good. But she was a real nice aircraft and did us proud.[277]

However, there were only two squadrons of these aircraft in the Far East, 5 and 155, and they had to perform many tasks in addition to bomber escort and interdiction: tactical reconnaissance; ground support and air defence to accompany the Hurricane squadrons. Furthermore, they were heavily committed at the end of 1942 and beginning of 1943 supporting the Army during the first Arakan campaign and resisting Japanese air attacks on airfields and installations.

The lack of entirely suitable aircraft in sufficient numbers resulted in a counter-air offensive by medium and heavy bombers which had mixed effects. Initially, the heaviest British bomber in India was the Vickers Wellington, a twin engine medium bomber capable of carrying a 4,500 lbs bomb load over a normal range of 1,470 miles. From September 1942 it was joined by R.A.F. Consolidated B-24 Liberators, an American built four-engine heavy bomber capable of carrying an 8,000 lbs bomb load over a normal range of 1,540 miles.[278] While such ranges encompassed Japanese bases and the bomb loads represented lethal capabilities, if such aircraft were used by day they needed long-range fighter escort which was lacking. Whilst using these aircraft (and others such as the Blenheim and Lockheed Hudson) to attack the main Japanese bases by night may have destroyed facilities, equipment and runways, it did little to

275 TNA, Supp 9/2, American Types 1941-1945.
276 Ibid and Supp 9/1 British Types 1941-1945. Both these figures represent the range without auxiliary fuel tanks. See Appendix IV.
277 Squadron Leader Guy Hogan quoted in Franks, *Hurricanes over the Arakan*, p.159.
278 *Jane's Fighting Aircraft of World War II*, p.146 and p.216.

destroy Japanese aircraft on the ground as the Japanese dispersed their aircraft to airfields out of range of the attacks, or kept them on well concealed airstrips. However, there were positive effects from the bomber offensive. By pushing Japanese aircraft to rearward areas it gave Allied aircraft some room to operate in central and upper Burma without fear of interception. It also reduced the weight of air attack against India; and enabled Allied aircraft to operate from advanced airfields.[279] However, the effects of the counter-air offensive did not seriously reduce Japanese air strength. What was required were more suitable aircraft the first of which became operational at the beginning of 1943.

The Beaufighter met some of the attributes for a suitable long-range fighter. It was heavily armed with four 20mm cannons and six .303 inch machine guns, was capable of carrying a 1000 lb bomb load or eight rocket projectiles and, in addition, the aircraft had a range of 1,480 miles and a top speed of 315mph at 14,000 feet.[280] These specifications set the aircraft apart from existing British types but there were operational difficulties. The Beaufighter whilst fast enough to outrun Japanese aircraft at full throttle was not manoeuvrable enough to engage single-engine Japanese fighters in aerial combat.[281] The second problem was that between January and September 1943 only 27 Squadron was equipped with interdictor Beaufighters and an examination of this unit's Operations Record Books shows it being tasked with a wide range of targets including rail, road and coastal transport.[282] The lack of Beaufighter numbers combined with the J.A.A.F. being stationed in rearward areas resulted in only a handful of sorties being flown against airfields and even fewer Japanese aircraft claimed as destroyed.

The combination of heavy bombers and a few suitable fighter aircraft being used in the counter-air offensive did not produce any tangible effect on Japanese air strength and Craven and Cate observed, "the interdiction program in central Burma had not succeeded by the end of 1943."[283] Clearly long-range fighters were required which could take the fight to the Japanese, and just as the introduction of the Spitfire represented a significant advance to air defence, so did the introduction of the American Lockheed Lightnings and North American Mustangs for counter-air operations.

The Lightning was a single-seat twin engine fighter that was armed with one 20mm cannon and four 0.5in machine guns and could carry up to 1,600 lbs of ordnance; significantly it had a range of up to 1,512 miles that could be increased with the addition of auxiliary fuel tanks.[284] The 459th F.S. who flew the Lightning was activated

---

279 TNA, Air 41/36, *The Campaigns in the Far East Volume III, India Command*, p.116.
280 TNA, Supp 9/1, British Types, 1941-1945.
281 Innes, *Beaufighters over Burma, No.27 Squadron, R.A.F. 1942-1945*, p.56.
282 TNA, Air 27/326, 27 Squadron Operations Record Books, 1st January 1924 to 31st December 1943 and Air 27/327, 27 Squadron Operations Record Book, 1st January 1944 to 31st December 1944.
283 Craven and Cate, *The Army Air Forces in World War II, Volume Four*, p.492.
284 Appendices 4 and 5.

in India in September 1943 with a core of experienced pilots supported by some new pilots from training schools. Along with their R.A.F. colleagues they attended the A.F.T.U. to learn about air and ground firing, their instructors becoming impressed with the rapid development of their techniques.[285] At the end of 1943 they were joined by the 530th F.S. equipped with the P-51A Mustang, a single-engine fighter which was armed with four .5 inch machine guns and could carry 1,000lbs of bombs or rockets; crucially the aircraft had a basic range of 1,500 miles which could be increased with the addition of two drop tanks.[286] Furthermore, the Allies' capability was increased at the beginning of 1944 with the arrival of the 1st A.C.G. also equipped with Mustangs and experienced pilots. The deployment of both these aircraft types would lead to a fundamental shift in counter-air tactics during the crucial first six months of 1944.

Prior to the beginning of 1944 the counter-air campaign was defined by its aircraft, bombers capable of attacking known airfields but with a lack of suitable long-range fighters able to act as escorts or to attack Japanese aircraft on their airstrips. With the introduction of the Lightning and Mustang, Japanese aircraft were vulnerable to attack in most locations and by aircraft that were their equal or superiors in aerial combat. The offensive was assisted by the intelligence services locating Japanese airstrips and units, and the Japanese bringing their aircraft forward to support their westward campaign. However, the Lightning's and Mustang's importance should not be underestimated. The air defence of the various landing strips was compromised by an inconsistent early warning system so the capability to reduce and interfere with Japanese air assets was vital, but now:

> These aircraft were now able to seek out the enemy at his forward airfields and owing to the apparent ineffectiveness of the Japanese warning system, they could often destroy his aircraft before they were airborne.[287]

Apart from airfield strikes and aggressive patrolling, tactics were also adopted to make best use of the Lightning's range and capabilities. For example, on 3rd March 1944 224 Group issued an instruction to the 459th F.S. which had its intention, "To operate 459 Squadron both on offensive and defensive sorties making full use of their long endurance and high performance at altitude."[288] In the event of a Japanese attack half of the 459th's aircraft would be scrambled for local defence, whilst the others would be despatched, with the help of intelligence, to intercept the Japanese aircraft as they returned to their bases short of fuel and ammunition. This reaped dividends

285 Stanaway, *P38 Lightning Aces of the Pacific and CBI*, p.79.
286 The 530th were also equipped with the A-36 Apache, a dive-bomber version of the Mustang.
287 TNA, Air 41/64, *The Campaigns in the Far East; Volume IV South East Asia November 1943 to August 1945*, p.69.
288 TNA, Air 25/950, 224 Group Operations Record Book (Appendices), 1st January 1944 to 31st March 1944. 224 Group Operation Instruction No. 4.

on 25th March when ten Lightnings were diverted to Shwebo and then to Anisakan where they found 36 Oscars returning to their base; the American pilots claimed nine probably shot down, three damaged and two aircraft destroyed on the ground.[289]

As the war continued the capabilities of American aircraft increased. At the start of 1945 the Mustang had evolved to the D variant, now armed with six 0.5in machine guns and powered by the British Merlin engine, which gave it superior performance, and a range, depending on tankage and load, of up to 2,250 miles.[290] In March 1945 aircraft from 2nd A.C.G. attacked the Japanese airfield at Don Muang in Siam, a trip equal to flying to Vienna and back from London.[291] Also introduced to service in the Far East during 1944 was the U.S. Republic P-47 Thunderbolt, another single-engine fighter, armed with eight .5 inch machine guns, the capability to carry 2,500 lbs of ordinance and a range extending from 737 to 2,100 miles depending on its fuel capacity.[292] Furthermore, the 1st A.C.G. occasionally used a variant of the North American B-25 Mitchell medium bomber on airfield interdiction operations which was equipped with eight fixed forward firing 0.5in machine guns and one .75mm cannon, in addition to its six 0.5in flexible machine guns.[293] Given the capabilities of these kinds of aircraft it was natural that the Americans would take a larger share in airfield attacks with only occasional sorties being flown, by the Beaufighter and later the Mosquito. The R.A.F.'s main fighters did not possess such ranges and this was commented on by a delegation from the Central Fighter Establishment following a visit to the theatre between February and April 1945, reporting:

> [M]ost of strategic bombing is done by long range heavies. To escort them, the R.A.F. in Burma has no fighter with sufficient range except the Thunderbolt. Escort is normally confined to airborne or supply operations … The lack of range of British fighters is a limiting factor on their full offensive role in this theatre. [294]

Apart from the Thunderbolt being used in R.A.F. service for ground attack as a Hurricane replacement, there was one other British type occasionally used in the counter-air role. The Mosquito F.B.VI was a high performance twin-engine fighter-bomber made almost entirely of wood which started to be delivered to India at the end of 1943. Armed with four 20mm cannons, four .303in machine guns, a 1000lb bomb load and a range of 1,120 miles, the aircraft was destined to replace the Beaufighter in the long-range interdictor role, but its introduction and subsequent Far Eastern

---

289 TNA, Air 41/64, *The Campaigns in the Far East; Volume IV South East Asia November 1943 to August 1945*, p.75.

290 TNA, Supp 9/2, American Types 1941-1945.

291 Don Muang was 780 miles away from the nearest Allied airfield.

292 Appendices 4 and 5.

293 The B-25H carried six 0.5in flexible machine guns, two in a turret, two in the tail, and two firing from waist positions in the fuselage. In addition it could carry 1000lbs of bombs.

294 TNA, Air 23/2835, Tactics Branch Visit to S.E.A.C., 1st February to 7th April 1945.

service was blighted by technical difficulties. It was originally thought that the glue holding the airframe together was susceptible to the high humidity in the Far East as it melted with disastrous results, but later it was found that the problem was actually insufficient glue.[295] By the beginning of 1945 these aircraft were being used for interdiction operations, one of their targets being Japanese airfields, and 221 Group's Mosquitos were proposed to be used in a similar role as 459th's Lightnings; after Japanese raids aircraft were to be despatched to specific airfields with intelligence assistance to intercept Japanese aircraft as they returned to their bases.[296] However, by the time the aircraft was fully operational the Japanese air threat had reduced leaving the Mosquito to concentrate on communication targets.

The counter-air offensive had vindicated the need for a high performance long-range fighter capable of carrying heavy weapons and taking part in aerial combat over the enemy's territory. Lack of development of British types resulted in an offensive for eighteen months limited to heavy and medium bombers bombing main airfields with minimal effect on Japanese air strength. When the Beaufighter was introduced it was in small numbers and it did little to reduce Japanese air assets. However, the need for a long-range fighter was met by the American Lightning and Mustang at just the right time at the beginning of 1944 when its squadrons addressed the difficulties of defending airstrips by attacking Japanese aircraft at their bases. The first half of 1944 represented the most crucial months of the counter-air campaign and, although the results may not have been as severe as previously thought, it hindered and thus reduced the Japanese air threat. Without the long-range fighter this result would have been harder to achieve.

Conclusions

Although this chapter has dealt with the factors of aircrew, tactics and aircraft separately for clarity, it has demonstrated that they were interdependent. Furthermore, the chapter has shown that each of the factors needed to be addressed and to achieve the same high standard if air supremacy was to be gained and maintained.

Japan achieved air superiority in 1941 and 1942 through having well-trained and experienced aircrew flying aircraft types which were suitable for combat tasks. Furthermore, their air tactics had been refined against Chinese and Soviet adversaries. The R.A.F. possessed no such advantages. Fighter pilots in Malaya were a mixture of inexperienced men fresh from training schools, those who had transferred from other aircraft and a small number who were experienced but in campaigns fought in Europe and the Middle East. Although their air fighting tactics were quickly adapted to counter Japanese fighters' manoeuvrability, this was not made easier because of their

---

295 Bowman, *Mosquito; Fighter/Fighter-Bomber Units 1942-1945*, p.82.
296 TNA, Air 20/5670, Survey of 221 Group Operations, 4th December 1944 to 3rd May 1945, p.7.

aircraft. Owing to priorities being greater to other theatres combined with undue optimism or refusal to accept intelligence reports, the Buffalo was sent to the Far East, and although some experienced pilots achieved good results, the majority could not. It must also be remembered that the dive and zoom tactic depended on height advantage which the early-warning system could not always supply, and which the Buffalo could not consistently reach. Taken together these factors represented a dangerous weakness in air defence terms.

The situation did not improve when reinforcements were sent. Pre-war plans to reinforce the Far East from the Middle East failed because at the end of 1941 the Middle East command was engaged in fierce fighting, and ships and aircraft were in short supply. The Hurricanes that were diverted to the Far East were not of the most advanced type and, again, many of the pilots were inexperienced, so the reinforcements did not represent a significant improvement over the Buffalos and their crews. Furthermore, as A.V.M. Maltby later wrote, there was no time for either acclimatisation or for using the Hurricanes in mass formations.[297] Admittedly the Hurricane units performed better over Palembang and Burma when the early-warning system gave more time, but attrition rates eventually reduced the R.A.F.'s defensive efforts.

This early period had demonstrated how important the relationship between aircrew, tactics and aircraft were. Squadrons quickly realized that tactics used against the Germans and Italians would not work against manoeuvrable Japanese fighters and made efforts to adopt the effective dive and zoom manoeuvre. However, the deficiencies in early warning combined with their fighters' limited performance restricted opportunities to gain the height necessary for capitalizing the dive and zoom tactic. This chapter has demonstrated that once the problem of gaining height had been addressed successfully, this tactic was accepted as the most relevant and effective when dealing with Japanese fighters down to the end of the war. Despite Japanese pilots trying to find counter-measures, Allied pilots' responses were essentially adaptations of their basic tactic.

From October 1942 the situation improved in terms of aircrew, tactics and aircraft quantity. Better trained pilots started to arrive, or men with previous combat experience, and the formation of the A.F.T.U. ensured they were trained in relevant combat tactics. However, while the quantity of aircraft improved, the quality did not as the Hurricane remained the principal day fighter until the beginning of 1944. This remained a crucial weakness. However, while the Hurricane fought on, the Beaufighter's first night interceptions demonstrated what was achievable when aircrew, aircraft and tactics combined successfully together.

The value of the correct aircraft for the task was demonstrated in late 1943. Defensively the Spitfire capitalized on the improved early-warning systems in eastern

297 TNA, Air 23/2123, Operations of the R.A.F. during the campaigns in Malaya and
     Netherlands East Indies: report by Air Vice-Marshal P.C. Maltby, 1st January 1941 to
     31st December 1942, paragraph 376.

India to intercept reconnaissance aircraft, and it proved a match for Japanese fighters. Until the Spitfire arrived Allied fighters were unable to intercept the Dinah, but from December 1943 Dinah sorties were virtually neutralized and so Japanese commanders were deprived of important intelligence. Later, when the Japanese devised methods to counter the Spitfire's performance and tactics, the R.A.F. was capable of adapting their tactics accordingly and this was made easier with the Spitfire's high performance capabilities. The Spitfire's introduction was thus of significant importance as it provided the missing link in the defensive chain. The contribution of the long-range American fighter to offensive operations was also of crucial importance.

The counter-air campaign was of vital importance in supporting defensive operations, particularly during the siege at Imphal when the early warning capability was restricted and transport aircraft required protection. Until their introduction the counter-air campaign had achieved little except dispersing Japanese resources, but Mustangs and Lightnings had the performance, range and armament to successfully attack Japanese units in their own territory. Chapter 3 of this book will analyse the counter-air campaign and show how its eventual success was achieved, but there can be no doubt that without the long-range U.S. fighters, the counter-air campaign would have been much harder to successfully prosecute.

Whilst Allied aircrew, tactics and aircraft improved, the Japanese did not keep pace and so lost their early advantage. Japan's industry was unable to produce aircraft in both quality and quantity to match the Allied resources leaving the Oscar as the main fighter in Burma until May 1945. If properly handled, as it was by Japanese pilots whose quality did not appear to deteriorate, the Oscar was a dangerous opponent and was respected by Allied pilots to the end. The hindrance for the Japanese was the lack of more modern aircraft and replacement pilots rather than the quality of their aircrew.

3

The Counter-Air Campaign

The counter-air campaign waged by the Allies in Burma was an integral component of gaining air superiority. The lack of an effective bomber offensive against the Japanese aircraft industry until early 1945, the inconsistencies of Allied early warning, particularly in the sieges at Kohima and Imphal, and the difficulties of finding aircraft in the air and destroying them made counter-air interdiction a priority. This chapter will assess the overall effect of the counter-air campaign on Japanese strength and its eventual contribution to attaining air superiority.

The benefits of a counter-air campaign had been first realized during the First World War and its doctrine developed through the formulative inter-war years before reaching operational maturity in the first years of the Second World War. The Japanese successfully used their Army and Navy air arms in pre-emptive strikes against British and American airbases in 1941 and 1942, rendering their enemies' air strength impotent. From October 1942 the Allies embarked on their counter-air campaign against Japanese air resources, but initially this was ineffective owing to the types and numbers of aircraft at their disposal. However, with the introduction of American long-range fighters in late 1943, assisted by an efficient intelligence organisation, the Allies were able to prosecute a robust campaign, which destroyed Japanese aircraft and forced units to disperse. During the period between March and June 1944 significant claims were made by Allied aircrews of Japanese aircraft destroyed in the counter-air strikes, with Bengal Command quoting 96 aircraft being destroyed in six weeks.[1] Furthermore, Air Historical Branch narrators wrote that the six month period of air fighting in the Far East at the beginning of 1944 broke the back of

---

1   TNA, Air 23/4681, Despatch covering operations of Bengal Command, 15th November 1943 to 17th December 1943 and 3rd Tactical Air Force 18th December 1943 to 1st June 1944, p.7.

Japanese air strength.[2] This chapter will examine the veracity of such claims in order to ascertain the role and importance of the counter-air campaign.

Definition of the term, the benefits, and the offensive requirements

A counter-air offensive can be described as the destruction of an enemy's air assets and also his ancillary organisation on the ground, which includes personnel, maintenance facilities, munitions stores, runways and fuel stocks. Bolkcom and Pike wrote that engaging aircraft in air-to-air combat is difficult as it involves fighting them in the environment they were designed to fight in and countering their attributes of speed, manoeuvrability and armament.[3] In contrast the authors wrote that an aircraft on the ground is vulnerable as it is out of its environment and therefore presents a relatively easy target. This can be taken further as aircraft are also vulnerable in two crucial stages of flight. During take off the aircraft is making height and flying speed, and is not in a good position to defend itself against attack from the air. Secondly after an operation on its approach to its home base, an aircraft is vulnerable to attack as it is low on fuel and short of ammunition and the crew is potentially fatigued.

There are significant benefits to be derived from a counter-air offensive either as a precursor to war or as part of an ongoing air superiority campaign. By attacking enemy aircraft over and on their bases the attackers gain the initiative as to where and when the encounter is fought, whereas the defender is presented with the difficulty of providing adequate defensive measures whilst waiting for an attack. Successful attacks have the capability of forcing the defenders to disperse to safer areas, thereby increasing the attacker's aircrafts' range of operations. This has beneficial effects on flying time, pilot fatigue, fuel consumption and aircraft serviceability. Furthermore, an airforce's logistical infrastructure is open to damage or destruction, as essential communications present vulnerable targets. Highly trained aircrew, technicians and mechanics, together with intelligence and communications staff are also viable targets and their loss can present insuperable problems for the enemy as skill and experience cannot be quickly or easily replaced. In addition, attacking an air force over its own territory and on its airfields has an important effect on morale by promoting uncertainty and insecurity.

There are a variety of requirements for a counter-air offensive. Good intelligence concerning the enemy's airfields, whether permanent or temporary, together with knowledge of ancillary maintenance establishments and supplies is a necessity. Some airfields' location may be known, as in the case of those in Burma vacated by the British in 1942, but other airfields require finding and this can be achieved by a variety

2   TNA, Air 41/64, *The Campaigns in the Far East Volume IV: South East Asia November 1943 to August 1945*, p.71.
3   Bolkcom and Pike, *Attack Aircraft Proliferation: Issues for Concern*, Chapter 7.

of measures from photo reconnaissance, clandestine intelligence gathering groups, and communications interception organisations. The ability to attack aircraft and their weapons system was a vital factor. Heavy bombers had the potential to cause more damage, but such attacks presented problems of protection particularly if the raids were carried out by day. Flying by night had the advantage of not requiring fighter escorts, but would suffer from difficulties in finding the target. A better option was using heavily armed fighter aircraft that had the capability of inflicting destruction on enemy aircraft and installations on the ground, whilst also being able to defend themselves against enemy aircraft and win an aerial battle. This was an approach often favoured by the Allies in both World Wars.

Tactically the attackers in a counter-air offensive have the initiative and create the battleground.[4] However, for the offensive to be successful, attacks must be concentrated and sustained for long enough that an effect in replacing losses can be imposed. To carry out this function the attackers must firstly have the right kind of aircraft, and sufficient resources to maintain concerted pressure.

This chapter will demonstrate that whilst there was a counter-air offensive in Burma between 1942 and 1943, it had little overall effect on Japanese air strength. In comparison, during the first six months of 1944 the predominately American led counter-air offensive was sustained and concentrated enough to cause an effect on Japanese air strength.

The Counter-Air Offensive during the First World War

In 1914 Winston Churchill (First Lord of the Admiralty) reported to the House of Commons that "Passive Air Defence against aircraft is perfectly hopeless and endless. You would have to roof the world to be sure."[5] Whilst the credit for counter-air strategies cannot be attributed to Churchill, it is not surprising that consideration was given to the prospect of attacking aircraft when at their most vulnerable and relatively easy to find. In September 1916 the lessons learned by the Royal Flying Corps (R.F.C.) were reflected in Major General Hugh Trenchard's *Future Policy in the Air*, which encapsulates a counter-air offensive:

> An aeroplane is an offensive and not a defensive weapon. Owing to the unlimited space in the air, the difficulty one machine has in seeing another … it is impossible for aeroplanes, however vigilant their pilots, however powerful their engines, however mobile their machines, and however numerous their formations, to prevent hostile aircraft from crossing the lines if they have the initiative

4   Ibid, Chapter 7.
5   TNA, Air 41/64, *The Campaigns in the Far East Volume IV: South East Asia November 1943 to August 1945*, p.72.

and determination to do so. The aeroplane is not a defence against the aeroplane; but … the aeroplane as a weapon of attack cannot be too highly estimated.[6]

It is clear that the aeroplane cannot defend a territory against aeroplanes across a wide front in the absence of an effective early warning system and it follows that one defence against attacking aircraft is an attack on its source.

During the First World War the theory was put into practice. After the Zeppelin raids on Britain bombing raids were carried out on their hangars, and in September 1917 the R.F.C. bombed the German Gotha airfields at Gastrode following their attacks on London.[7] On 19th July 1916 aircraft from the R.F.C. attacked the German aerodrome at Douai where a petrol store and hangars were set alight.[8] In April 1917 the German fighter dominance was such that the month was termed 'Bloody April' by the R.F.C. and to counter this R.F.C. aircraft were fitted with one-pounder quick firing pom-poms, "they succeeded in wrecking hangars and buildings on Richthofen's aerodrome at Douai, keeping Richthofen out of the air for a day or two."[9] The R.F.C.'s day to day summary shows the efforts to fight the German fighters during offensive patrols; on 26th September:

> It was impossible to bring the fast German scouts … to fight today as they continually dodged in and out of clouds, and except in the case of the Gothas and their escorts there were practically no German machines above the clouds.[10]

The Germans also participated in counter-air activity; on 17th November 1916 they bombed the French aerodrome at Cachy and "21 of their machines were put out of action, eight of which … were completely destroyed."[11] However, although both sides attacked aerodromes neither offensive was concentrated or sustained enough to make a significant difference to the respective air strength. Furthermore, because each side's aircraft industry was able easily to replace damaged and destroyed machines and aircrew training was uncomplicated, any counter-air offensive was only likely to result in temporary inconvenience.

---

6   Jones, *Official History of the War in the Air, Volume Three*, p.472. At the time Trenchard was Officer Commanding of the R.F.C. in France.
7   TNA, WO 158/35, Summary of Operations 8th April to 30th September 1917. The Gotha was a heavy bomber aircraft.
8   Jones, *fficial History of the War in the Air, Volume Three*, p.259.
9   Barker, *The Royal Flying Corps in World War 1*, p.259. Richthofen was Manfred von Richthofen.
10   TNA, WO 158/35, Summary of Operations 8th April to 30th September 1917.
11   TNA, WO 158/34, Summary of Operations 10th February to 17th November 1916.

Inter-War Thinking

The inter-war period is associated with strategists advocating the use of heavy bombers to destroy an enemy's army, its means to wage war and its population's morale.[12] However, Guilio Douhet, the Italian air power advocate, wrote that as the aircraft had no limitations to its movement it was therefore was the offensive weapon par excellence.[13] However, because of this freedom, "There is no practical way to prevent the enemy from attacking us with his air force except to destroy his air force before he has a chance to strike at us."[14] This was written before radar had been invented, but the basis of a counter-air offensive is unmistakable:

> This is the logical and rational concept which should be recognized, even for simple defence – namely to prevent the enemy from flying or from carrying out any aerial action at all. Achieving command of the air implies positive action – that is offensive and not defensive action, the very action best suited to air power.[15]

and:

> The one effective method of defending one's own territory from an offensive by air is to destroy the enemy's air force with the greatest possible speed.[16]

Douhet did not mention how this offensive would be carried out or specifically what kind of aircraft would be used, but a fellow air power advocate argued for the use of fighters.

American General William Mitchell had spent time with Trenchard, the first Chief of the Air Staff, during the latter stages of the First World War and, whilst appreciating the use of strategic bombers, he saw the importance of first neutralising an enemy's air resources. In 1920 he wrote:

> The principal mission of aeronautics is to destroy the aeronautical force of the enemy, and, after this, to attack his formations, both tactical and strategical, on the ground or water.[17]

In 1921 Mitchell wrote:

---

12   Douhet, Trenchard and Mitchell being the most prominent.
13   Douhet, *The Command of the Air*, p.18.
14   Ibid, p.21.
15   Ibid.
16   Ibid, p.94.
17   Futrell, *Ideas, Concepts, Doctrine: A History of Basic Thinking in the United States Air Force 1907-1964*, p.19.

As a prelude to any engagement of military or naval forces, a contest must take place for control of the air. The first battles of any future war will be air battles. The nation winning them is practically certain to win the whole war, because the victorious air service will be able to operate and increase without hindrance.[18]

Mitchell's themes were developed by Major William Sherman, an officer at the Air Service Field Officers' School, who wrote that the first duty of the air force was to, "gain and hold control of the air, by seeking out and destroying the hostile air force wherever it may be found."[19] Agreeing with Mitchell that the answer lay with fighter aircraft he wrote that the "backbone of the air forces on which the whole plan of employment must be hung is pursuit."[20]

Despite this and Mitchell's books, United States theorists debated the best use of air power throughout the 1930s.[21] A bomber's potential superior speed and defensive fire power was repeatedly seen as the key to attacking enemy's lands, and furthermore, the use of bombers was the best way to destroy enemy aircraft on the ground. However, it is important to recognise that the Americans knew a key to air superiority was to destroy the enemy's aircraft at source rather than in the air. Significantly in 1935 the Air Corps Board recommended that defences against hostile aircraft should be developed in the form of quick, cannon equipped fighters that were 20 per cent faster than the bomber aircraft they were likely to encounter. One of the fighters subsequently ordered in 1937 became the P-38 Lightning, which was to play a significant role in Allied attacks on Japanese airfields in 1944.

In Britain the creation of the first independent air force had strategic bombing as one of its raisons d'être. The inter-war period is remembered for Britain debating the idea of the bomber being always able to get through, but it is also clear that thought was given to how the enemy's airforce could be effectively neutralised.[22] In the 1922 R.A.F. Operations Manual the basis of a counter-air offensive was made clear:

The destruction of his air forces at their bases on the ground is the most effective method of attaining the main object, to it must be subjected all other independent uses for aircraft until this destruction has at least partly accomplished.[23]

---

18   Ibid, p.20.
19   Ibid, p.23.
20   Futrell, *Ideas, Concepts, Doctrine: A History of Basic Thinking in the United States Air Force 1907-1964*, p.23.
21   Mitchell wrote *Winged Defense* in 1925 and *Skyways* in 1929.
22   Prime Minister Stanley Baldwin told the House of Commons on 10th November 1932 "I think it is well also for the man in the street to realise that there is no power on earth that can prevent him from being bombed. Whatever people may tell him, the bomber will always get through."
23   TNA, Air 5/299, R.A.F. Operations Manual 1922, (CD22), p.54.

and:

> [T]he tactical offensive in aerial war is a continuous policy; to seek out and destroy the enemy's air forces by a continuous and unremitting offensive is the guiding principle of tactics in the air.[24]

First World War lessons had been learned as the manual writes of moving aircraft closer to the enemy as circumstances dictated, moving the point of contact from airfield to airfield so as not to give the enemy a chance to consolidate a defence, and the importance of offensive patrols, "The object of these patrols is to seek out and destroy enemy aircraft, thus securing the necessary degree of security for co-operative and independent aircraft."[25] Thus the British, like the Americans, had recognized the importance of eliminating an opponent's airforce and the theory was about to be put into practice in 1939.

The Second World War

The first counter-air offensives of the Second World War demonstrated the attributes of the strategy. In Poland and the Low Countries the *Luftwaffe's* superior aircraft types and numbers proved too strong for the defending fighter forces when encountered in aerial combat. In France, German numerical superiority in frontline aircraft combined (in some cases) with superior aircraft types and anti-aircraft artillery fighting over a sustained period eventually wore down the British and French fighter forces. However, German losses were significant:

> On 10th May, the Germans lost 83 aircraft (not including Ju52s) including 47 bombers and 25 fighters, equalling the worst losses for a day in the Battle of Britain. On the following day, the Germans lost a further 42 aircraft, including 22 bomber, 8 dive bombers and 10 fighters.[26]

Ultimately it was *Luftwaffe* numbers which counted as Buckley writes, "by engaging the fighter strength of the Allies in attritional battle the *Luftwaffe* consigned the attempts by the Allied bombers to disaster."[27] The relentless weight of German attack in the air and on the ground had a decisive effect on Allied air strength which could not be sustained.

---

24 Ibid, p.62.
25 Ibid, p.63.
26 Murray, *Strategy for Defeat, The Luftwaffe 1933-1945*, p.39.
27 Buckley, 'The Air War in France', in Bond and Taylor (eds), *The Battle for France and Flanders 1940*, p.123.

Within two months of the fall of France, Britain was threatened by Germany and the pre-requisite for invasion was air superiority. Here the *Luftwaffe* did not possess superior aircraft and its sustained attacks did not reduce the R.A.F.'s strength as factories replaced lost aircraft at an acceptable rate. Similarly attacks on airfields caused some disruption and subsequent discussions about moving airfields away from the south-east, but they never fully inconvenienced the defenders. However, the *Luftwaffe's* offensive caused profound difficulties because the number of R.A.F. fighter pilots steadily decreased and those that were not killed or wounded quickly became fatigued as a result of the sustained air attacks.[28] Missing or fatigued aircrew were much harder to train and replace. However, the important factor to consider was the damage sustained by the *Luftwaffe* whilst carrying out their offensive.

The Germans had entered into the battle weakened by serious losses from the offensive in the Low Countries and France; Murray shows that between May and June 1940 *Luftwaffe* single-engined fighter losses amounted to 19% of its strength, whilst 30% were damaged in the same period. For bomber aircraft the figures were 30% and 41% respectively.[29] The fighting over Britain was hard and caused severe losses to *Luftwaffe* aircraft as, for example, between July and September, 47% of single-engine fighters were destroyed and 64% were damaged.[30] Furthermore, in August out of 229 Bf109 aircraft written off, 57 pilots were killed, 41 injured, 3 were captured, 84 were missing and 47 listed as uninjured.[31] This was an important lesson. The other offensives had been relatively short campaigns and The Battle of Britain had shown that attackers, if undertaking a long-term offensive, had to have sufficient material and personnel resources to carry it out.

Pre-emptive strikes were a prelude to the German invasion of the Soviet Union in Operation BARBAROSSA and the *Luftwaffe* was able to surprise the defences and catch unprepared Soviet aircraft lined up on airfields. Those Soviet aircraft which managed to get airborne were soon despatched by German aircraft of superior capabilities. During June 1941 German records claimed 800 aircraft destroyed on 23rd; 557 on 24th; 351 on 25th; and 300 on 26th:

> The *Luftwaffe* claimed to have destroyed 1,489 aircraft on the ground on the first day; a first attempt to retaliate by bombing German targets cost the Russians 500 aircraft. On the day after the battle opened one commander of a Russian bomber group committed suicide after losing 600 aircraft to only twelve German.[32]

---

28   Terraine, *The Right of the Line*, p.189.
29   Murray, *Strategy for Defeat, The Luftwaffe 1933-1945*, p.42.
30   Ibid, p.50.
31   Ibid, p.49.
32   Ibid and Calvocoressi, Wint, and Pritchard, *Total War*, p.195.

By the end of August the Soviets had lost approximately 5,000 aircraft and as Murray points out, whether the Germans had actually destroyed that many aircraft is beside the point as, "a defeat of immense proportion had overtaken the Red Air Force."[33] However, catastrophic these losses, their effects only lasted for a limited period as the Germans lacked the strength to cover the whole Soviet front which covered 2,000 miles or to destroy the Soviet aircraft manufacturing capability. The inability to stop Soviet aircraft being replaced whilst at the same time failing to adequately replace their own losses resulted in German aircraft strength dropping from about 4,300 to 1,500 at the end of 1941 whilst in the Moscow sector alone the Soviets had assembled twice as many aircraft.[34] Therefore while the initial offensive had successfully allowed the German land forces to progress eastwards without undue interference from Soviet aircraft, in the longer term the Soviets were able to make good their losses and eventually meet the *Luftwaffe* on equal terms.

Japan attacks and the Allied response

The first Japanese attacks from 7th December 1941 employed all the requisites of a counter-air campaign: surprise; economy of force; momentum; and shock effect.[35] In addition the qualities of their aircraft were superior to almost anything the Allies possessed in the theatre. It was not likely to cause a long lasting effect as there was no possibility of destroying the American or British aircraft industry, but it resulted in Japan seizing air superiority for their island invasions. For the Americans the first Japanese attacks were devastating. During the initial attacks on Pearl Harbor J.N.A.F. pilots took advantage of U.S.A.A.F. aircraft parked wing to wing on Oahu airfield for security against sabotage attempts, whilst the U.S. Marines' aircraft were similarly parked on Ewa airfield. Furthermore, the Japanese were assisted by American early warning deficiencies and warnings which were ignored or dismissed by operations staff. The resulting attacks cost the Americans 188 aircraft destroyed and 159 damaged.[36] Similarly on the Philippines' Clark Field, American aircraft were lined up undergoing servicing and refuelling following a morning alert. The Japanese subsequently destroyed nearly 100 aircraft in the air and on the ground, including much of the American heavy bomber force at Clark Field, as well as fighter aircraft at Iba and Del Carmen.[37] The success of these raids ensured the Japanese bomber and torpedo carrying aircraft could carry out their attack on Pearl Harbor without interruption, whilst their invasion of the Philippine islands was able to take place with virtual air superiority. Similar Japanese attacks in the Far East were to prove highly successful.

33 Murray, *Strategy for Defeat, The Luftwaffe 1933-1945*, p.69.
34 Calvocoressi, Wint, and Pritchard, *Total War*, p.196.
35 Bergerud, *Fire in the Sky; The Air War in the South Pacific*, p.14.
36 Tolland, *Rising Sun*, p.235.
37 Peattie, *Sunburst: The Rise of Japanese Naval Air Power, 1909-1941*, p.170.

During attacks on the British airfields in the Far East the Japanese enjoyed similar advantages: surprise; superior numbers; superior aircraft; and an opponent whose early warning system was inefficient. On 8th December Japanese aircraft attacked airfields in northern Malaya in concentrated bombing attacks using anti-personnel and frag-mentation bombs. These attacks caused considerable damage to aircraft and personnel without damage to the runways which would be required for future operations once captured. Covert intelligence assisted the Japanese attacks as their attacks were coor-dinated to occur when aircraft were landing or taking off and were therefore at their most vulnerable.[38] The Japanese attacks were effective and devastating; out of the 110 serviceable aircraft available at the start of 8th December, only 50 remained service-able at the end of the day, a reduction in strength of 55%.[39] Individual squadrons were decimated; for example at Alor Star only two Blenheims remained serviceable, whilst at Sungei Patani only four Blenheims remained operational. This tide of events continued as the Japanese continued their assaults on Singapore, Sumatra and Java, their counter-air strikes giving them the initiative, and forcing R.A.F. fighters onto the defensive. When Buffalos were replaced by Hurricanes, the Japanese strength in numbers and superiority at their optimum operating heights resulted in a steady attri-tion rate which the British were not able to sustain. The latter point became crucial in Burma. The intelligence organisation estimated that the Japanese possessed between 450 and 500 aircraft in Burma and Siam, whereas the R.A.F. had only 42 operational aircraft on 21st March 1942.[40] A.V.M. Donald Stevenson admitted that the Japanese long-range fighters were able to fly great distances, destroying Allied fighters on the ground:

[T]he enemy fighters achieving surprise, would come in and by deliberate low flying attacks and good shooting could be relied upon to cause great damage to first line aircraft, if not destroy them all.[41]

Furthermore, it was not just low-level raiders which caused destruction to Allied aircraft. On 21st March 1942 a Japanese force of 59 bombers and 24 fighters attacked Magwe in three waves and succeeded in destroying six Blenheims and a Hurricane on the ground, whilst two further Hurricanes were lost in the air.[42] In addition, a 1,000 gallon oil dump was destroyed and all telephone communications were put out of

---

38   Richards and Saunders, *The Fight Avails*, p.22.
39   Ibid, p.22 and Probert, *The Forgotten Air Force*, p.43.
40   TNA, Air 2/7787, Operations: Far East; Air Operations in Burma, January to May 1942; Despatch by Air Vice-Marshal Stevenson, p.6. Stevenson admitted he thought this figure was an over-estimate, which is agreed by the A.H.B., who gave a probable figure of 350 aircraft and a daily effort of between 240 and 250 aircraft.
41   Ibid.
42   TNA, Air 41/63, *The Campaigns in the Far East, Volume II, Malaya, Netherlands East Indies and Burma 1941-1942*, p.198.

action. The Japanese returned on 22nd March with 27 bombers and a fighter escort; the raid caused damage to ground installations and the warning system, and three more Blenheims and an American P-40 were destroyed on the ground. The Blenheim losses were particularly severe; out of 20 Blenheims, nine had been destroyed, five were damaged and the remaining six were operationally unserviceable.[43] Stevenson wrote that these actions, "effectively terminated the R.A.F. activities based in Burma" and Richards agreed, "These two disasters virtually wiped out the air force in Burma" with the remaining aircraft being withdrawn to India.[44]

The Japanese air offensive against the Allies in the Far East between December 1941 and May 1942 had been as effective as the Germans' offensive in Europe in 1940. Using a mixture of sustained high and low-level attacks they had destroyed or severely damaged many R.A.F. aircraft and in some instances forced units to withdraw to safety. Airfields had been rendered unusable or captured, whilst important ancillary facilities such as fuel dumps and communications had been destroyed. Undoubtedly their successes were assisted by the Allies' lack of credible early warning systems, inferiority of many aircraft types, and the Japanese superiority in aircraft numbers and types. The Allies' efforts through this period to counter the Japanese air attacks were in comparison small and ineffective.

Despite mounting losses the R.A.F. engaged their enemy in a limited counter-air offensive which sought to reduce the scale of air attack, but Allied counter-air attacks were likely to fail during this period as they were not sustained owing to a shortage of aircraft. Conversely the Japanese had sufficient resources to replace lost aircraft quickly and were going to succeed in a war of attrition. Furthermore, the Allies' air effort was diluted by its many roles of air defence, reconnaissance, and close support all of which reduced the number of aircraft needed to mount a counter-air offensive.[45]

On 9th December 1941 a force of Blenheims was despatched from Tengah and Butterworth to attack the Japanese at Sangkla and Singora. Of the Tengah force three Blenheims were shot down by Japanese defenders when escort fighters failed to materialise. Of the Butterworth force, all the aircraft barring one were either destroyed or seriously damaged as they took off during a well timed high level Japanese bomber attack. The remaining Blenheim, flown by Squadron Leader Arthur Scarf, flew to Singora where the crew bombed the target although the aircraft was damaged and had to land at Alor Star where Scarf eventually succumbed to his injuries.[46] The loss of these Blenheims was grievous and further showed that the Blenheim itself was unsuitable to engage in this type of operation as Probert wrote:

43 Ibid.
44 TNA, Air 2/7787, Operations: Far East; Air Operations in Burma, January to May 1942; Despatch by Air Vice-Marshal Stevenson, p. 17, and Richards and Saunders, *The Fight Avails*, p.65.
45 Probert, *The Forgotten Air Force*, p.50.
46 Ibid p.44 and Bowyer, *For Valour: The Air VCs*, p.263. Scarf was the only aircrew recipient of the Victoria Cross in the Far East campaign 1941-1945.

His sortie [Scarf] had been part of a valiant attempt to show that the Blenheim could still hit back, but the lesson was clear: without fighter escort such missions were doomed and AHQ ordered no more.[47]

Various small scale attacks were carried out on Japanese airfields but none had a significant effect on either reducing or slowing down the Japanese onslaught. Stevenson decided to move some of his forces closer to the enemy where they could attack a number of target systems, one being Japanese airfields. However, the weight of Japanese strength quickly overwhelmed A.V.M. Stevenson's plans, the attack on Mingaladon providing a prime example. Reconnaissance had detected over 50 Japanese aircraft at Mingaladon and Stevenson decided to mount a raid to reduce the scale of Japanese attack. The subsequent raid was mounted by ten Hurricanes and nine Blenheims which Stevenson admitted represented all available serviceable aircraft.[48] The Blenheims fought their way to the target where they dropped 9,000 lbs of bombs on the airfield and claimed two Japanese aircraft destroyed, two probably destroyed and two damaged in aerial combat. The Hurricanes mounted a low-level attack and claimed 16 Japanese aircraft destroyed or damaged on the ground and nine claimed destroyed in the air.[49] This was a "small but heartening victory" but realistically did not inflict a decisive loss on the Japanese, because as the R.A.F. aircraft refuelled and rearmed in preparation for a return attack the Japanese attacked their base at Magwe.[50] The attacks accounted for most of the R.A.F. aircraft left in Burma and they subsequently withdrew to Akyab where a series of attacks further reduced Stevenson's force before it withdrew to India.[51]

The limited offensive had proved unsuccessful and its effects on the Japanese air offensive were negligible. Apart from aircraft numbers and the inability to maintain a sustained effort, the attacks showed the types of aircraft suitable for a counter-air offensive. The R.A.F. had long requested a long-range fighter aircraft for either escort or interdiction work, but none had been designed or were available. The Blenheim had the range and a reasonable bomb load, but did not have the speed or manoeuvrability to defend itself against fighter attacks. The Hurricane did not have sufficient range to reach Japanese airfields; the early versions did not have overload tanks that could be jettisoned and the extra weight and drag of such tanks caused the aircraft to lose performance. Squadron Leader Cedric Stone recalled an interception when his drop tank equipped Hurricanes were attacked by Japanese fighters:

47   Probert, *The Forgotten Air Force*, p.45.
48   TNA, Air 2/7787, Operations: Far East; Air Operations in Burma, January to May 1942; Despatch by Air Vice-Marshal Stevenson, p.17.
49   Ibid.
50   Richards and Saunders, *The Fight Avails*, p.63.
51   Probert, *The Forgotten Air Force*, p.150. The withdrawal to India came after similar attacks on the R.A.F. on Akyab further reduced aircraft numbers.

We were promptly jumped by about ten of them. Couldn't do a damned thing with the tanks on, never got a shot while the little buggers queued up on my tail and filled me full of holes.[52]

Later that day Stevenson called for Stone to lead an attack with his Hurricanes on the Japanese airfield at Bangkok:

He wanted me to take some long-range Hurricanes to Bangkok and strafe the aerodrome there, of all the bloody stupid ideas. I made him come up and look at my aircraft after the combat, and he thought perhaps it wasn't such a good idea after all. We whipped the tanks off the other two that night.[53]

The lessons were clear for Allied air plans; a counter-air offensive would require sufficient aircraft of the right type and attributes to attack Japanese airfields successfully. Such aircraft were not available until the end of 1943. Nevertheless the Allies carried out a limited counter-air offensive from April 1942 until January 1944 with unsuitable aircraft types.

June 1942 to December 1943

By June 1942 the British had withdrawn to India and the Japanese had halted their western advance. The British and their Allies began the process of re-equipping with men and matériel whilst the Japanese halted; having outrun their supplies they had no immediate plans to continue their conquests to the west. The situation was therefore in stalemate, a predicament assisted by the monsoon period which would hinder operations. Despite the limited offensive in the Arakan at the end of 1942 and Colonel Orde Wingate's first Chindit expedition in 1943, the Allies were in no position to contemplate an invasion of Burma until 1944, but they did wage a counter-air offensive throughout the period in review.

The Allies' counter-air offensive during this period had the basic aim of neutralising the Japanese air threat by attacking their aircraft, airfields and infrastructure. There were good reasons for the offensive. The Allies' air strength was below that of their enemy both in quality and quantity. Reinforcements were on their way from other theatres but would not arrive quickly, so every effort to reduce the Japanese air threat with surgical, low risk attacks was crucial. Throughout 1942 the air defence was being established in India and to assist this process attacks on Japanese bases were vital to reduce the risk of aerial attack. Furthermore, the airfield building programme in India had to be allowed to proceed unmolested if plans were to succeed. It was also recognized that the Japanese air threat had to be subdued if future offensive plans were to

---

52   Shores and Cull, *Bloody Shambles Volume One*, p.262.
53   Ibid, p.263.

have a chance of success. General Archibald Wavell, C. In C. India, and General Joseph Stilwell, commanding general of all U.S. forces in China, Burma, and India, agreed in October 1942 that the combined British and American air effort should be directed against Japanese airbases to gain control of the air and thereby acquire cover for future land and naval operations.[54] Similarly at the TRIDENT conference in May 1943 one of the five recommendations for the Far Eastern campaign was a rigorous air offensive against the J.A.A.F. in Burma.[55] Moreover, a successful air campaign in Burma would assist the Americans in the Pacific by diverting Japanese resources away from that theatre. When Admiral Lord Louis Mountbatten took charge as Supreme Allied Commander his first directive from Churchill on 24th October 1943 called for the wearing down of Japanese air strength in Burma so that "he would be compelled to divert reinforcements from the Pacific Theatre."[56]

However, throughout this period the Allies were unable to fully participate in a sustained counter-air offensive owing to a shortage of suitable aircraft types in significant numbers. The R.A.F. had requested a long-range fighter while the Americans did not have aircraft of the Mustang or Lightning types in the Far East until the end of 1943. In the meantime the R.A.F. continued to reinforce the Indian Command with Hurricanes which were not suitable for long-range interdiction sorties whilst the more suitable aircraft, the American built Mohawk, was only available in limited numbers. While both these fighters were occasionally engaged in the counter-air offensive, they were also needed for other tasks such as close air support and defensive duties. The other significant British long-range fighter available was the Beaufighter which did not arrive in the Far East until December 1942; in January 1943 there was only one squadron and a flight of a night-fighter variant available for operations.[57] By September 1943 there were two intruder squadrons and the night-fighter unit, and in December 1943 the number had increased by one extra night-fighter unit.[58] However, the variety of targets for attack outnumbered the amount of available and suitable aircraft with the result that the counter-air offensive could not be fully sustained.

In the absence of suitable fighter aircraft counter-air attack was left to the small number of bombers in the theatre. In early-September 1942 there were four squadrons of Blenheims, two squadrons of Hudsons and one squadron of Wellingtons in the Far East.[59] By January 1943 this number had been increased by another squadron of Wellingtons and two squadrons of R.A.F. Liberators.[60] In addition, two squadrons

---

54   Kirby (ed), *The War Against Japan, Volume II*, p.291.
55   Ibid, p.381.
56   Ibid, p.22.
57   Shores, *Air War for Burma*, p.383.
58   Ibid, p.388. December 1943 saw the introduction of the first Mosquito aircraft to the Far East but it was a while before technical difficulties were overcome to allow the aircraft to properly enter service.
59   The Hudsons were used in a bomber-reconnaissance role.
60   Shores, *Air War for Burma*, pp.382-385.

of American Mitchells and two squadrons of American Liberators had arrived in India.[61] This constituted a fairly weak bomber force and the Allied command was faced with a dilemma. If the force was to be conserved for future operations, the Japanese would inevitably suffer less disruption and would be in a position to use their resources against the Allies whilst building up stronger forces and reserves.[62] A compromise was agreed, namely to use the bomber force against selected targets in suitable tactical circumstances, "Enemy occupied airfields and airfield installations in Burma therefore became first priority for R.A.F. light and medium bombers, and Rangoon for heavy bombers."[63] However, the types of available aircraft would pose difficulties as these bombers required fighter escort if attacking by day, as they could not adequately defend themselves against Japanese fighters. The solution was to have Wellingtons and Liberators attack Japanese airfields by night, whilst the Blenheims, with their better speed and manoeuvrability, attacked by day and night. However, there was a serviceability problem with Blenheims and Wellingtons. The Blenheim was largely obsolete by the end of 1942 and posed maintenance problems for Far Eastern ground crews owing to spares shortages and ageing airframes. The Wellingtons were also obsolete and the tropical climate did not suit the aircraft or its engines resulting in inconsistent service rates. This situation was summed up by 99 Squadron in December 1942:

> It would not be possible to maintain in India that same high operational service-ability that prevailed in England. This was due firstly to the very tight supply position in India, and secondly to the variety of technical difficulties encountered in the new climate, not all of which had been fully overcome by the end of this month.[64]

As a result 99 Squadron was rarely able to have eight or nine Wellingtons out of 16 serviceable machines available for operations at any time which posed an additional problem of how to keep 31 operational aircrews occupied. The planned and important counter-air offensive against the Japanese in Burma from June 1942 to December 1943 was therefore bedevilled by two basic problems; lack of aircraft quantity and unsuitable aircraft types. However, the offensive did have an effect on Japanese air operations.

As the monsoon began in June 1942 the British and American air forces embarked on a counter-air offensive against Japanese airfields in Burma. The task was daunting as a report estimated the Japanese had 134 aerodromes, landing grounds, emergency

61   Ibid.
62   TNA, Air 41/36, *The Campaigns in the Far East, Volume III: India Command*, p.115.
63   Ibid.
64   TNA, Air 27/790, 99 Squadron Operations Record Book, December 1942 summary.

landing grounds, seaplane stations and seaplane alighting areas in the region.[65] Nevertheless during June, Blenheims and Wellingtons raided Magwe four times, Akyab three times, and Myitkyina once but with limited effects.[66] Following a 1st June raid on Magwe the Daily Air Summary reported, "Bombs fell in target area. One petrol fire started", whilst a return visit on 20th resulted in, "Bombs seen to burst on runways and aerodrome."[67] On 22nd June Magwe was raided again and the Daily Air Summary states, "Photos showed one direct hit on aircraft, one near miss. Runway hit."[68] In July Myitkyina was raided four times by American Mitchells and the attacks elicited familiar results, "Barracks claimed obliterated", "6 hits on recently paved end of runway", and "direct hits on aerodrome."[69] While the attacks were regular they were only made by two aircraft on each occasion and it is unlikely any damage was inflicted on Japanese aircraft. The offensive continued after the monsoon period in August for the rest of 1942 in a similar fashion. Akyab and its satellite airfield were raided in bomber attacks seven times, Myitkyina four times and various other Japanese airfields once or twice. In August Mohawk fighters joined the offensive with armed reconnaissance patrols and interdiction attacks on Mawlaik, Myitkyina, Dabaing, Akyab, and Mawdaung, but the number of raids throughout the final six months of 1942 was not large and the effect on Japanese air strength was minimal.

Japanese records are unreliable for this period, but they suggest between August and December 1942 only three Japanese aircraft were destroyed in the air over Burma, whilst four were destroyed on the ground.[70] The largest single Japanese loss resulted from an overnight raid by Wellingtons on Toungoo airfield on 19th/20th December during which two Dinahs and one Oscar were destroyed.[71] The minimum loss of seven aircraft in a six month period was negligible, and the Allied intelligence organisation's estimates of Japanese air strength only showed one marked decrease when 120 aircraft were moved out of the theatre prior to the monsoon in July 1942.[72] Intelligence estimates for the rest of 1942 shows an increase of Japanese aircraft from 182 in July to 279 on 1st December 1942. Clearly the offensive had had little effect on aircraft strength but did have an effect on Japanese air operations as the Allies' bombing effort forced them to withdraw aircraft into Siam. The regular Allied bombing concerned the Japanese who had little defence against night attacks and their shortage of reserves "forced the Japanese to adopt the uneconomical policy of bringing forward squadrons

65   TNA, Air 40/1735, Intelligence Reports and Papers: Airfields, Landing Grounds and Seaplane Bases, Asia, 24th July 1942.
66   TNA, Air 24/1280, Daily Air Summary, 1st April 1942 to 31st October 1942.
67   Ibid.
68   Ibid, 22nd June 1942.
69   Ibid, 1st July to 31st July 1942.
70   Shores, *Air War for Burma*, pp.19-48.
71   Ibid, p.133.
72   TNA, Air 40/1431, Japanese Air Services Order of Battle, 1942-1943.

to mount attacks and to retreat back to Siam again."[73] A.H.Q. Bengal reported on the bombing success and the scale of Japanese aerodrome construction:

> Enemy air activity for October to December 31st was on the increase, but did not reach the scale that had been anticipated. Possibly our constant bombing of his forward aerodromes by day and night made things difficult for him, although his aerodrome and pen construction had been so widespread and thorough that he had accommodation for over 1000 aircraft in Burma by December.[74]

Japan never had 1,000 aircraft in the theatre, but it did mean that all these airfields were available for dispersal during operations against Allied forces which would be a feature of the counter-air offensive during the next two years. However, these first attacks did establish an important pattern for counter-air operations for the next twelve months as attacks on airfields resulted in the J.A.A.F. being dispersed and only brought forward when operations were mounted.

Essentially the counter-air offensive in 1943 was a continuation of the series of attacks carried out in 1942. Despite the Allied commanders' recognition of the campaign's benefits the Allied air forces were handicapped by aircraft types, serviceability problems and dilution of effort. However, the limited campaign continued to force the Japanese to withdraw aircraft to distant bases to avoid attack in the front lines. By October 1943 the Allies' air strength was considerably improved particularly in terms of long-range fighters which would prove important in the counter-air operations in 1944.

January 1943 saw the resumption of the counter-air offensive, notably beginning with a series of daytime attacks carried out by Hurricanes and Mohawks in conjunction with light and medium bombers. These aircraft were able to attack the Japanese airfields thanks to an airfield building programme nearer to the borders which reduced the flying distance to their targets. From January to the middle of March Japanese airfields at Magwe, Akyab, Prome, Toungoo and Heho were attacked during the day by fighters but this had little material effect on Japanese air strength. On 2nd January, Hurricanes strafed Magwe and claimed two aircraft on fire; on 22nd January Mohawks attacked Prome and claimed a Sally probably destroyed; and on 13th February Hurricanes were engaged on an offensive patrol over Akyab when Oscars were engaged, two being destroyed in combat.[75] During this same period R.A.F. night bombers attacked main Japanese aerodromes at Akyab, Magwe, Heho, Maungdaw, and Tennant. The effects of these attacks were not substantially to reduce

73   TNA, Air 41/36, *The Campaigns in the Far East, Volume III: India Command*, p.105.
74   TNA, Air 23/1918, Miscellaneous Reports Covering Operations During 1942; Despatch of A.H.Q. Bengal 21st May 1942 to 31st December 1942, p.7.
75   Shores, *Air War for Burma*, pp.49-60.

Japanese air strength, but they forced the Japanese to move aircraft to and from bases in Siam especially for operations.

From mid-December 1942, Calcutta had been attacked by Japanese night bombers whose effect on the civilian population was out of proportion to the attacks. Following the destruction of four Japanese bombers by Beaufighters in two nights the Japanese commander ordered that the night raids on Calcutta should stop at once.[76] However, the Air Historical Branch narrative suggests the reason why such attacks did not stretch into 1943 was the counter-air attacks on Japanese aerodromes.[77] The Japanese aircraft had flown from Magwe which was attacked four times at day and night before the end of January along with a number of main airfields, so it is possible that the combination of airfield attack and efficient night-fighters had proved too much of a disincentive.[78] Interdiction Beaufighters were also assigned to airfield attacks, but during sorties against Heho on 17th February and Prome on 21st February a Beaufighter was lost on each occasion demonstrating the risk of low-level airfield attacks. While the combined day and night attacks continued to put pressure on the J.A.A.F., events on the Arakan coast would serve to reduce the R.A.F. counter-air effort.

At the end of 1942 British forces started a campaign along the western coast of Burma (Mayu Peninsula) principally to drive the Japanese out and to recapture Akyab Island and its airfield. At first the operation went well but as the first months of 1943 progressed the Japanese used their familiar tactic of encircling the advancing forces and this eventually pushed the British back into India. Throughout the operation, and particularly when the British were in retreat, the R.A.F. were engaged in close support sorties. Single-engine fighters and light bombers were assigned to support the Army and provide battlefield air superiority cover, and as there were not enough aircraft in the theatre these were taken away from the campaign against airfields. Nevertheless although the Allied day effort was reduced, R.A.F. bombers continued to attack main Japanese bases mainly by night from January to April.[79] The raids were carried out by all the available bombers in the command; Wellingtons, Liberators, Blenheims and Hudsons, the latter two regularly used in a light bomber role in this period during the day. The bombing raids were frequent, every two or three nights, a planned tactic. A.V.M. Thomas Williams, A.O.C. Bengal Command, reported that 99 and 159 Squadrons were to attack enemy airfields on two nights out of three, whilst 34 Squadron would attack on the third night.[80] However, Williams acknowledged that this was not always possible due to poor serviceability rates. The raids were

76   Ibid, p.53.
77   TNA, Air 41/36, *The Campaigns in the Far East, Volume III: India Command*, p.116.
78   TNA, Air 24/1282, Daily Operational Summaries, summary numbers 141-250, 1st January 1943 to 30th April 1943.
79   Ibid.
80   TNA, Air 23/1925, Bengal Command Despatch 1st January 1943 to 20th June 1943, p.135. 99 Squadron flew Wellingtons; 159 Squadron flew Liberators and 34 Squadron flew Blenheims.

usually carried out by six or seven aircraft, although overnight on 25th/26th January 10 Wellingtons attacked Heho, on 14th/15th 10 Blenheims attacked Shwebo, and on 15th/16th February 10 Wellingtons attacked Heho again.[81] These raids were exceptions rather than the norm. Other raids showed fewer aircraft involvement. On 25th/26th February three Liberators attacked Toungoo; on 23rd/24th March three Wellingtons attacked Magwe; and on 6th/7th March three Hudsons bombed Meiktila.[82] Lack of aircraft numbers combined with serviceability problems placed a heavy restriction on operational availability; at the beginning of 1943 the average availability in Bengal Command for night attacks was four heavy bombers (Liberators) and 13 medium bombers (Wellingtons), whilst there were 50 light bombers (Blenheims) available for day attacks.[83] The Americans had more at their disposal, 30 heavy bombers and 34 medium bombers, but these were quickly reduced when some were diverted to the China Theatre.[84] Furthermore, the Americans had their own supply and mainte-nance problems caused by low priorities allocated to the theatre and difficult lines of communications:

> But nowhere were the advantages of a highly industrialized society close at hand, as they were for air forces operating out of England or Italy … The stories of ingenious improvisations in maintenance and modification have become almost legendary; but there were times when, in spite of Yankee ingenuity and the plen-tiful use of baling wire and tin cans, an uncomfortable number of planes were inoperable.[85]

Despite these difficulties the raids continued on Japanese airfields with such typical post-raid comments as, "Bursts seen on runway and dispersal"; "Four bursts on runway" and "Hits observed on N.E. and N.W. of dispersal and extreme end of runway."[86] What then were the effects of the attacks?

The aim to reduce Japanese air strength was essentially a failure as the Japanese mounted a series of well supported raids during the First Arakan Campaign initially against Allied airfields. On 25th February 1943 a mixed force of 30 Oscars and nine Sallys raided northern Assam; on 2nd March 30 Oscars raided Feni; and on 4th April 15 Lilys and 15 Oscars raided Dohazari.[87] These numbers were indicative of

---

81 TNA, Air 24/1282, Daily Operational Summaries, summary numbers 141-250, 1st January 1943 to 30th April 1943.
82 Ibid.
83 TNA, Air 41/36, *The Campaigns in the Far East, Volume III: India Command*, p.116.
84 Ibid.
85 Craven and Cate, *The Army Air Forces in World War II, Volume Two*, p.xii.
86 TNA, Air 24/1282, Daily Operational Summaries, summary numbers 141-250, 1st January 1943 to 30th April 1943; raids were 19th/20th January on Heho; 22nd/23rd February on Mingaladon; and 5th April on Meiktila.
87 Shores, *Air War for Burma*, pp.61-79.

many of the raids of that period and while not large by European standards they were enough to cause trouble for defending R.A.F. fighters which were inferior in certain conditions to their opponents. The counter-air attacks were thus at best only causing damage or destruction to one or two aircraft, whilst some Allied defensive day fighter actions were destroying more aircraft during Japanese raids. The Allies were aware that Japanese aircraft numbers were not reducing despite the heavy fighting as their own intelligence estimates of Japanese air strength showed that on 1st January 1943 there was a total number of 260 aircraft of all types in the Burma/Siam area of operations. On 1st May this number had reduced to 216, largely due to Japanese units leaving the theatre for the monsoon rather than attrition.[88] Furthermore, an indication that the counter-air campaign was unsuccessful was the marked increase in Japanese air activity during April and May, which A.C.M. Pierse acknowledged.[89] However, while Japanese air strength was not significantly reduced, the counter-air attacks did force the Japanese to move their air strength around Burma and Siam to avoid either attack or detection. This dispersal caused precious fuel to be wasted and potential aircraft losses in a country where flying conditions were harsh and flying accidents common to both sides.

The monsoon period beginning in May saw a marked reduction in air activity over Burma. The Allies continued a limited air campaign in support of ground forces with virtually no opposition from the Japanese air forces but this was not due to attrition:

> By June 1943 the Allied air forces did, in fact, rule the skies over Burma but this situation was really the result of the Japanese custom of retiring for the monsoon rather than the result of the air battles fought during the dry season.[90]

The Japanese had withdrawn to replenish aircraft numbers, in some cases updating older types, and to prepare for the forthcoming dry season operations with training exercises.[91] Richards and Saunders also point out that some Japanese units were utilized during the monsoon period to reinforce Japanese units fighting in the Pacific campaign. In the case of the 50th *Sentai* which was withdrawn in June to Java and Singapore, detachments were sent to New Guinea, but in August they returned to Burma with the main body of their squadron.[92] However, some Japanese units still remained active in the Far East Theatre defending sea transportation off the Burmese coast and defending Rangoon against Allied bombing attacks.

For the Allies the monsoon season was a period of reinforcement with greater numbers being made available and also new aircraft types that would play an

88   TNA, Air 40/1431, Japanese Air Services Order of Battle, 1942-1943.
89   TNA, Air 23/4308, Despatch on Air Operations India Command by Air Chief Marshal R.E.C. Pierse, 1st January 1943 to 30th June 1943.
90   TNA, Air 41/36, *The Campaigns in the Far East, Volume III: India Command*, p.112.
91   Ibid, Appendix 13, p.6.
92   Richards and Saunders, *The Fight is Won*, p.305 and Shores, *Air War for Burma*, p.426.

important part in the counter-air offensive at the beginning of 1944. The R.A.F. began a programme of replacing the Blenheim types with Hurricanes, which were becoming available from other theatres, as well as increasing the number of Beaufighters and heavy bombers, particularly the Liberator. In September, the first fighter Spitfires were introduced to India which heralded the beginning of a defensive capability the Allies had been seeking for over a year. Important though these new arrivals were, it was the expansion of American aircraft strength, in particular long-range fighters, which started to tip the counter-air balance in favour of the Allies. The following table shows the increase of American aircraft in the Indian-Burma Theatre:

	20th June 1943		15th November 1943	
	Assigned	Combat Ready	Assigned	Combat Ready
Liberator	47	36	58	51
Mitchell	47	38	55	40
Apache	0	0	30	24
Mustang	0	0	22	20
P-40	76	67	80	62
Lightning	0	0	8	8[93]

From a counter-air view the introduction of the Apache, the Mustang and the Lightning would give the Allies a long-range, heavily armed fighter capability which would prove valuable in the forthcoming year. The arrival in Assam in September of the 80th Fighter Group with its three P-40N squadrons and its Lightning squadron together with the 311th Fighter Bomber Group and its three squadrons, two Apache and one Mustang, meant that:

> The fighter strength of the Tenth Air Force was greatly increased in the space of a few weeks. The number of squadrons jumped from two to seven, and instead of having old model P-40's for every conceivable kind of mission, P-40N's, P-51A's, A-36's and P-38's were available.[94]

Thus as 1943 progressed the numbers increased, and they were to receive a substantial boost at the beginning of 1944 with the introduction of the 1st A.C.G. which was principally to support Major General Wingate's second expedition as it possessed a long-range capability with its Mustangs.

As the monsoon ended in October the Allies were better equipped to conduct a counter-air offensive. In addition to better equipment, the Allied forces in the theatre were reformed at the start of December into a united Anglo-American organisation

---

93   TNA, Air 2/7907, Despatch of Air Operations India Command, 21st June 1943 to 15th November 1943, p.15.
94   Craven and Cate, *The Army Air Forces in World War II Volume Four*, p.467.

called South East Asia Command (S.E.A.C.) under the overall command of Admiral Lord Louis Mountbatten. The orders he issued to the air forces were that their objectives were to guard the air route to China, to interfere with enemy communications and to deliver supplies by air, all of which were paramount in preparation for support of the 1944 land campaign. To allow the bombers, transports and ground support aircraft to do their jobs protection against enemy interference was vital, "To accomplish these objectives with the maximum speed and minimum loss, [and] it became necessary to neutralize the Japanese Air Force as effectively as possible."[95] Again it was recognized that a counter-air offensive should be pursued but it would be a few months before the new American aircraft were available for these operations. The Apaches and Mustangs were initially used in a close air support role against Japanese troops moving south towards the Ledo Road and were not in action against Japanese airfields.[96] The 459th F.S.'s Lightnings did not fly their first operations until 20th November 1943 on a bomber escort mission to Kalewa. They mainly continued in this role until February 1944 when they were withdrawn for gunnery training.[97] However, the P-40s of the 80th Fighter Group participated in a number of bombing and strafing raids against the Japanese airfield at Myitkyina throughout October, November and December to reduce the risk aircraft based there posed to U.S. transport aircraft flying over the 'Hump' into China. This series of attacks was only one measure designed to assist the transports but it is possible that it had an effect:

> It is impossible to determine which of the precautions was most effective in stopping depredations on the Hump flyers, but in November no transports were shot down, and in December only two were lost to enemy action.[98]

The Allied counter-air offensive in 1943 had hardly been more effective than in 1942 and it is likely that more Japanese aircraft were destroyed and damaged as a result of defensive air-to-air combat than on the ground. Given that Japanese records are incomplete and inaccurate, analysis of the figures quoted in Shores' *Air War for Burma* suggest that approximately 46 Japanese aircraft were destroyed in defensive air battles over the entire year, with only about 13 being positively recorded as destroyed on the ground.[99] These figures do not include those aircraft destroyed during bomber escort sorties or those lost due to mechanical fault or accident whilst in flight, but it is doubtful that counter-air losses matched those in the air.

At the beginning of the year, the few operational Allied aircraft suitable for counter-air attacks were required for a multitude of tasks, but principally in close support

95   TNA, Air 41/64, *The Campaigns in the Far East Volume IV: South East Asia November 1943 to August 1945*, p.29.
96   Craven and Cate, *The Army Air Forces in World War II Volume Four*, p.467.
97   Stanaway, *P-38 Lightning Aces of the Pacific and CBI*, p.79.
98   Craven and Cate, *The Army Air Forces in World War II Volume Four*, p.468.
99   Shores, *Air War for Burma*, pp.49-142.

roles to assist the Army in the First Arakan campaign. The counter-air effort was therefore largely handed to medium and heavy bombers who, despite causing disruption and damage to Japanese airfields, had little material effect on enemy aircraft strength. It must be stressed that the raids did have a positive effect on forcing the Japanese to move aircraft to bases in their rear areas to avoid the attacks and this had a potential of increasing aircraft flying hours, fuel consumption and risk of flying accidents. When the monsoon began in June, Japanese air strength had not reduced fundamentally from January 1943, despite aerial combat, the counter-air offensive, and some transfers to other theatres of war. The maintenance of air strength can be attributed to a low-level of losses which were replaced from available reserves. By the time the monsoon ended in October, the Japanese returned to the area with 380 aircraft concentrated at the Burmese airfields at Heho, Anisakan and Rangoon, and at the Siamese airfield of Chieng Mai, whilst others were located at airfields further back in Siam, in Malaya and in the Dutch East Indies.[100] This figure of 380 is in contrast to a figure of 216 for the area in May 1943. Thus Japan was clearly able to increase the size of the J.A.A.F. in the Far East despite claims for increased numbers in other areas, and the Air Historical Branch authors point out that aircraft production actually increased during the first part of the war reaching a peak in September 1944.[101] The ability to reinforce and replace lost aircraft at the end of 1943 was observed during a series of coordinated attacks by the R.A.F. and U.S.A.A.F. on Rangoon docks, industry and airfields during a four day period in November 1943. Referring to the Allied air forces' claims of the destruction of fifty Japanese aircraft Craven and Cate wrote, "owing to [the] arrival of reinforcements during the operation, Japanese air strength was greater at the finish than on the first day."[102] Even given the propensity to over-claim, the Japanese clearly had sufficient reserves and this was demonstrated in a series of raids against Allied bases and docks from the beginning of December. On 5th December a combined force of 128 fighters and bombers took off to attack Calcutta: 59 fighters and bombers attacked bases in Assam on 13th; 65 attacking Kunming on 22nd December; and 99 attacking Chittagong on 26th.[103] The increase in Allied aircraft numbers was evidently forcing the Japanese to strengthen their forces in the region as a precursor to the planned campaign in 1944 as at the end of 1943 Japanese air strength numbered 370 in Burma and Siam, the majority (200) being fighters, all of which were superior to Allied transport aircraft.

Thus 1943 ended with the Japanese in a stronger position with regard to aircraft strength whilst the Allies' counter-air offensive had failed to significantly reduce Japanese strength owing to problems with quality, quantity and diversion of effort.

100 TNA, Air 41/64, *The Campaigns in the Far East Volume IV: South East Asia November 1943 to August 1945*, p.28.
101 Ibid, p.30. The figures quoted showed 642 Japanese aircraft constructed during the first nine months of war rising to a peak of 2,572 during September 1944.
102 Craven and Cate, *The Army Air Forces in World War II Volume Four*, p.482.
103 Shores, *Air War for Burma*, pp.125-139.

However, the prospects for 1944 were more encouraging. The combined effort had already been felt in the combined raids on Rangoon in November, whilst the air defence of important docks and establishments in India had been competently performed by Spitfires. Finally the arrival of American long-range fighter aircraft squadrons gave Allied commanders the ability to strike effectively at Japanese airfields in rear areas.

1944

Winning and maintaining air superiority in Burma was crucial for the Allies during the first six months of 1944. As land forces fought during the Battle of the Admin Box, the sieges at Kohima and Imphal, and the second Chindit incursion, transport and close support aircraft required protection against Japanese air attack. Lieutenant General Slim had formulated plans to counter Japanese infiltration tactics which called for surrounded troops to remain where they were whilst being re-supplied by air and supported by ground attack aircraft. At the Admin Box this tactic was successful. It was first time an Allied Army had won in Burma and it was a psychological victory which had a beneficial effect on the Fourteenth Army. Slim later wrote:

> It was a victory, a victory about which there could be no argument and its effect, not only on the troops engaged but on the whole Fourteenth Army was immense.[104]

At Kohima and Imphal transport aircraft were vital in moving supplies into the besieged areas as well as transporting the 5th Indian Division which was moved from one front to another by air. The importance of the transport effort can be gauged by two days' sorties on 14th April and 25th April at the height of the Kohima and Imphal sieges as seen in this graph of tactical operations:[105]

Air supply was the soldiers' lifeline during these engagements and it must be remembered that the loss of any aircraft had a potentially serious effect as there was a shortage of such equipment not only in Burma but throughout the rest of the world in 1944.[106]

At the beginning of 1944, Allied intelligence estimated the Japanese had an approximate total of 277 aircraft in the Central Burma, Rangoon, Siam, Malaya and

104 Slim, *Defeat into Victory*, p.246.
105 TNA, Air 24/1286, Daily Operational Summaries, summary numbers 596 to 656, 1st April 1944 to 31st May 1944. Graph drawn from figures contained therein.
106 Badsey, *Utah Beach*, p.43 and Richards and Saunders, *The Fight is Won*, p.108. For instance the two American airborne divisions (82nd and 101st) dropping on the Allied right flank in Normandy on 5th/6th June 1944 required 839 aircraft and the British 6th Airborne Division required 264 aircraft on the left flank. These figures do not include the additional glider combinations.

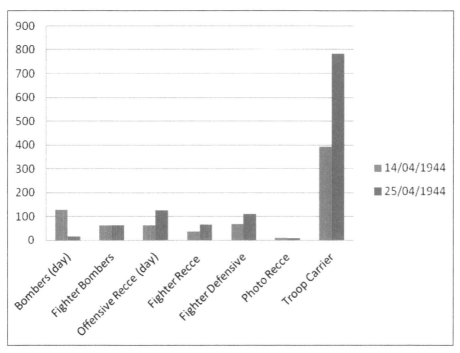

Allied tactical operations, 14th and 25th April 1944. (Source: TNA, Air 24/1286, Daily Air Summary, April and May 1944. Graph rendered from figures therein)

Sumatra area, of which 88 were single-engine fighters and 108 medium bombers.[107] This figure was to oscillate over the next two months reaching a peak in the week of 30th January of 333 aircraft (117 single-engine fighters) and a low point of 234 aircraft (81 single-engine fighters) on 27th February.[108] Some of these fluctuations were due to the attrition caused by Allied defensive operations and some to the arrival of extra fighter *Hikosentai* at the end of January and to the departure of other units to reinforce Japanese theatres elsewhere. Whilst the number of Japanese fighters was small in comparison to Allied numbers, if deployed correctly they posed a threat by exploiting early warning deficiencies and interrupting air supply operations.

At the end of 1943 the arrival of long-range American Lightnings and Mustangs promised an effective counter-air offensive, which was enhanced by the introduction of the American 1st Air Commando Group and its additional Mustangs. The A.C.G. was initiated by General Henry 'Hap' Arnold, commanding officer of the U.S.A.A.F.,

107 TNA, Air 24/1295, Weekly Intelligence Summaries, 1st January 1944 to 28th February 1944.
108 Ibid.

following a meeting with Colonel Orde Wingate during the QUADRANT conference in 1943. Appalled by stories of wounded troops being left behind on the first Chindit operation in 1943, Arnold formed the A.C.G. with the purpose of supporting Wingate with a wide mix of aircraft specifically chosen for the task.[109] These aircraft were: 25 transports (C-47 and C-46); 225 gliders; 100 light aircraft (for communications and casualty evacuation); 4 helicopters; 30 Mustangs and 12 Mitchell medium bombers.[110] Although principally formed to support Wingate in a ground attack role, the Mustangs and Mitchells could also be used against air targets as specified by the unit's joint commander, Colonel Philip Cochran:

> Thirty P-51 fighters and thirty fighter pilots were assigned to the project to furnish primary close support assault work for the columns and in cases where necessary to form air protection for our own forces and to gain air superiority in the area in which the force operates. These fighter planes are equipped with rockets for close support work and the pilots are of the highest caliber. Twelve B-25s equipped with 75mm cannon supplement the fighters for close support and assault missions.[111]

From the Group's inception, the maintenance of air superiority was a recognized function and one in which it played a part prior to and during the Chindit operations in 1944. However, despite its role the unit was unpopular in some quarters as it was thought of as Wingate's 'private airforce' at a time when the theatre was short of resources and such resources could be used for the good of many rather than a few.

The first two months of 1944 continued the pattern of heavy and medium bombers attacking Japanese airfields by night. Wellingtons and Liberators varying from two to 27 aircraft attacked airfields from Aungban to Zayatkuin with mixed results; whereas some raids reported that bursts were seen on runways and buildings, but others were much less successful.[112] The weather conditions over targets also made it difficult for intruder operations flown in the early morning or evening periods. During the evening of 5th February four Beaufighters attacked Heho airfield but could not find the target owing to poor weather. On the 7th February a Beaufighter visited Heho airfield and could not find any enemy aircraft or the airfield's flare path visible. The intelligence report noted that the "Visibility was bad throughout due to ground haze."[113] Overnight on 17th and 18th February 13 Wellingtons flew to Heho where

109 Wagner, *Any Place Any Time Any Where*, and Y'Blood, *Air Commandos Against Japan*. Both books give good accounts of how the Air Commando Group was formed.
110 TNA, WO 203/4719, Provision of Air Commandos, Air Commandos Letter from Colonel Cochran 22nd January 1944.
111 Ibid.
112 TNA, Air 24/1285, Daily Operational Summaries, summary numbers 505-563, 1st January 1944 to 28th February 1944.
113 Ibid, 7th February 1944.

only two aircraft found the target "due to very dark conditions and ground haze" and the results of their bombing was not observed.[114] Although these operations may have had some effect in disrupting the Japanese air effort, they did not reduce Japanese aircraft numbers.

However, new tactics were tried. In the early morning of 5th February four Beaufighters followed up an overnight bombing raid on Aungban airfield by flying across the base at 50 feet and attacking aircraft in dispersal pens; one aircraft was reported to have probably been set on fire.[115] This tactic however was soon dispensed with because it was equally affected by poor visibility and ground haze.[116] The raids by night or in marginal weather conditions were clearly not productive. Catching Japanese aircraft on the ground required attacks being carried out with an element of surprise, and therefore at low-level to beat the Japanese early warning system, and in better visibility conditions, and therefore during daylight hours. An indication of future operations began in February 1944 when the A.C.G. was starting to train to operational readiness in a series of multi-role sorties from reconnaissance to communications attacks. On 5th February, 12 Mustangs armed with 500 pound bombs attacked the rail junction at Wuntho and subsequently flew to Shwebo airfield, where no enemy aircraft were located.[117] On the 12th February, six Mustangs made an armed reconnaissance of the Shwebo-Monywa area where they machine gunned the airfield target area, but "results were not observed."[118] These flights, whilst unsuccessful, began the link between the heavy bomber phase and the daylight long-range fighter offensive which became an important part of the counter-air battle during the next three months.

The first counter-air sorties of March involved heavy bombers and began overnight on the 3rd/4th when a mixed force of R.A.F. Wellingtons and Liberators attacked Mingaladon and Zayatkwin airfields, their crews reporting bursts on runways and dispersal areas.[119] From then until overnight on the 17th April, periodic overnight raids were carried out on airfields with inconclusive damage caused to runways and dispersal areas.[120] It is not clear how much damage these raids inflicted on Japanese

114 Ibid, 18th February 1944.
115 Ibid, 5th February 1944.
116 TNA, Air 23/1921, Despatch on Air Operations South East Asia Command, 16th November 1943 to 31st May 1945, p. 23.
117 Y'Blood, *Air Commandos Against Japan*, p.77. There is no mention of this raid in the Daily Operational Summary.
118 TNA, Air 24/1285, Daily Operational Summaries, summary numbers 505-563, 1st January 1944 to 28th February 1944. Interestingly the 1st A.C.G. was already thought of as Wingate's property as an unattributed handwritten comment appears after this entry which states "Wingate's Show."
119 TNA, Air 23/4945, Daily Operational Summaries, March 1944.
120 TNA, Air 24/1286, Daily Operational Summaries, summary numbers 596 to 656, 1st April 1944 to 31st May 1944.

aircraft but Shores writes that an R.A.F. raid on Zayatkwin on 4th March destroyed 70% of the 64th *Sentai's* weapons and radio equipment storage.[121]

The daytime counter-air offensive began on 3rd March 1944, two days before Operation THURSDAY (the second Chindit expedition) was due to commence. 12 A.C.G. Mustangs, followed by four A.C.G. Mitchells, attacked the Japanese airfield at Shwebo, but as no aircraft were located, buildings and facilities were strafed and bombed.[122] A similar result was obtained on 7th March when ten Mustangs and ten Mitchells visited Bhamo airfield, east of the Broadway landing ground, where no aircraft were found, but buildings and runways were damaged. So far little had been achieved in terms of aircraft damage, but this was to change on 8th March.

The Japanese had moved forward a number of bombers and fighters in preparation for a raid on Ledo and the airfields at Maymyo, Shwebo, Anisakan and Onbaik were crowded. Aided by an intercepted 'live talk' transmission heard by an American technician and Allied Y-Service intercepts, 22 A.C.G. Mustangs were despatched each being armed with a pair of 1,000 lb bombs. Initially Anisakan was attacked and on the return flight to their base, the A.C.G. visited Shwebo and Onbaik where both bases were covered with Japanese aircraft.[123] After their attack the A.C.G.'s commander called for a follow up raid and nine Mitchells and 15 Mustangs were despatched; only two Mustangs were able to find Onbaik, but the Mitchells found and bombed Shwebo.

The claims from these raids indicate the difficulties in establishing a reliable estimate of Japanese aircraft attrition and this became a feature of the next few months. The Americans claimed 27 Oscars, six Dinahs, one Sally and an unidentified twin-engined aircraft destroyed on the ground, with an additional Oscar destroyed and two each probably destroyed and damaged in the air.[124] Furthermore, Wagner reported that the Mitchells' follow up raid on Shwebo claimed another 12 Japanese aircraft destroyed on the ground, whereas both Shores and Y'Blood state only that fires and explosions were started with no further claims of aircraft destroyed or damaged.[125] The American claim of over 45 aircraft destroyed was commented on by Allied intelligence analysts:

> On WEDNESDAY, March 8th, was delivered the heaviest blow that the Japanese Army Air Force has ever suffered in this theatre. The wreckage of 46 enemy aircraft lies strewn over the airfields of SHWEBO and ONBAUK [sic]

121 Shores, *Air War for Burma*, p.172.
122 Y'Blood, *Air Commandos Against Japan*, p.108.
123 Shores, *Air War for Burma*, p.175.
124 Ibid, p.175 and Y'Blood, *Air Commandos Against Japan*, p.111.
125 Shores, *Air War for Burma*, p.175; and Y'Blood, *Air Commandos Against Japan*, p.111; Wagner, *Any Place, Any Time, Any Where*, p.57.

– to say nothing of destroyed petrol bowsers and installations. It was a devastating attack – Malaya and Magwe in reverse![126]

46 aircraft represented approximately 22% of all Japanese aircraft in the theatre and the loss of 27 Oscars 33% of the Japanese fighter strength. Taken together these would have represented a notable victory, but the actual Japanese losses were likely to have been smaller. According to both Shores and Y'Blood between 15 and 18 Japanese aircraft were destroyed on the ground and in the air over Anisakan and Onbaik, whilst an unspecified number were only damaged at Shwebo, whilst Wagner makes no mention of the number of Japanese aircraft actually lost.[127] Intelligence analysts were aware that these raids did not spell the end of the Japanese effort as reinforcements or replacements were expected:

> That the Japanese will make good the losses there can be no doubt, but it will be interesting to see with what rapidity this is done or whether new units will come to the assistance of those temporally depleted.[128]

So with doubts about the actual Japanese losses and replacements expected, what had the raid achieved and what lessons were learned?

The raid had showed how future counter-air raids should be mounted. Intelligence about Japanese airfield and aircraft locations were crucial if the enemy was to be caught at its most vulnerable. The best weapon had proved to be agile, long-range, well armed fighters, particularly the American aircraft in the theatre. However, whilst both of these elements were tangible, there was clearly a problem in estimating actual losses claimed by the attacking fighters, which was always likely to be difficult to assess during confused raids. As subsequent attacks showed there was a disparity between the Japanese losses claimed by American pilots and those recorded by the J.A.A.F. in the area. Despite this there were positive results. The minimum actual loss of 15-18 Oscars represented about 19% of the Japanese fighter strength in the theatre which would need to be replaced. It does not take into account the bigger problem for the Japanese of replacing pilots who may have been lost with their aircraft.

The offensive continued in a similar manner in March with the 459th F.S.'s Lightnings. On 11th March 12 Lightnings attacked the Japanese airfield at Aungban and submitted claims of 13 destroyed and five probables in the air, with seven destroyed and two damaged on the ground. The actual Japanese loss was one Oscar from the 50th

---

126 TNA, Air 24/1296, Weekly Intelligence Summary, March 1944, No 17, Week Ending 12th March.

127 Y'Blood, *Air Commandos Against Japan*, p.111. Y'Blood gives the breakdown of losses as 12 Oscar fighters and six Helen bombers – these had been mistaken as Dinahs.

128 TNA, Air 24/1296, Weekly Intelligence Summary, March 1944, No 17 Week Ending 12th March.

Sentai caught as it was climbing to meet the American raid.[129] By now, if American claims were correct, the J.A.A.F. should have been severely weakened, but on the same day the Japanese were able to deploy 60 fighters to cover their troops crossing the Chinwin River during the advance on Imphal and between 12th and 17th March to raid the Allied airfields at Silchar, Broadway and Imphal with formations of bombers and fighters numbering between 15 and 72 aircraft. Evidently the Japanese had sufficient reserves and the Allied airfield attacks were not severely limiting enemy aircraft activity. On 25th March Japanese fighters and bombers flew to the Chittagong-Cox's Bazaar area; Lightnings were scrambled to meet this threat, but when no interception was made the American fighters were ordered to fly to Shwebo and Onbaik in an attempt to catch the enemy raiders as they landed. When the two formations met the American pilots claimed seven aircraft destroyed in the air and one on the ground, with three probables and two damaged in the air, whereas Japanese records show a destroyed tally of three fighters in the air and one on the ground.[130]

March 1944 saw the termination of night bomber attacks against Japanese airfields and the start of long-range fighter attacks from, mainly, the A.C.G. and 459th F.S., with some R.A.F. Beaufighters playing a small part. Approximately 142 daylight sorties were flown against Japanese airfields by these units with aircrews claiming a tally of 63 destroyed aircraft in the air and on the ground. Incomplete Japanese records give a minimum total of 20 Japanese aircraft destroyed as a result of the counter-air attacks in March.[131] At this stage of 1944 the J.A.A.F. had sufficient reserves to replace such losses from bases in their rear areas and Allied intelligence put Japanese fighter strength at 81 aircraft throughout March. This figure did not alter until the beginning of May. Gauging the actual attrition is obviously difficult when only incomplete records are available, however, it is likely that the raids caused some further damage to aircraft which necessitated rebuilding, or their being written-off. In addition the losses of ancillary equipment and death and injury to air force personnel must be weighed in the balance.

What effects had the March raids had? The Chindits' landings had been made in secret without interference from Japanese fighters but this was unlikely to have been as a result of the counter-air strikes. Allen wrote:

> Tazoe's airfields had been literally plastered by Cochran's air commando before the landings began, but in spite of the planes destroyed on the ground he could muster enough for a riposte.[132]

---

129 Shores, *Air War for Burma*, p.177.
130 Ibid, p.190.
131 Shores, *Air War for Burma*, pp.172-195.
132 Allen, *Burma: The Longest War*, p.328.

However, the Air Commandos had found no Japanese aircraft on the ground during the pre-5th March attacks, and had only damaged buildings and ancillary equipment. Whilst it is not known for certain it is more likely that the success of the Chindit landings was due to surprise, and the Spitfire's superiority against Japanese reconnaissance aircraft had been significant in curtailing their activities. Y'Blood claims that the 8th March raid had delayed the "Japanese … attacking the Chindit landing zones until Wingate's men were already in place" but this was, again, more likely to have been the result of the Japanese not being in a position to find the landing strips rather than a lack of numbers.[133] On 10th March two Japanese bombers escorted by 20 fighters tried to find Broadway, but missed and found Chowringhee instead, and on 11th March 60 Japanese fighters covered the crossing of the Chindwin. Broadway was not discovered by the Japanese until 13th March and during that day 40 Oscars were sent from Meiktila to attack the landing grounds.[134] The Japanese had therefore not been deprived of numbers, but had been deprived of eyes in the sky; on both 4th and 6th March Spitfires had destroyed a Dinah reconnaissance aircraft which might have revealed Allied preparations.[135]

The results of the counter-air offensive in March had therefore not been as effective as thought but had shown the necessity for future operations. The importance of protecting transport and ground support aircraft would take on an added urgency in April when the sieges of Kohima and Imphal increased in intensity. Despite the relative strength of Japanese air power, their fighters were capable of causing problems to such aircraft as witnessed on 17th March. Taking advantage of the lack of early warning cover 15 Oscars attacked the Broadway strip and caught the Spitfires of 81 Squadron just taking off or on the ground; one Spitfire was destroyed in the air and five destroyed on the ground, the remaining airborne Spitfire suffering severe damage.[136] If these kinds of losses could be inflicted on Allied fighters by surprise attack, then the necessity of reducing the air threat against transport aircraft required an efficient counter-air offensive.

The counter-air offensive intensified in April. The Chindits continued their operations behind Japanese lines depending on Allied aircraft for resupply, casualty evacuation and offensive air support. Whilst the Battle of the Admin Box had finished, the sieges at Kohima and Imphal had started and in the case of Imphal the siege would continue until June. Both these battlefields required close air support and re-supply from the air and the scale of the contribution made during the period by the Troop Carrier Command transport aircraft was profound as this graph demonstrates:[137]

---

133 Y'Blood, *Air Commandos Against Japan*, p.111.

134 Shores, *Air War for Burma*, p.179.

135 TNA, Air 27/678, 81 Squadron Operations Record Book, 4th March 1944 to 6th March 1944.

136 Shores, *Air War for Burma*, p.183.

137 TNA, Air 23/4681, Despatch covering operations of Bengal Command 15th November 1943 to 17th December 1943 and 3rd Tactical Air Force 18th December 1943 to 1st June 1944, Appendix A. Graph drawn from figures contained therein.

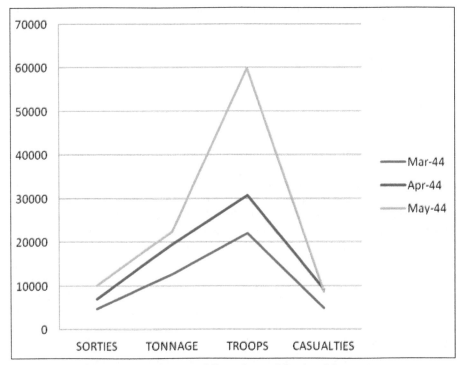

Troop Carrier Command Contribution March to May, 1944.
(Source: Ibid, Appendix A. Graph rendered from figures therein.

Air superiority was imperative to protect the transports and it must not be forgotten that the few land supply routes also had to be protected from enemy air action. The potential consequence is shown by a surprise attack by Oscars made on Zubza on 28th April:

> The attack highlighted the risk of using a single road to support five brigades plus divisional and corps troops. Were the Japanese to make a concentrated effort to disrupt this thread of communication by air action, maintenance of the forward troops would become practically impossible.[138]

The counter-air campaign assumed greater importance when the air defence of the forward areas was restricted as radar stations and observer posts were overrun and warning times were reduced.

138 Latimer, *Burma: The Forgotten War*, p.293.

The first counter-air attack occurred on 2nd April when 14 Lightnings attacked Heho and found a number of Japanese aircraft in the air returning to their base. During the attack American pilots claimed a total of 13 aircraft destroyed, four in the air and nine on the ground. Once again the American pilots over-claimed as Japanese records show only four aircraft were destroyed, two in the air and two on the ground.[139] The next notable raid occurred on 4th April when 19 1st A.C.G. Mustangs attacked Aungban where they found the Japanese 50th *Sentai's* fighters on the ground refuelling following earlier sorties. Once American claims had been assessed, a total of 24 Japanese aircraft were claimed as destroyed, 19 of which were fighters, and a number of others were claimed as probably destroyed or damaged.[140] Although Japanese records do not mention bomber losses they record 15 of their fighters destroyed and the effect of this successful raid was significant as "the whole unit [was] obliged to withdraw to Saigon to re-equip; it would return a week or so later with new aircraft."[141] This was the highest confirmed number of Japanese aircraft destroyed in a single operation during April and it would not be repeated.

From 4th April onwards the airfield offensive continued largely without the participation of the A.C.G. which reverted to supporting the Chindits in ground support operations although its aircraft visited Anisakan on 16th April and Naung on the 19th. The long-range operations were now largely left to the Lightnings from the 459th F.S. and their results showed a familiar pattern of disparity between claims and actual Japanese losses. For example, on 15th 12 Lightnings visited Heho and claimed seven destroyed, whereas Japanese records show one aircraft destroyed on the ground. On 25th 28 Lightnings attacked Heho in two waves, one at 07:12 and the other at 11:40; the first attack found nothing at Heho but engaged some Japanese fighters over Imphal during their return journey. The second attack, consisting of 11 Lightnings, flew to Heho to catch Japanese raiders refuelling following their earlier attack on Allied airfield targets at Silchar and Hailakandi. Following their attack American pilots claimed nine Japanese aircraft destroyed in the air and on the ground whereas Japanese records only show one fighter destroyed.[142] Adding to the Allied air forces' efforts in April was a combined attack of 83 Fleet Air Arm and United States Navy aircraft on the Japanese base at Sabang in Sumatra on the 19th. The pilots claimed a total of 24 Japanese aircraft destroyed on the ground and, while there are no Japanese records available, an ULTRA intercepted report of 8th May sheds doubt to the claims:

Two out of 12 aircraft inside blast pen damaged. Outside blast pen eight out of eight (including six out of six any aircraft) and rear repair shop (two out of

139 Shores, *Air War for Burma*, p.198.
140 TNA, Air 24/1286, Daily Operational Summaries, summary numbers 596 to 656, 1st April 1944 to 31st May 1944.
141 Shores, *Air War for Burma*, p.201. The Japanese ability to replace aircraft during this period will be discussed in Chapter Four.
142 Ibid, pp.210-212.

two). The remainder of the message appears to deal with damage to hangars and requests direction to be given for aircraft to be housed in blast pens.[143]

Including the Navy's attack the cumulative claims of 83 aircraft destroyed during April may have been good for morale and propaganda, but there were no signs that the counter-air offensive was having a decisive effect.

The first indication of the lack of success was that the weight of Japanese air attacks on the Allies did not substantially decrease. Even following the successful Allied attack on Aungban on 4th April when the Japanese lost 15 fighters, 30 Oscars from the 64th *Sentai* performed a sweep over Imphal positions on 12th, whilst on the 17th 50 Oscars and 12 Sallys attacked the Imphal plain. This indicated that either the Japanese had adequate reserves to replace losses or that the counter-air offensive was not destroying as many enemy aircraft as claimed. The Japanese ability to attack in such numbers and the early warning deficiencies around the Imphal area led to transport losses on 25th April when 30 Oscars attacked Imphal. There they were intercepted by Spitfires but a number of the Oscars managed to engage Dakotas flying in the area and five of these aircraft were lost.[144]

The counter-air offensive in May was conducted by the American long-range fighters supported by a few R.A.F. sorties. During the month the 1st A.C.G. withdrew to rest and refit, but the American 530th F.S.'s Mustangs became operational and this unit joined the offensive. However, the counter-air offensive began to wane as the month progressed owing to deteriorating weather as the monsoon period approached. On 19th May a joint R.A.F. and U.S.A.A.F. attack on Meiktila was aborted owing to bad weather, as were plans for the Americans to attack Japanese airfields on 18th and 21st. There was also the familiar story of claim against actual loss. For example, on 10th May 16 Lightnings attacked Aungban in two waves and claimed five Japanese aircraft destroyed in the air and on the ground, whereas Japanese records only show three aircraft lost.[145] By the end of May the Allies flew 340 sorties on counter-air operations and claimed a maximum of 63 Japanese aircraft destroyed against a minimum of 20 destroyed according to incomplete Japanese records.[146] This figure represented a one third ratio of actual Japanese loss against Allied pilots' claims recorded in March and April.

Despite these losses, claimed or actual, the Japanese were able to mount various heavy fighter sweeps against Allied positions throughout the month.[147] On 23rd May

---

143 TNA, Air 40/2682, Far East Special Air Intelligence, No 113.
144 This action subsequently resulted in the introduction of the air corridor, see Chapter 1, p.89.
145 Shores, *Air War for Burma*, p.224.
146 Ibid, pp.218-237.
147 On 5th May 30 Oscars attacked Kohima; on 14th May 25 Oscars attacked Kohima; on 18th may a mixed force of 41 bombers and fighters attacked Imphal; and on 21st May 24 bombers and fighters attacked army positions in the Bishenphur area.

35 Japanese fighters flew over the Burmese battle areas leading Shores to write, "The month's raids on the Japanese by the U.S.A.A.F. fighters still did not seem greatly to have diminished the J.A.A.F.'s ability to strike back despite the effective demise of the 87th *Sentai*."[148] This brings into question how effective the counter-air offensive of the March to May period had been.

The period between March and June 1944 is regarded as the important period of the counter-air offensive against the Japanese Air Forces in Burma. A.C.M. Pierse wrote in his Despatch that the 1st A.C.G. alone claimed 90 Japanese aircraft destroyed in the air and on the ground and the Bengal Despatch also referred to the 459th F.S.'s achievements:

> One squadron of P-38s alone, operating from Chittagong, destroyed 96 enemy aircraft in this way within six weeks of coming into operations in 224 Group.[149]

and:

> I would mention the P-38s of No 459 Squadron USAAF which subsequent to the attachments to 224 Group Chittagong achieved the following successes in a matter of 11 weeks, 121 enemy aircraft destroyed; 21 probably destroyed and 48 damaged.[150]

Craven and Cate wrote, "By June 1944 Allied air superiority in Burma was no longer challenged."[151] Despite this statement there was clearly a disparity between the claims made and the actual losses suffered by the J.A.A.F. during the counter-air offensive. Allied claims as a result of interdiction sorties against Japanese airfields alone amounted to 213 aircraft destroyed, whilst according to available Japanese records the minimum number of destroyed aircraft was approximately 66.[152] Aircrew claims must therefore be considered inaccurate but this should not be surprising as they were made in the heat of battle.[153] However, the disparity bears detailed analysis.

To analyse statistically the actual scale of Japanese losses during the three months in review is difficult owing to the lack of Japanese military records. While there were some unit records which survived most military records were destroyed leaving only

---

148 Shores, *Air War for Burma*, p.233.
149 TNA, Air 23/4681, Despatch covering operations of Bengal Command 15th November 1943 to 17th December 1943 and 3rd Tactical Air Force 18th December 1943 to 1st June 1944, p.7.
150 Ibid, p.20.
151 Craven and Cate, *The Army Air Forces in World War II Volume Four*, p.511.
152 Shores, *Air War for Burma*, pp.172-237.
153 Y'Blood, *Air Commandos Against Japan*, p.114. Y'Blood wrote, "The wide variance in claims just illustrates the difficulty in accurately assessing the actual damage incurred to an opposing force in a fast-moving aerial battle."

Japanese civilian production and manufacturing tables for analysis. The post-war United States Strategic Bombing Survey (U.S.S.B.S.) used, "the best Japanese figures and the estimates made by Allied intelligence agencies" to compile their report and wrote of their difficulties:

> All but a few Japanese Army and Navy records relating to losses have been burned, and the statistics on wastage furnished by the Japanese are based on almost nothing but the memory of a few Japanese officers. Moreover during the war, Allied intelligence on wastage was much less reliable than intelligence checks on the Japanese figures and many of the loss figures contained in this report may be subject to an error of 25 per cent or more.[154]

The U.S.S.B.S. report showed Japanese monthly aircraft production rose during the first half of 1944 from 1,622 in January to 1,786 in July which increased the size of the Japanese Air Forces from 4,050 to 5,500 during the same months.[155] Furthermore, it concluded that the Japanese were able to steadily increase the size of the J.A.A.F. during 1944 until the Philippines campaign in August and, "Then for the first time losses exceeded the number of planes reaching tactical units, and overall strength fell off."[156] This would indicate that Japanese industry was building aircraft in sufficient quantities to replace wastage during the first half of 1944, and it is therefore likely that losses in Burma were replaced. These are, of course, post-war figures which the Allied intelligence agencies did not have and Ford shows that the available wartime data from signal intelligence, captured documents and aircraft registration plates was fragmentary and did not allow firm calculations.[157] This data led the Chiefs of Staff Committee to deduce in May 1944 that "in spite of heavy aircraft losses, a rise in strength was possible thanks to increased output" whereas the Air Ministry representatives:

> [W]ere unable to put forward an educated critique, and the final conclusion was based on the deduction that only a small portion of the Japanese air forces had been engaged, and given their policy of conservation, wastage was unlikely to be high.[158]

A.C.S.E.A. intelligence on Japanese aircraft strength was based principally on signal intelligence, captured documents and registration plates taken from crashed aircraft. Although work had begun to break J.A.A.F. ciphers, it was not until mid-1944 that the difficulties involved in breaking Japanese codes and ciphers yielded

---

154 TNA, Air 48/69, U.S.S.B.S., *Japanese Air Power*, p.30.
155 Ibid, p.29.
156 Ibid.
157 Ford, *Britain's Secret War Against Japan 1937-1945*, p.83.
158 Ibid.

better intelligence of their intentions and actions. The level of accuracy can be seen in the A.C.S.E.A. Weekly Intelligence Summaries' figures which show varying levels of Japanese strength which do not always correspond with the counter-air offensive's claims which are themselves problematic.[159] The Intelligence Summaries showed Japanese air strength at a constant 216 aircraft in the theatre from mid-March until the second week of April when it increased to 288 and continued to rise to 321 at the end of April. The total then rose to 348 at the beginning of May before falling to 318 at the end of the month. Despite the claims made by Allied pilots the intelligence assessments never put the overall strength below 216, although various categories of aircraft were re-assessed as wastage claims were analysed. For example, in May the intelligence summary reported:

> Enemy fighter losses in Burma have been exceptionally heavy during the past week, some fifty being destroyed. There is reason to believe that full replacements have not been forthcoming and the fighter strength in Burma is marked down from 76 to 57 a/c.[160]

Although such adjustments were to be expected as information was collated it is also clear that the intelligence officers were aware of the shortcomings of their information. Typically in April:

> There are indications of two or three Army air units in Sumatra though it is not yet known whether they are complete units nor with what type of aircraft they are equipped. The present assessment of 72 single-engined fighters is therefore extremely tentative … It is estimated that the total number of aircraft in this area is now 270 as compared with 115 shown last week. It is most important to note, however, that the units comprising these increases, though newly identified in this area, have in fact been there for several weeks [161]

This would suggest that not only were the numbers suspect but that the Allies were facing more Japanese units than previously thought and this was actually admitted in June 1944:

> [T]he gradual increase in weekly figures over past months must not be taken as reflecting a gradual build-up by the enemy, but is due rather to an irregular flow of information from this area. In fact the greater part of air strength now shown is believed to have been there since early this year.[162]

159 TNA, Air 24 Series from Air 24/1295 onwards.
160 TNA, Air 24/1298, Intelligence Branch Appendices, May 1944.
161 TNA, Air 24/1297, Intelligence Branch Appendices, April 1944.
162 TNA, Air 24/1299, Intelligence Branch Appendices, June 1944.

This extract was taken from the intelligence summary of 25th June 1944 when the overall Japanese strength was assessed as 371, of which 196 were placed in Malaya and Sumatra undergoing rest and refitting.

The following graph which compares intelligence assessments with pilots' claims is of considerable value but cannot be regarded as anything better than a good approximation as intelligence estimates were estimates rather than firm figures. It shows the effect of the counter-air offensive on overall Japanese air strength in the theatre which includes aircraft on the Sumatra and Malayan airfields.[163]

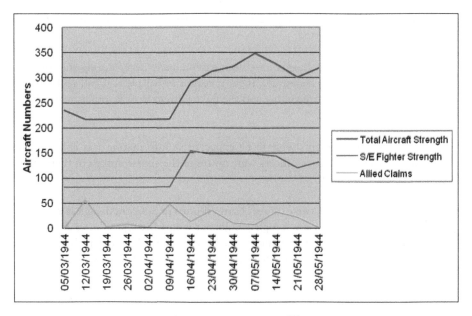

Strength against claims.[164]

The upper line shows overall Japanese air strength as assessed by Allied intelligence and the middle line shows the assessed fighter strength. The lower line shows Allied claims of destroyed aircraft from the counter-air offensive only, i.e. it does not include losses from air defence or escort sorties. The latter figure is likely to be higher than actual loss figures and we can assume this line could generally be two thirds lower. It will be seen that for the first six weeks Japanese air strength probably remained constant despite the claims made during the weeks ending on 12th March and 9th April. The strength then increased by 72 fighters as mentioned earlier and this can be explained in two ways; either the Allied counter-air offensive had forced

163 Ibid.
164 Ibid. Graph rendered from figures contained therein.

the Japanese to commit more fighters to the theatre, or, as Allied intelligence had stated, aircrafts' presence was tentative. However, this figure was not altered for the rest of the period, and given the June assessment of aircraft numbers it is likely that the 72 fighters had been there since the beginning of March. From mid-April Japanese aircraft numbers steadily increased particularly in terms of bombers and reconnaissance aircraft, whereas the numbers of fighters reduced slightly owing to attrition until 21st May when numbers started to increase prior to the monsoon period. Allied intelligence figures suggest that the increase in air strength rose to 389 aircraft in the week ending 2nd July 1944 which represents a greater figure than the Japanese had started the year with, 277. Therefore it must be concluded that it is probable that Japanese resupply combined with their policy of conservation had ensured a constant air strength within the theatre which the Allies had kept in check but not substantially reduced.

The preceding sections may give the impression that the counter-air offensive had failed in its objective. However, the 60 Japanese aircraft that were confirmed as destroyed even as a minimum was greater than the approximate number of 25 aircraft confirmed destroyed as a result of air to air attrition and showed the value of a counter-air offensive. In one unit's case the offensive had precipitated a demise and withdrawal. The 87th *Sentai* had arrived in Burma as a relatively inexperienced squadron on 8th May with its Ki-44 Tojo fighters which were considered an improvement over the Oscars. However, on 21st May the unit was forced to withdraw to Sumatra following the loss of six pilots killed and many aircraft destroyed as a result of "encountering the best Allied long-range fighters available in the area."[165]

At the beginning of this chapter the benefits of a counter-air offensive were described and many of these were relevant to the period under review. In addition to the 60 aircraft confirmed destroyed there were also the aircraft which had been damaged in the air or on the ground as a result of the airfield strikes. These required repair or replacement both of which placed a strain on the Japanese war effort. The U.S.S.B.S. concluded in 1946 that the Japanese failed to develop an adequate maintenance and repair organisation citing various problems such as over-extension of units and spare parts shortages.[166] If aircraft could not be repaired easily then they would have to be replaced, but the Japanese record of ferrying replacement aircraft was quite poor, as during the war they lost 4000 aircraft in ferrying operations. In comparison the Americans lost 909 in the European and Pacific Theatres combined.[167] Furthermore, there was the matter of replacing lost personnel, pilots in particular. In July 1944 an American MAGIC intercept showed the Japanese had set up a new training programme which was hoped would alleviate their pilot shortages by August 1944

165 Shores, *Air War for Burma*, p.232.
166 TNA, Air 48/69, U.S.S.B.S., *Japanese Air Power*, p.31.
167 Ibid, p.30.

but it was being hampered by lack of materials and suitable training aircraft.[168] The intercept showed that trainee pilots were not receiving advanced training, and that the 3rd Air Army in Singapore reported in May that the trainees had only 15 hours flying per month since leaving Japan in March. Similar shortages existed for other aircrew members and for the essential ground maintenance trades.[169] Finally in addition to material and personnel losses the offensive continued to force the Japanese to disperse their squadrons to avoid attack as reported in April:

> It is interesting to note that whereas not long ago the enemy had his fighter strength in Central Burma almost entirely concentrated at Anisakan, Heho and Aungban, he is now pursuing a policy of much wider dispersal, which is doubt-less due to the success of low-level attack by Allied fighters on airfields.[170]

Dispersing aircraft to smaller airfields away from main bases had a potential effect of increasing attrition from flying accidents as well as the effects of increased aircraft flying hours, pilot fatigue and fuel wastage.

June 1944 to June 1945

The last phase of the counter-air offensive was fought supporting the Allied offensive in Burma which led to the defeat of Japanese forces in 1945. The land offensive began on 21st June 1944 when the Japanese started to withdraw from around the Imphal Plain and continued after the road to Imphal was opened.[171] The Japanese were defeated and disorganized and suffering shortages of food and ammunition. The Allies sought to exploit these factors by pursuing them into Burma notwithstanding the monsoon period. They began their pursuit by clearing Japanese forces out of the hills surrounding Imphal in July before pressing on south-eastwards to retake Tamu on 4th August. The gathering momentum was maintained by two separate advances, one eastward towards Sittaung and the other southwards to Kalemyo through the Kabaw valley. Sittaung was captured on 4th September and Kalemyo on 14th November, before the port of Kalewa was taken on 2nd December. This had also been the objective of the Indian 5th Division which had fought its way southward from Imphal through Tiddim. The Allied advance to Kalewa had been hard against an enemy who fought a furious withdrawal which necessitated regular supply drops and close air support operations to sustain their troops:

---

168 TNA, Air 40/2682, Far East Special Air Intelligence Summary No 175 July 1944. MAGIC was the American equivalent of the British ULTRA signals intelligence organization.
169 TNA, Air 48/69, U.S.S.B.S., *Japanese Air Power*, p.34.
170 TNA, Air 24/1297, Intelligence Branch Appendices, April 1944.
171 Latimer, *Burma: The Forgotten War*, p.304.

It had taken 11 Division four months to cover the 100 plus miles from Tamu to Kalewa, and in face of constant opposition they had depended for their food and ammunition entirely on the transport squadrons, operating under conditions of almost unbelievable difficulty.[172]

The 5th Division's advance had "to be entirely supported by air-drop and provided with constant air support, again largely furnished by Hurricanes."[173] Air support would continue to play a vital role in the reconquest of Burma and this was taken into account in planning. By December 1944 the Fourteenth Army was at the banks of the Chindwin River and airfield construction to accommodate transport and fighter aircraft had begun, for instance, at the recently captured Kalemyo. Plans such as Operation CAPITAL (the reconquest of Central Burma), Operation ROMULUS (conquest of the Arakan), and Operation TALON (capture of Akyab Island) had been formulated and all emphasised the necessity of capturing airfields, or constructing makeshift airstrips for supply or casualty evacuation. Whilst these and subsequent plans were adapted or formulated over the next eight months they all made provision for air support from transport and attack aircraft, and synonymous with the air plan was a necessity for gaining air superiority. The primary task given to 221 Group was:

> [The] Destruction of the Japanese Air Force in Burma in order to maintain air superiority and to ensure protection against the enemy for transport aircraft engaged in essential air supply operations.[174]

Transport aircraft continued to be in short supply in the theatre whilst some ground attack aircraft required protection from enemy fighters. For example, while many of the newer types of Allied aircraft such as the P-47 Thunderbolt could adequately defend themselves in aerial combat, the Hurricane continued to provide sterling service in short range army support and as Probert wrote, "For short-range work at low-level *in conditions of air superiority* they remained invaluable."[175] Providing air superiority over such a vast area provided difficulties as it had done earlier in the campaign and as it was to do for the remainder of the Far Eastern war. Providing escort fighters to defend transport sorties was necessary but wasteful of fuel as not every flight encountered Japanese fighters. Such operations also increased wear and tear in airframe and pilot fatigue but there was no alternative. It was nearly impossible to depend on fighters being alerted from their bases in turn to intercept Japanese aircraft as the transports were operating a long way from Allied fighter bases, and early warning from radar and

172 Probert, *The Forgotten Air Force*, p.251.
173 Ibid.
174 TNA, Air 41/64, *The Campaigns in the Far East Volume IV: South East Asia November 1943 to August 1945*, p.256.
175 Probert, *The Forgotten Air Force*, p.259, my italics.

observer posts was unreliable owing to the distances involved, the speed of the Allied advance and limitations in the effectiveness of transportable radar equipment. The speed of the advance in early January 1945 towards Ye-U and Shwebo was a typical example as 221 Group's fighters were based in the Imphal area and the front line was 150 miles away. Given these circumstances counter-air strikes were vital.

The fighting in the 1944 monsoon period differed from the same period in 1942 and 1943 because neither side completely ceased military operations. Mountbatten ordered that fighting should continue during the monsoon as he was keen to exploit the Japanese withdrawal from Imphal. This strategy limited the effectiveness of air operations as the weather often precluded any flying and even when operations were mounted, targets were often not found.[176] Continual Allied advances also resulted in the Japanese not completely withdrawing their air strength as had been the case in previous years and this was recognized by the Allies. In May 1944 General Stratemeyer wrote:

> It became evident towards the end of the month that the Japanese were intending to keep a force of about 90 fighters in Burma during the monsoon and use them as opportunity offered.[177]

On 4th June Allied intelligence reported:

> As for the fighters, there is no sign as yet of any withdrawal, and it does not seem likely that any move will take place until the military situation becomes less acute.[178]

At the end of June 1944 the J.A.A.F. had a total of 371 aircraft in the S.E.A.C. area. This represented the highest total of Japanese aircraft in the theatre up until that time despite the losses inflicted on its forces during the intensive period of air operations during March, April and May.[179] On 16th July an intelligence report stated:

> It is believed that the only operational aircraft now remaining in Burma are approximately 62 single-engined fighters, Oscars and Tojos ... The heavier losses which they have suffered this year would have made their withdrawal for rest and training desirable from the Japanese point of view, but the military situation did not allow for it.[180]

---

176 Shores, *Air War for Burma*, p.238.
177 TNA, Air 23/1927, Despatch on Air Operations Eastern Air Command 15th December 1943 to 31st May 1944.
178 TNA, Air 24/1299, Intelligence Branch Appendices, June 1944.
179 Ibid.
180 TNA, Air 24/1301, Intelligence Branch Appendices, July 1944.

Successive Allied intelligence assessments showed that for the rest of the monsoon period the Japanese retained a single-engine fighter presence of approximately 70 aircraft between Central Burma and Rangoon and they were, as General Stratemeyer had predicted, occasionally used. For example on 7th July what was described as a strong force of Oscars attacked the Myitkyina airfield where they caught the American 80th F.S. on the ground damaging six P-40s.[181] On 17th and 18th August 20 Oscars attacked a bridge over the Salween near to Eitsu and although the bridge was not hit on either occasion, a Dakota was shot down and destroyed by the Japanese formation. Although none of these raids posed a significant threat they did demonstrate that the J.A.A.F. was prepared to fight, and, importantly, the threat it posed to transport aircraft.

The monsoon period precluded intensive Allied counter-air operations but given the occasional Japanese presence over the front some attacks were mounted when the weather was favourable. On 6th June 459th F.S. Lightnings attacked Meiktila and Heho airfields claiming two aircraft destroyed and six damaged, though Japanese records only show one aircraft destroyed.[182] Despite the Japanese strength in the area there was clearly a policy of conservation and dispersal as during two U.S. raids on Lashio on 11th and 13th July only five and two aircraft respectively were seen on the airfield.[183] Weather conditions in August restricted wide scale operations except on the 27th August when Spitfires were sent to Donbauk airfield to investigate a report that 36 Tojos were present; only one was found and that was claimed as destroyed.[184]

Despite the inability to find and draw the Japanese into battle their presence was occasionally felt later in the monsoon season. On 8th September 20 Oscars attacked army positions at Salween and on 10th a mixed force of 33 Japanese aircraft attacked Tengchaung and Langling.[185] Reacting to these raids 15 Lightnings flew a sweep to Rangoon on 13th September where an Oscar was confirmed as destroyed when it attempted to intercept the U.S. formation.[186] None of the Allied attacks posed a serious threat to Japanese air strength at this time as even the numbers claimed were very small. This is unsurprising given the weather conditions, low frequency of raids and difficulty of finding a small number of Japanese aircraft dispersed over many airfields in a vast country. However, as the monsoon began to abate during October 1944, the situation changed as Japan had built up its air strength for the

---

181 Shores, *Air War for Burma*, p.248.
182 Ibid, p.241 and TNA, Air 24/1287, Daily Operational Summaries, summary numbers 657-717, June and July 1944.
183 TNA, Air 24/1287, Daily Operational Summaries, summary numbers 657-717, June and July 1944.
184 TNA, Air 27/1026, 152 Squadron Operations Record Book, 27th August 1944.
185 TNA, Air 24/1288, Daily Operational Summaries, summary numbers 718-778, August and September 1944.
186 Shores, *Air War for Burma*, p. 260 and TNA, Air 24/1288, Daily Operational Summaries, summary numbers 718-778, August and September 1944.

new campaigning season. By 29th October Allied intelligence estimated Japanese air strength as 485 aircraft in the Far East: 100 in Burma; 60 in Siam/French-Indo China; and 325 in Sumatra/Malaya.[187]

As the weather improved, air supply and ground attack operations supporting Allied ground troops in their advance into Burma increased in intensity. Allied intelligence estimated between 45 and 55 Japanese fighters were based on three airfields around Rangoon (Mingaladon, Hmawbi and Zayatkwin) and it was decided to mount a series of attacks on these bases starting on 18th October and lasting for three days.[188] Importantly the attacks, called Operation 'L', would coincide with the start of the U.S. campaign in the Philippines and it was hoped that they would deter Japanese aircraft transfers to the Pacific region.[189] The first attack occurred on 18th October when a composite force of R.A.F. Beaufighters, Mosquitoes and Thunderbolts and U.S. Lightnings, Mustangs and Thunderbolts flew to the Rangoon airfields. There is some discrepancy with regard to the numbers of Japanese aircraft claimed destroyed. Shores writes of seven on the ground and three in the air, Y'Blood writes of six on the ground and three in the air, whilst Allied intelligence gave the figure as five on the ground and three in the air. Japanese records only show one aircraft destroyed during aerial combat.[190] Weather conditions prevented an attack on 19th October but a similar composite force of British and U.S. aircraft attacked the airfields again on the 20th. This time pilots claimed six destroyed on the ground and one in the air, the latter being confirmed as lost in Japanese records.[191] Over two days Allied pilots had claimed approximately 16 to 18 aircraft destroyed which the Eastern Air Command considered as a poor return for the effort expended. Some units, such as 58th F.S. and 459th F.S., were criticised for their lack of aggression, only the A.C.G. being praised.[192]

Such raids presented a problem to Allied commanders. In October the Allies had approximately 1,000 aircraft of all types in the South East Asia Theatre and by the end of the year this figure increased to 1,500.[193] The Japanese had approximately 410

187 TNA, Air 24/1305, Intelligence Branch Appendices, October 1944.
188 TNA, Air 24/1289, Daily Operational Summaries, summary numbers 779-839, October and November 1944 and Y'Blood, *Air Commandos Against Japan*, p.131.
189 TNA, Air 23/4665, Despatch on Air Operations by Air Chief Marshal Sir Keith Park, 3rd May 1944 to 12th September 1945.
190 Shores, *Air War for Burma*, p.273.
191 Ibid, p.274.
192 Y'Blood, *Air Commandos Against Japan*, p.133 and Wagner, *Any Place, Any Time, Any Where*, p.97. Y'Blood cites the H.Q. Army Air Force Report 'A Study of Operation L' as his source for this information. The conclusion is different to that of Wagner who wrote "The missions were the largest of their kind in South East Asia and proved highly successful."
193 In addition to the increase in forces, on 1st September 1944 the 1st Air Commando Group was re-activated and was joined by the 2nd A.C.G. in January 1945. Both groups brought much improved aircraft, notably the P-47 Thunderbolt and the latest variant of

aircraft according to intelligence estimates and this included all types from front line fighters to those relegated to training roles.[194] The Allies were forced to expend a disproportionate effort to neutralise what was effectively a smaller force, but one which was still capable of inflicting losses on transport aircraft and the resources committed to them were needed elsewhere in the ground attack role such was the nature of the advance over land and its dependence on air support.[195]

The disappointing consequences of disproportionate numbers of Allied aircraft being used to neutralize Japanese air strength became very apparent at the beginning of November. Intelligence noted that approximately 60 Japanese aircraft were based at the Rangoon series of airfields and it was decided to attack them at the same time as U.S. Liberators and Superfortresses raided docks and railway installations. On 3rd November Operation ERUPTION involved 21 459th F.S. Lightnings, 33 A.C.G. Thunderbolts and 24 R.A.F. Thunderbolts which attacked the airfields at Hmawbi, Mingaladon, Zayatkwin, and Heho. Despite the numbers involved the results were disappointing: at Hmawbi only a few aircraft were seen on the ground; cloud cover obscured Mingaladon; nothing was seen at Zayatkwin; and only a few aircraft were seen at Heho. Total claims by Allied pilots were one aircraft destroyed, four damaged and one probably destroyed. The following day a mixed force of 83 R.A.F. and U.S. Thunderbolts and Lightnings escorted bombers to Rangoon where similar dispro-portionate results were recorded; in air-to-air combat the escort fighters claimed four aircraft destroyed and six damaged, whilst in an attack on Zayatkwin and Hmawbi only two aircraft were claimed as destroyed, both in air combat over the airfields.

Despite the claims, the Japanese ability to disrupt Allied transport activities continued. During the morning of 8th November, 24 Oscars attacked British artil-lery positions at Kalemyo and whilst there engaged a formation of Dakotas, whilst in the afternoon 25 Oscars returned to the same area and engaged Allied trans-ports. On both occasions Spitfires were scrambled to intercept the Japanese aircraft and on both occasions failed to find them.[196] During the day Allied transport losses amounted to between five and nine aircraft leaving the air command little option but to provide escorts to subsequent transport sorties which 152 Squadron provided on 9th November.[197]

The counter-air offensive continued during November on six days but on no occa-sion did Allied pilots claim more than two enemy aircraft destroyed, and according to Japanese sources there was only one success.[198] The numbers claimed during these raids did little to significantly reduce Japanese air strength which was proving elusive

the Mustang, the P-51D. See Appendices 6, 7, and 8 for Allied aircraft strengths through 1944.

194 TNA, Air 24/1305, Intelligence Branch Appendices, October 1944.
195 TNA, Air 24/1311, Intelligence Branch Appendices, February 1945.
196 TNA, Air 27/1026, 152 Squadron Operations Record Book, 8th November 1944.
197 Ibid, 9th November 1944 and Shores, *Air War for Burma*, p.282.
198 Shores, *Air War for Burma*, pp.278-291.

in comparison with the intensive counter-air period at the beginning of 1944. For example on 15th November the Lightnings of 459th F.S. raided Heho airfield and failed to find any aircraft present. This trend was to continue in December. Counter-air operations only took place on four days and once again Japanese aircraft were hard to find; only four Japanese aircraft were claimed as destroyed overall and only one of these is confirmed by their records.[199] While such raids were keeping pressure on the Japanese to disperse and conserve their aircraft in Burma, and causing by the end of December 1944 their aircraft numbers in the South East Asia area to fall, this was not the only reason for such a decline.

Allied intelligence started to record a reduction in Japanese aircraft numbers caused by the escalation of the war in the South-West Pacific area. While a full appreciation of the effect the Pacific war had on the Far East will be discussed in Chapter 4 it is useful to record how Japanese numbers gradually decreased in the S.E.A.C. area.

Based on intelligence estimates:

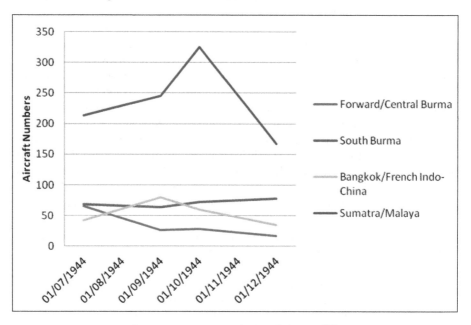

Japanese air assets in the S.E.A.C. area.[200]

199 TNA, Air 24/1290, Daily Operational Summaries, summary numbers 840 to 901, December 1944 and Shores, *Air War for Burma*, pp.290-300.

200 TNA, Air 24/1299, onwards, Weekly Intelligence Summaries July to December 1944. Graph rendered from figures contained therein.

As always care should be taken with the intelligence assessments of Japanese air strength as it is clear from their contents that there were continual reassessments of numbers owing to ongoing intelligence reports. However, such a large readjustment had never been witnessed previously and intelligence was clearly pointing to transfers to other Japanese theatres of action. In an intelligence report summarising the last six months of 1944 the analysts pointed out that figures in Burma had remained "remarkably static" and they surmised that the Japanese could replace losses from rear areas and had not been called upon to transfer any aircraft away from the theatre.[201] However, the same report showed a reduction in fighter aircraft in Sumatra and Malaya from 263 in November to approximately 100 in December. Although the report concluded that the aircraft in Malaya and Sumatra were "never an actual threat on the Burma front" it suggested that aircraft transfers to Burma from these countries could have been undertaken if circumstances had dictated.[202] Therefore if aircraft were removed from Malaya and Sumatra it presented a situation in which potential reserves for the Burma front were no longer available. The Burma area was split by A.C.S.E.A. into forward/central and South Burma (Rangoon) but numbers should be regarded as fluid from week to week owing to the Japanese ability to move aircraft around the country within a few hours.

Japanese aircraft in Malaya and Sumatra were ignored by the U.S.S.B.S., and were often dismissed in Allied documents as not being in a position to affect operations in Burma, but this is an error.[203] As with most aircraft in the theatre, it was possible to transfer them within a few days via staging posts to most areas in Burma to disrupt Allied land and air operations. Furthermore, whilst those aircraft were guarding important oil fields they provided a threat to any proposed Allied invasion of Malaya.

Allied intelligence officers had been reporting on the migration since November:

> It is very possible that with the Allied advance into the Philippines and the destruction of so many Japanese aircraft both here and in Formosa and the Rykus, the Japanese may have been obliged to withdraw some aircraft from the Sumatra/Malaya area to bolster up their defences.[204]

Similar weekly reports continued into December where on 10th the report stated:

> It is believed that several aircraft, particularly fighters, have been withdrawn from the Sumatra/Malaya area to assist the 4th Air Army in the Philippines and Netherlands East Indies.[205]

---

201 TNA, Air 23/4682, Third Tactical Air Force: Enemy Air Strength and Activity, 1st June 1944 to 4th December 1944.
202 Ibid.
203 R.A.F. Museum Hendon, U.S.S.B.S., *Air Operations in China, Burma, India, World War II*.
204 TNA, Air 24/1306, Intelligence Branch Appendices, 19th November 1944.
205 TNA, Air 24/1308, Intelligence Branch Appendices, 10th December 1944. The 4th Air Army was a land-based force of the J.A.A.F. It was formed in Rabaul in June 1943

All the reports had only mentioned aircraft drawn from Malaya and Sumatra but this was to change. In the 24th December report it was stated that:

> There is now good reason to believe that the fighter strength in Burma/Siam has also suffered and now amounts to no more than 75 aircraft. These have recently been divided between Rangoon and Central Burma, but latest intelligence indicates that they are now all concentrated in the Rangoon area.[206]

Various intelligence sources from Y Service wireless intercepts to interpretations of Japanese coded messages were used to form a picture of the J.A.A.F.'s movements. On 19th November the reduction of 55 aircraft in the Malaya and Sumatra area was noted and attributed to the transfer of two units to the Philippines and Borneo.[207] On 3rd December Japanese air strength in Malaya and Sumatra reduced by 45 aircraft as the 26th *Hikosentai* and part of the 21st *Hikosentai* had moved to the Philippines.[208] These reports also made use of intelligence gathered from U.S. sources to track the movement of Japanese units as seen on 17th December:

> The only change in the Burma Sumatra zone is that 204 Hikosentai (30 fighters) has been well identified in the Philippines and has, therefore, transferred accordingly. Backdated information recently available shows that both this unit and another Army unit (shown by Air Ministry as having moved some weeks ago from Sumatra to the Philippines) were in fact ordered to transfer as early as October 6th – i.e. before any landings on the Philippines and even before the preceding air strikes on Formosa.[209]

There was thus clearly a transfer of aircraft away from the South East Asia area towards the Pacific and this would have a fundamental effect on Japanese air assets in Burma. Whilst such aircraft moved there was a reduction in likely reserves and whilst losses were mounting in all theatres it was unlikely that replacement aircraft would be available for transfer to Burma, which in turn placed an onus on Japanese air chiefs to conserve aircraft and not use them wastefully. The rate of loss of Japanese aircraft being transported from one area to another has been covered earlier in this chapter as an effect of poor pilots who had not been sufficiently trained for their task. Intelligence analysis of Japanese aircrew returns had shown in July 1944 nearly 50% of pilot personnel in Burma and China were formed from category C crews, which were

and was responsible for covering the Solomon Islands, Netherland East Indies and the Territories of Papua and New Guinea areas of operations.

206 TNA, Air 24/1309, Intelligence Branch Appendices, 24th December 1944.
207 TNA, Air 40/2690, 'U' Weekly Summary, No 55, 19th November 1944.
208 Ibid, No 57, 3rd December 1944.
209 Ibid, No 59, 17th December 1944.

defined as unfit for operations.[210] This meant front-line squadrons were engaged in operations whilst at the same time training new pilots. This problem of inexperience continued in 1945 as, for example, on 24th April four new Ki-84 Frank aircraft of the 50th *Sentai* were forced to crash-land as a result of navigational errors which "given the shortage of aircraft remaining to the J.A.A.F., was something of a disaster."[211]

Despite the reduction in Japanese aircraft numbers in the theatre, for the first few months of 1945 the J.A.A.F. in Burma were still fighting and inflicting damage on Allied resources. At the beginning of January 1945 intelligence estimates of aircraft stationed in Burma amounted to 75 fighters and 20 reconnaissance aircraft, and during the month the fighters were used in a series of attacks against Allied positions.[212] The successful Allied landings on Akyab Island in late December 1944 together with the rapid advance in the Shwebo area had precipitated Japanese attacks which were larger than at any time since June 1944 and relatively free from interception. As the Allies' advance had been so rapid, 221 Group's fighters were still based on the Imphal airfields, which meant the squadrons were 150 miles from the Army's front line. Eventually the fighters were able to move forward to advanced landings grounds but until that happened in January 1945, Japanese fighters, "appeared in greater numbers than had been seen since June-July 1944 strafing almost with impunity."[213] On five occasions during January formations of between 18 and 35 Japanese bombers and fighters attacked Allied positions in strafing and bombing operations. Together with the threat posed to ground troops the raids posed problems for the transport supply aircraft. For example, on 12th January 17 Oscars attacked a forward landing strip where they encountered a formation of Dakotas; two Dakotas were destroyed on the air and a further two on the ground. As fighters were unable to assist in defence, the counter-air campaign continued and Japanese airfields in the Meiktila and Zayatkwin areas were attacked on five occasions during the month by R.A.F. and U.S. aircraft. During the attacks Allied pilots claimed nine Japanese aircraft destroyed and surviving Japanese records show that two of their aircraft were confirmed as lost.[214]

According to intelligence estimates at the end of January, Japanese aircraft numbers in Burma had reduced to 51 aircraft of which 35 were fighters, eight reconnaissance and eight light bombers of which only two reconnaissance and the light bombers were in the forward and central Burma area.[215] The 51 aircraft compares to a total of 95 (75 fighters and 20 reconnaissance) at the beginning of January a reduction of 44 aircraft, of which 24 were fighters, over the month.[216] Total Allied counter-air claims did not match the figure of 44 so the reduction in Burma based aircraft was due to some

210 TNA, Air 40/2689, Monthly Reports on Japanese Air Force 'U', 1st April 1945.
211 Shores, *Air War for Burma*, p.355.
212 TNA, Air 24/1310, Intelligence Branch Appendices, 7th January 1945.
213 Shores, *Air War for Burma*, p.302.
214 Ibid, pp.302-323.
215 TNA, Air 24/1311, Intelligence Branch Appendices, February 1945.
216 TNA, Air 24/1310, Intelligence Branch Appendices, January 1945.

other already noted factors. There was some attrition caused by defensive and offensive sorties but Allied air power was forcing Japanese squadrons to withdraw to Rangoon airfields in the south and only to bring aircraft forward to their central and forward bases for specific operations. Once the missions were completed the Japanese aircraft returned to their Rangoon bases to avoid being caught by Allied fighter-bombers.[217] Furthermore, Japanese aircraft also transferred to airfields in Siam and French-Indo-China which were considered out of range of Allied aircraft.[218] The following graphs show that as aircraft numbers started to fall in Burma at the end of January 1945, a corresponding increase appears in Siam and French-Indo-China.

It should be remembered that as the Fourteenth Army continued its rapid advance eastwards, Japanese forward airstrips were captured forcing the Japanese to withdraw from the front line and fly from distant airfields.[219]

From the beginning of February 1945 Japanese air power in the South Sea Asia Theatre, particularly in Burma, continued to decline. The Japanese aircraft industry, airframes and engine, was beginning to suffer from falling production and the output from its factories were allocated to priority areas such as the Pacific and the defence of the Japanese homeland; this aspect will be analysed in Chapter 4. The Allied counter-air offensive in Burma, as A.C.M. Sir Keith Park wrote, "aggravated" the losses caused by the transfer of Japanese units away from the area.[220] Allied intelligence officers estimated no Japanese aircraft were based in the forward or central areas of Burma, around the Rangoon series of airfields, or in Siam or French-Indo-China. Japanese aircraft were brought forward from these airfields for specific operations which eventually declined in both frequency and the number of fighters and bomber sorties flown. In February the Japanese attacked Allied positions on five occasions, using between 13 and 24 aircraft, in March on two occasions using three and 14 aircraft and in April four occasions using between 10 and 15 aircraft.[221] This activity was on a small scale and was unlikely to affect the Allied advance, but it caused the Allies a disproportionate effort to provide escort patrols or defensive flights to counter the attacks.[222] The counter-air attacks continued with mixed results but did not achieve the level of destruction witnessed during the early part of 1944. It was difficult to find Japanese aircraft on the airfields as there were so few dispersed around so many locations and the problem was exacerbated by Japanese orders. Faced with the prospect of meeting large formations of superior Allied fighters, the Japanese

217 TNA, Air 24/1310, Intelligence Branch Appendices, 14th January 1945.
218 Ibid. Allied Intelligence reported that aircraft from Mingaladon had transferred to Saigon to assist forces there.
219 TNA, Air 23/4665, Despatch on Air Operations by Air Chief Marshal Sir Keith Park, 3rd May 1944 to 12th September 1945, p.13.
220 Ibid, p.17.
221 TNA, Air 24/1291, Daily Operational Summaries, summary numbers 902 to 960, February and March 1945.
222 TNA, Air 24/1311, Intelligence Branch Appendices, February 1945.

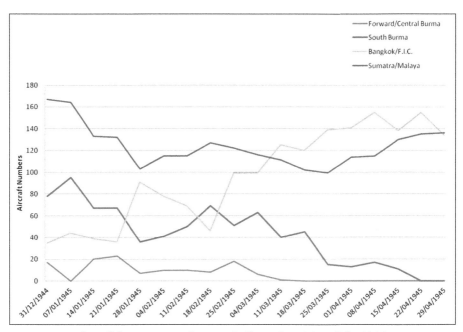

Overall Japanese aircraft strength, December 1944 to May 1945.

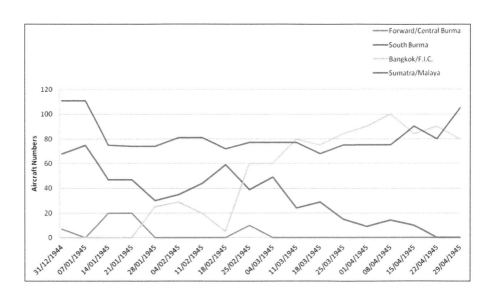

Japanese single-engined fighter strength, December 1944 to May 1945.

5th Army Headquarters issued instructions on 1st March 1945 that their aircraft should only engage single Allied aircraft so as not to risk the loss of their precious fighters.[223] In March the Allied determination to counter the remaining Japanese air threat increased. On 8th March Heho, Mingaladon and Hmawbi were attacked and three aircraft were claimed destroyed and hangars were strafed, whilst on 18th March the 2nd A.C.G. attacked Mingaladon, Hmawbi and Hlegu where three were claimed destroyed. However, some visits to Japanese airfields resulted in no Japanese aircraft being found, for example, on 26th March when U.S. aircraft raided Hmawbi and Mingaladon finding no targets.[224] This was the result of the Japanese policy of conservation and dispersal, but whilst Japanese targets were almost impossible to locate in Burma they were not so in Siam where the Japanese had moved their aircraft to save them from Allied attack.

Intelligence officers were aware that aircraft from Siam were brought forward to Burma for periodic attacks and had been watching airfield activity there with daily photographic reconnaissance sorties over Japanese airfields. On 4th March photographic reconnaissance and reports from the Thai underground revealed over 50 Japanese aircraft on Don Muang airfield, 12 miles north of Bangkok.[225] Even though this location was 780 miles away from the nearest Allied airfield at Cox's Bazaar, plans were formulated to send 40 Mustangs from the 2nd A.C.G. with long-range fuel tanks to attack the airfield. Carefully flying to conserve fuel the A.C.G. attacked the airfield on 15th March and although they only planned to strafe on one pass, conditions were so favourable that some Mustangs made two. Using available sources the U.S. pilots claimed between 17 to 20 Japanese aircraft destroyed, four probably destroyed and between 6 to18 damaged. On 16th March a Mosquito flew over the airfield on a photographic reconnaissance sortie and the crew reported seeing 11 damaged or burnt out aircraft.[226] There are no available Japanese records to confirm the losses but even if a third of them had been destroyed it represented a serious blow to Japanese air strength as it was considered that Japan "was not in a position to replace fully or quickly their losses in the S.E.A.C. Theatre."[227]

This raid did more than aggravate the reduction in Japanese air power as it had been conducted by single-engine fighters at a vast range which surprised the Japanese who thought their aircraft were safe in Siam from Allied attack. Furthermore, it reinforced the view that Japanese aircraft were not safe from Allied attack wherever they were based, for those in Sumatra and Malaya had been targeted by Fleet Air Arm aircraft. On 24th January an attack on the oil fields and facilities near to Palembang included an attack on the airfield, where claims of 13 destroyed, four probably destroyed and

---

223   Shores, *Air War for Burma*, p.336.
224   Ibid, p.344.
225   TNA, Air 27/2213, 684 Squadron Operations Record Book, 4th March 1945, and
         Y'Blood, *Air Commandos Against Japan*, p.175.
226   TNA, Air 27/2213, 684 Squadron Operations Record Book, 16th March 1945.
227   TNA, Air 24/1312, Intelligence Branch Appendices, 25th March 1945.

10 damaged were, "remarkably close to the figures of aircraft apparently submitted by the J.A.A.F. as shot down."[228] While the exact scale of the losses is in doubt, it is clear that the Japanese would find it hard to replace aircraft and pilots at this crucial time. Such attacks by F.A.A. aircraft would continue intermittently through the remaining months of 1945 serving the dual purpose of reducing Japanese air strength, and preventing aircraft being sent from the Sumatra/Malaya airfields to Burma or the Philippines.

April 1945 saw the virtual end of Japanese air operations in Burma. The Japanese attacked Allied positions on four occasions during the month using formations of 10 to 15 fighters with the last of these raids taking place on 29th April. This date was significant as it marked the last aerial combat over Burma and the last time the Fourteenth Army was attacked by Japanese aircraft.[229] Allied attacks against Japanese airfields continued and can be regarded as mopping up operations. On 1st April the 2nd A.C.G. visited Mingaladon and Hmawbi where no aircraft were claimed, but airfield facilities were destroyed to prevent their use as staging posts. On 2nd April 2nd A.C.G. raided Nakhon Sawan where they left a twin-engined aircraft in flames and on 9th April revisited Don Muang and another airfield at Nakhon Pathan, the pilots submitting claims of 21 single-engined and nine twin-engined aircraft destroyed.[230] There are no Japanese reports to confirm these claims but at a time of severe shortage any losses added to Japanese difficulties in the theatre. However, April saw the last of Japanese aircraft involvement in Burma and with it the end of the Allies to conduct a counter-air offensive.

In the week ending 22nd April there were no Japanese aircraft left in Burma and whilst a warning was given that this did not preclude the risk of air attack, a report emphasized that Japanese air strength was stationed in Siam, French-Indo-China, Malaya or Sumatra.[231] The exodus of Japanese *Sentais* was now complete with even long established units such as the 64th and 50th leaving the country.[232] Furthermore, the withdrawal did not solely involve flying units as intercepts of Japanese code messages reported a migration of Japanese headquarter units. In May a unit responsible for Japanese navigational aids in Burma had moved from Mingaladon to Lopburi in Siam, whereas during the same month the 5th Flying Division, which was the senior command in Burma, moved its headquarters to Phnom Penh in Indo-China.[233]

228 Ibid.
229 Kirby (ed), *The War Against Japan, Volume IV*, p.360.
230 TNA, Air 24/1291, Daily Operational Summaries, summary numbers 902 to 960, February and March 1945.
231 TNA, Air 24/ 1314 (Part Two), Intelligence Branch Appendices, 29th April 1945.
232 Shores, *Air War for Burma*, p.426. The 64th *Sentai* had been stationed in Burma with its Oscars since 1942 but in April 1945 moved via Thailand to Cambodia and its sister unit, 50th *Sentai*, after operating from various bases in Thailand moved to Formosa in July 1945.
233 TNA, Air 40/2689, Monthly Report on Japanese Air Force 'U', May 1945.

The withdrawal of the 5th Flying Division left the 4th in sole command, but it was reported in June that this command unit had itself withdrawn to Siam to direct the few remaining operations against the Allies.

Although there were occasional sightings of Japanese aircraft over the Burma battlefields, the small number of Japanese aircraft aided by monsoon conditions meant in May 1945 that Allied air supremacy had been achieved. This meant ground forces could operate without disruption from the air, freed defensive fighters for ground support operations and gave transport aircraft the chance to operate safely. As a result some Spitfire squadrons were converted to the ground attack role by carrying bombs while in June transport aircraft flew without any fighter escorts.[234]

The period between June 1944 and June 1945 had witnessed an initial increase of Japanese air power in the S.E.A.C. area followed by a steady decline which ended in late April 1945.[235] While there were Japanese aircraft stationed in Siam, French-Indo-China, Malaya and Sumatra from May to August 1945, shortages of fuel, spares and aircrew prevented serious operations. The neutralisation of Japanese air power in the S.E.A.C area in this period had been achieved by a combination of aircraft transfers to the Pacific region and offensive action in the S.E.A.C. Theatre.

In conclusion, although the Japanese air strength during the period 1944-1945 was not likely to seriously affect Allied operations, its continued presence with occasional nuisance raids on troops and transport aircraft provided the Allies with a series of difficulties. The counter-air offensive played its part in reducing Japanese air power by destroying aircraft and creating circumstances which forced the Japanese to disperse aircraft away from airfields liable for attack.

Air Intelligence and the Counter-Air Offensive

Allied airfield attacks benefited from intelligence sources to identify where Japanese units were based. This section will describe the role intelligence played with specific relation to the counter-air offensive and will identify which methods of information gathering were available and which proved the most beneficial.

The Allies employed various methods to gather intelligence for the prosecution of their air operations: human intelligence from agents and prisoners of war; captured documents; aircraft identification plates; photographic reconnaissance; and signal intelligence. Some of these sources relied on deciphering Japanese codes particularly signal intelligence, which proved to be a crucial element in identifying Japanese airfields and units for the counter-air offensive. The activities of the code breaking organisations was kept secret until 1974 when Winterbotham wrote *The Ultra Secret* which detailed the work played by the staff of Bletchley Park in breaking German

---

234 TNA, Air 23/4665, Despatch on Air Operations by Air Chief Marshal Sir Keith Park, 3rd May 1944 to 12th September 1945, p.13.
235 TNA, Air 24/1314, Intelligence Branch Appendices, 29th April 1945.

and Japanese Army and Navy codes.[236] The publication of this book lifted the veil of secrecy on the work of code breakers and a series of books have subsequently been published chronicling development of message interception and code breaking; authors such as Elphick, Smith, Erskine and Stripp have all produced informative works.[237] Whilst this section will not detail the history of Far East code breaking, it is clear from these works that Japanese codes started to be broken in the 1930s by British, American and Australian scientists, mathematicians and linguists so that by 1941 many Japanese military and diplomatic messages could be intercepted, decoded and read by the Allies.

Each piece of collected information was potentially useful. Crashed aircraft could provide experts with information on the vulnerability of certain types, their armament and performance, whilst the aircraft identification plate could provide clues on aircraft production. Captured documents were prized as they would provide analysts not only with information contained therein, but also with corroboration that codes had been correctly deciphered or that intelligence assessments had been successful.

Prisoner of war interrogations could provide a cross section of information about which individuals and units had been stationed at bases and about aircraft types and details about the airfield layout. When linked with other intelligence sources, such as photographic reconnaissance, an accurate picture could be made of an airfield's layout which could be passed to attacking units so as to enable them to approach from particular directions to avoid anti-aircraft fire. In fact regular Japanese airfield reports were published using these and other intelligence sources which gave their layout in detail.[238] Two typical Japanese prisoner interrogation reports from August 1944 provide great detail of all the airfields they were based at, together with unit numbers, aircraft and individual's names.[239] However, dates of the prisoners' postings were anything from three months to a couple of years old by the time they were interrogated which provided some information but were not immediate enough for an airfield attack.

Despite the importance of these areas of intelligence, clearly not all of it was useful for informing a counter-air offensive as this required timely information. It is important, therefore, to make a distinction between the less immediate pieces of

236 Winterbotham, *The Ultra Secret*.
237 Elphick, *Far Eastern File, The Intelligence War in the Far East 1930-1945;* Smith and Erskine (eds.), *Action This Day;* Smith, *The Emperor's Codes;* Stripp, *Code Breaker in the Far East.*
238 TNA, Air 24 series for regular updates on Japanese airfields were given in the weekly Intelligence Reports in the Intelligence Branch Appendices and, for example, Air 24/1318 Intelligence Branch Appendices Air Bulletin No 171 gives a report entitled *Japanese-Held Airfields in South Burma*, which attributes its information to captured Japanese documents.
239 TNA, Air 24/1302 Intelligence Branch Appendices, No 41, August 1944, R.A.F. Section Intelligence Reports Number 150 and 151.

intelligence, which nonetheless had a role to play, and that which could be used to organize effective strikes.

Keightley wrote of the necessity for timeliness of intelligence in air operations saying of tactical air intelligence:

> Accurate, timely and relevant intelligence forms the base for sound planning and is essential to the conduct of air operations.[240]

and:

> [O]f an immediate nature and is directly concerned with the operation of aircraft, the capabilities and immediate intention of the adversary and the current environmental conditions.[241]

To maximize the destructive effect of attacking airfields, it was essential to catch as many Japanese aircraft on the ground as possible at the time of attack. The more immediate the information the better the plan of attack, and in a pre-satellite age the three methods were human intelligence, photographic reconnaissance and signal intelligence.

Timely intelligence from human sources was the least reliable factor. Clandestine groups, such as Force 136, were considered to be purely operational groups dealing with sabotage until November 1944, and its "collection of intelligence was more of an incidental nature."[242] Furthermore, the R.A.F.'s 224 Group did not act on Force 136's intelligence until mid-March 1945 for airstrikes on tactical targets such as troop concentrations.[243] Although there does not appear to be specific records for operations in Burma relating to Japanese airfields, between 1943 and 1945 Force 136 were inserted in Malaya on 12 operations, all bar one submitting airfield information, but there were no airfield strikes mounted on the strength of the intelligence.[244]

A more reliable source was photographic reconnaissance (P.R.) which had to be built from scratch in 1942 terms of experience, material and aircraft. Owing to the comparative lack of ground intelligence in the theatre the P.R. unit's work assumed great importance and "provided an indispensable factor in the maintenance of Allied air superiority."[245] Regular reconnaissance flights were flown over enemy airfields

240 Keightley, *Intelligence Support for Air Operations*, p.xii.
241 Ibid p.33.
242 TNA, HS 7/120, S.O.E. Histories and War Diaries, Force 136 Misc. Missions, 1944-1946.
243 TNA, Air 23/4375, Operations in Support of Force 136, 1945.
244 TNA, HS 7/165, Force 136 Operations in Malaya 1943-1945.
245 TNA, Air 41/7, *Photographic Reconnaissance, May 1941 to August 1945, Volume II*, p.170.

which provided information on aircraft numbers, and the imminence of Japanese air attacks.[246] For example, in 1943 the Bengal Command reported:

> [S]pecial attention was paid to MEIKTILA aerodrome and its satellite KANGUANG, where P.R.U. cover has revealed a continued concentration of JAPANESE Fighter aircraft. MEIKTILA was raided on two occasions (5 sorties) and KANGUANG also on 2 occasions (15 sorties).[247]

Similarly at the beginning of 1944 airfields came in for a "large share of the P.R. Squadrons' attention ... due to the necessity of neutralising enemy air efforts against our ground forces", and during January 80 airfields were covered in one day.[248] Furthermore, in March 1945 P.R. Mosquitos from 684 Squadron located a number of Japanese aircraft on Don Muang airfield in Siam, thus precipitating the long-range attack by Mustangs from the 2nd A.C.G.[249]

Whilst P.R. intelligence was important it had various drawbacks. Flights were limited by aircraft range and enemy opposition and were only possible when weather allowed. A review of the squadrons' record books shows visibility difficulties; for example, "The weather in operational area was cloudy with poor visibility."[250] The intelligence was limited to what could be seen and interpreted and often could not provide all the details required.[251] However, these drawbacks were balanced by signals intelligence.

Signals intelligence started with the Y-Service whose operatives listened to Japanese wireless transmissions and passed them to code-breakers who interpreted the messages.[252] A.C.M. Pierse wrote of their work in the early part of 1944:

> In this task the "Y" Service was employed to its full extent and proved of great value, eighty-one aircraft being destroyed in seven weeks as a result of briefing information passed from this source.[253]

---

246   Ibid, p.72 and Air 23/4308, Despatch on Air Operations India Command, by A.C.M. Pierse 1st January to 30th June 1943, p.10.

247   TNA, Air 23/1925, Despatch on air operations Bengal Command, 1st January 1943 to 20th June 1943, p.2.

248   TNA, Air 23/1988, Despatch on Operations carried out by Units of the Photographic Reconnaissance Force, Eastern Air Command, 1943-1944.

249   TNA, Air 27/2213, 684 Squadron Operations Record Book, 4th March 1945 to 16th March 1945.

250   Ibid, 11th March 1945.

251   TNA, Air 41/7, *Photographic Reconnaissance, May 1941 to August 1945, Volume II,* p.171.

252   A useful account of the British Y-Service and associated units can be found in Smith, *Spies of the Airwaves.*

253   TNA, Air 23/1921, Despatch on Air Operations, S.E.A.C., 16th November 1943 to 31st May 1944, p.13.

Similarly A.V.M. Thomas Williams wrote of the American long-range fighter attacks:

> Owing to the unavoidable delay between P.R.U. cover and the receipt of first phase interpretation reports ... most of their attacks have been based on information passed from W.O.U. "Y" Units and I would here like to pay tribute to the work done and accuracy achieved by these Units.[254]

The signals were intercepted by wireless units who passed them onto analysts and Stripp writes of the Japanese using 21 codes and six ciphers, not all of which were broken by the Allies.[255] However, one J.A.A.F. three-digit code which was read until December 1944 and given the codeword BULBUL provided, for example, information on unit location and Japanese aircraft ferrying information.[256]

Unfortunately, examples of the information decoded in early 1944 do not appear to be available and it is likely that it was destroyed either at the time or after the war. However, an idea of the intelligence gathered can be seen in entries in the 358 Wireless Unit's Operations Record Book from late 1944 onwards. On 4th October they demonstrated how the information was used for airfield attack:

> In the morning an enemy aircraft of the 81st was airborne. Meiktila asked Shwebo where the aircraft was going, and was informed that Heho was its destination. Group were informed ... and despatched Mosquitoes [sic] to attack the aircraft on the 'drome. Unfortunately the Mosquitoes were unable to reach Heho owing to adverse weather.[257]

However, two days later:

> On the strength of information supplied by this unit, a sortie was arranged, with the result that one Dinah just taking off from Heho 'drome was destroyed by a Mosquito.[258]

Furthermore, aircraft were tracked:

---

254 TNA, Air 23/4681 Despatch covering operations of Bengal Command 15th November 1943 to 17th December 1943 and 3rd Tactical Air Force 18th December 1943 to 1st June 1944, p.20.
255 Stripp, *Code Breaker in the Far East*, p.79.
256 Ibid, p.76.
257 TNA, Air 29/163B, 358 W.U. Operations Record Book, 4th October 1944.
258 Ibid.

The presence of this aircraft in Heho was confirmed later today by a ... message in which Heho indicated that the aircraft would leave for Mingaladon at 0630hrs BST.[259]

Examination of other units' record books for this period reveal similar information of aircraft movements and unit transfers which was of particular importance in 1945 in showing the decline of Japanese units in the theatre. For example for 7th July 1945, "From complete absence of 64th F.R. (fighter) activity in Siam and F.I.C. since 30th June it would appear that this unit has withdrawn."[260]

The intelligence reports from photographic and signal sources provided interdiction squadrons tasked with counter-air operations with relevant and timely information. As Cox says "the most valuable sources during the war were ... signals intelligence, or SIGINT, and photographic reconnaissance, or PR."[261] Although its mechanism is not recorded, the work of the intelligence organisation in analysing all these forms of intelligence whether photographic, signal or others must be acknowledged as this information provided forces in the theatre with valuable knowledge of their enemy. In a campaign where resources were limited and in demand, such information was vital for avoiding unnecessary waste whilst, at the same time, ensuring interdiction sorties had the maximum impact.

Conclusions

The counter-air campaign played an integral part in the Allies gaining air superiority in Burma in conjunction with the other factors of early warning, aircraft, aircrew and tactics. However, like these elements the counter-air campaign faced various difficulties in the level of efficiency required for destroying Japanese air assets.

Air power doctrine had drawn upon the experience of the First World War and the subsequent debates of the inter-war period to show how crucial a well executed counter-air offensive could be. The Germans demonstrated this in the Low Countries and the Soviet Union by using their superiority in aircraft quality or quantity to overwhelm poorer equipped forces in pre-emptive and sustained attacks. However, they failed in the Battle of Britain owing to range deficiencies with their aircraft and unsustainable attrition rates. The Japanese took advantage of Allied weaknesses in 1941 and early 1942 with their superior aircraft types and numbers to achieve air superiority in a manner every bit as dominant as the Germans in the Low Countries and Soviet

259 Ibid.
260 TNA, Air 29/163A, 368 W.U. Operations Record Book, 7th July 1945.
261 Cox, Sebastian, 'The Organisation and Sources of R.A.F. Intelligence,' Paper presented to the Air Intelligence Symposium , Royal Air Force History Society, Bracknell, 22nd March 1996.

Union. The Germans and Japanese shared both quantity and quality of aircraft and aircrew in their successful attacks, which the Allies, initially, did not possess.

The R.A.F. was aware of the benefits of a counter-air offensive, but their attempts in late 1941 and early 1942 to stem the Japanese attacks in this manner were handicapped by the small number of unsuitable aircraft at its disposal which were no match for Japanese aircraft. Whilst the attempts were undeniably gallant, they did not slow Japanese progress through Malaya into Burma.

From October 1942 until January 1944 the lack of suitable aircraft in sufficient numbers hindered the Allied counter-air campaign. Craven and Cate wrote that by the end of 1943 the airfield interdiction had not succeeded and this is a correct appraisal.[262] Japanese air strength hardly reduced as a result of the airfield attacks and this can be attributed to the lack of suitable long-range fighters. Bomber attacks by day or night were relatively easy to defend against, and often aircraft on airfields had been dispersed before attacks commenced. While these attacks may have destroyed ancillary equipment and disrupted airfield life, they did not reduce air strength as Japanese records make clear. At best, the bomber attacks forced Japanese units to disperse to temporary locations or to airfields in rear areas, before being brought forward again for specific operations. However, the dispersal was likely to raise the risk of flying accidents, particularly in such a difficult environment, as well as waste fuel and increase airframe wear and tear. In addition the aircraft that were suitable for prosecuting a counter-air offensive at that time, notably the Mohawk and Beaufighter, were in short supply and had a number of other roles to fulfil. This was demonstrated during the First Arakan campaign in 1942-1943 when the counter-air offensive reduced in intensity owing to aircraft flying sorties in support of the Army. Clearly until the Allies obtained long-range fighters in sufficient numbers their counter-air campaign would not be fully effective.

The inability to equip India with long-range fighters was due to a lack of suitable British aircraft whilst American priorities were in other theatres. The R.A.F. did not have a long-range fighter of the Lightning or Mustang variety even though one had been requested from the Air Ministry.[263] The Spitfire whilst an excellent defensive fighter had a relatively short range, whilst the Beaufighter, had a long-range and heavy armament, but lacked the manoeuvrability of a single seat fighter. American P-40s were largely based in the north-east of India engaged on operations against the Japanese in China, but these aircraft did not represent an advance over their Japanese adversaries and the Americans' priority for their Lightnings and Mustangs lay in Europe, North Africa and Italy rather than the Far East. Without the introduction of the long-range, multi-role fighter in numbers, the counter-air campaign would continue to only play a minor disruptive role.

---

262 Craven and Cate, *The Army Air Forces in World War II*, *Volume Four*, p.492.
263 Please see Chapter 2, p.171 of this book.

The introduction of new Allied aircraft at the end of 1943 changed the counter-air campaign at the right time. Whilst the Spitfire improved defensive operations, the American Lightning and Mustang tipped the balance in the counter-air offensive in favour of the Allies. During the first battles and sieges of 1944, protection of vulnerable transport and close support aircraft could not be guaranteed by defensive fighters especially when the early warning system could not provide sufficient cover. Later working with the aid of relevant and timely intelligence gathered from the Y-Service and photographic reconnaissance, long-range fighters were able to attack Japanese units at their airfields and over their own territory. Damage and destruction of enemy aircraft and property was caused, and the Japanese were forced to disperse to avoid attack. The value of high performance, long-range fighters which carried large weapon payloads and a clear superiority over their opponents at great range cannot be overstated, and it is no wonder that Pierse had preferred receiving Mustangs to Spitfires in his command.[264] Thus for the first time in the Far East the Allies had sufficient and relevant aircraft to prosecute a counter-air campaign but the results should be viewed with caution.

The A.H.B. authors wrote that the counter-air campaign of March to June 1944 broke the back of Japanese air power in Burma but it is clear from Japanese records that not as many aircraft claimed as destroyed were actually lost.[265] Over claiming by Allied pilots was understandable on low-level high speed passes, as was two pilots claiming the same destroyed aircraft and intelligence officers counting it for two. Allied intelligence estimates never reflected severe losses even given the time delays of accrued information, and the Japanese were able to mount fighter sweeps throughout the period which often exceeded 40 aircraft. Furthermore, Allied intelligence reported replacements for lost aircraft were available from other areas of the theatre as at a time Japanese industry was reaching its peak production figures.

Despite this the counter-air campaign between March and June 1944 was important in reducing Japanese air operations. The minimum figure of 60 Japanese aircraft destroyed on counter-air operations was over two times higher than that destroyed in air-to-air combat, and the figure does not take into account those aircraft that were damaged. Damaged aircraft needed repair which put an additional strain on maintenance units and the supply of spare parts, neither of which the Japanese were efficient at mobilising. Long-range fighters created an additional problem when the Japanese dispersed their aircraft, as Allied fighters were harder to defend against than their slower bombers, and so the Japanese were forced to move units to wider locations.

From October 1944 until the end of Japanese air operations in May 1945 the counter-air offensive continued but it did not have the same destructive results as obtained in the first months of 1944. Japanese air strength steadily reduced mainly

264 TNA, Air 23/2153, Minutes to S.A.C.S.E.A. 1943-1944.
265 TNA, Air 41/64, *The Campaigns in the Far East Volume IV: South East Asia November 1943 to August 1945*, p.71.

through large scale transfers to other theatres of war and with those units left facing the prospect of receiving no replacements or spare parts, aircraft conservation became the dominant policy. Although Allied fighters continued counter-air sorties aided by the intelligence organisation, Japanese units were harder to locate as they had fewer aircraft dispersed around many airfields, though these started to diminish in number as the Fourteenth Army advanced eastwards. However, the ability to maintain pressure on the J.A.A.F. throughout this period was crucial. The ground forces were heavily dependent on air transport for their supplies during the advance but defensive fighters were based up to 150 miles away from the front lines leaving transport aircraft vulnerable to attack. By maintaining constant pressure on the J.A.A.F. by interdiction patrols and airfield strikes, the Allies forced the Japanese to withdraw further away, but even then they were not safe. If proof were required of the benefit of a long-range fighter it was demonstrated in the attacks on Don Muang in March 1945 which involved a round-trip of over 1500 miles and which proved the Japanese were not safe, even in remote locations.

The counter-air offensive in the Far East had positively contributed to the air superiority campaign's success. The Japanese were forced to disperse valuable aircraft around a country where flying conditions were harsh and flying accidents common to both sides. During the first months of 1944 in the absence of defensive certainty, airfield interdiction attacks carried out by superior aircraft reduced Japanese air assets during a crucial period and in the last phase from October 1944 counter-air operations continued to put pressure on diminishing Japanese numbers and their support organisations.

4

Japan's War, Industry and Strategy

An air superiority campaign in any theatre of war can be divided into three elements. Firstly there are the events which occur in the theatre which involves attrition inflicted on aircrew and aircraft in air-to-air and ground-to-air operations, and this element and its constituent parts have been analysed earlier in this book. The second element is the results caused by actions in other theatres which have an effect. For the Japanese, fighting in the Pacific and in China stretched their resources so that the J.A.A.F. in Burma were seldom assisted by the J.N.A.F. and did not receive substantial reinforcements or newer aircraft types. This element also encompasses the bombing and blockade campaign against industry and supplies as, unlike the Allied campaign against the German aircraft industry in Europe, the American bombing campaign against the Japanese aircraft industry did not begin to have a serious effect until March 1945 by which time air superiority had been won in Burma. Similarly the American blockade of Japanese shipping did not begin to have a damaging effect on the Japanese aircraft industry until mid-1944. The third element concerns how the participating countries dealt with their war. The Japanese had entered the war with limited aims of a quick victory followed by a negotiated peace settlement, but as this did not happen, they were forced to participate in a longer war. This affected their industrial capacity to produce matériel and in particular aircraft of sufficient quality and quantity. The third element includes how the country used its forces to their best effect. For example the Japanese in the Far East in late 1942 had better aircraft than the Allies but failed to make the most of the advantage at a time when the east coast defences of India were relatively weak. Furthermore, these effects have an important bearing on what priority was given to a theatre. Japan's priority was to prevent the Americans retaking Pacific islands or gaining ground in China to deny them the opportunity to establish airfields from which they could fly bombing operations against the Japanese mainland. This priority affected the Far East in matériel terms as numbers of aircraft and units were denied to the J.A.A.F. leaving them with limited resources which had to be used carefully as it was unsure if and when replacements would be forthcoming.

This book has concentrated on various combat and technical factors in the Far East which affected the air superiority campaign. The early warning organisation, a robust counter-air offensive and air-to-air combat all played a part in the Allies eventually gaining air superiority in Burma during 1944. However, activities in the Burma Theatre itself were only part of the story as the Japanese war in other areas, notably the Pacific, and Japanese strategy had significant effects on the J.A.A.F.'s performance in the Far East. This chapter will bring together the factors and strategies which assisted the Allies in attaining air superiority and will analyse the impact each factor played in the campaign. Such an analysis will then allow a clearer appreciation of the relative value and impact of all factors in the winning of air superiority.

Part One – Japan's War

The effect of the war outside Burma cannot be underestimated even though it is overlooked. For example, in *The Forgotten Air Force* Probert fails to mention any external influences from June 1942 until October 1944 when he refers to Japanese units transferring to the Philippines as a result of MacArthur's campaign.[1] However, the effects on the Burma air war started in 1942.

Before the war the nature of the air campaign was set when the Japanese Army and Navy agreed to divide their responsibilities. The Navy identified the American bases in the Philippines as being the greatest threat, whilst the Army established the oil fields in Palembang and Balikpapan in the Indies as principle targets. From 7th December 1941 this division continued although, as will be discussed later, the J.A.A.F. was eventually requested to assist the Navy when attrition became unsustainable. Following the first months of their campaign against Allied bases in Malaya and the Indian Ocean, the J.N.A.F. withdrew to the Pacific Theatre and the Japanese Navy were occupied in a series of battles on land and sea which would ensure their non-involvement in Burma. During the Battle of the Coral Sea, (4th to 8th May 1942), the Japanese lost 77 aircraft, 1,074 dead, one aircraft carrier and two other carriers which had to be put into port for repair.[2] During the Battle of Midway, (3rd to 6th June), the Japanese Navy lost 332 aircraft, four aircraft carriers, and a number of its best pilots who went down with the carriers.[3] The loss of these airmen was profound:

> These airmen, many veterans of the China Incident and years of training, were irreplaceable. Midway marked a turning-point in the fortunes of the Pacific War, and the Japanese Navy never again fought from a position of strength.[4]

---

1   Probert, *The Forgotten Air Force*, p.242.
2   Calvocoressi, Wint, and Pritchard, *Total War*, p.1057.
3   Ibid, p.1070.
4   Ibid.

Furthermore, for seven months from August 1942 the J.N.A.F. were involved in the attritional struggle for Guadalcanal whilst simultaneously fighting in the east of New Guinea. This involvement would continue through the Solomon Islands, Marshall Islands, Saipan, Marianas, into the Philippines and eventually to Iwo Jima and Okinawa in 1945. Japan's priority was to deny the Americans access to any of the defensive ring of islands around Japan whose airfields would provide bases from which heavy bombers could strike against the Japanese homeland and industry, and the outcome of these actions was to remove the threat for the Allies in Burma of any meaningful participation by the J.N.A.F.

The J.N.A.F.'s presence in the Pacific and the defence of Japan resulted in the J.A.A.F. being the principle agent engaging the Allies in South East Asia, but events elsewhere would affect the air force's involvement. On 18th April 1942 16 U.S. Mitchell bombers flew from the aircraft carrier U.S.S. *Hornet* to attack Tokyo in a morale boosting propaganda exercise. The attack caught the Japanese by surprise and although the damage caused was not severe, it highlighted the inadequacies of Japanese air defences and for the next few months four air units were either transferred to Japan or reformed from training units to constitute a defensive capability. For example, the 47th Independent *Chutai* was recalled from Burma in September 1942 to be placed under the command of 17th Air Brigade to defend Tokyo.[5] The units sent to Japan were not used again until late 1944 despite calls from the Japanese Navy for reinforcements to the Solomon Islands and so it is doubtful if these units would have been made available for Burma. The J.A.A.F., like their naval counterparts, was engaged throughout various operational areas which stretched their resources and this had an effect on the Burma Theatre. In December 1942 the 11th *Sentai* transferred from China to New Guinea, and on the way took aircraft from both the Burma based 50th and 64th *Sentais* to bolster their numbers.[6] After the Battle of the Philippine Sea in June 1944 the J.A.A.F. responded to requests from the Navy for reinforcements by sending four *Sentais* from Japan and China between June and August 1944.[7] This situation would continue as the war progressed with J.A.A.F. units transferring from their bases to reinforce hard-pressed areas in addition to their own commitments in, for example, China. The following table taken from Allied intelligence assessments shows the combined Army and Navy fighter strength in different theatres, noting that there were no Naval fighters in the Far East:

5   Sakaida, *Japanese Army Air Force Aces 1937-1945*, p.63 and Hata, Izawa and Shores, *Japanese Army Air Force Fighter Units and their Aces 1931-1945*, p.85.
6   Hata, Izawa and Shores, *Japanese Army Air Force Fighter Units and their Aces 1931-1945*, p.27.
7   Ibid, p.45. The *Sentais* sent were 17th, 19th, 30th and 31st.

	15/07/44	15/09/44	15/11/44	18/03/45
Japan/Muriles/Manchuria/Korea	845	1060	325	1420
China/Haiman/Formosa/ N Indo-China	260	305	459	410
Burma/Siam/Malaya/Sumatra/ S Indo-China	230	275	320	240
Philippines/N.E.I./Bismarcks/ Micronesia	545	540	595	90[8]

The figures show that the fighter strength in the Far East was clearly lower than other theatres and by March 1945 the fighters had moved from Burma into Malaya and Siam. These statistics show Japan's priority lay in the theatres from which the greater danger was posed to their homelands and the potential of bombing by U.S. aircraft and raises the question of how Burma and the Far East were viewed by the Japanese high command. This factor will be analysed later in this chapter.

The War in Japan

The campaigns away from Burma ensured that valuable aircraft resources were used in areas of greater need, with the J.N.A.F. taking practically no part in the Far East after July 1942, and the J.A.A.F. suffering from a lack of priority for resources. However, similar direct effects on Japanese aviation did not occur as a result of the campaign on Japanese shipping whilst transporting raw material for the aircraft industry, or American bombing operations on Japanese aircraft manufacturing until late 1944 and early 1945, by which time air superiority had been won in Burma.

Attacks on Japanese shipping began with a limited American submarine force which gradually expanded into 1944 when it was joined by land-based and carrier-borne aircraft and eventually these attacks accounted for 3,000,000 tons of shipping between September 1943 and the end of 1944, an average loss of 192,000 tons per month.[9] Despite the loss of valuable imports the Japanese aircraft industry did not appear to be affected as the graph of monthly production demonstrates:[10]

---

8   TNA, Air 24/1300, S.E.A.C. Intelligence Branch Appendices, July 1944; Air 24/1303, S.E.A.C. Intelligence Branch Appendices, September 1944; Air 24/1308, S.E.A.C. Intelligence Branch Appendices, December 1944 and Air 24/1312, S.E.A.C. Intelligence Branch Appendices, March 1945.
9   TNA, Air 48/183, U.S.S.B.S., *The War Against Japanese Transportation 1941-1945*, p.2.
10 TNA, Air 48/69 U.S.S.B.S., *Japanese Air Power*, using figures on p.222.

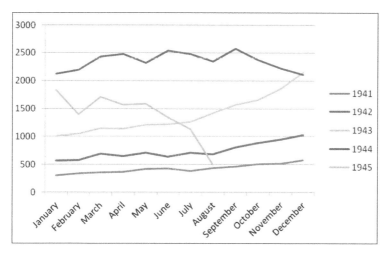

Monthly Japanese aircraft production, 1941-1945. (Source: TNA, Air 48/69, U.S.S.B.S., Japanese Air Power. Rendered with figures on p.222)

The Japanese aircraft industry was not put on a wartime footing until early 1943 and as the graph shows, production increased monthly until a peak was reached in September 1944 when 2,572 aircraft of all types were produced. Total aircraft production peaked in the third quarter of 1944 with a total of 7,391 aircraft:[11]

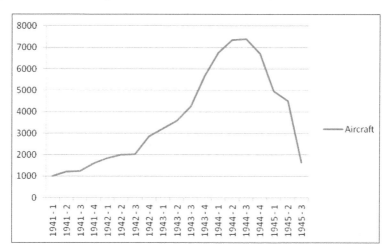

Total aircraft production by year/period. (Source: TNA, Air 48/69, U.S.S.B.S., Japanese Air Power. Rendered with figures on p.222)

11   TNA, Air 48/69 U.S.S.B.S., *Japanese Air Power,* using figures on p.222.

Furthermore, by the third quarter of 1944 Japanese fighter production exceeded bomber production as would be expected whilst the Japanese air services were fighting a defensive war throughout the theatres:

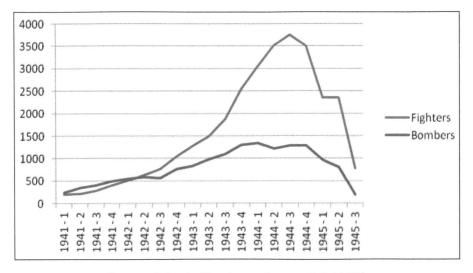

Japanese fighter and bomber production, 1941-1945.[12]

The increase in production in 1944 correlated to the level of losses incurred by Japanese air services as the Americans moved westwards towards Japan, but although the figures show completed aircraft were leaving the factories, they were not sent in large numbers to Burma.[13] These figures only represented aircraft leaving the factories, not all of which were necessarily available to operational units as there was evidence of aircraft losses during ferrying to the fronts. U.S.S.B.S. authors estimated that total Japanese ferrying losses amounted to 4,000 aircraft during the war as opposed to the total American losses in all theatres of 909 aircraft.[14] As fuel and resources decreased there was less emphasis on testing aircraft before delivery resulting in the ferry flight being the test flight "and a high ferrying loss rate was inevitable."[15] Pilot quality obviously had an effect on these losses as training decreased, as did the general construction of aircraft which deteriorated as the war progressed:

12   TNA, Air 48/104, U.S.S.B.S., *Effects of Strategic Bombing on Japan's War Economy*, using figures on p.24.
13   See p.283.
14   TNA, Air 48/69, U.S.S.B.S., *Japanese Air Power*, using figures on p.30.
15   Ibid.

The two principal weaknesses constantly encountered in the forward areas were landing gear and poor brakes. These constructional weaknesses were apparently never overcome even in the new aircraft types.[16]

The figure of 4,000 aircraft lost in ferry flights amounted to approximately two months' worth of aircraft during industrial output, and when combined with the poor repair and maintenance system represented unsustainable waste.

The impact of attacking raw material imports for the aircraft industry did not make a significant difference until late 1944 and early 1945, and the same can be said of the bombing campaign against Japanese industry. Japan's aircraft industry was concentrated in their homeland which was outside the range of American bombers owing to the depth of the conquered islands' defensive perimeter. Once those islands were seized from late 1944 the U.S.A.A.F. were able to deploy their long-range Boeing B-29 Superfortresses against Japan but at first the results were not good, as the crews' accuracy was poor, the bomb loads light and opposition was "serious."[17] However, a portent of the future occurred on 25th February 1945 when explosive bombs were exchanged for incendiaries against Tokyo; 202 Superfortresses dropped 454 tons of incendiaries which destroyed nearly 28,000 structures and left 35,000 people homeless.[18] From March 1945 the U.S.A.A.F. changed their bombing tactics from high-level, daytime raids dropping explosive ordnance to low-level, night-time incendiary raids designed to capitalize on the inflammable nature of Japanese construction; overnight on 9th/10th March 1945 279 Superfortresses dropped 1,665 tons of incendiaries onto Tokyo's urban areas from 4,900 to 9,200 feet. The defences and civil defence organisations were overwhelmed leaving a fearful aftermath:

> In ten previous attacks since November, Tokyo had sustained fewer than 1,300 deaths. Then, literally overnight, some 84,000 were killed and 40,000 injured. More than a quarter-million buildings were destroyed, leaving 1.1 million people homeless.[19]

The tactic of low-level incendiary attack was obviously a success and paved the way for subsequent attacks on Japanese towns and main industrial centres from March until the war's end with similar devastating results. The bombing attacks were joined by carrier-borne aircraft on transportation, particularly railways, which until February 1945 had not been targeted. While these concentrated series of attacks in early 1945 affected Japanese aircraft production in conjunction with the campaign against Japanese shipping, it was clearly too late to directly influence the air war over Burma

16   Ibid, p.31.
17   Ibid, p.36.
18   Tillman, *Whirlwind: The Air War Against Japan 1942-1945*, p.102.
19   Ibid, p.153.

and in particular, the crucial first six months of 1944. By the middle of 1944 the Allies began to gain air superiority owing to their increasing strength and the J.A.A.F.'s attrition rates, in combination with their war in the Pacific, which eventually led to Japanese units withdrawing to other areas in late 1944. Even though Japanese aircraft production rates grew in September 1944 the priority for Japan's finished aircraft was despatch to the Pacific rather than Burma.

The war away from Burma had a clear effect on the numbers of aircraft and units available to the Japanese commanders in the Far East. Another factor which affected numbers was the inability of Japanese industry to produce sufficient aircraft of comparable quantity and quality to the Allies.

Pre-war Japan was essentially a poor country which lacked raw materials and depended on imports of rare metals, coal, oil and machinery for its industrial use, many of the products of its industry being exported and Japan depended on its exports for revenue.[20] Despite this the Japanese aircraft industry in the 1930s was able to produce sufficient aircraft of good quality to fight China and the Soviet Union, and in 1939 its aircraft production figures exceeded that of the United States by approximately 2,000 aircraft.[21] In 1940 Japan produced 7,800 aircraft of all types which included the Zero and the Oscar which were both to play a leading role in the initial attacks during 1941 and early 1942. Furthermore, during the initial 1941 attacks the Japanese were able to take advantage of their aircraft strength at the time British commitments in Europe and the Middle East required Spitfires and Hurricanes, and also American aircraft in the Pacific area which were, with some exceptions, largely obsolete. The quantity and quality of both the Japanese aircraft and aircrews in the initial attacks on Allied bases during the first few months of the war has been discussed in chapters 2 and 3 of this book and it is not necessary to repeat it again.

Japan believed that the United States did not have the willingness to enter a long war and would press for a peace settlement at the first opportunity, whilst its conquest of an outer ring of islands, "rich in resources" provided a defensive barrier against American attack.[22] However, Japan underestimated the United States' desire for war and its actions over Pearl Harbor stirred a sleeping industrial giant whose resources Japan could not match. Overy wrote:

> Japan's war against the Western powers possessed a strong sense of military unreality. It was clear that the United States would be able to use its vast material superiority to defeat Japan ... but defeat came through the fact that from the outset Japanese strategy had been a gamble for which resources were demonstrably inadequate.[23]

20   Calvocoressi, Wint, and Pritchard, *Total War*, p.654.
21   Overy, *The Air War 1939–45*, p.21.
22   Ibid, p.87.
23   Ibid, p.85.

This material superiority was able to quickly accelerate American aircraft figures from pre-war manufacture to full war production as the following graph shows:[24]

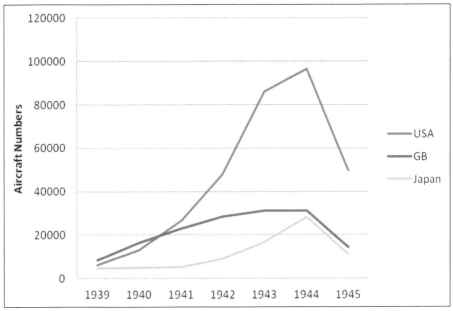

(Great Britain figures includes production by Commonwealth Countries)

Aircraft production 1939-1945.

By the end of 1941 U.S. production started to increase until it reached a peak in 1944 of 96,318 aircraft of all types, although it must be remembered that these were also destined for Europe, the Mediterranean, and service with other countries. The Japanese had not planned for, nor anticipated, a long war and thus their aircraft production at first did not alter greatly from pre-war levels. However, their losses beginning at the Battle of Midway in 1942 galvanised the Japanese into expanding the aircraft industry to produce better aircraft in greater numbers. Notwithstanding that production in 1943 was three times higher than in 1941, and five times higher in 1944 it still lagged behind American production sixfold. Overy uses aircraft weight as a comparison; the 5,000 Japanese aircraft produced in 1941 represented 26 per cent of the weight of total American aircraft produced, and the 28,000 produced in 1944 only 8 per cent.[25] Comparison with the Allied aircraft production output, and, in particular, the Americans may be unfair as the Japanese could not hope to match or

---

24   Ibid, from figures on p.150.
25   Overy, *The Air War 1939-45*, p.93. One reason for the disparity in 1944 was the larger number of lighter fighter aircraft built by the Japanese over bombers.

exceed the figures involved. However, Japanese production was hindered by a series of difficulties which prevented larger numbers of aircraft leaving the production lines.

Authors such as Overy, Tillman and the A.H.B. and U.S.S.B.S. narrative writers since the Second World War have identified Japan's aircraft industry problems as being the lack of resources, a shortage of skilled workers and an inability to mass produce aircraft on a large scale. However, these problems had been identified by the German Air Attaché and visiting members of the German aircraft industry in 1944. The Allies intercepted a document sent by the German Air Attaché to the High Command of the *Luftwaffe* on 3rd November 1944 and it is worth quoting the report's conclusions in full:

a)   Available workingarea [sic] and manpower warrant a higher production of aircraft and accessories.

b)   The raw material situation, in spite of the bottleneck in steel, and despite transport difficulties, does not show particular cause for alarm at present nor in the near future.

c)   Efforts to increase the output of aircraft are greatly hindered by the ignorance on the part of technical designers of mass-production and standardization methods, by a shortage of skilled factory workers and special machine tools, all of which result in an antiquated production system.

Since the Japanese have recognized these shortcomings, they are endeavoring to acquire patent rights for the manufacture of modern German machine tools and are enlisting the aid of German experts in the establishing of modern mass-production systems.[26]

The inefficiency of Japanese industry has been illustrated by Overy, who wrote that the Japanese munitions minister Fujihara carried out an administrative inspection in the middle of 1943 and "calculated that the available capacity if properly utilized could produce not the 8-10,000 currently produced, but 53,000 per year."[27] It is clear that Japan did not have the infrastructure to produce this many aircraft, but even if half that number had been manufactured it would have represented a substantial increase in Army and Navy capabilities.[28] The post-war Japanese view substantiates the difficulties. Lieutenant General Saburo Endo, a senior Japanese official, was interviewed by Allied intelligence officers in September 1945 and told his interrogators of the difficulties of the predominance of "hand-work" methods in most Japanese factories.[29]

26   TNA, Air 40/2203, Production-Japanese Aircraft, Translated Report from German Air Attaché to German Air High Command, November 1944.

27   Overy, *The Air War 1939-45*, p.155.

28   Ibid, p.232. Overy makes this point in a footnote.

29   TNA, Air 40/323, Japanese Air Force Strength and Distribution of Aircraft, Intelligence Memorandum Number Four, 17th September 1945. Endo held various posts in

The spinning-mills represented practically the only efficient pre-war mechanized industry, but as the factories were taken over for munitions work the organizations were broken up and became less efficient. Crucially Endo stated that the bottleneck in aircraft manufacture was not in airframe production but in engine manufacture, "Although there was never a safe margin of engine production over airframe production, engines were practically always available for completed airframes until October 1944."[30] It will be remembered that from October 1944 as the Japanese situation in the Pacific was worsening and supplies were deteriorating, aircraft were transferred from Burma units to make up shortages in other areas in the Pacific Theatre.

Another significant problem was the tension between the Japanese Army and Navy as Endo pointed out:

> After the outbreak of war, the Army and Navy each planned a huge (aircraft) expansion program. However, the production rate was greatly hampered due to the rivalry between the Army and Navy in respect to the limited national strength.[31]

Fundamentally the two services were two entirely separate entities that did not cooperate over aircraft production, raw materials and resources. Even when the Munitions Ministry was created in November 1943 to coordinate the services' demands into a single production capability for the benefit of the war effort, both sides largely ignored the new powerless organization and continued as before.[32] The failure to pool resources led to a diversification of effort at a crucial time for the Japanese war effort as both services produced their own types and specifications of aircraft. The two most widely produced Japanese aircraft, the Oscar and Zero, never served as a standard fighter for the two services and were developed independently of each other with separate resources and production facilities. For a small country with limited resources it would have been prudent to develop and produce fewer types of aircraft that could be used by all forces. The Americans, for example, produced 18 aircraft models for their Army and Navy together whilst the J.N.A.F. produced 53 basic models with 112 variations and the J.A.A.F. produced 37 basic models with 52 variations.[33]

As the quantity of aircraft suffered so did the quality of aeroplanes developed for the Army and Navy. Both the Oscar and Zero served throughout the war and the basic aircraft types were upgraded with better engines, armament and armour plating. However, such improvements were counter-productive as weight increased, which

---

the Japanese War Ministry from 1940, being Chief of General Affairs of Army Air Headquarters from May 1943 to November 1943, and head of the Aircraft Section in the Ministry of Munitions from November 1943 to August 1945.

30   Ibid, p.2.
31   Ibid, p.3.
32   TNA, Air 48/69, U.S.S.B.S., *Japanese Air Power*, p.28.
33   Overy, *The Air War 1939-45*, p.178.

therefore affected the high levels of manoeuvrability which categorized both types in the early months of the war. While the Oscar and Zero could be effective in certain circumstances, as the air fighting in Burma had shown, neither type could be developed to be truly effective against the improving Allied types such as the Spitfire or Mustang. Newer types were needed but owing to the belligerence of the Army and Navy, the lack of resources and the rush to bring new designs into service none of the later aircraft were able to make an effective contribution. The Army produced the Tojo, a single-seat fighter similar in configuration to the Oscar, which was eventually effective over Japan in countering American heavy bombers. Despite first flying in August 1940, developmental problems through the first types resulted in acceptable versions not reaching units until late 1943, but the aircraft suffered from high-landing speeds, high-wing loading and a violent reaction to high-speed manoeuvres which made it unpopular with its pilots. The Ki-61 Tony, another Army aircraft, was powered by a licence built version of the German Daimler-Benz engine and was found in trials in early 1942 to be superior in performance to the American P-40E and German Bf 109E. However, despite early promise the aircraft's development was troubled by various different unreliable engine types, and later structural wing failure problems, resulting in a reversion to an earlier design. Although production continued with various armament configurations, the engine problems proved insurmountable and the delivery of later aircraft was delayed.[34] However, when the engine plant was destroyed by American bombing, Japanese engineers fitted a radial engine to spare Tony airframes to produce the Ki-100, thought to be one of the best Japanese fighters produced, but the aircraft only came into service in February 1945 in limited numbers.[35] Furthermore, the Army's Ki-84 Frank, first flown in April 1943 and introduced into service in 1944, possessed a better climb rate and manoeuvrability than either the American Mustang or Thunderbolt, but owing to its success was overworked which led to unserviceability and maintenance problems.[36] Apart from a brief appearance by the Tojos of the 87th *Sentai* in May 1944 and the Franks of the 50th *Sentai* in late 1944, none of these aircraft were deployed in substantial numbers to Burma to reinforce or replace the J.A.A.F.'s Oscars. Similar problems were encountered by the J.N.A.F.'s fighters. The J2-M Jack's prototype first flew in March 1942, but owing to continuous design change and production difficulties did not enter service until December 1943. Although later versions were heavily armed and capable against American bombers, its unreliability due to constant design changes and engine problems detracted from its potential. Finally the J.N.A.F.'s N1K1-J and N1K2-J George aircraft possessed excellent performance and manoeuvrability, but was rushed into service in early 1943

---

34 Japanese aircraft figures taken from Mondey, *Axis Aircraft of World War II*, and *Jane's Fighting Aircraft of World War II*.
35 Because the Ki-100 was produced in small numbers and was a derivative of the Tony it was not given an official Allied codename.
36 Mondey, *Axis Aircraft of World War II*, p.228.

before it was properly developed giving its users problems with unreliable engines and landing gear. However, as earlier discussed apart from the Zero in 1941 and early 1942, none of the J.N.A.F.'s fighters served in Burma.

Fundamentally the Japanese were capable of designing and building fighter aircraft which could match Allied aircraft. However, the rush to bring them into service, combined with the conflicting Army and Navy demands for manufacture ensured the later types were not ready for combat in large quantities. An idea of how few of these fighters were manufactured can be seen in this table:

Oscar	Army	5919
Tojo	Army	1225
Frank	Army	3514
Tony	Army	2666
Ki100	Army	371
Zero	Navy	10449
George	Navy	1007
Jack	Navy	476 [37]

In comparison with these figures the Americans produced 15,000 Mustangs of all types, and the British 20,351 Spitfires of all types, 6,500 Mark Vs alone.[38] The diversity of Japanese fighters and aircraft in general, was a fundamental mistake committed by the Japanese high command as one centralised body earlier in the war could have identified one suitable aircraft for development and use by both the Army and Navy. This affected the Japanese in Burma as the J.A.A.F. had to continue with the Oscar in lieu of a better developed fighter which could match the Allied aircraft deployed in the theatre. It should be recognized that although Japanese aircraft numbers declined as the Burma campaign progressed there is no evidence that Japanese pilot and aircrew quality decreased. Chapter 2 of this book showed that the majority of Japanese aircrew in the theatre maintained a high standard until their eventual withdrawal, gaining respect from their Allied adversaries as dangerous foes.

Part Two – Japanese Use of Air Power

Japanese industry could not supply sufficient aircraft for all the J.A.A.F. and J.N.A.F.'s requirements and fighting in priority areas took first claim on resources from the Far East. Despite this the Japanese at various times between 1942 and 1945 failed to take advantage of their superiority in aircraft types and numbers against weaker Allied airforces. From 7th December 1941 until May 1942 the J.A.A.F. and J.N.A.F.

---

37   Mondey, *Axis Aircraft of World War II* and *Jane's Fighting Aircraft of World War II*, for Japanese aircraft figures.
38   Price, *The Spitfire Story*, p.139.

soundly beat two world powers, and their initial operations were well executed. However, when the J.A.A.F. was left to fight the Allies in Burma from October 1942, their operations were compromised by doctrine, a lack of appreciation of air power, and inflexibility. This section will show how these factors affected the campaign in relation to the Japanese use of bombers and fighters, and also how Allied air action contributed to limiting Japanese commanders' options.

The Japanese air services had defined roles. The J.N.A.F. was equipped to protect the fleet and project air power from the decks of its aircraft carriers and the J.A.A.F. was to provide support for ground troops.[39] After the J.N.A.F. had left Asia in 1942 the J.A.A.F. continued alone but was hampered by its commanders' insistence to adhere to its Army support role. The result was the Japanese failed to fully capitalize on their advantages of aircraft quality and quantity, and the Allies' early defensive weaknesses. The J.A.A.F. was under the command of ground commanders at the Imperial Headquarters in Tokyo who had little or no experience of air operations; in post-war interrogations it emerged that many were infantry or artillery officers who had been transferred to the J.A.A.F.[40] The result was that operations in support of ground troops took precedence over air operations, for example, strategic bombing raids on Allied targets:

> Some Japanese air force officers did, in fact, realize the value of strategic bomber attack but were hampered ... by the refusal of air commanders, who held the whip hand, to consider long-term air operations.[41]

According to the U.S.S.B.S. narrative the Japanese commanders in the theatre thought things could have been done differently:

> The Japanese officer in charge of air operations in southeast [sic] Asia at the end of the war has stated that, in his opinion and in the opinion of other air officers, the planes used for ground support might better have been used against Calcutta and the Hump route. Those officers always were overruled by ground officers on the staff of the Southern Army which controlled air operations in southeast Asia.[42]

Furthermore, this lack of appreciation of air power also resulted in the Japanese failing to learn the "art of assembling large numbers of planes and attacks involving more than 100 aircraft were few and far between."[43] The inflexibility of thought

---

39   TNA, Air 48/69, U.S.S.B.S., *Japanese Air Power*, p.1.
40   TNA, Air 41/36, *The Campaigns in the Far East, Volume III: India Command*, p.34.
41   Ibid.
42   TNA, Air 48/69, U.S.S.B.S., *Japanese Air Power*, p.20.
43   Ibid, p.3.

combined with piecemeal use of resources had a detrimental effect on Japanese air operations.

In addition to command difficulties the J.A.A.F. was hampered with the lack of suitable aircraft for their tasks, "It was a force well adapted for the close support of advancing armies, but totally unsuited to defensive warfare or strategic bombing."[44] Japanese fighters possessed long-range and manoeuvrability, and despite limitations with armour and armament proved a dangerous adversary in skilled hands to the end of the war. Japanese bomber aircraft such as the Lily, Helen and Sally could only be described as medium types fitted with two engines and bomb capacities of between 1,764 and 2,205 lbs.[45] Self-protection and armour was sacrificed for long-range, speed and manoeuvrability, and it will be recalled that during the first exchanges between R.A.F. Buffaloes and Japanese bombers over Malaya, the bombers were able to draw away from the fighters.[46] No heavy Japanese four-engine bombers such as the Allies' Lancaster or Flying Fortress were developed and this would limit the destructive power of bomber operations against Allied targets.[47]

In order to appreciate the difficulties of rigid doctrine and unsuitable equipment, it is pertinent to examine the J.A.A.F.'s use of bombers and fighters separately for clarity.

Bombers

The first indication that the Japanese failed to appreciate the significance of air power in Burma occurred during the Commonwealth armies' retreat from Burma into India in May 1942. Whilst R.A.F. and U.S.A.A.F. fighters maintained a degree of air superiority for the Army to escape, it found operations difficult owing to fatigue and a growing shortage of aircraft. Their task was made easier as when the Japanese could have concentrated its air forces on the retreating troops, they chose to mount a series of raids on towns and cities "in order to disrupt the public services."[48] When the 1942 monsoon ended the initiative was in favour of the J.A.A.F. who possessed a number of long-range bombers that carried a reasonable bomb load for the purpose and fighters that were capable of flying long-range operations. The R.A.F.'s Hurricanes in 1942 and 1943 had inadequate performance for interceptor duties, except in the dive and at certain heights, and relied on an efficient early-warning system in order to gain sufficient height to employ the dive and zoom tactic. Furthermore, the limited number of R.A.F. fighters had to defend a 700 mile front which had gaps in the early-warning

44   TNA, Air 41/36, *The Campaigns in the Far East, Volume III: India Command*, p.152.
45   The Ki-48 Lily carried 1,764lbs bomb load and the Ki-21 Sally 2,205lbs. The similar two-engined British Wellington III had a bomb load of 4,500lbs.
46   See Chapter 2, p.150.
47   Overy, *The Air War 1939-45*, p.125. "The standard bombers lacked range or carrying capacity and the proposed trans-oceanic bomber, the *Fugako*, was judged to be too demanding on limited production resources."
48   Probert, *The Forgotten Air Force*, p.94.

system as the organisation was developed through 1942 and beyond. This represented an ideal opportunity for the Japanese to capitalize on Allied weakness and attack Indian cities, in particular Calcutta into which large amounts of supplies and troops were arriving for the forthcoming campaigns. However, between October and mid-December 1942 Japanese aircraft did not appear over the cities, but instead mounted a limited number of tactical raids against airfields in Assam. The lack of effort suggested that the Japanese were saving their aircraft for future operations, or were uncertain when replacements or reinforcements were likely to be supplied to the area. U.S.S.B.S. authors suggested that the J.A.A.F. was not strong enough to mount attacks against Calcutta without the assistance of the J.N.A.F. but this suggestion should be reviewed. The J.A.A.F. mounted two raids on airfields on 25th October 1942 consisting of two formations; in the first 24 Sallys were escorted by 32 Oscars, and the second 30 Lilys escorted by 30 Oscars.[49] Therefore, a potential formation of 54 bombers escorted by, at least, 30 fighters would have presented Calcutta's defenders with an interception problem during October 1942. Whatever the reason it is clear that an opportunity to disrupt the Allies' reinforcement plans during these months was missed and this was repeated in late December. Between 20th and 28th five night attacks, using no more than nine bombers at a time, were carried out on Calcutta which caused minimal damage, but serious effects to the civilian population's morale.[50] There was no R.A.F. night-fighter force to defend Calcutta, and the few Hurricanes engaged in visual searches looking for the bombers' exhaust flames for identification had limited success. The Japanese did not take advantage of this potential weakness by overwhelming the night defences with larger raids of 20 to 30 bombers which would have provided more destructive and morale-threatening effects. Even after Beaufighters arrived in January 1943 and destroyed four Japanese bombers in two nights, mass raids could have over-whelmed the defences in a concentrated campaign, but instead the Japanese chose to switch focus to attacking Allied airfields:

> There is no doubt that successful raids on Calcutta would have paid hand-some dividends and it was therefore surprising that the enemy made no further attempts to bomb targets west of Brahmaputra.[51]

Even allowing for a policy of conserving aircraft this was a risk worth taking, but in the event Calcutta returned to normal within a few days. As Calcutta was ignored and air supply to the Chindits in early 1943 was missed, the Japanese then switched their efforts yet again to airfields and supporting ground troops, ignoring the oilfields

49   Shores, *Air War for Burma*, p.29.
50   Kirby (ed), *The War Against Japan, Volume II*, p.259.
51   TNA, Air 41/36, *The Campaigns in the Far East, Volume III: India Command*, p.106.

at Digboi (Assam) and, for the most part, the 'Hump' air route from India to China.[52] The U.S.S.B.S. authors wrote:

> Had the Japanese air force been more determined and aggressive in the early days of Hump operations and had it appreciated the ultimate value of the Hump, it undoubtedly could have inflicted far more damage than it did.[53]

These general examples show various traits; a misunderstanding of air power; inflexibility of thought and an adherence to their role. The A.H.B. narrators wrote:

> At no time after the initial invasion of Burma were the Japanese able to take the initiative in the air … Indeed, in studying the Japanese air force it is difficult to escape the conclusion that, despite the continuous improvement of aircraft types, Japan remained at least twenty years out of date in her conception of the role of an air force in modern warfare. She persisted in regarding her air forces as mere handmaids of the ground and sea forces and in Burma, as elsewhere, she eventually paid the penalty.[54]

Japan's use of bombers has attracted comment from historians. In 1949 the A.H.B. narrators wrote that the Japanese air actions of early 1942 had "exploded the theory that the Japanese were out of their element in the air", whilst admitting their aircraft were useful air weapons.[55] However, for the end of 1942 the narrators wrote, "Perhaps their greatest weakness lay in their air commanders who failed to make the best overall use of the available strength."[56] Probert added that the Japanese had concentrated their efforts on tactical targets and Allied airfields in the first half of 1943 ignoring strategic targets further afield:

> Admittedly they lacked an effective long-range bomber, but more imaginative use of their medium bombers might have posed the RAF and USAAF defences serious problems at this crucial stage of the build-up in India. As it was, by concentrating their efforts mainly on counter-air and to a lesser extent on tactical operations they showed an inflexibility of thought which boded ill for the future.[57]

These are valid views when applied to Japanese bomber operations. Japanese bombers were used largely against tactical targets and when used against strategic

---

52   Ibid, p.112.
53   TNA, Air 48/69, U.S.S.B.S., *Japanese Air Power*, p.25.
54   TNA, Air 41/36, *The Campaigns in the Far East, Volume III: India Command*, p.152.
55   Ibid, p.63.
56   Ibid.
57   Probert, *The Forgotten Air Force*, p.131.

targets were not used in force or in sustained attacks. For example, the lessons of saturating defences with large formations at night as witnessed in Europe during this period were not learned as the raids on Calcutta in 1942 and 1943 demonstrated. Japanese bomber operations went through two phases, firstly between October 1942 and December 1943 when the J.A.A.F. held the advantage over the Allies but failed to take their opportunities, and secondly from November 1943 when increasing Allied air superiority virtually nullified the Japanese bomber force threat. However, whilst these phases may be distinct, some earlier Allied air actions affected Japanese bomber operations, particularly by night, for the rest of the war.

As most of the world's airforces discovered in the Second World War, the key to successful daylight bombing operations by medium or heavy bombers was effective fighter escort. For example, the American Eighth Air Force in Europe with its heavily armed bombers failed at first against superior German fighters, but ultimately were successful when escorted by long-range fighters such as the Mustang. This also applied to the Japanese as their Oscars supplied an essential barrier of protection against R.A.F. fighters who were inferior until the introduction of better aircraft in late 1943. However, the Hurricane had proved itself to be a good gun-platform whether equipped with eight or twelve machine guns or later with four cannons and so if Japanese bombers were attacked the advantage switched to the Hurricane. For example on 27th March 1943 a formation of Lilys raided Cox's Bazaar without fighter escort which had failed to rendezvous with the bomber formation; eleven Hurricanes met the bombers and nine bombers were destroyed (one by AA fire), and two badly damaged.[58] Similarly on 1st April 17 Hurricanes intercepted 27 Sallys escorted by Oscars in a raid on Feni; the escorting screen was breached and three Sallys were lost and a fourth was damaged for the loss of one Hurricane.[59] However, for most of this period Japanese bombers were escorted by fighters giving the Japanese an advantage they did not exploit owing to choices of tactical targets. From September 1943 onwards the Allies introduced better fighter aircraft and the Japanese lost their potential bomber advantage. The Spitfire was largely superior to Japanese fighters and was able to take full advantage of the improved early-warning systems when used defensively over India. Furthermore, the Spitfire squadrons were used in conjunction with the Hurricane, as in Europe, to attack the fighters whilst the Hurricane attacked the bombers. Also introduced at the same time as the Spitfire, the American Mustangs and Lightnings had the performance to deal with Japanese fighters and firepower to destroy bombers and these aircraft would play an important role during counter-air operations in early 1944.

While the daytime advantage did not begin to pass to the Allies until the beginning of 1944, R.A.F. night fighters had dissuaded Japanese commanders from night attack as early as January 1943. Although the raids on Calcutta in December 1942

---

58   Shores, *Air War for Burma*, p.74. Two bombers collided at the start of the attack.
59   Ibid, p.78.

had been conducted by small Japanese numbers, the R.A.F.'s response had a profound effect. Overnight on the 22nd/23rd December 1942, patrolling Hurricanes from a day-fighter squadron intercepted three Sallys raiding Calcutta; two of the bombers were hit and were forced to crash land.[60] The night raids on Calcutta continued into January 1943 and earlier it was described how the loss of four bombers over two nights to R.A.F. night-fighter Beaufighters calmed the city's populace and curtailed further raids on the city for a year. It would appear that the threat posed to bombers by the night-fighters persuaded Japanese commanders to curtail night operations, except in small numbers, for the rest of the war. Calcutta should have been attacked again, probably in greater numbers, and the successful day raid of 5th December 1943 warranted a follow-up night attack but neither was forthcoming. The reticence to attack strategic targets at night may be explained by J.A.A.F. commanders focussing on tactical targets, but the need to conserve aircraft must be recognized and, clearly, attacking at night proved costly. A combination of inflexibility, role adherence, and decisive R.A.F. action had therefore removed a potentially valuable weapon from the J.A.A.F.'s armoury, and this was to occur again during the critical first months of 1944.

At the beginning of 1944 Allied intelligence services estimated the J.A.A.F. had approximately 108 medium bombers and 36 light bombers stationed in the theatre from Burma through Siam into Malaya and Sumatra.[61] Although most of the bombers were based in rear areas it was feasible to bring units forward, as per the normal Japanese practice, for specific operations. However, the non-appearance of bombers from 4th to 15th February resulted in this intelligence appreciation:

> Lack of any bomber offensive at such an opportune moment remains something of a mystery. No completely satisfactory explanation has so far been forthcoming. It cannot be entirely a matter of conservation of first-line strength for there are occasions when the Japanese must realise that offensive action is the cheapest in the long run.[62]

Similarly, during the fifteen days from 23rd February to 9th March the Japanese "undertook no offensive action."[63] Examination of the Japanese air offensive during the first six months of 1944 reveal few occasions when bombers were used in significant numbers by day or night against the Chindit landing rounds, Kohima or Imphal. This represented a wasted opportunity for low-flying bombers, particularly at night when landing grounds were most vulnerable. The early-warning systems at Imphal

---

60   Ibid, p.44.
61   TNA, Air 24/1295 Weekly Intelligence Appendices, January to February 1944, No 8, 9th January 1944.
62   Ibid, No 14, 20th February 1944.
63   TNA, Air 24/1296, Weekly Intelligence Appendices, March 1944, No 17, 12th March 1944.

had a reasonable ability to detect high or medium flying raiders by day but could not cope with attacks flown at lower heights and this defensive flaw was made worse at night:

> Night interceptions were never actually attempted over the plain itself owing to the many blind spots in our radar devices, save on one occasion when the attempt was made to guide the Beaufighter to its target by means of indicator shell bursts.[64]

However, despite this, Japanese night raids were occasionally intercepted, for example, overnight on the 3rd/4th April four 62nd *Sentai* Helens were intercepted by two Beaufighters over Imphal and two bombers were destroyed.[65] Although this was an exception, like Calcutta in January 1943 it dissuaded the Japanese from night bombing raids on landing grounds at a time when such attacks may have been profitable.

There was a growing need for conservation. In February 1944 Allied intelligence considered that the Japanese reticence to use their bombers was due to logistic problems and conservation of resources.[66] Japan faced difficulties producing sufficient aircraft to meet the services' requirements and Japanese commanders were aware that aircraft replacements and spare parts were becoming difficult to obtain. The difficulties of logistics and the maintenance of complex multi-engine aircraft would be complicated by aircraft losses in combat and Japanese bombers had shown themselves vulnerable to modern high powered and heavily armed Allied fighters. On 27th March nine Helens from the 62nd *Sentai* escorted by 60 Oscars attacked Ledo airfield and were intercepted by a mixed formation of American Mustangs, Apaches and P-40s; while the Oscars were engaged, the American fighters shot down all nine bombers which "was a further blow to the 5th *Hikodan*, from which its bomber arm was never fully to recover."[67] This *Sentai* had already lost five aircraft destroyed and five damaged in a ground strafing operation by American fighters on 8th March. Combat attrition was also increased by wastage during ferry operations and flying accidents; on 6th April one of the 8th *Sentai's* Lilys crashed on take-off, whilst three more were lost presumably to the "vagaries of the weather."[68] Lastly it must not be forgotten that the landing ground at Imphal was defended by a number of anti-aircraft guns which were able to put up a barrage; during a raid on Imphal on 26th April Shores writes that of

---

64   TNA, Air 41/64, *The Campaigns in the Far East Volume IV: South East Asia November 1943 to August 1945*, p.88. A flight of A.I. Beaufighters were based on Imphal on 8th March 1944.
65   Shores, *Air War for Burma*, p.199.
66   ¹TNA, Air 24/1295, Weekly Intelligence Appendices, January to February 1944, No 14, 20th February 1944.
67   Shores, *Air War for Burma*, p.192.
68   Ibid, p.202.

the two Lilys destroyed and eight damaged most if not all were accounted for by the anti-aircraft defences.[69]

Although target selection, air-to-air attrition and conservation explain some of the bombers' non-appearance during the first half of 1944, another important factor was the intensive counter-air campaign carried out by long-range American fighters. Initially the Japanese brought bombers forward from rear bases where they were relatively safe, before carrying out raids and then returning to their original base. This worked until the beginning of 1944 when the introduction of the Lightning and Mustang, supported by an efficient intelligence organisation which plotted the bombers' progress to the forward airfields, resulted in bomber units being attacked on the ground. On 8th March 1944 a large collection of Japanese aircraft had gathered on Maymyo and Shwebo airfields in preparation for a raid on Ledo when A.C.G. Mustangs and Mitchells attacked the airfields; the Japanese lost five Helens destroyed, one damaged, with ten Oscar fighters lost.[70] Similarly on 4th April Lightnings attacked Aungban and Heho airfields where a number of Lilys, Helens and Oscars were assembling; the Americans claimed four Helens, 19 Oscars and one Tony destroyed.[71] This kind of attrition reduced aircraft numbers at a time when replacements were becoming scarce and made the process of bringing bombers forward to the advanced airfields extremely hazardous, as the range of the American fighters precluded such journeys. This resulted in a minimal use of bombers, often in only formations of twos and threes in supply dropping sorties and night nuisance raids.[72] As the monsoon approached Japanese bombers started to be withdrawn from the theatre:

> [A]fter what must have been for them a most unsatisfactory season with very little accomplished and serious losses which still have not been fully replaced. The monsoon may give them the opportunity to build up again.[73]

The appreciation that the monsoon would allow the Japanese to build up their bomber force was mistaken. Although the intelligence service reported that the units spent their time training for night operations as they believed "the enemy can no longer expect to attack … by day without incurring severe losses", from October 1944 until May 1945 Japanese bomber operations reduced to small and occasional nuisance raids.[74] Intelligence reports indicate that bombers were brought forward from rear bases occasionally for raids, but often returned without carrying out a mission. There

---

69   Ibid, p.214.
70   Shores, *Air War for Burma*, p.175.
71   Ibid, p.201. No details of bomber casualties were available, but the 50th *Sentai* lost 15 fighters in the attack.
72   TNA, Air 24/1297, Intelligence Branch Appendices, 1st April 1944 to 30th April 1944, No 21, 9th April 1944.
73   TNA, Air 24/1299, Intelligence Branch Appendices, No 29, 4th June 1944.
74   TNA, Air 24/1303, Intelligence Branch Appendices, No 43, 10th September 1944.

were various factors responsible for the reduction in sorties. The attrition caused to Japanese forces in the Philippines had become serious and aircraft from the Far East Theatre had begun to be transferred further east. From September 1944, Japanese industry started to switch its production to fighters at the expense of other aircraft resulting in fewer bombers and their spares being available for front line use. Allied air power had become too dominant for Japanese bombers to operate by day or night and so superiority over the Japanese bomber force in Burma had been gained.

Fighters

Japanese use of fighters was hindered by the same inflexibility and necessity to support ground operations. However, while the bombers passed through the phase of failing to capitalize on their advantages before entering a decline, the fighters were still capable of inflicting losses on Allied air power, particularly transport aircraft, through the critical months of 1944 and the advance into Burma in 1945. Two factors eventually affected this ability, the quality of the fighters and their employment.

At the start of the war Japan had fighter aircraft noted for their long range and manoeuvrability which proved superior to the Allied Buffalo, Hurricane and P-40 aircraft. In October 1942 the J.N.A.F. had withdrawn, taking its Zeros and Claudes to the Pacific, leaving the J.A.A.F.'s Oscars as the only single-engine fighter after the obsolete Nate was replaced. The Oscar remained in service in Burma until the end of the war undergoing several upgrades to the original airframe which had positive and negative effects. Although the first Mark had outstanding range and manoeuvrability it lacked self-sealing fuel tanks, armour plate and heavy armament, only being equipped with two .303 inch machine guns. This light armament was in contrast to the 12-gun battery of the Hurricane IIB and would have found difficulties dealing with the Allied aircraft's robust airframes. However, Japanese pilots were aware of their armament shortcomings and knew where the weak points of their enemy's aircraft were:

> The Hurricane was a unique plane with twelve 7.7mm (0.303in) machine guns which caused deadly damage if we were shot from behind ... when we fought with Hurricanes we attempted to counter its fire power with the better manoeuvrability of the 01 [Ki-43 Oscar] and tried to hit its radiator, bringing the engine to a stop. Even with the poor fire power (two 12.7mm guns) of the 01, Hurricanes could be shot down merely by a hole in the radiator.[75]

The armament deficiency was addressed in the Mark 1b and Mark 1c which were fitted with one .303 and one .5 and two .5 inch machine guns respectively.[76] However,

---

75 Sergeant Yoshito Yasuda quoted in Shores, *Air War for Burma*, p.15.
76 Mondey, *Axis Aircraft of World War II*, p.222.

improving the fire-power of the Oscar was insufficient to deal with improving Allied fighters and so the Oscar II was developed, with an improved engine, armour plating, a form of self-sealing tank and two .5 inch machine guns. This aircraft represented an improvement over the Oscar I as it was 12 mph faster and dispensed with the tele-scopic gunsight in favour of an internal sight which was easier to use and caused less drag.[77] The downside of fitting self-sealing tanks and pilot armour was extra weight which made the Oscar II's rate of climb and turning ability inferior to the earlier variant. At the end of 1943 as the Spitfire was introduced, the Oscar was still the main Japanese fighter in Burma and as there were no new aircraft to take its place, it had to continue. Oscar pilots were disappointed in the late-production Oscar II which was some 15 mph slower than the previous version because of the additional wind resistance caused by new drop tank installations.[78] The final version of the Oscar to reach Burma was the Mark III in August 1944 which had an improved engine giving the aircraft an extra 30 mph over the Mark II, a shorter take-off run and extra power to maintain full combat throttle for 40 minutes. However, compared to the Allied fighter aircraft in service, the Oscar was neither quick enough nor adequately armed to make a substantial difference although it did retain its high manoeuvrability.

The Oscar remained the main fighter in service although others did make appear-ances. In late 1943 intelligence sources reported sightings of the Tojo, a faster and better armed single-engine fighter which sacrificed the Oscar's manoeuvrability for higher speed and a better rate of climb. However, the higher speed resulted in a high wing loading and violent reactions to high-speed manoeuvres, which proved unpopular with pilots.[79] The 87th *Sentai* arrived with this aircraft in May 1944 in an attempt to counter the better Allied types, but was forced to withdraw after a fortnight following severe losses in aerial combat and Allied ground attacks.[80] While the Tojo did not stay long, the 50th *Sentai* re-equipped with the Frank during the 1944 monsoon and returned to Burma in October. The Frank, armed with twin 0.5 machine guns and twin 20mm cannons, was considered to be better than either the Mustang or Thunderbolt in terms of climb rate and manoeuvrability in the Pacific theatre. However, the Frank did not possess the Oscar's turn rate which led to the Oscar pilots' ire:

A *Hayate* pilot would simply drop the nose [when attacked] and be off in a flash. They couldn't avoid an attack if it came from above, however, because of the Ki-84's poor rate of turn. This meant that the *Hayates* would routinely head for

---

77   Ichimura, *Ki-43 Oscar Aces of World War 2*, p.28.
78   Ibid, p.42.
79   Mondey, *Axis Aircraft of World War II*, p.224.
80   Shores, *Air War for Burma*, p.232.

home while we were left to dogfight with the Spitfires. 50th *Sentai* pilots became notorious for firing a few cannon bursts at the enemy and then fleeing the scene.[81]

However, despite the Frank's potential it had arrived too late and by the end of December 1944 the 50th *Sentai* had started its withdrawal from Burma to its eventual destination in Formosa. The last fighter worthy of mention was the Ki-45 Nick, a twin-engine aircraft armed with various combinations of front firing cannons and heavy machine guns depending on the Mark. This aircraft was especially effective against heavy bombers, such as the Liberator or Superfortress and was eventually equipped with airborne interception radar in the night-fighter role. The 21st *Sentai* were equipped with the Nick, but despite its potential as a night-interdictor, was not used offensively as a study of operations in Shores' *Air War for Burma* shows it being used for the defence of Rangoon and Sumatra, and this was identified by the intelligence service in April 1944, "NICKS have still not been used in attack and appear to be reserved for airfield defence."[82]

Despite the relative failure of the Tojo and the brief (and late) appearance of the Frank the Japanese had a competent fighter in the Oscar which, if properly handled, could provide severe difficulties for the Allies. During the first six months of 1944 Oscars were able to break through the early warning belt and attack transport aircraft without detection, eventually prompting the Allies to institute the patrolled air corridor as described in Chapter 2. However, instead of concentrating on the transport fleet and landing grounds, the Oscars were routinely used against airfields and in support of ground troops with little benefit. Similarly the Nick with its heavy cannon armament had great potential as an interdictor, especially at night, against transport aircraft but the Japanese high command failed to grasp the advantages this aircraft could provide.

In earlier chapters this book has described the Japanese fighter superiority over the Buffalo, Hurricane and P-40 during the early stages of the war and it is not intended to repeat the events again. At the end of the monsoon in 1942 the Japanese possessed an air superiority advantage with their aircraft at the same time the Allies were constructing an early warning organisation on the east coast of India. Furthermore, during the last six months of 1942 there were as many as four Japanese Oscar fighter *Sentais* operating in Burma so there was no shortage in aircraft numbers.[83] Despite

---

81 Sergeant Toshimi Ikezawa quoted in Ichimura, *Ki-43 Oscar Aces of World War 2*, p.50. *Hayate*, translated as 'Gale', was the official Japanese name for the Ki-84 Frank. This quote would appear to contradict the general opinion that the Frank was comparable to Allied fighters, and it is possible that Sergeant Ikezawa was mistaken or the combat took place above 30,000 feet at which height the Frank was at a disadvantage.

82 TNA, Air 24/1297, Intelligence Branch Appendices, No 21, 9th April 1944. Capital letters in report.

83 Shores, *Air War for Burma*, pp.425-428 and Hata, Izawa and Shores, *Japanese Army Air Force Fighter Units and their Aces 1931-1945*, pp.102-187.

this the defences at Calcutta were not troubled until December and the night bomber raids, which gave the R.A.F. fighter squadrons at Alipore the chance to practice battle formations and combat tactics.[84] In other areas Japanese fighters and bombers were engaged on a series of raids against airfields which achieved little success in air superiority terms owing to a lack of intensity which the Allies had been expecting.[85] This was demonstrated by the Japanese conserving their resources by attacking for a few days and then having a week of inactivity which gave the R.A.F. time to grow stronger. A.C.M. Pierse reported in the Spring of 1943 that R.A.F. Hurricanes had received V.H.F. radios, the early warning organisation and the ground control systems had improved which in turn gave the Hurricanes more time to achieve height for interceptions.[86] During the first Arakan campaign the Japanese had dissipated their fighter effort between supporting their ground troops repelling the British advance and attacking airfields in a counter-air campaign. Whilst these were logical targets other vulnerable targets were left untouched.

In February 1943 Colonel Orde Wingate's first Chindit expedition walked into Burma with the intention of being re-supplied by air. At the time the R.A.F. was short of transport aircraft, only three Dakotas and three Hudsons being available for operations which subsequently flew 178 sorties, dropping 300 tons of supplies.[87] The Japanese, either through a lack of air intelligence or a failure to appreciate from where this force was receiving its supplies, did not intercept any supply flights; General Geoffrey Scoones, IV Corps Commander, wrote, "enemy air opposition was not encountered and the R.A.F. was fortunate not to lose a single aircraft from any cause."[88] Providing protection for the transports would have been difficult given the range and the Hurricane's performance at low altitude, and so the Japanese failed to take the initiative, "Up to the point of the Arakan crisis in February 1944 the Japanese failed completely to understand the possibilities of air supply."[89] Similarly American transport aircraft flying supplies into China over the Hump did not receive the level of attention they merited.

At the end of the 1943 monsoon the Japanese maintained air superiority over the Allies in aircraft quality and quantity, but the situation started to change from October 1943 with the introduction of better Allied fighters. The combination of the Spitfire and an efficient early-warning organisation meant Oscar pilots had to develop new tactics such as the 'squirrel cage' and 'beehive' to counter the R.A.F. fighter and these tactics effectively slowed down the rate of attrition inflicted by Spitfires.[90] The initial

---

84   Probert, *The Forgotten Air Force*, p.128. Alipore was outside Calcutta.
85   TNA, Air 41/36, *The Campaigns in the Far East, Volume III: India Command*, p.150.
86   TNA, Air 23/1919, Despatch on Air Operations India Command, 1st January to 30th June 1943, p.7.
87   Probert, *The Forgotten Air Force*, p.134.
88   Ibid, p.135.
89   Craven and Cate, *The Army Air Forces in World War II, Volume One*, p.500.
90   See Chapter 2, p.142.

confrontations took place between these aircraft during January and February 1944 when Japanese fighters attacked Allied airfields and supported ground operations. However, from March 1944 Japanese commanders were presented with large scale operations which tested their command's flexibility and their air power perception.

From March to June 1944 four significant actions took place in the theatre; the Battle of the Admin Box; the second Chindit raid; and the sieges at Kohima and Imphal. In March the Japanese had four single-engine fighter *Sentais* and one twin-engine fighter *Sentai* based in Sumatra and the Japanese commanders were faced with how best to use their fighters.[91] The Chindit landing grounds and advance had to be attacked; the Japanese Army required close support during their westwards advance; home airfields and territory required defending; Allied transport aircraft carrying supplies to Kohima and Imphal required interception; and bombing raids had to be escorted.[92] Of these targets the transport sorties presented the biggest threat to Allied operations because of aircraft shortages, and the importance of supply flights to Lieutenant General Slim's 'stand and fight' strategy. Ideally the Japanese should have concentrated their efforts into intercepting these aircraft and targeting the supply dumps on the landing grounds. However, Allied action prevented Japanese intervention.

Operation THURSDAY, the second Chindit incursion, started on 5th March 1944 but it was not until 13th March that the Japanese discovered the main Allied presence at Broadway. Although Allied security had been tight, Japanese reconnaissance Dinahs had been routinely intercepted by Spitfires thereby blinding Japanese commanders to Allied intentions. Despite subsequent raids on the Chindit landing grounds the Japanese failed to take advantage of the poor early-warning organisation and fighter cover from distant airfields, and the attacks on Broadway "failed to prevent the routine fly-in of supplies to the stronghold and supply dropping to elements of Wingate's Special Force continued unhindered."[93] Priorities switched for the Japanese as their westward advances toward Imphal and Kohima were in progress and their fighter force was committed to supporting the Army's ground offensive. Furthermore, the Japanese had finally appreciated the value of air supply and began a series of attacks in April against transport aircraft supplying Kohima and Imphal. The threat posed by fighters on the transport aircraft was profound. Earlier on 8th February, Dakotas flying re-supply sorties during the Admin Box battle had been met in force by Japanese Oscars and only 12 of the 30 transport sorties flown during the day had reached the drop zones. The Dakota pilots were disconcerted by the appearance of the fighters and to improve their morale, it took the commanding officer of Troop Carrier

91   The 87th *Sentai* moved to Burma with its Tojos for a fortnight in May.
92   From February 1944 some Oscars carried bombs on raids.
93   TNA, Air 41/64, *The Campaigns in the Far East Volume IV: South East Asia November 1943 to August 1945*, p.79.

Command, Brigadier General William Old, to personally lead a subsequent flight.[94] In April Japanese fighters flew sweeps of as many as 50 aircraft, sometimes escorting bombers, to the landing grounds at Imphal occasionally benefitting from the lack of radar cover following the capture of Tamu on 23rd March. Defending fighters had protected many Dakota flights up until 25th April when five Dakotas, three R.A.F. and two U.S.A.A.F., were destroyed by Japanese fighters who had reached the transport formations.[95] The outcome was the formation of an air corridor from Silchar to Imphal which would be patrolled by fighters whenever transport aircraft were due to fly in or out of the Imphal Plain airfields.

If the patrolled air corridor had prevented transport losses over the battlefield, the intensive counter-air campaign reduced Japanese commanders' options. The difficulties of destroying Japanese fighters in aerial combat had already been experienced during the first two months of 1944 even though the Spitfire was operational. Improved Japanese tactics resulted in fewer 'kills' and, as described earlier, the threat experienced to transport aircraft in February was fully appreciated. The solution was the counter-air campaign conducted principally by the long-range fighters of the U.S.A.A.F. as analysed in Chapter 3. Allied intelligence was able to intercept Japanese radio traffic and knew the location of aircraft brought forward for specific raids. For example on 4th April following intelligence information, 459th F.S. Lightnings attacked Aungban and Heho airfields where a number of Japanese bombers and fighters were gathered; although no record of bomber casualties are available, Japanese records consulted for Shores' *Air War for Burma* show the 50th *Sentai* lost 15 Oscars and had to withdraw for a week to re-equip.[96] In addition to the pre-planned raids, American fighters flew counter-air patrols over enemy territory to catch Japanese aircraft on known airfields, or to intercept them in the air. Finally, the 459th F.S. and ground controllers received instructions on 3rd March 1944 that the squadron was to be scrambled when Japanese raids were in progress, not to intercept over the target but to proceed to the known enemy airfields and catch the homeward formation on landing.[97] The outcome of these operations caused attrition to the J.A.A.F. even though the intelligence service thought the losses were replaced, "Japanese fighters suffered heavily in our surprise attacks ... but P.R. cover indicates they have since been reinforced."[98] Furthermore, the attacks forced the Japanese to disperse their fighters over a wide area, thereby increasing flying time and creating logistic difficulties.[99]

94   Shores, *Air War for Burma*, p.158.
95   Ibid, p.211.
96   Ibid, p.200.
97   TNA, Air 25/950, 224 Group Operations Record Book (Appendices), 1st January 1944 to 31st March 1944, Group Instruction No 41, 3rd March 1944. On 10th May 1944 this order was extended to the 530th Fighter Squadron, Group Instruction No 45.
98   TNA, Air 24/1297, Intelligence Branch Appendices, No 20, 2nd April 1944.
99   Ibid, No 30, 30th April 1944.

The outcome of attrition and robust Allied offensive measures removed the initiative from Japanese commanders to deploy their fighters against the transports, landing grounds or other local targets directly involved with the Japanese advance. Not only did the supply flights continue, but Allied airfields were kept open:

> These raids on our airfields achieved little, none of our strips was unserviceable for more than two or three hours, he did little material damage and personnel casualties were comparatively few.[100]

Japanese commanders appeared to attack Allied targets in familiar ways without imagination or making use of the available resources thereby handing over a measure of air superiority. Could the Japanese in Burma have disrupted the supply operations during March to May 1944? Much would have depended on their ability to bring aircraft forward in total secrecy imposing a radio blackout, and hiding aircraft from Allied photographic reconnaissance sorties. Firstly single-engine fighters could be used to evade the limited early-warning coverage and attack the transport aircraft as supplies were being unloaded or as they were landing. Losses would have switched the daytime sorties to fly at night therefore decreasing the tonnage of supplies delivered as well as making the transports vulnerable to attack by the twin-engine Nicks acting as interdictors in the transport stream. Lastly, bomber aircraft could have flown at low-level under the limited radar cover bombing landing grounds and supply dumps. All these operations would have found difficulties in their execution considering Allied strength and expertise, but it is telling that not one was tried by the Japanese.

Once the 1944 monsoon was over, the J.A.A.F. fighter force suffered from a series of transfers to other areas of Japan's war. At first the four fighter *Sentais* engaged during the Imphal and Kohima battles returned and appeared to be settled:

> The enemy were able to replace their losses without having to bring in new units, nor was Burma called upon to send any of its strength elsewhere. This holding force responsible for both offensive and defensive operations consisted of approximately 90 fighters, 35 light bombers and 15 reconnaissance aircraft.[101]

By January 1945 three of the four *Sentais* had left Burma; the 33rd had gone to Sumatra; the 50th to Siam; and the 204th to the Philippines.[102] Steady attrition to the fighters in air and ground operations combined with their non-replacement and

---

100 TNA, Air 41/64, *The Campaigns in the Far East Volume IV: South East Asia November 1943 to August 1945*, p.82.
101 TNA, Air 23/4682, Despatch covering operations of 3rd T.A.F. from 1st June to 4th December 1944, Appendix C, Enemy Air Strength and Activity, p.37.
102 Shores, *Air War for Burma*, pp.425-427 and Hata, Izawa and Shores, *Japanese Army Air Force Fighter Units and their Aces 1931 – 1945*, pp.102-187.

transfer to other theatres forced the Japanese commanders to conserve their aircraft and perform hit-and-run nuisance raids:

> The scale of enemy activity during the month of December and, in some measure the tactics employed by enemy fighters, confirm the necessity for conservation of aircraft imposed upon the enemy by the wastage of his strength in the Philippines and the consequent withdrawal of aircraft, particularly fighters, from the S.E.A. Theatre.[103]

Despite the reducing force Japanese fighters were still capable of causing loss to the important transport fleet. On 12th January 1945 17 64th *Sentai* Oscars attacked a forward landing airstrip at Onbauk where Dakotas were overhead dropping supplies and on the ground unloading; during the attack four Dakotas on the ground were destroyed.[104] Transport aircraft were absolutely vital to the Fourteenth Army's pursuit of the Japanese across Burma, and losses of supply aircraft could potentially hinder the advance. Japanese commanders chose instead to attack Allied ground forces to support their own retreating troops which brought criticism from Air Chief Marshal Sir Keith Park:

> Had the enemy used his fighters effectively instead of frittering away their efforts on infrequent low-level attacks against forward troops he would have been able to do great execution among our Dakotas and Commandos and seriously impede the advance.[105]

By February 1945 the J.A.A.F. was not in a position to do more than mount nuisance raids which while tying up Allied resources in counter measures, did not prevent the Fourteenth Army's advance eastwards and in May the final Japanese fighters left Burma.

Part Three – Japanese Priorities

Industrial capacity, strategy and the war in other theatres affected Japan's ability to wage an effective air war in Burma. Another factor was whether Japan had given a low priority to the Burma Theatre as U.S.S.B.S. authors suggest:

---

103 TNA, Air 24/1310, *Intelligence Branch Appendices*, No 61, 14th January 1945.
104 Ibid, No 62, 21st January 1945.
105 TNA, Air 23/4665, Despatch on air operations by Air Chief Marshal Sir Keith Park, 1st June 1944 to 2nd May 1945, p.20. The Curtiss C-46 Commando was a twin-engine U.S. transport aircraft.

Meanwhile, the Japanese high command had given air operations in China and Burma a low priority and in those theatres the Allies won air superiority in 1944 almost by default.[106]

Later the authors wrote:

The best replacement pilots were sent to Rabaul and New Guinea in preference to southeast [sic] Asia, and some of the best units from southeast Asia were moved as reinforcements to Rabaul and New Guinea.[107]

These views were also shared by the A.H.B. authors who repeated and referred to them in Volume IV of their narrative in 1956.[108] Whilst there is some truth in the first comment, the second is misleading, whilst both require analysis. This section will examine whether Japan deliberately gave the J.A.A.F. in Burma a low priority for aircraft and aircrews, or whether circumstances in other theatres defined Japanese decisions. Firstly it is pertinent to examine Burma and the Far East's value to the Japanese, both economically and politically.

Part of Japan's decision to go to war in 1941 had been to obtain essential raw materials from its neighbours:

Japan … had never been, and never would be, self sufficient in raw materials, least of all those materials on which an industrial revolution, in the throes of which Japan laboured, most urgently depended – non-ferrous metals, rubber, and above all, oil.[109]

Their solution for self sufficiency was simple:

Japan would acquire the resources it needed from its neighbours and assure its supply by the most direct of all methods, imperial conquest.[110]

Future economic survival lay with the formation of the Greater East Asia Co-Prosperity Sphere which was formed from Japan, China, French Indo-China, Siam, the Philippines, Malaya, and Hong Kong. Despite some potential in foodstuffs other resources caused difficulties:

106 TNA, Air 48/69, U.S.S.B.S., *Japanese Air Power*, p.9. This view was also shared by Robert Mikesh, *Broken Wings of the Samurai*, p.22.
107 TNA, Air 48/69, U.S.S.B.S., *Japanese Air Power*, p.19.
108 TNA, Air 41/64, *The Campaigns in the Far East Volume IV: South East Asia November 1943 to August 1945*, p.30.
109 Keegan, *The Second World War*, p.199.
110 Ibid.

In summary, the evaluation of potential self-sufficiency in the Co-Prosperity Sphere concluded there would be little to worry about in foodstuffs, difficulty in meeting fibre and non-ferrous metal requirements, and serious problems in disposing of certain agricultural surpluses, namely rubber, beans and sugar.[111]

Despite that, invading and subjugating their neighbours gave the Japanese huge resources, for example, in 1937 China supplied 14% of Japan's iron ore imports and in 1941 this had increased to 50%.[112] Similar advantages were found in Burma and Siam who between the two countries provided Japan with rice, tin, rubber, tungsten, oil, a topping plant for motor fuel, oil refineries, arsenals and power plants:

> Burma and Siam … not only exported raw material to Japan but supplied perhaps as much as 50 percent of the food and material required by the enemy forces defending Burma.[113]

Furthermore, conquest of South East Asia and the East Indies gave Japan the bulk of the world's supply of rubber, tin, antimony, jute and quinine, and vast supplies of petrol, iron ore, coal, phosphate, bauxite, sugar, corn and rice:

> This storehouse of raw materials, supplementing the materials and manufacturing capacity of the Inner Zone, gave Japan a position of strength in the waging of war as long as sea transport to the south remained unmolested.[114]

Although the sea links deteriorated as 1944 progressed, retaining and defending these important resources was clearly an important war aim.

Politically the region was also important to Japan. Burma had to be conquered in order to cut off supplies that were transported into China from India and Burma itself. Additionally Japan's initial planning foresaw a potential link-up with the Germans after the fall of Singapore, Ambassador Oshima suggested to Hitler that their operations be synchronized:

> When Japan attacks India from the east, it will be most advantageous if German troops threaten India from the west. Hitler refused to commit himself but did promise to drive over the Caucasus as far as Iraq and Iran.[115]

---

111 TNA, Air 48/183 U.S.S.B.S., *War Against Japanese Transportation*, p.20.
112 TNA, Air 48/104, U.S.S.B.S., *Effects of Strategic Bombing on Japan War Economy*, p.13.
113 R.A.F. Museum, Hendon, U.S.S.B.S., *Air Operations in China, Burma, India World War II*, p.20.
114 TNA, Air 48/183, U.S.S.B.S., *War Against Japanese Transportation*, p.20. The largest applications for metallic antimony are as alloying material for lead and tin and for lead antimony plates in lead-acid batteries.
115 Toland, *Rising Sun*, p.245.

The territory gained would realize another goal of a Great Asia empire. After Singapore fell in February 1942 Prime Minister Tojo told the Japanese Diet that Burma and the Philippines would be granted independence and said:

> The objective in the Great East Asia war … is founded on the exalted ideals of the founding of the empire and it will enable all the nations and peoples of Great East Asia to enjoy life and to establish a new order of coexistence and co-prosperity on the basis of justice with Japan as the nucleus.[116]

Japan had to establish alliances with the independence parties of Burma and India, led respectively by Dr Ba Maw and Chandra Bose, and in return for their support grant their countries independence. Eventually Burma was granted its token independence by Tojo on 1st August 1943 when the Japanese military administration was withdrawn, and on 21st October the Provisional Government of Free India under Bose was established. Japanese expansion into India in early 1944 through Kohima and Imphal was intended to "forestall an ultimate offensive against themselves" by Allied divisions in India and China.[117] This suited Bose, who pressed for the rebel Indian National Army (I.N.A.) to be in the vanguard of the attack which, he hoped, would eventually corrupt the loyal Indian Army to rise against British rule. In the event not only did the Japanese lose the fight at Imphal but the I.N.A. failed in combat and the Indian Army remained loyal to its officers, oath of service and regimental pride.[118] Therefore one of Japan's greatest failures in both Burma and India was its inability to win the full support of each country against their pre-war imperial masters.

Given the economic and political importance of Burma and India to Japan's expansion plans it would be logical to regard the region as deserving a high priority for military resources particularly defensive ones such as aircraft. Why then, did the Japanese give it a low priority for air resources, as U.S.S.B.S. and A.H.B. authors claim?

As the British had found in 1941, Burma and the Far East represented a lower priority to Japan in relation to threats closer to home. From June 1942 Japan and the Allies fought a defensive campaign in Burma, neither side being strong enough to advance into each other's territory and establish a firm foothold. For the Japanese the threat to their homeland began in May 1942 with the disastrous engagement at Midway which precipitated a series of Naval and land battles from Guadalcanal in 1942 to the Philippines in late 1944 which consumed vast numbers of Army and Navy aircraft which industrial deficiencies found hard to replace. Japan's defensive perimeter consisted of a number of small islands on which it was impossible to base a large airforce:

---

116 Ibid, p.277.
117 Calvocoressi, Wint, and Pritchard, *Total War*, p.1121.
118 Ibid, p.1130.

When the Allies attacked the perimeter, the Japanese ... were unable either to assemble a large land based airforce in the threatened sector or to retire to land masses where such an assembly might have been possible. They committed and lost their best air units in piecemeal fashion on the perimeter.[119]

In contrast with the war against this defensive perimeter, the Japanese homeland was in no danger from invasion from the Allies in India, although the raw materials in the Far East had to be defended against periodic bombing attacks, which was achieved by keeping air units for the defence of Rangoon and Sumatra.

Whilst the U.S.S.B.S. was correct, with qualifications, that the Burma Theatre's air operations were given a low priority by the Japanese, issue should be taken with its statement that the best pilots and units were transferred to other theatres. The statement gives the impression that Japanese pilots in the Far East were below standard, however, as described in Chapter 2, the quality of Japanese aircrew in the Far East was high and this was corroborated in another U.S.S.B.S. publication:

Japanese pilots and aircrews, with the possible exception of those based in the extreme rear areas, were tough, experienced and resourceful fighters.[120]

The official United States Army Air Force historians agreed:

The Japanese aircraft were manned by pilots and crews who were experienced and resourceful fighters and they were regarded as a courageous and worthy foe.[121]

Furthermore, Allied pilots fighting in Burma were in no doubt about the threat their adversaries posed in May 1944:

The Oscars were very agile, very light ... To dogfight with the Oscars was a recipe for disaster. We couldn't keep with them in a turn, but we didn't do too badly.[122]

The quality of Japanese pilots was analysed in Chapter 2 and so it is not necessary to repeat the findings at length again here, but it is clear that the overall quality of pilots in the Far East comprised a serious threat until their withdrawal in 1945. As described earlier in this chapter, if the quality and quantity of aircraft had been better the Allies would have faced hindrances in their advance into Burma.

---

119 TNA, Air 48/69, U.S.S.B.S., *Japanese Air Power*, p.3.
120 R.A.F. Museum, Hendon, U.S.S.B.S., *Air Operations in China, Burma, India World War II*, p.13.
121 Craven and Cate, *The Army Air Forces in World War II Volume Four*, p.510.
122 Squadron Leader Dave Davies quoted in Franks, *The Air Battle of Imphal*, p.115.

The alleged transfer of the best Japanese units from the Far East to other theatres requires clarification. Japanese units committed to the area actually remained in the region for much of the war with minimal transfer after late 1942.[123] In the case of bomber units the 8th *Sentai* served from January 1942 until mid-July 1945, while the 12th *Sentai* remained in the region until late July 1944. The 34th *Sentai* served from October 1942 until February 1944 and the 62nd *Sentai* was sent to the area at the start of March 1944 as reinforcements, but was withdrawn two months later after suffering severe losses.

Japanese fighter units also showed a remarkable longevity. Both the 50th and 64th *Sentais* served in Burma from 1942 until their withdrawal in January and April 1945 respectively. The 33rd *Sentai* flew a detachment from Tavoy, Burma from October 1943 and was joined by the rest of the unit a month later serving in Burma until June 1944; following the monsoon it moved to Siam and finally to Sumatra. The 204th *Sentai* was first posted to Burma as a training unit becoming fully operational in February 1944 continuing to serve in Burma until August 1944 until its move to Siam and the Philippines. Therefore none of these units transferred from Burma until the fighting became serious in other areas, notably the Philippines, in late 1944. Both the 21st and 87th *Sentais* were based as defensive units in Sumatra from late 1942 and early 1943 occasionally operating in Burma, whilst the 26th *Sentai* operated in Sumatra and French Indo-China from October 1943. The mass transfer of units did not occur as described by U.S.S.B.S. while Japanese operations were taking place in early 1944. The 1st *Sentai* moved from Burma in late 1942, 11th *Sentai* to Rabaul in November 1942, and the only unit to transfer in early 1944, the 77th *Sentai*, had moved from Sumatra to Burma in January 1944 and only served there for a month until transferring to New Guinea in February.

The longevity of Japanese units also applied to the aircrews. Allied aircrews flew a set number of operations or an agreed period of time on combat missions before being rested or sent to non-operational duties. The J.A.A.F., like the *Luftwaffe*, did not have this policy and continued to fly operationally. An Oscar pilot who served in Burma, Sergeant Yoshito Yasuda, was interviewed by Canadian historians in 2000 who wrote:

> Yasuda noted that only four of his classmates who completed flying training with him survived the war. Like the Luftwaffe, they continued flying until they were killed, or were so severely wounded or struck down by tropical diseases that they were unfit for further service. They envied our system of operational tours and the so-called rest periods available to Allied aircrew.[124]

---

123 Shores, *Air War for Burma*, pp. 425-428 and Hata, Ikuhiko, Izawa, Yasuho and Shores, Christopher, *Japanese Army Air Force Fighter Units and their Aces 1931 – 1945*, pp.102-187, for J.A.A.F. units.

124 Brown and Rodney, 'Burma Banzai: The Air War in Burma through Japanese Eyes', *Canadian Military History*, 2002, Volume 11, Issue 2, Article 6, p.57.

As discussed in Chapter 2, some operational training was carried out by the Japanese squadrons which removed the need for sending experienced aircrew to teach at training schools.

The available evidence would therefore suggest that the J.A.A.F. in the Far East was a consistent force of locally well-led aircrews and aircraft who only started to transfer away from the region in late 1944 owing to pressures in other theatres. Whilst reinforcements were not received from the homeland or the Pacific, both the 33rd and 204th *Sentais* were moved into Burma in time for the Japanese advance towards India, while the 87th was moved up from Sumatra in May 1944 in an attempt to counter improved Allied fighters. Furthermore, while reinforcement units were not forthcoming, Allied intelligence services indicate from radio and photo recon-naissance sources that the Japanese were able to quickly replace lost aircraft. For example in March 1944, "that the Japanese will make good the losses there can be no doubt" and in May, "the destructive intruder raids that continue to whittle down Japan's air strength in Burma in spite of the enemy's well-known tendency for speedy replacements."[125] Although Allied intelligence believed only 50% of the *Sentais'* pilot strength were fully trained, those remaining had adequate aircraft with a capability for replacements when required.

Conclusions

By May 1945 the J.A.A.F. had virtually withdrawn from Burma leaving the Allies with total air supremacy, air superiority being theirs since the middle of 1944. Whilst Allied air forces had played their part in establishing air dominance, events in other theatres and in Japan affected the eventual outcome as Shores identified:

> So, in conclusion, the campaigns in Burma may be seen ultimately to have repre-sented a great success for Allied air power. However, it was a success which perhaps needs to be considered not on its own, but in the integral context of the Pacific war as a whole, for this had impacted so greatly on the efforts and abilities of Japan's own air forces in sustaining the war here.[126]

While Shores is correct to identify the Pacific it is clear that Japan's problems were on a wider scale as the J.A.A.F.'s ability to wage an effective air war in Burma was hindered by a variety of factors away from the Far East and by the policy and strategy of its high command.

The root of the problems was Japan's underestimation of the Allies', particularly the Americans', determination to fight rather than press for an early peace settlement.

---

125 TNA, Air 24/1296, Intelligence Branch Appendices, No 17, 12th March 1944 and TNA,
      Air 24/1300, Intelligence Branch Appendices, No 37, 30th July 1944.
126 Shores, *Air War for Burma*, p.381.

Japanese industry, even when eventually placed on a war footing, could not hope to match the huge industrial capability and manpower resources of the Americans and British, and even though great efforts were made to increase output it was never enough to reach any kind of parity. Outmoded industrial techniques which desperately required modernisation, even in the Germans' view, linked with a squabble for resources by the Army and Navy condemned production to a lower level than was potentially possible to achieve. Furthermore, the division between the Army and Navy, which would appear to have no deeper reason than simply rivalry, resulted in separate aircraft types for each service which diverted industrial effort and split basic manufacturing resources. There were no common types flying with the Japanese air arms, whilst, for example, the British 'navalised' both the Hurricane and Spitfire for aircraft carrier service with the Fleet Air Arm.[127] Limited resources combined with the urgency to bring new aircraft types into operation to match superior Allied aircraft resulted in further difficulties. The Frank, Tony and Ki-100 were allegedly as good as if not better than later American aircraft such as the Mustang or Thunderbolt, but all suffered early technical difficulties which had delayed their service introduction. Additionally, once in service their superiority over other Japanese types resulted in over-use which highlighted various technical problems, such as engines, which should have been identified in the design and test stages. The ability to test aircraft properly was hindered by the need to bring aircraft quickly into service as well as diminishing fuel stocks which started to reduce in mid-1944, and priority for petrol was given to operational squadrons. As fuel stocks started to reduce the Japanese experimented with fuel mixtures containing alcohol and petrol. Training units were using 20 per cent alcohol and 50 per cent petrol mixtures in early 1945, but by the end of the war the Japanese had not used alcohol mixtures in combat operations.[128] Furthermore, there is no evidence that the quality of Japanese fuel affected J.A.A.F. operations in the Burma Theatre during the period between mid-1944 and May 1945.

The difficulties in Japanese aircraft production had an effect on air operations in Burma. There was never more than four single-engine fighter *Sentais* in the country, whilst Sumatra had a couple of single-engine fighter *Sentais* boosted by the Nicks of the 21st *Sentai*. Reinforcements or additional *Sentais* were unlikely to be sent while units were desperately required in the Pacific, and the uncertainty of replacement aircraft being despatched influenced the frequency of Japanese operations. Crucially the numbers of aircraft available to the J.A.A.F. in Burma was not totally due to manufacturing difficulties but where the Japanese set their priorities. Despite the Allied blockade on Japanese resources and their own manufacturing deficiencies, Japanese aircraft production grew steadily from 1942 until it reached its peak in September 1944. From October 1944 until April 1945 Japanese units transferred away

---

127 Whilst both the Sea Hurricane and Seafire served with the F.A.A., American naval types were purchased for operational use by the British. The United States did not have any common types, but given its vast resources did not need to.
128 TNA, Air 48/69, U.S.S.B.S., *Japanese Air Power*, p.41.

from Burma to reinforce other units fighting in the Philippines, Pacific and in defence of Japan itself because of the growing attrition rates. Japan's priority was to protect its homeland and the defensive barrier of islands surrounding Japan, and this policy required the majority of its air units and the best aircraft available.

However, at the beginning this did not matter too much. For much of the period between June 1942 and December 1943 Japan's interests in the Far East were under no immediate threat from the Allies and although Allied intelligence services reported occasional sightings of Tonys and Tojos, air combat had shown the Oscars to be more than a match for the Hurricane. There was, therefore, no need to bring additional units equipped with later types of aircraft into Burma owing to the tempo of operations and the Oscar's advantages. However, at the end of 1943 the situation changed when the Allies started to receive superior defensive and offensive fighters such as the Spitfire, Mustang and Lightning. Japanese *Sentais* were not able to counter these aircraft in quantity or quality with better equipped, experienced units. Moreover, by early 1944 the introduction of potentially better aircraft came too late to make a difference. For example, the 87th *Sentai* was despatched in May with Tojos to counter the Allies, but the *Sentai* was relatively inexperienced and it was their misfortune "to encounter the best Allied long-range fighters available in the area."[129] Whilst the quality of Japanese pilots, according to contemporary reports and subsequent analysis, was good and the majority of the units experienced in the theatre, they were handicapped against numerically superior Allied fighters. The lack of modern aircraft in terms of quality and quantity was an obvious handicap to Japanese operations in Burma, particularly after December 1943, as no air force could operate for long under such circumstances against a better equipped foe. However, such deficiencies must be balanced against how the resources were used. While Japanese aircraft were sent to priority areas, the use of their available air resources in Burma has to be questioned. The intrinsic difficulty of a service having its own air arm was demonstrated with the J.A.A.F. being used almost exclusively for direct support of ground operations, operating aircraft that were designed principally for that purpose. Although initially successful in that role, there was little chance, for example, of using bombers in an effective strategic bombing campaign and owing to the manufacturing difficulties no opportunity to develop a heavy bomber fleet. In addition to aircraft types Japanese air actions were hindered by a traditional Army high command who failed to grasp the possibilities of air power outside the confines of ground support. During the 1942-1943 period they failed to identify important targets and exploit the various Allied air defence weaknesses in eastern India, particularly Calcutta. Although commanders may have been conscious that replacements were unlikely to be sent and conservation of their resources was important, the inability to use their aircraft boldly at crucial times gave the Allies time to build their own resources and defences. Similarly by using fighters in ground support roles instead of concentrating on vulnerable transport operations

129 Shores, *Air War for Burma*, p.232.

during the early 1944 campaigns the Allies were handed the opportunity to supply their ground forces and prevent the Japanese advance towards India. From late 1944 Japanese air power in Burma started to diminish, although even then the remaining fighters could have been used to hinder the Fourteenth Army's advance by attacking the transport fleet, but were used, as A.C.M. Park described, in small numbers in ground support roles.[130] A concerted effort in 1945 to disrupt Allied supply flights with the few available Japanese fighters, at a time when the early warning systems were unable to maintain pace with the rapid advance, would have caused considerable supply difficulties. This factor had more to do with policy and strategy rather than aircraft numbers or types, as a bolder approach between October 1942 and May 1945 may have paid dividends in hindering Allied plans.

Whilst these influences played a part in reducing Japanese strengths and capabilities in combination with the inability or unwillingness to use their resources effectively, they must be balanced against Allied actions in the theatre. For fourteen months from October 1942 the Allies held their own against Japanese air attack whilst at the same time building their resources and experience. Once Allied air forces had been resupplied with numbers of better, relevant aircraft in late 1943, they started to take the initiative from the Japanese both in attack and defence, particularly between March and May 1944 with the aggressive counter-air campaign which destroyed Japanese resources and forced their units' dispersal. Once the 1944 monsoon was over the migration of Japanese resources combined with sustained Allied counter-air operations reduced Japanese commanders' options further, although as discussed earlier, more emphasis could have been placed on attacking transport aircraft. Therefore, whilst the Japanese had missed their opportunities in 1942 and 1943, the initiative had been taken from them with the increase in Allied strength from December 1943 leaving Japanese commanders, with their misunderstanding of air power capabilities, with fewer options for action.

The Japanese commanders' inability to use what resources they possessed effectively had the most immediate influence on Japan's air war in Burma. Although they did not possess sufficient resources and the potential lack of replacements may have affected commanders' decisions, it would have been possible to hinder and disrupt Allies' plans at crucial times with the equipment they had available. This factor can only be judged on the available resources they had at the time, but this chapter has effectively shown that they failed to take advantage of Allied weaknesses with equipment and resources that were potentially superior given the circumstances from 1942 to the middle of 1944. Consequently, the winning of air superiority by the Allies was significantly assisted by Japanese passivity at crucial moments and evaluation of the success or otherwise of R.A.F. measures and activity must incorporate this into any overarching analysis.

---

130 TNA, Air 23/4665, Despatch on air operations by Air Chief Marshal Sir Keith Park, 1st June 1944 to 2nd May 1945, p.20.

Conclusion

The aim of this book has been to answer fundamental questions which have at their core how the Japanese won air superiority in 1941 and 1942, and then how the Allies reversed the situation, winning air supremacy by June 1945. The book has shown how the early warning organisation was developed from June 1942, despite supply and technical difficulties, to becoming an efficient system in India by February 1944, and then how it coped with new challenges when the Allies were on the offensive. The book has demonstrated how and why the factors of aircrew, tactics and aircraft were important to the air superiority campaign, and how each was successfully developed. The counter-air campaign played a crucial role, particularly after February 1944, and this book has demonstrated why it was unsuccessful prior to then and argued why Allied claims of destroyed Japanese aircraft may not have been correct during the period between March and June 1944. It has also shown that the Japanese contributed to their eventual defeat in the air campaign. The principle factors were difficulties in aircraft production, fighting a war on several fronts and the use to which commanders used their air resources in India and Burma.

Since the First World War air superiority and air supremacy have been recognized as essential factors in allowing air, sea and land operations to be prosecuted. During the initial attacks in 1941 the Japanese were able to gain air superiority in a series of well planned and executed air raids, the R.A.F. alone losing 55% of its air strength during the first day's attacks.[1] The J.A.A.F. and J.N.A.F. consisted of modern aircraft suitable for the campaign, and aircrew that had considerable experience from air combat against the Chinese and Soviets during the late 1930s. This gave them an advantage over the British and Americans. As the Germans had found in their initial attacks on the Soviet Air Force in 1941, a pre-emptive counter-air offensive is successful against a weaker adversary and the Japanese were able to capitalize on Allied weaknesses. The British in the Far East had an early warning system that was inconsistent, obsolete fighter aircraft, and aircrew whose courage could not be doubted but who largely lacked flying and combat experience. Attempting to reinforce Malaya and Burma with radar and aircraft once the Japanese had seized air superiority proved a failure as equipment could not be deployed in time and the aircraft sent there were mainly

---

1   Probert, *The Forgotten Air Force*, p.43.

unsuitable. The early exchanges emphatically demonstrated the importance of an integrated air defence system as existed in Britain, where all the factors were in place and efficiently working prior to an enemy attack.

From May 1942 until the end of 1943, the quest for air superiority reached stalemate. While the R.A.F. built up their air defence system in India with an early warning organisation, more aircraft and better aircrew, the essential supporting factors did not develop at the same rate. The monumental effort to establish an effective early warning chain despite technical and supply difficulties was matched by more aircrew who arrived better trained and then received relevant air fighting training in the theatre. However, while the quantity of aircraft improved, the quality did not as Hurricanes were not a match for the more manoeuvrable Japanese Oscars they faced. The deficiency in suitable aircraft also affected the counter-air campaign and added to the stalemate. The lack of long-range fighters both in quantity and quality resulted in small numbers of medium and heavy bombers being deployed on raids on enemy airfields which, at best, caused some disruption to Japanese operations by forcing the J.A.A.F. to disperse aircraft around their network of airfields. Loss of Japanese aircraft as a direct result of these raids was minimal and it is possible that more Japanese aircraft were lost in flying accidents than during interdiction raids.

The stalemate in the air superiority campaign also owed something to the Japanese failing to seize the initiative. Their aircraft were largely superior to Allied aircraft in quality and quantity, and from October 1942 until late 1943 the air defences in eastern and north-eastern India were susceptible to air attack. Concentrated fighter and bomber operations against Indian cities or against the transport operations over the Hump route into China could have disrupted Allied supply plans. For example, the few night raids on Calcutta in December 1942 and January 1943 had caused panic and evacuation of the city's population and it is clear that concentrated raids by larger formations could have overwhelmed the defences precipitating further disruption. Similarly if day raids had been properly coordinated to capitalize on weaknesses in early warning and fighter defences, the Japanese might have severely hindered the Allied campaign. However, these operations, and those against the Hump, were not pursued and the Japanese missed a vital opportunity. It is not clear whether they failed to appreciate Allied weaknesses and their own strengths, or whether they were cautious because aircraft replacements were likely to be unavailable, but it is arguable that the Japanese could have assumed air superiority and its benefits throughout this period.

The balance in air superiority began to swing in the Allies' favour in late 1943 with the introduction of better British and American aircraft. Although priorities in other theatres had prevented the Spitfire fighter's arrival until October 1943, the eventual deployment marked the final establishment of an integrated air defence system in India and Burma. Once the ground controllers adapted to the fighter's higher performance in combination with the improving early warning systems in eastern India, Japanese raids were regularly intercepted. Moreover the Spitfire played a crucial role intercepting and destroying Japanese reconnaissance Dinahs that had previously flown too high and fast to be intercepted by existing fighters. Thus, Japanese commanders were denied vital intelligence of Allied ground activity which proved crucial once the Fourteenth Army began its advance into Burma in mid-1944. Accordingly, by February 1944 the R.A.F. had a much improved early warning organisation, better trained and experienced pilots and aircraft that were capable of utilising improved air fighting tactics. However, subsequent events in 1944 showed the Spitfire was not the sole answer to attaining air superiority.

Defending transport and ground support aircraft around the Imphal Plain and Chindit landing grounds in the absence of adequate early warning proved difficult. The lack of fighters coupled with the need to conserve fuel meant inefficient and wasteful combat air patrols were a last resort. The introduction of the patrolled air corridor was clearly a success, but represented a compromise between full combat air patrols and interceptions. Although successful in protecting the transport aircraft within the corridor, the tactic did little to reduce Japanese air strength. However, at the same time as the Spitfire changed air defence capabilities in India and Burma, the introduction of the American long-range Lightnings and Mustangs played a crucial part in the counter-air offensive. These fighters had the capability to strike at Japanese airfields in a concentrated offensive which had not been possible prior to December 1943. Although the available figures suggest that Japanese losses in the airfield raids were not as high as originally claimed, the offensive reduced Japanese air strength in a manner that air-to-air combat did not match. The minimum figure of 60 Japanese aircraft destroyed on counter-air operations was twice as high as those destroyed in air-to-air combat, and it does not take into account those aircraft that were damaged and needed repair. This put an additional strain on maintenance units and allocation of spare parts, neither of which the Japanese were efficient at. Furthermore, the interdiction attacks continued the earlier trend of forcing Japanese units to disperse to other airfields, thereby increasing flying time and the risk of flying accidents. The counter-air offensive continued to play an important role in the air superiority campaign as a tactic which complimented air defence, but it was clear it could only be effective with suitable aircraft.

When was air superiority and air supremacy gained by the Allies? The A.H.B. authors were correct to point out that it was not won in the middle of 1943 with the beginning of the monsoon.[2] The Allies were able to continue very limited air operations through the monsoon not through air superiority but simply because the Japanese had withdrawn for the monsoon season, as they had done in 1942, to re-supply their units and train their personnel. The J.A.A.F. returned to Burma in October 1943 with a potentially potent force that if properly handled could have caused the Allies considerable problems, but from that time the situation gradually changed as better Allied aircraft were introduced to the theatre. Most of the literature relating to the air campaign agrees that by June 1944 blanket air superiority had been won by the

2   TNA, Air 41/36, *The Campaigns in the Far East, Volume III: India Command*, p.112.

Allies in India and western Burma with the J.A.A.F. never again being a credible force. However, this statement is only partially accurate. When the monsoon began in May 1944 Japanese air strength had not been crushed and there were 123 aircraft, of which 54 were fighters, in forward and central Burma, and 348 in the entire theatre.[3] When the monsoon ended in October the Japanese air strength, according to intelligence estimates, had risen to 485 in the entire theatre, which, if properly directed, could have caused difficulties for the Allies.[4] Successive transfers and attrition caused this number to diminish so that eventually the J.A.A.F. ceased to be a credible force and this will be discussed later in this conclusion. However, air superiority had been gained in localized areas as early as February 1944.

The introduction of the Spitfire in combination with the improved early warning organisation had provided air superiority over much of eastern India by February 1944, ensuring ports were safe and Japanese reconnaissance aircraft were likely to be intercepted. Similarly, during the Battle of the Admin Box in February and March 1944, transport aircraft were able to fly their vital supply sorties protected by friendly fighters that were within the range of the early warning systems, which included the radar units based offshore on barges. However, providing local air superiority over the Chindit landing grounds, Kohima and Imphal, proved harder owing to the perilous state of the available early warning. The deficiencies in air defence were successfully offset by a rigorous counter-air campaign which attacked Japanese airfields destroying and damaging aircraft, and forcing Japanese units to disperse to other locations. The combination of the interdiction programme, air defence and the patrolled air corridor had thus ensured localized air superiority which enabled transport and close air support sorties to be flown. However, it should be remembered that Allied air superiority during this period was assisted by Japan's tactical inflexibility and lack of imagination. Given their aircraft numbers, concentrated attacks with fighters and bombers on the Allied transport effort by day and night might have paid dividends, particularly when the Allies lost much of their early warning capability to the east of Imphal. As in 1942 and 1943, the Japanese failed to make effective use of their resources at a crucial time in the land battle.

According to intelligence sources Japanese units and their aircraft returned to the Far East in October 1944 in greater numbers, but from November 1944 systematic transfers and withdrawals to other areas significantly reduced Japanese air strength. From October 1944 the Japanese were out-matched in aircraft quantity and quality, and were not able to materially alter the ground or air operations in a substantial way. These months saw air superiority gained in Burma, as the localized superiority widened to the entire country and the advancing Allied operations. Air supremacy was gained by May 1945 when Japanese air strength had virtually vanished leaving the Allied air forces in command of the air. The process was complete in June 1945

3   TNA, Air 24/1298, Weekly Intelligence Summary, May 1944.
4   TNA, Air 24/1305, Weekly Intelligence Summary, October 1944.

when transport aircraft were able to fly on supply dropping sorties without any fighter escort.

One factor which affected both the Allies and the Japanese in the Burma theatre was the level of priority afforded to the campaign. The R.A.F. lacked modern fighter aircraft in Malaya and Burma in 1941 because Spitfires and Hurricanes were required in Great Britain and the Middle East. As the campaign developed this trend was continued especially when the Allies decided to make defeating Germany their first priority at the expense of the Far East Theatre. For example, India Command was denied radar equipment until other commands had been equipped and there was a delay in supplying Spitfire fighters to the theatre, with even supplying the Soviet Union being given a higher priority. Similarly it took the Americans until the end of 1943 to equip the forces in their China-Burma-India theatre with the very efficient Lightning and Mustang fighters. This book has thus demonstrated that the campaign to achieve air superiority was delayed in reaching a high level of success because these fighters were denied to the theatre until nearly two years after the Japanese first attacked.

The lack of resources committed to the British campaign in Burma has resulted in the epithet of 'forgotten' being attached to it. Japan's attitude to the theatre was similar. The U.S.S.B.S. authors pointed out that air superiority was won almost by default as the Japanese gave the theatre a low priority for equipment, but it is unlikely that the Japanese deliberately gave Burma and India such a low priority owing to their economic and political importance. As the British had found in 1941 when equipping Malaya with aircraft, greater priorities in the home islands and Middle East had taken the better Spitfires and Hurricanes, leaving only the Buffalo. From November 1942 the Japanese were faced with a growing threat from American forces in the Pacific and eventually the home islands which resulted in more aircraft and units being deployed to those theatres. This was exacerbated by the limited numbers of aircraft produced from Japanese factories which had to be shared between fractious Army and Navy commands.

Air superiority in India and Burma was ultimately won by a combination of inter-relating factors rather than one outstanding element. The campaign was not like the Battle of Britain where the Germans suffered high, unsustainable attrition rates of both aircraft and aircrew over a period of time. It could also not be compared to the air superiority campaign against Germany in 1944, where a vigorous counter-air campaign was assisted by a strategic bomber offensive against the German aircraft industry and its supporting organisations. The air superiority campaign in Burma did not rely on an offensive against Japanese aircraft manufacturing or on high attrition rates inflicted in aerial or interdiction operations. Air supremacy was won by a number of factors acting together.

While the early warning organisation only played a supporting role in the campaign it was still vital. The lack of an efficient early warning system during the initial Japanese attacks, and later in 1944 when cover over the battlefront proved difficult, had shown that modern air defence depended on an early warning organisation to act as a force multiplier. Although never completely perfect the system had assisted fighters in disrupting Japanese raids and then, in combination with the Spitfire, to intercepting raiders and reconnaissance aircraft. Without the organisation costly air combat patrols would have been flown at considerable cost in fuel and airframe life which the R.A.F. and its Allies, with their limited resources, could ill afford. Building on the foundation of the early warning organisation were the factors of aircrew, aircraft and air fighting tactics. Air fighting over Malaya in 1941 and early 1942 had shown the interrelationship between these factors. Even when the radar units gave adequate warning of Japanese raids, without a fighter capable of climbing to advantageous heights to intercept enemy aircraft and destroy them using the accepted dive and zoom tactic, the defenders were at a disadvantage. Furthermore, the fact that many of the pilots lacked flying and combat experience meant another part of the overall air defence capability was deficient. One of the essential requirements for achieving air superiority was an improvement in these elements. The dive and zoom air tactic was clearly the best manoeuvre to counter Japanese fighters and this was recognized and taught to aircrew as they became operational. Although it took until the end of 1943 for the quality of fighters to improve, the introduction of Spitfires, Lightnings and Mustangs meant that therefore both defensive and offensive operations were capable of attaining new levels of efficiency. It took some time for an integrated air defence system consisting of elements of early warning, aircraft, aircrew and tactics to bed down, but the Allies now had all the necessary factors to prosecute an integrated air superiority campaign, whilst the addition of the long-range fighter was to give operations an important flexibility.

By February 1944 the combination of these factors gave the Allies better tools to prosecute an air superiority campaign, but the contribution made by the Japanese to their air defeat cannot be discounted. Japan's aircraft industry was unable to produce sufficient aircraft for the Army and Navy and their many areas of operations even before the American Naval blockade and bombing campaign took effect. A combination of limited resources, which included aircrew, a diversion of effort between the Army and Navy, and a lack of central control reduced the numbers of aircraft that were produced. It is clear that a few more hundred, well directed, Japanese fighter aircraft could have provided the Allies with a number of difficulties even to the end of May 1945. Aircraft types were also a problem. It is clear that given sufficient resources and development time the Japanese were capable of producing efficient aircraft that could have matched most Allied fighters. Aircraft like the Frank and Ki-100 proved to be equivalent to or better than some American types in the Pacific, and there can be little doubt that if these aircraft had been properly developed and deployed in sufficient numbers, the Allies in Burma would have faced a formidable foe. Finally the Japanese failed to use their resources in Burma to the best effect. This book has shown that they failed to take the initiative in 1942-1943, and failed to attack the Allies whilst at their most vulnerable in the first six months of 1944. As A.C.M. Sir Keith Park stated, even at the end of the air superiority campaign in 1945 the Japanese were capable of hindering the Allied supply operations by properly using their resources instead of concentrating on ground support. Ultimately the Japanese had contributed to their air campaign downfall in Burma and assisted the Allies in their goal for air supremacy.

This book represents an original study of the air superiority campaign in Burma between 1941 and 1945. Although the early warning organisation has been covered in other publications, it has not been analysed in depth before and this book has effectively demonstrated its overall contribution to the campaign. Whilst the factors of aircrew, tactics and aircraft have been addressed separately, this book has discussed all three elements together and has shown how they impacted on the Allies' eventual success. The book has corroborated most sources' view that the counter-air campaign was unsuccessful prior to February 1944 and how and why it was successful after that date. However, it has clearly shown that Allied claims of destroyed Japanese aircraft in the counter-air campaign after that date may have been excessive, even though the effects of the campaign were still beneficial to the eventual outcome. This book has also corroborated existing evidence that the Japanese industry failed to produce suffi-cient aircraft in quality and quantity, but it has also argued that Japanese commanders were forced to give the J.A.A.F. in Burma a lower priority owing to pressing demands in other theatres. As a whole, the book represents an original contribution to current historical knowledge of the air superiority campaign in Burma during the Second World War.

Appendix I

Comparative Table of Fighter Types 1941-1942

	Wingspan	Length	Maximum Weight	Rate of climb	Maximum Speed
Buffalo	35	26	6703	Time to 10000 feet – 7.6 mins	321 mph at 18989 feet (6388lbs)
Hurricane IIB	40	31.6	7340	Time to 20000 feet – 8.4 mins	342 mph at 22000 feet
P-40B	37.3	31.7	7778	Time to 15000 feet – 7.1mins	345 mph at 15000 feet
Nate	37.1	24.6	3946	Time to 20000 feet – 6.6 mins	292 mph at 11485 feet
Oscar	35.7	29.2	5500	Time to 16405 feet – 5.5 mins	329 mph at 13125 feet
Zero	36.1	29.7	6330	Time to 20000 feet – 6.6 mins	340 mph at 19700 feet

Dimensions in feet
Weight in pounds

Appendix II

Comparative Dimensions of Fighters Far East May 1942 to September 1943

	Wingspan	Length	Maximum Weight	Rate of Climb	Maximum Speed
Hurricane IIB	40	31.6	7340	Time to 20000 feet - 8.4 mins	342 mph at 22000 feet
Hurricane IIC	40	31.6	7640	Time to 20000 feet - 9.1 mins	339 mph at 22000 feet
Beaufighter IV	57.9	41.9	21322	Time to 15,000 feet - 7.8 mins	333 mph at 15,600 feet
Spitfire V	36.8	30	6737	Time to 20000 feet - 7 mins	374 mph at 20000 feet
Ki-43 Oscar	35.7	29.2	5500	Time to 16405 feet - 5.5 mins	329 mph at 13125 feet

Dimensions in feet
Weight in pounds

Appendix III

Comparative Dimensions of Principal R.A.F. and Japanese Fighters

	Wingspan	Length	Maximum Weight	Rate of Climb	Maximum Speed
Buffalo	35	26	6703	Time to 10000 feet – 7.6 mins	321 mph at 18989 feet
Mohawk	37.3	29	6717	Time to 15000 feet – 8 mins	298 mph at 13000 feet
Hurricane IIB	40	31.6	7340	Time to 20000 feet – 8.4 mins	342 mph at 22000 feet
Hurricane IIC	40	31.6	7640	Time to 20000 feet – 9.1 mins	339 mph at 22000 feet
Spitfire Vc	36.8	30	6737	Time to 20000 feet – 7 mins	374 mph at 20000 feet
Spitfire VIII	40.2	30	7800	Time to 20000 feet – 7 mins	408 mph at 20000 feet
Beaufighter IV	57.9	41.9	21322	Time to 15,000 feet – 7.8 mins	333 mph at 15,600 feet
Mosquito IV	54.1	44.5	22300	Time to 15,000 feet – 8 mins	362 mph at 5,500 feet
Nate	37.1	24.6	3946	Time to 20000 feet – 6.6 mins	292 mph at 11485 feet
Oscar	35.7	29.2	5500	Time to 16405 feet – 5.5 mins	329 mph at 13125 feet
Zero	36.1	29.7	6330	Time to 20000 feet – 6.6 mins	340 mph at 19700 feet
Tojo	31	28.9	6598	Time to 20000 feet – 5.5 mins	383 mph at 17000 feet

Dimensions in feet
Weight in pounds

Appendix IV

Comparative table of Allied fighter aircraft ranges

	Basic Range	Maximum Range when applicable	Aircraft internal tankage
P40B (Tomahawk IIA)	600 miles	805 miles	133 IG
P40D (Kittyhawk I)	750 miles	1308 miles	166.6 IG
P38 (Lightning)	810 miles	1512 miles	279 IG
P51A (Mustang)	640 miles	1500 miles	186 IG
P51B (Mustang)	950 miles	2250 miles	150 IG
P51D (Mustang)	950 miles	2190 miles	150 IG
P47 (Thunderbolt)	835 miles	2100 Miles	254 IG
Mohawk	620 miles	860 miles	132 IG
Hurricane IIB	480 miles	1090 miles	97 IG
Hurricane IIC	460 miles	1090 miles	97 IG
Spitfire Vc	469 miles	1135 miles	84 IG
Spitfire VIII	660 miles	1530 miles	120 IG
Beaufighter	1480 miles	1640 miles	550 IG
Mosquito FB.IV	1120 miles	1500 miles	536 IG

IG = Imperial Gallons

Appendix V

Comparative Dimensions of Principal U.S. and Japanese Fighters

	Wingspan	Length	Maximum Weight	Rate of Climb	Maximum Speed
P40B	37.3	31.7	7778	Time to 15000 feet – 7.1 mins	345 mph at 15000 feet
P38 (Lightning)	52	37.9	15500	Time to 16000 feet – 6.75 mins	400 mph at 16800 feet
P51A (Mustang)	37.25	31.5	7708	Time to 20000 feet – 8.8 mins	388 mph at 16500 feet
P51B (Mustang)	37	32.3	9190	Time to 20000 feet – 7.5 mins	395 mph at 20000 feet
P51D (Mustang)	37	32.3	9478	Time to 20000 feet – 7.5 mins	407 mph at 20000 feet
P47D (Thunderbolt)	40.9	36	14600	Time to 15000 feet – 5.1 mins	440 mph at 29000 feet
Oscar	35.7	29.2	5500	Time to 16405 feet – 5.5 mins	329 mph at 13125 feet
Zero	36.1	29.7	6330	Time to 20000 feet – 6.6 mins	340 mph at 19700 feet
Tojo	31	28.9	6598	Time to 20000 feet – 5.5 mins	383 mph at 17000 feet

Dimensions in feet
Weight in pounds

288

Appendix VI

Average Number of Aircraft on Strength of Operational R.A.F. and U.S.A.A.F. Squadrons

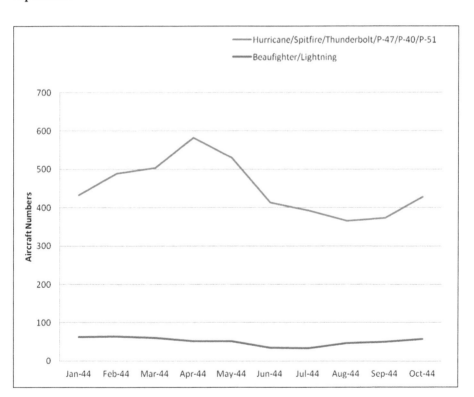

Appendix VII

Average Number of Serviceable Aircraft in R.A.F. Operational Squadrons, Eastern Air Command

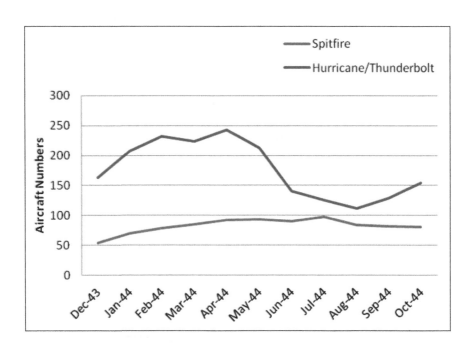

Appendix VIII

Average Number of Serviceable Aircraft in R.A.F. Operational Squadrons, 222 and 225 Groups

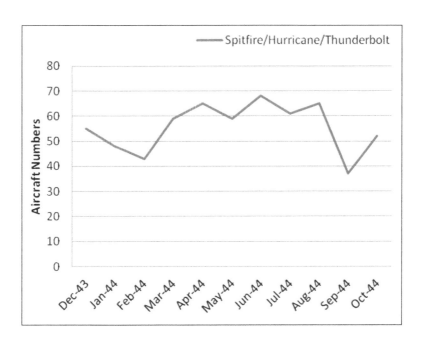

Bibliography

PRIMARY SOURCES: ARCHIVE MATERIAL

The National Archives, Kew

ADM 53   Admiralty and Ministry of Defence, Navy Department; Ships Logs.

Air 2   Air Ministry and Ministry of Defence: Registered Files.

Air 8   Air Ministry and Ministry of Defence: Department of the Chief of the Air Staff; Registered Files.

Air 10   Air Ministry and predecessors: Air Publications and Reports.

Air 20   Air Ministry and Ministry of Defence: Papers accumulated by the Air Historical Branch.

Air 23   Air Ministry and Ministry of Defence: Royal Air Force Overseas Commands; Reports and Correspondence.

Air 24   Air Ministry and Ministry of Defence: Operations Record Books, South East Asia Command.

Air 25   Air Ministry and Ministry of Defence: Operations Record Books, Groups.

Air 26   Air Ministry: Operations Record Books, Wings.

Air 27   Air Ministry and successors: Operations Record Books, Squadrons.

Air 29   Air Ministry and Ministry of Defence: Operations Record Books, Miscellaneous Units.

Air 40   Air Ministry, Directorate of Intelligence and related bodies; Intelligence Reports and Papers.

Air 55   Air Ministry, British Air Forces of Occupation, Germany and Allied Commission for Austria (British Element), Air Division: Papers.

Avia 7   Ministry of Aviation, predecessors and successors: Royal Radar Establishment and predecessors; Registered Files.

Avia 12   Ministry of Supply and Ministry of Aviation: Second World War and Miscellaneous Unregistered Papers.

Avia 15   Ministry of Aircraft Production and predecessor and successors; Registered Files.

Avia 38   Ministry of Supply and Ministry of Aircraft Production: North American Supply Missions, Second World War, Files.

CAB 21   Cabinet Office and predecessors: Registered Files (1916 to 1965).
SUPP 9   Aircraft Data Sheets and Photographs.
WO 106   War Office: Directorate of Military Operations and Military Intelligence,
and predecessors; Correspondence and Papers.

The Royal Air Force Museum, Hendon
Papers of Air Chief Marshal Sir Richard Edmund Charles Peirse KCB, CB, DSO,
AFC.

The Churchill Archive, Churchill College, Cambridge University
Slim, Field Marshal William Joseph, 1st Viscount (1891-1970); Private correspondence, military papers, articles.

Christ Church College Library, Oxford University
Lord Portal of Hungerford; Personal Papers.

PRIMARY SOURCES: OFFICIAL PUBLICATIONS

The National Archives, Kew
Air 41/4, Air Ministry and Ministry of Defence: Air Historical Branch: Narratives
and Monographs. *Flying Training – Aircrew Training, 1934-1942*, (1945).
Air 41/6, Air Ministry and Ministry of Defence: Air Historical Branch: Narratives
and Monographs. *Photographic Reconnaissance, 1914 to April 1941, Volume I*, (1945).
Air 41/7, Air Ministry and Ministry of Defence: Air Historical Branch: Narratives
and Monographs. *Photographic Reconnaissance, May 1941 to August 1945 Volume
II*, (1948).
Air 41/12, Air Ministry and Ministry of Defence: Air Historical Branch: Narratives
and Monographs. *Signals, Volume IV: Radar in Raid Reporting*, (1950).
Air 41/35, Air Ministry and Ministry of Defence: Air Historical Branch: Narratives
and Monographs. *The Campaigns in the Far East, Volume I: Far East Defence Policy
and Preparations for War*, (1948).
Air 41/36, Air Ministry and Ministry of Defence: Air Historical Branch: Narratives
and Monographs. *The Campaigns in the Far East, Volume III: India Command*,
(1949).
Air 41/37, Air Ministry and Ministry of Defence: Air Historical Branch: Narratives
and Monographs. *The Campaigns in the Far East, Volume V: Air Supply Operations
in Burma, 1942-1945*, (1949).
Air 41/38, Air Ministry and Ministry of Defence: Air Historical Branch: Narratives
and Monographs. *The Campaigns in the Far East, Volume VI: Air Transport in the
S.W. Pacific Area, 1945-1946*, (1949).
Air 41/63, Air Ministry and Ministry of Defence: Air Historical Branch: Narratives
and Monographs. *The Campaigns in the Far East: Volume II, Malaya, Netherlands,
East Indies and Burma 1941-1942*, (1954).

Air 41/64, Air Ministry and Ministry of Defence: Air Historical Branch: Narratives and Monographs. *The Campaigns in the Far East: Volume IV South East Asia November 1943 to August 1945*, (1956).

Air 41/69, Air Ministry and Ministry of Defence: Air Historical Branch: Narratives and Monographs. *Flying training during World War II: Volume 2 (organisation) part 1; Basic Training in UK*, (1952).

Air 41/70, Air Ministry and Ministry of Defence: Air Historical Branch: Narratives and Monographs. *Flying training during World War II: Volume 2 Part 2; Basic Training Overseas*, (1952).

Air 41/71, Air Ministry and Ministry of Defence: Air Historical Branch: Narratives and Monographs. *Flying training during World War II: Volume 2 Part 3; Operational Training*, (1952).

Air 41/88, Air Ministry and Ministry of Defence: Air Historical Branch: Narratives and Monographs. *Signals, Volume V: Fighter Control and Interception (The Second World War, 1939-1945, Royal Air Force)*, (1952).

Air 48/69, United States Strategic Bombing Survey: Reports. Military Analysis Division Reports. *Japanese Air Power*, (1946).

Air 48/73, United States Strategic Bombing Survey: Reports. *Morale Division Reports. The Effects of Strategic Bombing on Japanese Morale*, (1947).

Air 48/104, United States Strategic Bombing Survey: Reports. *Overall Economic Effects Division Reports. Effects of Strategic Bombing on Japan War Economy*, (1946).

Air 48/183, United States Strategic Bombing Survey: Reports. *Urban Areas Division Reports: effects of air attacks. War Against Japanese Transportation*, (1947).

The Royal Air Force Museum, Hendon
United States Strategic Bombing Survey: Reports. *Military Analysis Division: Air Operations in China, Burma, India, World War II*, (1947).

PRIMARY SOURCES: PRINTED WORKS

Books
Anon, *Wings of the Phoenix*, London, H.M.S.O., 1946.
Calvert, Michael, *Fighting Mad*, Barnsley, Pen and Sword, 2004 edition.
Chapman, F.S., *The Jungle is Neutral*, London, Corgi, 1965.
Chennault, Claire, *Way of a Fighter*, New York, Putnam's, 1949.
Douhet, Guilio, *The Command of the Air*, London, Faber and Faber edition, 1943.
Fergusson, Bernard, *Beyond the Chindwin*, London, Fontana, 1975.
Fraser, George MacDonald, *Quartered Safe Out Here*, London, Harper Collins, 2000 edition.
Harris, Sir Arthur, *Bomber Offensive*, London, Greenhill Books, 1990 edition.
Kelly, Terence, *Hurricane over the Jungle*, Barnsley, Pen and Sword, 2005 edition.
Kelly, Terence, *Hurricanes Versus Zeros*, Barnsley, Pen and Sword, 2007 edition.
Sakai, Saburo, *Samurai*, London, New English Library edition, 1969.

Slim, Viscount William, *Defeat into Victory*, London, Grub Street, 2005 edition.
Stripp, Alan, *Code Breaker in the Far East*, Oxford, Oxford University Press, 1995 edition.
Tedder, Lord Arthur, *With Prejudice*, London, Cassell, 1966.

Articles

Royal Air Force Quarterly
Harden, R.J., 'The Use of Allied Air Power in the War Against Japan,' 1945, Volume 17, Only one issue, pp.131-136.
Leigh-Mallory, Trafford, 'The Maintenance of Air Superiority in a Land Campaign, April 1931, Volume 2, Number 2, pp.245-252.

Royal United Services Institution Journal
Baldwin, Sir John, 'Air Aspects of the Operations in Burma,' Volume XC, No 558, May 1945, pp.195-203.

SECONDARY SOURCES

Official Publications
Craven, Wesley, and Cate, James (eds.), *The Army Air Forces in World War II, Volume One, Plans and Early Operations, January 1939 to August 1942*, Chicago, University of Chicago Press, 1964.
Craven, Wesley, and Cate, James (eds.), *The Army Air Forces in World War II, Volume Four, The Pacific: Guadalcanal to Saipan, August 1942 to July 1944*, Chicago, University of Chicago Press, 1964.
Craven, Wesley, and Cate, James (eds.), *The Army Air Forces in World War II, Volume Five, The Pacific: Matterhorn to Nagasaki, June 1944 to August 1945*, Chicago, University of Chicago Press, 1964.
Craven, Wesley, and Cate, James (eds.), *The Army Air Forces in World War II, Volume VI, Men and Planes*, Chicago, University of Chicago Press, 1964.
Craven, Wesley, and Cate, James (eds.), *The Army Air Forces in World War II, Volume VII, Services Around the World*, Chicago, University of Chicago Press, 1964.
Kirby, Woodburn (ed.), *The War Against Japan, Volume I: The Loss of Singapore*, London, H.M.S.O., 1957.
Kirby, Woodburn (ed.), *The War Against Japan, Volume II: India's Most Dangerous Hour*, London, H.M.S.O., 1958.
Kirby, Woodburn (ed.), *The War Against Japan, Volume III: The Decisive Battles*, London, H.M.S.O., 1961.
Kirby, Woodburn (ed.), *The War Against Japan, Volume IV: The Reconquest of Burma*, London, H.M.S.O., 1965.
Kirby, Woodburn (ed.), *The War Against Japan, Volume V: The Surrender of Japan*, London, H.M.S.O., 1969.

Books

Allen, Louis, *Burma, The Longest War*, London, Phoenix Press, 2000.

Aldrich, Richard J., *The Faraway War*, London, Doubleday, 2005.

Annett, Roger, *Drop Zone Burma*, Barnsley, Pen and Sword, 2008.

Anon, *The Japanese Air Forces in World War II*, (A reprint of a 1945 intelligence paper.) London, Arms and Armour Press, 1979.

Badsey, Stephen, *Utah Beach*, Stroud, Sutton Publishing, 2004.

Baker, Alan, *Merrill's Marauders*, London, Pan, 1972.

Barker, Ralph, *The Royal Flying Corps in World War 1*, London, Robinson, 2002 reprint.

Bayly, Christopher and Harper, Tim, *Forgotten Armies*, London, Penguin, 2005.

Bergamini, David, *Japan's Imperial Conspiracy*, London, Panther, 1971.

Bergerud, Eric M, *Fire in the Sky; The Air War in the South Pacific*, Colorado, Westview, 2001.

Bickers, Richard, *Ginger Lacey; Fighter Pilot*, London, Blandford, 1988 edition.

Birtles, Philip, *Hurricane, The Illustrated History*, London, Patrick Stephens Ltd, 2001.

Bond, Brian, and Taylor, Michael (eds), *The Battle for France and Flanders 1940: Sixty Years on*, Barnsley, Leo Cooper, 2001.

Boog, Horst (ed), *The Conduct of the Air War in the Second World War*, Oxford, Berg, 1992.

Bowman, Martin, *Mosquito Bomber/Fighter-Bomber Units 1942-45*, London, Osprey, 1997.

Bowman, Martin, *Mosquito Photo-Reconnaissance Units of World War 2*, London, Osprey, 1999.

Bowyer, Chaz, *Hurricane at War*, London, Ian Allan, 1974.

Bowyer, Chaz, *For Valour The Air V.C.s*, London, Grub Street, 1992.

Brown, Louis, *A Radar History of WWII; Technical and Military Imperatives*, Bristol and Philadelphia, Institute of Physics Publishing, 1999.

Buckley, John, *Air Power in the Age of Total War*, London, UCL, 1999.

Budiansky, Stephen, *Air Power*, New York, Viking, 2003.

Bungay, Stephen, *The Most Dangerous Enemy*, London, Aurum Press, 2000.

Calvocoressi, Peter, Wint, Guy, Pritchard, John, *Total War*, London, Penguin, 1995, revised 2nd edition.

Colvin, John, *Not Ordinary Men*, London, Pen and Sword, 2003.

Costello, John, *The Pacific War*, London, Pan, 1981.

Cox, Sebastian, and Gray, Peter, (eds.) *Air Power History: Turning Points from Kitty Hawk to Kosovo*, London, Cass, 2002.

Cull, Brian, *Buffaloes over Singapore*, London Grub Street, 2003.

Cull, Brian, *Hurricanes over Singapore*, London Grub Street, 2004.

Dean, Maurice, *The Royal Air Force and Two World Wars*, London, Cassell, 1979.

Elphick, Peter, *Far Eastern File, The Intelligence War in the Far East 1930-1945*, London, Hodder and Stoughton, 1997.

Foot, M.R.D., *S.O.E. The Special Operations Executive 1940-1946*, London, Arrow Books, 1993 edition.

Ford, Daniel, *Flying Tigers: Chennault and the American Volunteer Group*, Washington/ London, Smithsonian Institute Press, 1991.

Franks, Norman, *Hurricanes over the Arakan*, London, Patrick Stephens, 1989.

Franks, Norman, *The Air Battle of Imphal*, London, William Kimber, 1985.

Franks, Norman, *Spitfires over the Arakan*, London, William Kimber, 1988.

Franks, Norman, *Hurricane at War 2*, London, Ian Allen, 1986.

Franks, Norman, *Frank 'Chota' Carey*, London, Grub Street, 2006.

Futrell, Robert Frank, *Ideas, Concepts, Doctrine: A History of Basic Thinking in the United States Air Force 1907-1964*, New York, Arno Press, 1980.

Gooch, John, *Air Power Theory and Practice*, London, Cass, 1995.

Gruhl, Werner, *Imperial Japan's World War Two*, New York and London, Transaction Publishers, 2007.

Hallion, Richard, *Strike from the Sky*, Shrewsbury, Airlife Ltd & Smithsonian Institute Press, 1989.

Hastings, Max, *Nemesis*, London, Harper, 2007.

Hata, Ikuhiko, Izawa, Yasuho and Shores, Christopher, *Japanese Army Air Force Fighter Units and their Aces 1931-1945*, London, Grub Street, 2002.

Hata, Ikuhiko, Izawa, Yasuho and Shores, Christopher, *Japanese Naval Air Force Fighter Units and their Aces 1932-1945*, Grub Street, 2011.

Healy, Mark, *The Battle of Midway*, Oxford, Osprey, 1993.

Ichimura, Hiroshi, *Ki-43 Oscar Aces of World War 2*, Oxford, Osprey, 2009.

Innes, David, *Beaufighters Over Burma, No.27 Squadron, R.A.F. 1942-1945,* Poole, Blandford, 1985.

Jane's Fighting Aircraft of World War II, London, Bracken Books, 1989 reprint.

Johnson, J.E., *Full Circle; The Story of Air Fighting*, London, Cassell, 2001 edition.

Keegan, John, *The Second World War*, London, Pimlico, 1997.

Keightley, H.B., *Intelligence Support for Air Operations*, Canberra, Air Power Studies Centre, 1996.

Lake, Jon, *Blenheim Squadrons of World War 2*, London, Osprey, 1998.

Latimer, Jon, *Burma: The Forgotten War*, London, John Murray, 2004.

Lewin, Ronald, *Slim; The Standard Bearer*, Ware, Wordsworth, 1999.

Liddell Hart, Basil, *History of the Second World War*, London, Book Club Associates, 1975.

Liddle, Peter, Bourne, John, and Whitehead, Ian, (eds.), *The Great World War 1914-1945; Volume One; Lightning Strikes Twice*, London, Harper Collins, 2000.

Lyman, Robert, *Slim, Master of War*, London, Robinson, 2005.

Meilinger, Phillip, *Airwar: Theory and Practice*, London, Cass, 2003.

Mikesh, Robert C., *Broken Wings of the Samurai*, Shrewsbury, Airlife Publishing, 1993.

Miller, Russell, *Behind the Lines*, London, Pimlico, 2003.

Molesworth, Carl, *P-40 Warhawk Aces of the CBI*, London, Osprey, 2000.

Mondey, David, *British Aircraft of World War II*, London, Chancellor Press, 2004.

Mondey, David, *Axis Aircraft of World War II*, London, Chancellor Press, 2000.

Moreman, T.R., *The Jungle, The Japanese and the British Commonwealth Armies At War 1941 – 45*, Abingdon, Frank Cass, 2005.

Moser, Dan, *China-India-Burma*, Time Life, 1978.

Murray, Williamson, *Strategy for Defeat, The Luftwaffe 1933-1945*, London, Apple Press, 1986.

Nesbit, Roy Conyers, *An Illustrated History of the R.A.F.*, London, Colour Library Books, 1991.

Odgers, George, *Air War Against Japan 1943-1945*, Canberra, Australian War Memorial, 1966.

Overy, Richard, *The Air War 1939-45*, London, Europa, 1980.

Pearson, Michael, *The Burma Air Campaign 1941-1945*, Barnsley, Pen and Sword, 2006.

Peattie, Mark, *Sunburst: The Rise of Japanese Naval Air Power, 1909-1941*, Annapolis, Naval Institute Press, 2001.

Prange, Gordon, *At Dawn We Slept*, Harmondsworth, Penguin, 1981.

Prasad, Bisheshwar (Ed), *History of the Indian Air Force 1933-1945*, India and Pakistan, Combined Inter-Services Historical Section, 1961.

Preston, Diana, *Before the Fall-Out*, London, Corgi, 2006.

Price, Alfred, *Late Marque Spitfire Aces 1942-45*, London, Osprey, 1996.

Price, Alfred, *Spitfire Mark V Aces 1941-45*, London, Osprey, 1997.

Price, Alfred, *The Spitfire Story*, London, Arms and Armour Press, 1988.

Price, Alfred, *Spitfire*, London, Bookmark, 1991.

Probert, Henry, *The Forgotten Air Force: The Royal Air Force in the War Against Japan 1942-1945*, London, Brassey's, 1995.

Richards, Denis, *The Royal Air Force 1939-1945, Volume 1, The Fight at Odds*, London, HMSO, 1993 edition.

Richards, Denis, and Saunders, Hilary, St George, *Royal Air Force 1939-1945, Volume 2, The Fight Avails*, London, HMSO, 1993 edition.

Richards, Denis, and Saunders, Hilary, St George, *Royal Air Force 1939-1945, Volume 3, The Fight is Won*, London, HMSO, 1993 edition.

Rooney, David, *Wingate and the Chindits*, London, Cassell, 2000.

Rooney, David, *Burma Victory: Imphal and Kohima March 1944 to May 1945*, London, Cassell, 2002.

Sakaida, Henry, *Japanese Army Air Force Aces 1937-1945*, London, Osprey, 1997.

Shacklady, Edward, *Hawker Hurricane*, Stroud, Tempus, 2000.

Shores, Christopher, *Air War for Burma*, London, Grub Street, 2005.

Shores, Christopher, and Cull, Brian, with Yasuho, Izawa, *Bloody Shambles Volume One*, London, Grub Street, 1992.

Shores, Christopher, and Cull, Brian, with Yasuho, Izawa, *Bloody Shambles Volume Two*, London, Grub Street, 1993.

Sims, Edward, *Fighter Exploits*, London, Corgi Books, 1973 edition.

Smith, Michael and Erskine, Ralph (eds), *Action This Day*, London, Bantam Press, 2001.

Smith, Michael, *The Emperor's Codes*, London, Bantam Press, 2001.

Stanaway, John, *P-38 Lightning Aces of the Pacific and CBI*, London, Osprey, 2004.

Stanaway, John, *Mustang and Thunderbolt Aces of the Pacific and CBI*, London, Osprey, 2006.

Spick, Mike, *Fighter Pilot Tactics: The Techniques of Daylight Air Combat*, Cambridge, Patrick Stephens, 1983.

Spick, Mike, *Allied Fighter Aces of World War Two*, London, Greenhill Books, 1997.

Storry, Richard, *A Modern History of Japan*, Harmondsworth, Pelican, 1963.

Swinson, Arthur, *Mountbatten*, London, Pan, 1971.

Tamayama, Kazuo, and Nunneley, John, *Tales by Japanese Soldiers*, London, Cassell, 2003.

Taylor, C.G., The Forgotten Ones of South East Asia Command and Force 136, Ilfracombe,

Stockwell, 1989.

Taylor, Joe, *Air Supply in the Burma Campaign*, USAF Historical Division, 1957, www.afhrs.af.mil

Terraine, John, *The Right of the Line*, London, Sceptre Edition, 1988.

Thomas, Andrew, *Hurricane Aces 1941-1945*, London, Osprey, 2003.

Thomas, Andrew, *Spitfire Aces of Burma and the Pacific*, Oxford, Osprey, 2009.

Thompson, Julian, *The Imperial War Museum Book of the War in Burma 1942-1945*, London, Pan, 2002.

Thompson, Julian, *Forgotten Voices of Burma*, St Ives, Ebury Press, 2009.

Tillman, Barrett, *Whirlwind: The Air War Against Japan 1942-1945*, New York, Simon & Schuster Paperbacks, 2010.

Toland, John, *Rising Sun*, London, Pen and Sword, 2005.

Townsend, Peter, *Duel of Eagles*, London, Corgi, 1974.

Wagner, R.D., *Any Place, Any Time, Any Where*, Atglen P.A., Schiffer Publishing Ltd, 1998.

Webster, Donovan, *The Burma Road*, New York, Farrar, Straus and Giroux, 2003.

Winterbotham, F.W., *The Ultra Secret*, London, Weidenfeld and Nicolson, 1974.

Williams, Kathleen, *Army Air Forces in the War Against Japan 1941-1942*, Assistant Chief of Air Staff, Intelligence Division, U.S.A.A.F., 1945.

Y'Blood, William T., *Air Commandos Against Japan*, Annapolis, Naval Institute Press, 2008.

Ziegler, Philip, *Mountbatten*, London, Book Club Associates, 1985.

Online Books

Bolkcom, Christopher, and Pike, John, *Attack Aircraft Proliferation: Issues for Concern*, www.fas.org, Federation of American Scientists, 1996.

Articles

Canadian Military History
Brown, Sutherland, and Rodney, William, 'Burma Banzai: The Air War in Burma through Japanese Eyes', 2002, Volume 11, Issue 2, Article 6, p.57.

Royal Air Force Air Power Review
Richards, S, 'The Decisive Role of Air Power in the Pacific Campaign of WWII, Summer 2003, Volume 6, No.2, pp. 56-73.

Richie, Sebastian, 'Rising from the Ashes, Allied Air Power and Air Support for 14th Army in Burma 1943 to 1945', Autumn 2004, Volume 7, No.3, pp. 17-29.

Walton, David, 'The Royal Air Force and Air/Land Integration in the 100 days, August to November 1918', Summer 2008, Volume 11, No. 2, pp. 12-29.

Seminar Papers
Cox, Sebastian, 'The Organisation and Sources of R.A.F. Intelligence,' paper presented to the Air Intelligence Symposium, Royal Air Force History Society, Bracknell, 22nd March 1996.

David, Dennis, 'Burma: The Air Fighting,' paper presented to The R.A.F. and the Far East War 1941-1945 Symposium, Royal Air Force History Society, Bracknell, 24th March 1995.

Dick, David, 'Offensive Air Support for the Army,' paper presented to The R.A.F. and the Far East War 1941-1945 Symposium, Royal Air Force History Society, Bracknell, 24th March 1995.

Grant, Ian, 'Burma: The Land Campaign,' paper presented to The R.A.F. and the Far East War 1941-1945 Symposium, Royal Air Force History Society, Bracknell, 24th March 1995.

Groocock, Deryck, 'Air Supply,' paper presented to The R.A.F. and the Far East War 1941-1945 Symposium, Royal Air Force History Society, Bracknell, 24th March 1995.

O'Brien, Terence, 'A Personal Memoir,' paper presented to The R.A.F. and the Far East War 1941-1945 Symposium, Royal Air Force History Society, Bracknell, 24th March 1995.

Probert, Henry, 'Setting the scene,' paper presented to The R.A.F. and the Far East War 1941-1945 Symposium, Royal Air Force History Society, Bracknell, 24th March 1995.

Websites
Burma Star Website, www.burmastar.org.uk

United States Air Force Historical Research Agency, www.afhrs.af.mil

Index

INDEX OF PEOPLE

INDEX OF PLACES

INDEX OF ORGANISATIONS/FORMATIONS/UNITS

INDEX OF MISCELLANEOUS TERMS